AFTERWORDS

FROM A FOREIGN SERVICE ODYSSEY

GAR PARDY

◆ FriesenPress

Suite 300 - 990 Fort St
Victoria, BC, Canada, V8V 3K2
www.friesenpress.com

Copyright © 2015 by Gar Pardy
First Edition — 2015

All rights reserved.

No part of this publication may be reproduced in any form, or by any means, electronic or mechanical, including photocopying, recording, or any information browsing, storage, or retrieval system, without permission in writing from FriesenPress.

ISBN
978-1-4602-7094-3 (Hardcover)
978-1-4602-7095-0 (Paperback)
978-1-4602-7096-7 (eBook)

1. Political Science, Essays

Distributed to the trade by The Ingram Book Company

Table of Contents

Introduction xi

1. The Wars:
Afghanistan And Beyond 1

    When Diplomacy Turns Deadly 8
    Afghanistan: When to Stop 12
    Put a Lid on Afghanistan 16
    Afghanistan: Somalia Redux? 20
    Held Hostage by Afghanistan 23
    Book Reviews 27
    A Doomed Mission 35
    The Good Soldier 39
    Troublesome Neighbours 43
    The Manley Panel's Sharp Recipe of 'Ifs' Will Never Make Cake Today for Afghanistan 46
    The Bully General 50
    Book Reviews 54
    Over There 66
    Eyeless in Gaza 69
    A Nasty Little Middle Eastern War Brings More Evacuations 72
    Afghanistan: Beginning Again? 75
    Book Review 79
    Afghanistan: The Hole Gets Deeper 86
    Book Reviews 89
    Colvin is Just Doing His Job 98
    Speech 103
    Peter Kent goes to War 120
    Afghanistan: The Quagmire Gets Deeper 123
    Afghanistan: Canadian Sunset 129

Book Reviews 134
Afghanistan: Is the War Still Necessary? 144
Afghanistan: An Unnecessary War 150
An Unnecessary War 153
Tone Deaf Foreign Policy on Israel............................ 157
How Peace Came to Paradise 161
Book Review 166
The futility of war 173
Bibi Goes to Washington...................................... 176
Perpetual Wars 179

2. Inside the Shadows – The Quest for National Security 183

Bush's Power has Limits....................................... 190
The Same Old Mounties....................................... 194
The Commissioner Takes Us on a Musical Ride................. 198
Another RCMP Report for the Pile 202
National Security Wonderland 206
Arar Blame Game Continues 210
Iacobucci's Failure to Live Up to His Own Standard............. 214
The media aren't always a help 217
Book Reviews 220
Cannon's Misinformed Response to Guantanamo............... 227
Dangerous Work... 230
The Duty of Fairness... 233
Missing the Target... 236
The Biggest "But" in Canadian Judicial History................. 239
The Sad Reality of the Iacobucci Report 242
Torture and Public Policy 246
Iacobucci Appointment: Another Document Delay Tactic 253
Flimflam and Keeping Canadians Safe Act..................... 256
Khadr Saga is Far From Over 259
Ghosts of the Past Still Scare Today 262
The Politics of Geographic Perimeters......................... 266
Peace, Order and Windy Government......................... 269

Criminal Justice Without Reason 272
No job for the Mounties. 275
Lacking in Justice 279
Canada's Preventative Detention Scheme Akin to Internment Camps 283
Alfred Dreyfus and Omar Khadr, bookends of injustice 288

3. Canadian Abroad 293

Canadians Abroad 302
The Modernization of Consular Services: The Importance of
Technology. 312
Review 319
They Do More Harm than Good 329
Canadians in Foreign Places 333
Border Follies 337
Royal Prerogative and Consular Services 341
How to Save Ramin 348
Freedom to Travel. 352
Evacuations and Departures 356
The Rule of Law's Limits 361
Tears Are Enough 365
The Consular Game 368
Another Sad Chapter 372
The Real Reason to Bring Canadian Prisoners Home 375
At the Mercy of the Government 379
Some Will Be Helped, Others Not 382
All Aid Short of Help 385
Dragging Through the Courts. 388
When Tragedy Strikes in Paradise 391
Canadians Abroad Deserve Our Help 394
Are We Paying More for Consular Services than Necessary?. 397
Modernising the World of Consular Affairs 401

4. A Miscellany of Afterwords 405

Book Reviews 413

The Definition of a Nation. 422
Nuclear North Korea: The Road from Chalk River 426
A Species on the Move. 431
Book Review 435
A Little Tibetan Political Theatre Playing Out 442
Book Review 445
Change Isn't Always Good. 449
The Mobility of Labour 453
Toward Self-Determination. 457
The Border. 460
Cadillos and Balconies. 463
Canada's 2012 Bid for the Security Council 466
More Huffing and Puffing about Immigration 469
The New Nuclear World. 472
Canada Will Pay a Steep Price in Border Talks 478
How the U.S. Blackmailed Canada. 482
Harper Takes a Page from Assad Playbook. 485
Chain Reactions 488
Mission-Sharing: Baird was Ambushed by Brits 491
Canadian Cheerleaders on the Sidelines in Mid-East Diplomacy. . 494
Book Review 497
The Iran Caper: The Washington Scene - Getting the Americans
Interested in the Six 504
The Confusing World of Economics 511
No Slam Dunks with Uncle Sam 515
"Those Who Take Us Away" – and Those Who Look Away 517
Borders and Edges 520
The Canadian Legacy of Margaret Thatcher. 523
Qatar's Quiet Understanding of Canadian Politics 527
Obama: Pivots and Divots. 530
The Politics of Numbers. 533
Russian Roulette at the North Pole. 536
High Stakes in the High Arctic. 539
Gods, Caesars and Elections 543

The Break-Up of States and Lessons for Canada	547
The Malicious Concept of Mother Canada	551
Nigeria Beckons	554
Canadian Foreign Policy – The World to Come	558
Satire and Irony: Bedfellows for Today's World	563
Speech: Writing and Writers	566
Baird's Version of Harper's Kool-Aid	571
Book Review	574
Cuba: An island looking for more sun	583
Endnote	587

For Laurel, Michael and Julian

Companions on the Journey.

The Odyssey Continues

Other Books by Gar Pardy

"Consular and Diplomatic Protection in the Age of Terrorism: Filling the Gaps" by Gar Pardy in **The Human Rights of Anti-terrorism**, Edited by Nicole LaViolette and Craig Forcese, Irwin Law, Toronto, 2008

"The Long Way Home: The Saga of Omar Khadr" by Gar Pardy in **Omar Khadr, Oh Canada,** Edited by Janice Williamson, McGill-Queen's University Press, Montreal, 2012.

Introduction

THIS IS A RETIREMENT BOOK. ITS ORIGINS ARE IN THE MONTHS AFTER August 2003 when I retired from the Canadian Foreign Service following some thirty-six years wandering the world or contemplating its vicissitudes from the banks of the Rideau. Initially there were several years of tidying major controversies through commissions of *inquiry* before I began a second career of commenting on domestic and foreign policy issues. Pleasantly surprised, I learned there was a market for such work. The idea it would be remunerative quickly faded into the dreams that most often are occasioned by smoking something other than tobacco. But as doctors frequently remind us the brain needs as much help as we can give it and the ironies of Canadian policy over the past few years has been a rich coal face available for excavation, if not by a new worker then certainly an experienced one.

1967 was at the tag end of Mike Pearson's "golden" influence on the Canadian Foreign Service and the beginnings of Pierre Trudeau's acerbic approach to things foreign. As with most things with Mr Trudeau he had by then a well-honed perspective on the world. His own travels twenty years earlier to India and China, places undergoing great changes and, ultimately in diametrically opposite directions, provided him with perspectives and interests that differed from many Canadians. This was especially so with those in the Foreign Service whose leadership at the time was largely those with Second World War experiences if not service.

My peripatetic journeys to places foreign were the continuation of a journey that began in the most international of all towns in Newfoundland. Gander, the centre of post-war civilian aviation, perched on the western reaches of the North Atlantic. It was as idyllic as the lands of Kubla Khan. Those years opened my mind to the larger world symbolized by aircraft – DC-4s, and 6s and 7s, Boeing Stratocruisers and the gem of the fleet, Super Constellations - that landed daily having successfully overcome the perils of flying the North Atlantic. But as with today's technologies, aviation technology of the post war leaped forward and the piston engines that helped win the war and conquered the Atlantic gave way to the jet and its ability to conquer distances with almost the speed of the sun. Gander was soon bypassed by world aviation except for the eponymously named "non-scheds" or the planes of Soviet bloc maintaining air contact with Cuba.

For most of the passengers of the 50s there was little awareness that the North Atlantic was as much a graveyard of pioneering adventurous flyers as it was for sailors. Gander and Newfoundland became known to tens of thousands travelers of the North Atlantic who spent a few minutes of their long journeys safely on the ground. The airport survives and its value to the world was again demonstrated in the aftermath of 911 when thousands more found quick and safe landings from the scourge of terrorism.

Aviation remained a preoccupation with early journeys to the weather stations at the edges of Canada at Goose Bay, Labrador and Frobisher Bay on Baffin Island in the Northwest Territories. Years at those isolated places which at the time were major bases of the American Strategic Air Command (SAC) bastions of the Cold War before intercontinental missiles silently became the weapons of mass destruction. This small relationship with the strategic balance of mutually assured destruction help kindled the interest in the larger world and before long I was in the bucolic Annapolis Valley of Nova Scotia and formalizing my interest in things international at Acadia University. With Laurel, a lady of the valley whose family reached back to the early 1750s' we were soon in the sooty town of Hamilton where further study at McMaster paved the way for entry into the Foreign Service.

Assignments to India, Kenya, Washington, D.C. and the five countries of Central America (Honduras, El Salvador, Nicaragua, Costa Rica and Panama), now with Michael and Julian, provided experiences and knowledge that comes only with living with the peoples of the world. In between assignments in Ottawa where Asia, national security, international communications and consular along with the internal machinations of the government of Canada rounded out a well-lived life of infinite variety. It has been a wonderful journey and I have tried to reflect this in the articles making up this book. It is hoped that the reading is as fulfilling as the writing.

Gar Pardy, Ottawa
April 2015

Never interrupt your enemy when he is making a mistake.

—Napoleon Bonaparte

1. The Wars:
Afghanistan And Beyond

HISTORY SHOWS THE FIRST YEARS OF THIS THIRD MILLENNIUM WERE not particularly violent. Such records are normally suspect but even when casually compared with the first fourteen years of the 20th century, recent wars while more numerous have been much less deadly. Less than a million persons died in the recent ones, a figure at least five times smaller than those killed during the early years of the last century. But such numbers are of little value in making historical comparisons when the former period was capped by the start of The Great War with more than 20 million dead and, accepting the view of most historians that the Great War was only a precursors to the Second World War, twenty years later, with 55 million dead. A detached viewer might conclude we live in a fairly benign environment.

During war itself there is little opportunity or willingness to come to such a benign view. In the middle of conflict it is impossible to expect there is any traction for those who offer a view of war other than that promoted by government. Nevertheless, given the nature of contemporary wars there is a greater need for those who offer a different view to speak out and ensure that there is some understanding of outcomes other than those that see an invasion as a straight line into victory. Blowback, unintended consequences and the fog of war must be essential elements in our calculus.

Canadians never made a distinction between "support for our troops" and hard-headed conclusions on the likelihood of success for the West's collective policy in the war in Afghanistan. Instead, Canadian military and political leaders deliberately confused the two and ensured that anyone who wandered away from that confusion was tarred as undervaluing the valiant effort of Canadian troops and lacking in patriotism. In a country such as Afghanistan where there are numerous historical examples of the defeat of invaders by indigenous forces, this should have been apparent to those who promoted war with a constantly changing table of objectives.

* * *

My direct experience with things Afghan came at a time when Mohammed Zahir Shah sat comfortably on the Afghan throne. It was 1971 and talk of war on the sub-continent was rife but involved India and Pakistan and the future of East Pakistan which despite its name was not far from Burma and largely surrounded by Indian territory. Indira Gandhi was emerging from being a friendly face for the aging wallahs of the Congress Party, determined to rule in her own right and that of her father, Jawaharlal Nehru, the first Prime Minister of independent India. Indian policy was to see the dismemberment of post-partitioned Pakistan and from the limited information available to us in New Delhi it was apparent that India was making military arrangements accordingly.

The foreign military attaches were barred from the border regions and so it was decided a civilian diplomat driving a nondescript, aging Volkswagen bus might be able to drive through the border areas of India and Pakistan and provide a snapshot of the military buildup along the common border in the west. To give verisimilitude to the trip it was agreed that we would drive on to Afghanistan and return a few weeks later for a second look at the border. A hurried briefing by the Canadian military attaché, Col. Tony MacLaughlan, provided a quick understanding of Indian and Pakistan military unit nomenclature. At the time my life had very little to do with things military (except for the American air force at Goose and Frobisher Bays) and there was little understanding of the differences between a regiment and a division or a tank or armed personnel carrier.

It was "innocents abroad" as four of us (another colleague and our spouses) left Delhi on a brisk October morning for the long drive up the Grand Trunk highway to the border. As we neared the border copious notes were taken as Indian military traffic started to dominate. We deliberately lost our way beyond Amritsar as we neared Wagga, the only official crossing point, in order to see as much of the Indian military buildup as was possible. It was enormous and it was with some relief when we crossed the border without being closely questioned as to why we were going to Pakistan at this time. There was some initial consternation when Pakistani border guards kept asking for papers, but this faded when it was realized they were asking for recent copies of Indian newspapers. On the Pakistani side the military buildup was much less apparent and after a day wandering around Lahore we went on to Islamabad where we organized our notes and sent them on to Ottawa.

Afghanistan was a land of peace and tranquility. North out of Islamabad the road passes an old military installation, Attock Fort, where it is rumoured that Sheik Mujibir Rahman, the leader of the independence movement for East Pakistan, was imprisoned. We slowed but the raising of our cameras were matched by the raising of guns by soldiers in the area and we passed on none the wiser as to where Sheik Rahman was sequestered. Soon we were into the borderlands and before long the historic Khyber Pass with its silent memorials to foreign invaders - regimental plaques attached to the ancient stone. Perched high above the road was Ali Masjid Fort, remnant of the British failures in this ancient land.

In their silence the words of Shelly echoed:

> I met a traveller from an antique land
> Who said: "Two vast and trunkless legs of stone
> Stand in the desert. Near them on the sand,
> Half sunk, a shattered visage lies, whose frown
> And wrinkled lip and sneer of cold command
> Tell that its sculptor well those passions read
> Which yet survive, stamped on these lifeless things,
> The hand that mocked them and the heart that fed.
> And on the pedestal these words appear:
> `My name is Ozymandias, King of Kings:
> Look on my works, ye mighty, and despair!'
> Nothing beside remains. Round the decay
> Of that colossal wreck, boundless and bare,
> The lone and level sands stretch far away".

The words of Shelly soon fade as we cope with the sinuosity of the Kabul Gorge where switchbacks were the straight parts of the road. Soon we are on the flats surrounding Kabul, a dusty city in a dusty land. After a few days of wandering its byways – all about the same age as the old roads of Ottawa all built following the total destruction of Kabul by the British Army as retribution for the annihilation of its 1839 invasion force – we pointed our trusty Volkswagen northward and the Oxus River, then a border in the Cold War with the Soviet Unions. The Salang Tunnel and the associated roads were excellent, the results, as local wags put it, of Soviet forward planning, capable of accommodating their largest tanks. Several hours later we were in the courtyard of a small inn at Mazar-i-Sharif where small chickens clucked in anticipation of being our supper. Over the next few days we drove the byways of northern Afghanistan including Balkh a neighbouring city were Alexander paused before heading south to take on the Pashtuns. He quickly decided the wars of his homelands were more amendable to his generalship and lit out for the Arabian Sea and home. He did leave his favourite horse – Busephalus – buried at Balkh, another silent memorial to remind invaders of their coming despair.

A quick flight to the Bamyan Valley on a YAK-40 of Baktar Airlines completed our tour of Afghanistan. It was the highlight of what was already a tour of firsts. The YAK-40 was a relatively new Soviet aircraft and the flight between towering mountains of the Hindu Kush and lowering clouds illustrated why this remains one of the most isolated parts of the country. The sudden appearance of the valley with its high sides, wandering river and greenery to match that of Canada warmed our senses which by now had seen more than enough sand. A hotel of yurts and a herd of horses provided food and transportation and before long we were puffing our way up the inside staircase of the 55 meter-high standing statute of Buddha. A shorter version nearby was an easier climb. In a piece of barbaric religious narrow mindedness both statutes were destroyed by the Taliban government in 2001, a foretaste of the violence that still racks the country.

Before leaving the country we spent several days in the eastern city of Jalalabad, a much fought over place in Afghanistan's many wars. The stay was inadvertent; our trusty Volkswagen did not want to leave the country and in a mighty screech of metal a piston rod smashed through the engine and we were ingloriously towed into the city by a slow-moving bullock. The ingenuity of the Afghan mechanics knew no bounds and soon a new engine was assembled and we were on our way. Unfortunately, the engine timing mechanism was overlooked in the repairs and from time to time our journey was interrupted by loud backfiring which in this land could occasion return fire.

On the return trip we repeated our spying. On the Pakistani side the troop and tank carriers were readily evident on the sides of all roads and the only empty spaces were within a few miles of the border. The formalities on the Pakistani side were perfunctory with almost evident zeal in seeing us leave. There was some distance of no-man's land between the Pakistani border office and that of India. The drive was eerily bereft of anyone or anything. But Indian border officials were not welcoming. Who were we and why were we crossing the border at this time – this despite the Indian plates on the vehicle and our diplomatic identifications issued by New Delhi. In the end using more bluster than diplomacy we were allowed to enter India but as soon as we did we were in the middle of the Indian Army whose only instructions were readily understood – get of this road immediately. We did not question the instructions and headed of cross country using tracks that had not seen a Volkswagen before and disappeared in the warrens of Wagga. Later we discovered the Indian Minister of Defence, Jagjivan Ram, was in the area inspecting his army a few days before the 1971 War turned hot.

Afghanistan and wars returned to my daily fare in the last half of the 1980s. Then I was political director for the countries stretching from Afghanistan to New Zealand excluding Indochina, China,

Japan and Korea. These were the fading years of the decade-long Soviet invasion and issues associated with that invasion, the Western response and the millions of refugees were constant preoccupations. One issue did stand out; the Foreign Minister of the day, Joe Clarke, decided that Canada would reach into Afghan and rescue five Soviet soldiers being held by the Mujahidin. I was in charge of the rescue and along with several colleagues carried out a Canadian rescue of the five as difficult as the rescue of six American diplomats by other colleagues from Tehran in 1980. The rescue was a success and in the process there was not much about things Afghanistan and Pakistan that I did not encounter. Pictures of the five at my house in Ottawa broke the story for the world. [The rescue was detailed in David Prosser's book *Out of Afghanistan*, Eden Press, Montreal, 1987],

* * *

If nothing else, war should teach, and the issue for Canada and Canadians is whether or not we have learned anything over the past fourteen years. Certainly there is little indication that our leaders have learned much. We have had eight defence ministers, ten foreign ministers, three prime ministers and a host of ministers and presidents at CIDA, the latter having now disappeared into the bowels of Foreign Affairs. We have had also an Independent Panel of distinguished Canadians who were supposed to provide advice and guidance on Afghanistan. In all that time and with all of those eminent Canadians, not more than fifty per cent of Canadians, and often there was much less, were convinced that either the United States or NATO or Canada could succeed in the difficult and hostile environment of Afghanistan. Importantly, there are few signs that the Afghans themselves were prepared to even come close to meeting the "reasonable" expectations of Western leaders who expended large amounts of their treasuries and, tragically, the loss of the lives of thousands of their citizens. Equally, tragically, the Afghans lost in the war have yet to be fully counted.

We are now done with Afghanistan but Afghanistan is by no means done with us. Apart from several thousand Americans, Western troops have departed "the land in between" to give it its ancient name and there is little to suggest that ancient land has reached any degree of peace or equilibrium. There is a fragile coalition government perched in Kabul but the countryside is largely controlled by the Taliban, the government ousted by the 2001 invasion. Al Qaeda the ostensible justification for the invasion is still present. Ironically, its brand of extremism and violence has now been out-distanced by the forces of the Islamic State and al Qaeda is largely the boogey under the bed used to scare the uninformed.

But the wars of this millennium roll on. We were convinced that getting rid of the outlandish, cruel and corrupt leader of Libya would lead to peace, order and good government in that colonial era gerrymandered part of North Africa. Less than three years later Afghanistan is almost a peaceful place in comparison. Today we are fighting the successor forces to al Qaeda in Iraq and neighbouring Syria. Today's Iraq is the product of another invasion, a coalition of Western countries willingly coopted by the United States. Unfortunately the *Pax Americana* of the last century is of little value in dealing with the legacy of colonial era constructed countries. The government of Canada is now a willing partner in this fool-hardy enterprise. As with earlier such enterprises many Canadians are taken in by the jingoism and propaganda of fighting largely imaginary forces and rue the political leader who suggests that we are simply demonstrating that our CF-18s are bigger than theirs. In the wars of the 21st Century that is not so. (April 2015)

When Diplomacy Turns Deadly
May 6, 2006

THE DEATH OF CANADIAN DIPLOMAT GLYN BERRY IN KANDAHAR IN mid-January bought home to Canadians the dangers of representing Canada abroad. Canada's military have borne the brunt of such tragedies in places as diverse as the Balkans, Cyprus, the Congo and Haiti. Until Mr. Berry's death, the dangers for diplomats were thought to be less.

Unfortunately, Mr. Berry's death is a harbinger of things to come. The changing face of conflict as represented by places such as Afghanistan, Iraq and Haiti means his death will not be the last among civilians who serve their country overseas. Diplomats, or to use the more inclusive term, members of Canada's official foreign service community, which includes members of the police and aid workers from such organizations as CIDA and Health Canada, work on the unmarked and confusing lines between violent conflict and normal daily life. And in many places there is no line. In the words on one journalist after visiting Iraq, "conflict is everywhere and nowhere."

Canada's military will continue to bear the heaviest burden. The three young men seriously wounded at the time of Mr. Berry's death, and others who have died since, join a long line of comrades, stretching back to the very first days of peacekeeping in Kashmir following the Second World War. With the changing face of war, military and civilian commentators have tried to make their governments and their citizens understand that peacemaking is a more dangerous job still. And by its nature, peacemaking, with the attendant purpose of creating and supporting democratic governments, involves diplomats and their associated colleagues in the official Foreign Service community.

Press reports at the time of Mr. Berry's death, suggested he was the first diplomat to have died in the "line of duty" in more than 50 years although the reports were silent on those who may have died in that distant past. Those reports were partially correct; very few Canadian diplomats have died in the line of duty.

Diplomats, other governmental officials and others from the non-governmental aid community have died in accidents and other mishaps around the world and such deaths, tragic as they are, are similar to the perils that many Canadians face in many corners of the world. J. M. Boyer, a Canadian trade commissioner, was a casualty in the January 1952 rioting in Cairo. An old colleague, Wayne Hubble, died in the crash of a Japan Air Lines 707 near New Delhi's Palaam Airport in June of 1972. The pilot mistook a row of street lights for those of the runway. Only three survived. Mr. Hubble was returning to Delhi from Hong Kong to get married, a marriage that was clearly not to take place. Other Canadians killed in tragic circumstances include Ottawa NGO aid worker Timothy Stone, who died in the crash of a hijacked Ethiopian Airlines plane of the coast of the Comoros Islands in 1996. Vancouver's Nancy Malloy, one of six Red Cross workers was murdered in December 1996 in Chechnya as they ministered to those affected by that nasty war.

Prior to Mr. Berry's tragic death, research has shown that only one other Canadian diplomat died in the line of duty overseas – using a narrow definition of "line of duty" as relating to Canada's diplomatic service. John Douglas Turner died on October 18, 1965, when the plane he was on, disappeared during a flight between Vientiane, Laos and Hanoi, in then North Vietnam. Mr. Turner, who had just turned 30 the previous month, was one of Canada's representatives on the International Commission for Supervision and Control in Indochina and based in Hanoi.

There were twelve others on the flight; a French crew of four, five members of the Indian delegation and one member of the Polish delegation. With overtones of Kandahar, two other Canadians, both military members, were with Mr. Turner on the flight. Sgt. James Sylvester Byrne and Cpl. Vernon J. Perkin also perished when the aircraft, an old workhorse Boeing 307 Stratoliner from before the Second World War, owned and operated by French company CITCA, went down.

Neither the aircraft nor the crew and passengers have been found. Despite extensive air and ground searches, the foreboding, impenetrable jungles of eastern Laos and south western Vietnam yielded no answers as to how and why the aircraft disappeared or where it was located. It remains one of the mysteries from the Vietnam War era.

In 1998, the crash of a multi-engine aircraft was located just inside Laos on its Vietnam border. A Laotian military team trekked to the site and was able to retrieve a piece of the wreckage along with small bone shards. However, subsequent analysis by the Transportation Safety Board of Canada and Boeing in Seattle determined that it was not the aircraft that disappeared in 1965.

A detailed re-examination of the circumstances surrounding the flight was undertaken in 1995, the 30th anniversary of the disappearance of the aircraft. The common factors for such mishaps were considered including pilot error, engine or airframe failure, weather and contaminated fuel. All these possibilities were ruled out as being inconsistent with what was known from the contemporaneous records. It is highly unlikely any were the cause of the crash.

1965 was a pivotal year in the Vietnam War. The United States was increasing its combat troop levels while bombing, both military and industrial, in North Vietnam was increasing in ferocity. "Rolling Thunder," as the American air war was known, was a fact of daily life. The North Vietnamese and their allies in Laos, the Pathet Lao, countered with a sophisticated anti-aircraft system and the number of American planes downed and aircrew captured in the North, increased dramatically.

It was into this dangerous atmosphere that the aging Stratoliner carrying Mr. Turner and his military companions flew in the late afternoon of Oct. 18, 1965. Twenty minutes into the flight, Captain Henri Domergue radioed that he was on time for the scheduled arrival in Hanoi at 5 p.m. That was the last communication. Flying through the aerial battlefield of Indochina, the aircraft was most likely mistaken for a attacker and shot down, a victim of the fog of war. The only memorial to diplomat Doug Turner and his military colleagues, James Byrne and Vernon Perkin, has been 40 years of silence.

Their loss and that of others more recently, shows that service to Canada abroad has never been risk-free. The grimmer and more confusing circumstances of war, near-war and terrorism in today's world mean that those risks can only increase. Public recognition of this change is overdue.

Diplomat and International Trade

Afghanistan: When to Stop
November 16, 2006

ONE OF THE MOST DIFFICULT ISSUES IN PUBLIC POLICY IS ENDING A policy when it is clear that you are not going to obtain the desired result. In more specific terms, when does a government put an end to a military operation once it has become evident the expected objective will not to be reached?

American governments have faced such an issue twice in the past forty years. The first was, of course, Vietnam where, by the late sixties, it was evident that the North-Vietnam leadership had both the will and the way to sustain its aim to unite Vietnam.

The demilitarized zone agreed to in Geneva in 1954, allowing the French to straighten their *kepis* and withdraw, put an end to its seriously flawed hope that Indochina could remain a part of France's overseas domain. However, it did not end the objective of the North Vietnamese leadership for a united Vietnam. Unlike Korea, the geography of Indochina allowed the North to initiate a sustained war against the South – which the presence of hundreds of thousands of American troops could not withstand.

Misleadingly, some American commentators placed the blame for the defeat on the unwillingness of the American people to sustain a leader in Washington who refused to accept that the policy of ever-increasing war would not succeed. President Johnson's decision not to run in 1968 was the first American political casualty of Vietnam.

It took the election of President Nixon on a policy of getting out of Vietnam – despite the Cassandras of doom who continued to argue for more war – for the American government to change a badly flawed piece of public policy. Fortunately, the cost of doing so in Vietnam and Asia – except for the people of South Vietnam – was short-lived, and today it is difficult to understand why millions of people had to die.

A similar issue is again facing the United States in Iraq. A consensus among military and other experts is now emerging that the continued presence of American and other coalition forces in Iraq will do three things: First, the emergence of a coalition government will not succeed as long as foreign troops remain as its main source of support. Second, the presence of coalition troops provides the focus for an escalation of violence as is evident with the current increase in American casualties – and tens of thousands yet to die. And third, the ongoing war, in the words of a recently released American government assessment, will provide "a potential source of leadership for jihadists" elsewhere in the world.

Iraq is not Vietnam and 2006 is not 1968. But the public-policy issue is not dramatically different. As the old political adage puts it, "when you are in a hole the first order of business is to stop digging." Today it is simple to see the wisdom of the decision of the American people to get out of Vietnam in 1968; it is much more difficult to reach a similar conclusion five years after a terrorist attack on your principal cities – even though there is no evidence connecting the two sets of events. But, as witnessed by numerous examples around the world, such as the Philippines, the Congo, and Chechnya, it is highly unlikely that a determined "national"-liberation movement can be defeated by a foreign state at an acceptable price. And in Iraq it is not cynical to suggest that there are at least three such "national" liberation movements trying to get out from under the misguided decisions made in Paris in 1919.

The debate is intensifying in the United States and, two weeks away from the mid-term elections, it is not possible to forecast the impact of the results on the decision that has to be made regarding Iraq. Even if the Republicans retain control of the Senate and the House of Representatives, it cannot be assumed that would represent an endorsement of the current policy. There is an ever-increasing realization in the United States that the price of Iraq has now exceeded the possible benefits and the consequences of staying the course. "Saluting the flag" and "Supporting our troops" does not a rational national policy make.

And Canadians need to dismount from their high horses and begin the serious debate that is now necessary in this country about our war in Afghanistan. The early history of our involvement in that tragic country has little to do with any hard assessment at the political level of what was involved. The political assessments that were done had more to do with balancing the decision to go or not to go with other aspects of Canadian foreign policy, including relations with the United States and our allies and friends in Europe.

It was recently revealed that a military assessment concluded Afghanistan and the Caucasus were the two worst places in the world for the deployment of Canadian military forces. Not surprisingly many Canadians are more than ambiguous apropos their support for our involvement in a war that grows increasingly complex – and no longer amendable to influence by the "purity" of our motives.

Ever since Alexander III wandered through the area some 2300 years ago (he is credited with founding Kandahar), a variety of outsiders have come to grief in the lands and at the hands of the Afghans. The British (historically) and the Pakistanis (today) adopted a common policy of divide and influence, rather than divide and conquer. Afghans kill each other with some regularity, but the historical evidence is that they kill foreigners with greater alacrity and, as the Russians recently found out, with great success. A lesson that Canadians and their NATO allies are now learning. That thousands of Afghans die as well is not something that is covered by the most mischievous of recent Canadian, fatuous, foreign-policy initiatives – the Responsibility to Protect. R2P is now RIP.

The debate that there has to be more development and less military is at its best pious posturing and at its worst malevolently misleading. It totally misses the point. The debate must be about whether there is any expectation that foreign troops in Afghanistan

– supporting a weak coalition government of warlords, drug dealers, regional satraps and religious extremists and indirectly undermined by the strongest of the neighbouring countries – can succeed at a price that the troop-contributing countries are prepared to pay.

The very soft support in Canada for the war – where continuing casualties or an atrocity would turn existing support into Jello – the "after-you-Alphonse" attitude on the part of our European allies for increased support, the war-weariness in the United States, the spreading of the insurgency to most parts of Afghanistan, a Kabul government whose influence does not run throughout the capital city and the expectation that the government in Islamabad will expire anytime, all support the conclusion that the consequences of staying in Afghanistan are larger than the consequences of getting out.

Hopefully these realities will spark a public debate and put an end to the hubris of politicians who see war as part of a policy continuum. War is not; it is a world unto itself. It is not to be measured in the same way as support for clean air or tax reductions. When good men and women are asked to die for something, there should be every expectation that there will be a good end. In Afghanistan, there is no good end.

There is an alternative, however. It has stood the world in good stead for more than sixty years and, with patience, it can not only do the job in Afghanistan but could do the job in Iraq as well. This is "containment" – and while it does not have the glamour of war it does offer a real chance of success.

The hard question is whether a government in Ottawa can put an end to an unsuccessful military operation. The answer is no – so thousands will die and the operation will be ended by others. But in a few years the question will again be asked: "What was that all about?"

The Citizen

Put a Lid on Afghanistan
December 20, 2006

IN WASHINGTON, IRAQI SHOES ARE FALLING, BUT THERE IS LITTLE willingness to accept that the "point of no return" has been reached. Instead there is a danse macabre of political manoeuvring leading to the presidential election of 2008.

Unfortunately, the same unreality is evident in Ottawa. The Bloc Quebecois announcement that it would see the Conservative government fall over Afghanistan, unless it "modifies rapidly and profoundly" Canadian operations, has set the tone for the looming debate. The Liberals have little meaningful to say, reflecting either their confusion or the need to heal internal rifts.

The government, for its part, is not prepared to foster an atmosphere in which a national, informed debate on Afghanistan can take place. The prime minister, in responding to the Bloc's announcement, wrapped himself in the flag and reiterated earlier comments that such a debate would seriously undermine our troops on the ground.

Only a lachrymose Afghan President Hamid Karzai reflected the sad state of affairs when, recently on television, he lamented the deaths of Afghan children at the hands of both the Taliban and NATO forces.

Eggs and omelettes, anyone?

For Canada the results of the Riga NATO summit represented an enormous political failure – a failure as great as any Canada has experienced at the hands of its political and military allies since the end of the Second World War.

Out of the Nov. 29 Declaration's 46 paragraphs, only four dealt with Afghanistan. Even the words used in these paragraphs did not rise about the banal: "We welcome the continued contribution of partners and other nations to the ISAF and encourage ..."

In the aftermath of the summit there are few signs that there will be more European guns in Afghanistan. There is no succour for Canada or the Netherlands on the points pleaded by both prior to the meeting. Afghanistan has now joined Iraq as a point of division within the alliance.

The recklessness of the government's hasty, unconditional decision last May to extend the Canadian military commitment to 2009 demonstrated parliamentary one-upmanship and also a lost opportunity to engage Canadians on the matter. More fundamentally, the extension decision illustrated the ineptness of the new government in dealing with the international community.

What is missing is any relationship between the military and civilian resources on the ground, and the objectives of the mission. The idea that democracy can be established and spread throughout Afghanistan by outside forces or that those forces will be around long enough for it to happen is no more realistic there than it is for Iraq. And, to expect that significant social change is in the cards is highly delusional. The Bloc will become federalists first.

The central argument for the invasion of Afghanistan was regime change, and in most minds that has morphed into support for a dysfunctional government that will ensure the country does not become a base for international terrorism. In the words of some, "we fight them in Afghanistan or at home." But as events in a variety of places have demonstrated, we are already fighting them at home – and the longer the war goes on in Afghanistan, the more of them there will be to fight in both places. This conclusion was reached in relation to Iraq several months ago.

There is now a need to begin a strategy of containment for Afghanistan. Canada is well-placed to begin the thinking as well as taking the initiatives for this to happen – perhaps in co-operation with the Netherlands. The central objective would be to see all foreign troops removed from Afghanistan as soon as possible to permit Afghans to come to their own consensus. This they have always done. The presence of foreign troops delays and undermines that process. In the minds of many Afghans, support by foreign troops demonizes the factions associated with them and marginalizes forces for change.

The main points in a containment strategy are:

- Inclusion of the Taliban in the Afghan coalition. There are factions in the Taliban, based on in-versus-out-of-country presence and tribal differences, that probably could be brought into the coalition.

- Recognition that Pakistan is unable or unwilling to control its own and Afghan-related insurgencies (there is already a Pakistani Taliban in the Waziristan and other tribal areas) and to develop specific international-assistance programs, both civil and military.

- Changes in NATO military strategy from one of static positioning with occasional offensives to one of mobile border control and interdiction, and a significant increase in Afghan police and military training.

- Creation of a regional consultative group, involving Iran, Pakistan, India, China, Indonesia, Malaysia, Bangladesh, the central-Asian states and Afghanistan, to deal with cross-border issues, including terrorism.

- Creation of an international consultative group on Afghanistan under the auspices of the United Nations, inclusive of all NATO countries, Russia and China with a mandate to deal with political, military, economic and international terrorism issues.

- Broadening of co-operative surveillance by western countries of citizens (and visitors) who travel to Pakistan in order to identify persons who may be harbingers of terrorism.

- Acceptance by governments that their policies toward Afghanistan and Pakistan should be to minimize this region as a source of international terrorism.

Rudyard Kipling, more than a hundred years ago, knew a bit about Afghanistan and the fate of foreign soldiers. With apologies for some slight changes, he wrote:

> When you lie wounded on the Afghan plain
> And the women come out to slice up your remains
> Take out your rifle and blow out your brains
> And die like a soldier on the Afghan plain

The Citizen

Afghanistan: Somalia Redux?
February 8, 2007

GEORGE KENNAN, THE GREAT DIPLOMATIST OF THE LAST CENTURY who gave us containment as an alternative to war, wrote toward the end of his life that we always know where we are when we start a war, but we do not know where we will be when it ends. Sound words for democracies to keep in mind when wars are started for reasons that do not find wide public acceptance. The glory of the shock and awe of 2003 is now blighted by the bitter ashes of defeat, and the arguments against withdrawal have more to do with the consequences for George Bush than they have for Iraq.

The news that Canadian soldiers may have been less than correct in their treatment of Afghan prisoners should come as no surprise to anyone who closely follows military affairs. The robust and almost indignant responses of the Defence Minister and the Chief of Defence Staff offer little comfort to the many Canadians who continue to believe that our presence in Afghanistan will not achieve its original objectives. And the almost Keystonean stumbling of military police and judicial organizations offers even less comfort – as they fail to prove that they are capable of providing us with accurate, believable and reliable conclusions.

The treatment of prisoners in Afghanistan has been a Canadian story since as early as Christmas 2001 when it was revealed that Canadian soldiers were permitted to transfer captured persons to American forces. In some measure this was corrected through an agreement in 2005, requiring prisoners be transferred to the tender mercies of the new Afghan government – whose standards are certainly no better than those of the United States.

Widespread comment at the time pointed out the weakness of the agreement – since there was no provision for Canadian follow-up on post-transfer treatment of prisoners, suggesting instead that this was a role for the International Committee of the Red Cross (ICRC). At the time, officials stated this arrangement was the best that could be achieved, even though other NATO countries were able to obtain national follow-up in their bilateral agreements. Now the story is abuse of prisoners while in Canadian custody.

The information on which the current episode of the story is based is tenuous at best and vastly overblown at worse. Even the newspaper that broke the story has subsequently written that we must remember that "Canada is fighting a full-scale war in Afghanistan against a vicious enemy whose soldiers hide by dressing like ordinary farmers and blending in with civilians."

Perhaps the paper is now understanding of the little boy who shouted fire in a crowded theatre, or it has suddenly realized that the war in Afghanistan is slightly different than when the grand old Duke of York marched his soldiers up the hill and then down again.

More disturbing than this is the information contained in the various media reports on why the three men involved were taken prisoner by Canadian forces. One is said to have been taken because he was observing Canadian soldiers, while another reacted badly when discovered in a room with women and children and the third was a suspected maker of bombs.

Fortunately, only forty or so such persons have been captured by Canadian troops and transferred to the government of Afghanistan, suggesting that the standards used are not significantly abused, or perhaps there is limited contact with the local population. However, if one of the objectives is winning the "hearts and minds" of that population and if observing or being found with women and children becomes the basis for capture, then there is need for corrective action. More information is needed on the suspected bomb-maker before a judgement can be offered. However, one out of three is not bad during war.

The analogy of Somalia to the current stories has been peremptorily dismissed by most commentators. They are right to do so based on the nebulosity of the available information. Two young men died in Somalia at the hands of Canadian soldiers and one of those soldiers continues to live with its tragic consequences. The available information on Afghanistan is not in the same league.

Nevertheless, there is one aspect of the Somalia story that does have relevance and fuels the public uncertainty. At the time, military and political leaders reached new levels of obstruction and obscurantism in denying and hiding and confusing the events in Somalia. When there was some danger that the full story and the subsequent cover-up reaching into command and political levels would be unveiled by a commission of inquiry, the commission was summarily dismissed.

Public memories are long on such events. The resulting mistrust is such that it will take more than internal investigations by the military to reassure Canadians that our laudable expectations in Afghanistan, no matter if they are misguided, are not tarnished by the actions of a few. Hortatory statements by interested and responsible leaders will not do the job.

Canadians expect a high standard of behaviour from military, police and public officials. This is fuelled by a press that seldom applies the same standards to its own behaviour. As a result there is little tolerance or understanding when things do go bump in the dark hours and the shadows. In this case there may be very little in the shadows, but it will take a great deal of effort to reassure Canadians of that. However, with some certainty, it can be said that there will be other bumps in the Afghan night for Canada.

Held Hostage by Afghanistan
September 8, 2007

THE GOVERNMENT IS SLOWLY AND CRABBEDLY SIDLING TOWARDS A decision on Canada's future military role in Afghanistan. Defence Minister Peter Mackay told a TV audience a few days ago "The signal that has been sent already (to NATO)is that our current configuration will end in February, 2009." However, a DND spokesman later clarified the minister's statement by saying that this is not a new or recent signal but rather "there will be a vote in Parliament to decide the way forward after that."

These statements, which were echoed by Foreign Minister Maxime Bernier but not the prime minister, suggested the government is accepting the reality, evident for well over a year, that Afghanistan is not a place that can be put right by and undermanned, poorly led and disparate foreign military intervention force.

Canada with the highest casualty rate of any contributing country illustrates the inequality of the NATO deployment. In Uruzgan province to the north of Kandahar province, with a much smaller territory and population, the Dutch and Australians with an equal number of troops to Canada have had 11 deaths to Canada's 70. The lack of air transport and bomb clearing equipment today illustrates Canada's inability to provide troops with equipment appropriate for the fight. The ebb and flow of "captured" territory in Kandahar province is but the latest evidence of a doomed mission.

Equally, these recent ministerial statements represent an acknowledgement that there is insufficient political or public support in Canada for a continuation of the current military mission. The tenuous political scene and inability or unwillingness of the government to create a national consensus is merely a subplot to the evolving tragedy of Afghanistan. Bumper stickers on municipal service vehicles are a poor substitute.

Needless to say the government is now caught between the dog and fire hydrant, and the situation is largely of its own making. While it inherited a policy made by previous governments, it has made the current mess its own by divorcing the reality of Afghanistan from hoped-for electoral benefits at home. In the meantime, more Canadians will die without seriously affecting the outcome.

The continued lack of political progress in Afghanistan, the worsening military situation in the southwest and elsewhere and the refusal of allies to improve on their military commitments paints a dismal context for Canadian decision-making. The built-in deadline for the current Canadian military commitment provides a soft option that will be exercised by the government at the appropriate time.

Nor is there any succor to be had from other key countries.

The Americans are totally preoccupied with their danse macabre that is Iraq. To suggest that Afghanistan will receive appropriate attention and consideration in its ever-lengthening presidential selection process is a far-fetched as February grass in Newfoundland.

As for Pakistan, its perennial shift from military to civilian government offers no help on Afghanistan. While Benazir Bhutto and Nawaz Sharif appear as attractive alternatives to Gen. Pervez Musharraf, their history demonstrates that they are regional, parochial politicians who will do little to lead a deeply fractured and troubled state out of its decades-long miasma. They will make many of the same compromises that the generals made in order to obtain and maintain power.

Pakistan has from its earliest days copied the British policy of ensuring a weak and fractured Afghanistan on its artificial northern border. That is as close to a national policy as Pakistan has and there is no reason to believe the periodic retreat of the generals to their barracks will alter that primordial element in Pakistani politics. The Taliban is as much Pakistani as it is Afghan.

The increasing ability of the Taliban to take foreign hostages is another depressing aspect of the downward spiral. Equally troublesome was the reaction of Foreign Affairs Minister Bernier who gratuitously criticized the Korean government for negotiation with the Taliban. "We do not negotiate with terrorists, for any reason," the minister's statement read.

How short the memory. In 1996 the Canadian ambassador to Peru, Tony Vincent directly negotiated with the Tupac Amaru Revolutionary Movement in order to obtain the release of hostages at the residence of the Japanese ambassador. Many years earlier the Canadian government negotiated with the FLQ to end the kidnapping of the British trade representative in Montreal. In the intervening years Canada used any number of intermediaries (the Catholic Church and the Red Cross) to obtain the release of kidnapped Canadians.

There is a dilemma in such situations. However, Canada along with all other members of the G8 where the "no negotiations policy" originated, equally accepts that the safety of the hostages is paramount, and where necessary Canada has been prepared to sup with the devils. The only question is one of how long the spoon.

In this increasingly bubbling cauldron, no though is being given to other than a military solution for Afghanistan centered on foreign troops. There are occasional references to low level contacts between the government and the Taliban but these appear to be little more than will-o'-the-wisps.

Afghanistan as with the vast majority of post-Second World War insurgencies/civil wars, will only be resolved by a political deal between the contending parties. Maybe not enough people have yet died to bring home that reality.

If Northern Ireland and Palestine are susceptible to negotiated settlements, surely Afghanistan is worth a try. It is more than time for Canada to exercise the third "D" of its Afghanistan policy

and give Diplomacy a hard push, given the failure of Defence and Development.
The Citizen

Book Reviews
October 3, 2007

The Places in Between, by Rory Stewart. Penguin Canada, Toronto, 2004, 299 pp.

The Prince of the Marshes: And Other Occupational Hazards of a Year in Iraq, by Rory Stewart. Penguin Canada, Toronto, 2006, 196 pp.

A HUNDRED YEARS FROM NOW HISTORIANS WILL HAVE PASSED judgement on the two curious wars that began the 21st century. Will these wars then be as faded as the wars that surrounded the opening of the 20th century? Will they have been assembled into the welf and the warp of a quickly changing world in which there are few large historical consequences? Japan's wars with China and Russia, the Spanish-American War, the Boer Wars, and the Boxer Rebellions were relatively small affairs – relative to what was to come later in the first half of the 20th century. Today there are small footprints of these wars and their echoes – largely contained within historical footnotes. Curiously, only the British skirmishes with the Pashtuns on the Northwest Frontier of present-day Pakistan and Afghanistan can be tracked to today's troubles in the same region.

For those living at the time or for the participants, these wars were of some significance, involving as they did major European powers and, just as today's wars in Afghanistan and Iraq, they captured world-wide attention. Both of today's wars, involving the military might of the United States and major European powers, dominate the world's agenda almost to the exclusion of all else. In part, this is due to the amount of oxygen American interest consumes, but for other countries there are also significant national interests involved – ranging from keeping relations with the United States in good repair to, for some, the belief that the future of Western civilization depends on the outcome.

A consequence of the global preoccupation with the Afghan and Iraqi wars has been the proliferation of books, both good and bad, that detail the mites and the mightiest – and the labyrinthine motivations involved in these troublesome conflicts. For those who had forebodings of the demise of the printed word with the advent of the www, its dependent children of email, blogs and YouTube and their associated .com enterprises, the literary canon shows no signs of yielding to these neoteric devices and concepts. Very few, however, in the hurry to have the first, if not the definitive word contain mihrabs to give readers a sense of understanding, or a sense of the future of what is involved. Pre-emptive protection, regime change, elimination of nasty weapons and drugs, retribution, punishment, emancipation of women, the spread of democratic values and the security of oil supply have all been promoted as the reason or among the reasons for sending thousands of Western troops to Afghanistan and Iraq. Unfortunately, very few of these books have much to say about the Afghans and the Iraqis and their countries.

Enter Rory Stewart. Mr Stewart, a then-itinerant British diplomat, succeeds in fixing that troublesome imbalance. In short order he has given us two books: *The Places in Between,,* detailing a gruelling walk across most of central Afghanistan in 2002 and *The Prince of the Marshes*, memorializing a ten-month "governorship" in the Iraqi marsh-centered cities of Amarah and Nasiriyah in 2003-2004. These books provide a ground-up view of why Western interventions have been such failures in their objectives, and form part of the events that have altered the world's strategic balance. They should be required reading for all who deal with places foreign. Hopefully, the books will be read long after these wars come to some form of conclusion – as illustrations of what we don't know when we militarily engage societies, such as those in Afghanistan and Iraq.

In the opening of *Places,* Mr Stewart succinctly acknowledges the basic humanity of his journey and his hosts:

> But never in my twenty-one months of travel did they attempt to kidnap or kill me. I was alone and a stranger, walking in very remote areas; I represented a culture that many of them hated, and I was carrying enough money to save or at least transform their lives. In more than five hundred village houses, I was indulged, fed, nursed and protected by people poorer, hungrier, sicker, and more vulnerable than me. . . . I owe this journey and my life to them.

Stewart's Afghan journey began in the early winter months of 2002, just weeks after the fall of the Taliban. The route stretched from Herat in the northwest due east through the central mountains along the Hari Rud (river) through the lost Islamic capital of the Turquoise Mountain into the Bamiyan valley (the home of the destroyed cliff Buddhas), and onto Kabul. It was the route taken by Babur early in the 16th century (probably based on bad advice) as he began his wanderings that led to the establishment of his Mogul empire. Babur died in 1530 in India and, after a delay, his remains were buried in Kabul under the widely-quoted inscription, "If there is a paradise on earth, it is this, it is this, it is this." A more recent traveller is quoted by the author as writing that she was "reluctant to recommend this route without the gravest reservation."

The passes only lower to 14,000 feet and in the winter deep snows and 40-below temperatures are common. For most of the route, the Hazara people dominate. The Hazaras are Shia and descendants of Genghis Khan, an earlier traveller in the region. They are at the very end of the Afghan social scale and it is more the result of their isolation that they continue to survive at some ten percent of the population. They were the last to be dominated by the Taliban in 1996, which added further to their misery and downtrodden status.

The author's journey is blessed by the Herat governor and starts out with two minders from the local security authorities. Their's, and many other, conversations establish the strength of the book. As the author notes:

> *Yuzufi* [local official in Herat] *had an older view of an Afghanistan with a single national identity, natural frontiers, and ambassadors and a culture defined by medieval poetry. The Security Service saw my walk only as a journey to the edge of Ismail Khan's terrain. The Hazara area was as foreign to them as Iran. But for Yuzufi my walk was a journey across a united country. Perhaps this was why he was one of the only people who thought the walk possible.*

As the author leaves, Yuzufi remarked, "Record me in your book. As the Persian poets say: 'Man's life is brief and transitory. Literature endures forever.'"

The minders, Seyyad Qasim and Abdul Haq, related through marriage, are of a different order. Described with a touch that Cervantes would appreciate, they work now for the new regime in Herat, but their histories reflect the country: Probably they had been with the Taliban; before that they fought the Russians; and even earlier, as children, they enjoyed one of the few periods in recent Afghan history when there was reasonable peace throughout the land, and when the national buzkaski in Kabul had the status of Stanley Cup playoffs between Montreal and Toronto. Along the journey's route, the recent history of Afghanistan is also memorialized: destroyed Russian equipment, places were Russians died, places where the Taliban killed Hazaras and places were the Hazaras killed Taliban. And, from six-hundred years earlier or even nine-hundred years, there are still signs of Babur's journey and the wanderings of Genghis Khan's armies.

The author deftly gives Babur's journey currency by quoting from his journal (and those of many other previous and more recent travellers on the same route), demonstrating the endurability of the people and the land. In one quote, a local ruler in the 16th century was convinced of his invincibility and, without planning, believed he could defy the invading Uzbeks. Babur writes:

> *Zulnun . . . kept his ground against fifty thousand Uzbeks with a hundred and fifty men. A great body of the enemy coming up took him in an instant and swept on. They cut off his head as soon as he was taken.*

And today, the author observes:

> *No where in Afghanistan did the cruelty of the Taliban seem so comprehensive or have such an ethnic focus. In a three-day walk from Yakawlang, where the Taliban had executed four hundred to Sahidan, where eighty shop fronts had been reduced to blackened shells, every Hazara village I saw had been burned. In each settlement, people had been murdered, the flocks driven off, and the orchards razed. Most of the villages were still abandoned. The Hazara knew little and cared less about the World Trade Center.*

It is these riffs up and down the historical scale that provide a reality check for our current preoccupations with things Afghan. The folly and conceit of our coming is quietly and devastatingly illustrated by Mr Stewart's daily privations, and small courtesies that are extended by his hosts. "Only when he saw I was warm and had finished eating did he lean forward and ask, "And who are you? And where are you from?" As he ended his journey in Kabul, Mr Stewart, perhaps with journalistic opportunism, picks up a piece of paper from the street:

> *There is a consensus in Afghan society: violence must end, respect for human rights will form the path to a lasting peace and stability across the country. The people's aspirations must be represented in an accountable, broad-based, gender sensitive, multiethnic, representative government that delivers daily value.*

It was a draft proposal, in English, intended for the Afghan government! Needless to say there are many such draft proposals lying in the dirt of Iraq, too.

By 2003, Mr Stewart was looking for a new adventure (he had resigned from the British foreign service by this time) and thought that Iraq offered an antidote to tree-planting in the Highlands of Scotland. He was asked by the Foreign Office to be "deputy governorate coordinator" of Maysan, and by late September 2003, he was on his way via Basra. Maysan "lay in the marshes just north of the Garden of Eden. Or rather just north of the dead date palm and visitors' parking lot that Iraqis claimed marked the site of paradise." His mission was to create "a democratic Iraq at peace with itself and with its neighbors" – or, in the jargon popular in Baghdad, "a multi-ethnic, decentralized, prosperous state, based on human rights, a just constitution, a vibrant civil society, and the rule of law." "

The Prince of the Marshes is written as a series of journal entries and excerpts from documents still available to the author. It covers the period from September 28, 2003 to June 28, 2004. This was the time in which the brilliant military invasion of Iraq in early 2003 turned into the quagmire that deepened and broadened the fissures of Iraqi society into vast gulfs of irreconcilability. The author tracks this decline through the eyes of a civilian coalition team working within the confines of the supposedly homogeneous people of the marshes. Like the Hazaras in Afghanistan, the Marsh people were the outcasts of Iraqi society and in some ways were more harshly treated by the previous Baathist regime than were the Kurds in the north.

The team, when fully staffed, was made up of a disparate group of short-term aliens who were supposed to re-establish social and economic services until such time as elections could be held for Iraqis to take over. The author, through wit, understatement, satire, irony and naiveté, treats us to ten months of slipping and sliding that only dealing with an ancient, patient and knowing people could produce. The daily work ranged from the establishment of a local governing council, the appointment of police and security officials and local administrators to obtaining some measure of understanding of the various social and political forces and local personalities. The work made Lawrence Durrell's descriptions of a British embassy in central Europe between the wars appear as nursery play. Money was no object and tens of millions of dollars were available – and the author's accounting standards would have led Judge Gomery to early retirement.

It is the author's dealings with the Prince of the Marshes that is at the centre of the book and provides its sub title – *And Other Occupational Hazards of a Year in Iraq*. The Prince was a serious occupational hazard, having for the previous seventeen years fought the Baathists from Baghdad, and had considerable legitimacy both locally and with the new forces in the capital. The naming of the "Prince" (he was not) was attributed to Paul Bremer, but he subsequently denied it – as with so many other things for which he was responsible. The British military and more significantly minor civilian functionaries were of little consequence. The marsh Arabs could remember British soldiers from fifty and even a hundred years earlier and assess their true importance on the area's many millennia of recorded history. Upon Mr Stewart's introduction, the Prince "glanced at me and then looked away." While there were other occasions, it was clear that the Prince (although he was overcome by the new forces in the marshes and from the east) had an understanding of the relative order of things.

For Mr Stewart the new order crumbled when the invading forces failed to provide protection for the new local authorities he was instrumental in putting into office. Paralleling the "looting" in Baghdad a few months earlier, in the word of the new local governor: "You sent home my security force, dissolved the police line and took responsibility for the building. How did you then let the crowd get in and steal everything?" The author notes, "the governor left that meeting certain that we were not prepared to give him the level of protection we gave ourselves. And from then onwards almost any hope of cooperation was lost." A few lines earlier he notes: ". . . we thought property less important than life. And because we could not define the conditions under which we were prepared to kill Iraqis or have our own soldiers kill. Occupation is not a science but a deep art that can only be learned through experience." And clearly it is an experience that Western publics do not wish to learn.

In the middle of his Afghan journey, the author was presented with a dog, a "Sag-Jingo," a dog of war, as company for the last five weeks of his trek. It was the size of a small pony and named Babur by the author. When the author flew off to Scotland, he made arrangements for the dog to follow. It was not to be. Babur died before he got on the plane.

> *Someone had given him rack of lamb. After eating bread all his life, he had neither the teeth nor the experience to handle a bone. The shards cut up his stomach and killed him. I had thought that line of smells by unmarked boulders, stretching to a snow-ridge horizon, with ice holes for drinking, would finish with good meat, oak trees, rabbits, and a warm house. But it ended with his death.*

Perhaps fitting testimony to our own efforts in that ancient land.

Another Afghan host, when asked by the author to explain the Hazara, carefully unwrapped the Koran and read:

> *Unbeliever, I do not worship what you worship,*
> *Nor do you worship what I worship,*
> *I shall never worship what you worship,*
> *Nor will you ever worship what I worship,*
> *You have your religion and I have mine.*

Many have died to arrive at that understanding.

bout de papier Vol. 23, No. 2.

A Doomed Mission
October 20, 2007

THE TWO UNSPOKEN WORDS IN THE PRIME MINISTER'S RECENT announcement creating the Independent Panel on Canada's Future Role in Afghanistan were "exit strategy."

Unlike the daily litany of these words in the Iraq debate in the United States, in Canada the two words are only implicit in the announcement. Nevertheless the panel is a short-term exit strategy on the Afghan issue for the government to remove it from the feverish atmosphere surrounding the resumption of Parliament. Mackenzie King would be proud of the stratagem.

In one fell swoop the prime minister disarmed the Official Opposition. The panel broadens the fence on which the Liberals have been uncomfortably sitting and effectively removes the one issue of some consequence from forthcoming parliamentary debates. The NDP and the Bloc will remain consistent with their previous views but their voices will be of little consequence. The government will be sailing in blue waters in the coming months and Canadians may have a breather from the overheated debate on the possibility of a fall election.

The emphasis, however, is on the short term. Like the government stratagem in 2006 in obtaining parliamentary approval for the two-year extension of the Kandahar commitment in Afghanistan, the panel is a flawed instrument that may have some impact on some Canadians; however, it will have no effect whatsoever on events in Afghanistan. And before Canadians gets too comfortable with Mr. Harper's handling of the issue, it would be prudent to remember that is where the war is and Canadians are dying.

Others have pointed out that panel members have been carefully selected and are ideologically and sociologically coherent. They are not neophytes in Canada's political wars and, if past expressions are a guide, have strong views on Afghanistan.

Equally important they are not experts on Afghanistan or military affairs. It is easy to understand why it was not named and "expert" panel and shows that someone had a sense of humour with the use of the word "independent." This is especially so in light of comments in the Speech from the Throne on Tuesday when the government declared its intention to see the Afghan mission extended to 2011.

As such there can be every expectation that the panel will provide recommendations that closely adhere to the government's existing policy. Road to Damascus conversions should not be expected. And should there be, the manner in which President George W. Bush handled the recommendations of the Iraq Study Group provides the prime minister with a useful precedent on how quickly recommendations can be shunted into the archives.

The four options listed by the prime minister for study by the panel assume an almost benign Afghan and Alliance environment. The construction of the options – continue training the Afghan army and police so Canada can begin withdrawing its forces in February 2009; focus on reconstruction and have forces from another country take over security in Kandahar; shift Canadian security and reconstruction effort to another region in Afghanistan; withdraw all Canadian military except a minimal force to protect aid workers and diplomats – are all designed to beguile.

The options also assume that in the Afghan chess game, Canada can play both the white and black pieces.

Nothing could be further from the Afghan reality. The government is in its present pickle because the initial deployment decision by the previous government ignored that reality; nor was it a factor when the present government extended the mission. It is the same folly that led the Americans to their debacle in Iraq.

The government in instructing the panel states it should keep in mind the "potential' for deterioration in security and development. Obviously, this is a reality that has been with us for some time and its importance is undercut by its being boxed with such factors as the sacrifices already made and our obligations to NATO, the UN and our international reputation.

It is now close to six years since the first Canadian troops arrived in Afghanistan and the current war has exceeded the days of the Second World War. The lack of a coherent achievable objective still bedevils the mission and in its absence public ambiguity can only become more so. Rampant poppy production, the use of the death penalty, torture on prisoners and corruption are not influenced by the presence of western troops or episodic development efforts. These are issues Afghans know but they also know they are part of the social cohesion that will provide for the continued existence of Afghanistan in its historical framework.

There is only one real western objective in Afghanistan – to ensure that it is not again used as a base for al-Qaeda in its worldwide jihadist objectives. The idea that foreign troops can promote enormous social change is an enormous con and gets in the way of achieving the one thing that makes sense to most western audiences.

Recently the commandant of the U. S. Marine Corps suggested that his soldiers should bet out of Iraq and perhaps be used in Afghanistan since they fight best in an "expeditionary" role. The idea that Afghanistan six years after the fall of the Taliban still needs an expeditionary force should give pause to all, including the Panel. Perhaps such a pause might lead to a better understanding of what is possible in the the chaos of present day Afghanistan.

Lt-Gen. Ricardo Sanchez, former commander of American forces in Iraq spoke publically this month. He described American political leadership as "incompetent" and Iraq being a "nightmare with no end in sight."

Mr. Harper's Panel might wish to invite the general to Ottawa for a discussion of the commonalities with Afghanistan since he was responsible for part of that "nightmare."
The Citizen

The Good Soldier
October 30, 2007

THE RECENT FLAP OVER WHETHER THE GOVERNMENT INTENDS TO extend the term of office for the Chief of Defence Staff, General Rick Hillier, is a rare event in Canadian political life. Most of the time Chiefs come and go without making waves (even the occasional Admiral) and Canadians are hard pressed to remember their names – let alone anything significant they may have done. And it should be said that some have done well in a political environment where to be a member of the military was akin to being a skunk at a wedding.

General Hillier, who was recently nicknamed "the Big Cod", is a Chief of a different order. He was appointed in early 2005, following his tour in Afghanistan as Commander of the NATO-led International Security Assistance Force (ISAF) in Kabul. His appointment coincided with the Canadian change of mission in Afghanistan from one centred in relatively peaceful Kabul to the insurgency-plagued Kandahar province in the southwest.

The initial Kandahar arrangement was made by the previous Liberal government, but the new Conservative government in 2006 robed itself in the decision – and went an extra step by extending the deployment for a further two years. It has now indicated that it wants the mission extended to 2011. A rare example of a successor government willingly accepting a bad decision and making it its own in every conceivable way.

Leaving aside General Hillier's military acumen for the moment, it is his political skills that have been most public. Even here, an environmental word of caution is necessary. Since 2001 there have been six Ministers of National Defence and, except for Bill Graham, all had trouble distinguishing between Iltis and colitis. As such they were incapable of providing the political leadership and public face for the military that was needed during a time when men and women were being asked to die in the cause of a nebulous and forlorn adventure.

It is against this background of lacklustre political leadership that General Hillier has appeared as a colourful, articulate and decisive leader. Not surprisingly, Canadians have responded to his bright plumage with enthusiasm and widespread support. In many ways he is a bird of the government's own making – and he is one that they need more than the General needs them. As such it was not surprising that the Prime Minister avoided the issue of the General's future and took the time-honoured sidestep of stating that no one had brought the issue to his attention and denying that anyone in his office was so involved. Now the Minister has echoed similar vacuous comments.

But popularity at home does not make for a successful mission overseas. Appearing in a red t-shirt along with a huckster for a patented cold remedy, known for slagging French-speaking hockey players or calling the enemy "scumbags," plays well in North Bay. It does little to help the beleaguered detachment on the ground in Afghanistan. Even if the vast majority of Canadians supported the Afghan deployment, the inherent weaknesses of the Western mission drag everyone and everything into a quagmire that tarnishes all.

General Hillier and all current Canadian military leaders have little to no experience in dealing with the type of war they are facing in Afghanistan. Only the British (Northern Ireland) and the Russians (Chechnya) have such experience. The Americans, in turn, have learned that regime change is easier than new regime maintenance. This was recognized by others in the Canadian military when they wrote before the Kandahar mission that Afghanistan and the Trans Caucasus were the two worst regions in the world for Canada to deploy troops.

The issue of appropriate equipment for the troops has been a serious and ongoing problem. While the General and his recent predecessors have been outstanding in obtaining billions of dollars for new equipment, apart from vastly improved personnel carriers, they have done little for the troops in Afghanistan. The new personnel carriers have proven to be inadequate relative to the ability of the insurgents to upgrade their use of cheap, deadly landmines and rocket-propelled grenades. The present rush to provide mine-clearing equipment, which has been on the market for years, is an acknowledgement of the original planning failure.

General Hillier is not responsible for the sad, sorry tale of the efforts to obtain helicopters. However, he is responsible for not finding an interim solution that might have saved tens of Canadian casualties in the daily crapshoot of re-supply missions to outlying bases. Canadians have died and will continue to die for the historic helicopter debacle. There is no reason why, almost two years into the Kandahar mission, Canada still relies on other countries for such transport – and NATO is now scouring commercial markets for appropriate equipment. Ironically, one of the countries on which we rely uses helicopters sold by Canada a decade or so ago.

One would have thought by now that there would be a Canadian helicopter component to the mission. Leopard tanks have been deployed and the Sperwer Tactical Unmanned Aerial Vehicle is now part of the deployment. Both are marginal to the success of the mission, although they dazzle the public. There have even been suggestions, straight-faced, that Canadian submarines be made part of the mission. Until the past few days there has been almost total official silence on the timely provision of helicopters – the one piece of equipment that could make a significant difference in Canadian casualties.

In the comments concerning the future of General Hillier there are allusions to the firing of General of the Armies Douglas MacArthur by President Harry Truman in 1951. These allusions are misleading. General MacArthur, a battlefield commander, was fired for believing, after one of the most successful amphibious operations of the 20th century, he could invade North Korea with impunity. A million troops from China pricked that hubris, and for hundreds of United Nations troops "to die for a tie" was their epitaph.

General Hillier, warts and all, remains the only Canadian military leader – and the word military could be easily dropped – who provides any measure of confidence on the part of Canadians in the Kandahar mission. More than anyone else he has maintained a fixed point of believability. In that, he is almost solely responsible for maintaining close to fifty-percent support for the mission. One can only hope that the earlier comments on his future were trial balloons and that the government understands that the General represents the only lifebelt it has.

Troublesome Neighbours
January 3, 2008

THE GREEKS AND THE ROMANS SAW THEM AS "THE CRUEL FATES;" "accidents," Machiavelli called them in advice to his Prince; and in more modern times, Harold Macmillan described them as "events, dear boy, events" – the greatest vulnerability of any political leadership or country.

Pakistan has more than its share of events and the assassination of Benazir Bhutto is but the latest. Such events for a country as fragile as Pakistan, in such a problematic region and of such importance to Canada, promote them to the level of cruel fates.

Ms Bhutto was not the saviour that many hoped for – like many of her contemporaries who were never national politicians and had difficulty rising above parochial and regional interests. But she was on the brighter, modern side of Pakistani politics and culture – which is at times difficult to discern, overshadowed as it is by deeply historical tribal and linguistic differences. While she did represent a quickening of the need to return to democratic politics, she was a Hail-Mary policymaker far too beholden to the West, unlike her father, and too wounded by nagging corruption charges to create a national Pakistani psyche.

As with most things in the region, the British interregnum created the basis for most of today's problems. Their decision late in the 19th century to cut their losses in trying to dominate the Afghans and the imposition of a border that divided the Pashtun people laid the foundation for much that is wrong with the region today. The decision in 1947 to create two countries out of British India ensured that the earlier *realpolitik* decision was carried forward into today's world.

The people of British India of all faiths struggled collectively for independence and the Congress Party was the shamiana that had room for everyone. Moslems were not as comfortable as most, and Gandhi's promotion of mystical Hinduism sowed the seeds of disunity and the eventual creation of Pakistan and India. Fortunately, the Indians retained the Congress Party as a secular institution, which for a number of years successfully kept one of the most disparate of states together and moving ahead.

For Muhammad Ali Jinnah and Liaquat Ali Khan, leaders of Pakistan's first government, the best they could do was to convert the Muslim League into a political party. However, it soon proved that the League was less a political party than the lowest common unifying idea available to the new state.

The League was soon overtaken by other forces within the bicycle state (East Pakistan, now Bangladesh, was separated by a thousand miles of India) and civilian rule quickly gave way to frequent military interventions and rule – proving once again the fragility of religion in overcoming regional memories that are longer than history.

The death of Ms Bhutto represents an enormous failure, not only for the United States but also for Canada and the West generally. She was to be the bridge or at least the veil that provided legitimacy for the enormous Western adventure in Afghanistan. It is now clear, and has been for some time, that Pakistan is the key to any hope for success in Afghanistan. Ms Bhutto's death deepens the regional pit out of which there are no singular military escapes.

The intelligence and academic crowd are now telling us that Afghanistan may be the lesser of the two problems. There is a Pakistani Taliban and Al Qaeda, far from being a bastion of Arab and North African intrusion, has Pakistani colouration – drawing recruits as much from the Punjab and Sindh as from Bradford.

Western policy has all the sophistication of the Trailer Park Boys on a Saturday night in Sunnyvale. It has been dominated by a militarist mindset with occasional allusions to development and democratic institution building. It is dependent on Western proxies in both Kabul and Islamabad – both of whom have marginal national support and legitimacy. The NATO coalition spends more time negotiating amongst its members than it does on developing the necessary regional political agenda that might have some hope of containing the forces seething in both countries.

Like Iraq, there are enormous problems of national legitimacy in both Afghanistan and Pakistan. Also, like Iraq, there are external players who need to be included in a long-term diplomatic strategy of containment and cooperation.

Going into the seventh year of war in Afghanistan, no country has tried to rise above the false euphoria of the fall of Kabul in late 2001 in order to create a grand alliance, rather than a coalition of the half-willing. NATO and the military are tools not policy, driven by short-term domestic forces in Western countries needing a quick fix, ignoring the perspective and patience that problems of this magnitude require.

Most of the countries of the Middle East and North Africa have a deep interest in the outcome in Afghanistan and Pakistan, as do Iran, Turkey, Russia, China, India and the countries of Central Asia. Yet there is no coherent effort to include them in a process that might bring enough political force to bear which, in the first instance, could contain the forces we do not like in the region and begin the long-term cooperative effort that is clearly needed.

Canada has neither the influence nor the ability to initiate such a process. However, it does have the legitimacy to begin talks in concert with other interested countries. So far there is no evidence that this government is willing to try; rather, for domestic political reasons, it has turned over its responsibilities to superannuated politicians and officials with less than no experience or understanding of the issues involved.

The Citizen

The Manley Panel's Sharp Recipe of 'Ifs' Will Never Make Cake Today for Afghanistan
January 30, 2008

IN OTTAWA, RHETORIC AND REALITY SELDOM SHAKE HANDS. AND the sharp solipsism of the Manley report does not bring them any closer.

The report, despite all of its rhetoric to the contrary, is a Canadian-centric document that leaves the problems of Afghanistan and their possible impact on the rest of the world hostage to factors beyond the control of Canadians. In this report, Afghanistan provides the stage on which Canadians strut their deceptions, self and otherwise. John Manley and his fellow panellists may have provided a stop-the-clock picture – but the clocks of the world never stop.

Rudyard Kipling would have been proud to have authored such a wonder list of "ifs" as a basis for future action:

- If the prime minister were to take charge of the issue,
- If NATO members were to provide more troops,
- If the Afghan government were to become less corrupt and more effective,
- If Canada were to provide more airlift and high-in-the-sky intelligence,
- If Pakistanis were to put the needs of Afghanistan first,
- If regional players were to be more helpful,
- If the United Nations would be more coherent.

That is a recipe for cake possibly tomorrow, but it will never deliver cake today.

It is, however, a very sharp and appealing recipe that, with guile, puts the responsibility on others for the machinations of the Canadian political system. Earlier I wrote that the mandate for the panel was meant to beguile Canadians. The panel evidently agreed, breathlessly determining that all four options it was given were "deficient" – and then striking out in directions that border on fantasy.

The panel writes that the Canadian combat mission should "conclude when the Afghan National Army is ready to provide security in Kandahar province" and, more broadly, the aim is to "contribute with others to a better governed, stable and developing Afghanistan." It goes on to declare that there are no parallels with Iraq, since Afghanistan is based on the collective decisions of the UN, NATO and the legitimacy of the Afghan government – even though, as recent history has shown, decisions by such bodies are as reliable as the American mortgage system.

With a sense of Never-Never Land, the panel suggests that Canada should take "concerted diplomatic action" to establish "clearer, more comprehensive strategies and better co-ordination of the overall effort in Afghanistan by the international community, the Afghan authorities and other governments in the region." Then, recognizing that it had left a most important player out of the equation, the panel lamely ducks and states that the situation in Pakistan is difficult to assess – and the "government will have to monitor events there very closely and adjust its Afghanistan strategy as events warrant."

The panel's prescriptions are all linear when the situation requires the precepts of dynamic systems to create new solutions. The bumblebee in Indonesia affects the weather in North Bay, and the reality of Afghanistan requires more complex answers than those prompted by the hand-wringing of Canadians who hope beyond reason for relief from others in Kandahar.

And now the weighing of the report will go on, largely in terms of whether or not it provides the Liberals and/or Conservatives with sufficient rhetoric around which to craft new policy. If they cannot do that, then clearly we need new parties and politicians. In the meantime, Canada will stay in Afghanistan and, if there is any expectation that the American Marine Corps will ride to their rescue in Kandahar, then Canadians should expect to pay an even larger price. Playing second fiddle to American marines will not see the winning of many hearts and minds.

In the meantime, the world moves on. It has been clear for some time that NATO and other member governments are considering issues of greater importance than Afghanistan. Even in Iraq, the Americans finally decided that the Sunni had to be re-armed, and through the "Awakening" movement have provided equipment and training. This reverses American policy from the first days of the war and will ensure that the Sunnis will be heavy-handed participants in all future developments in Iraq. The Shia and the Kurds are already there. A National Army is as nebulous an Iraqi concept as it is an Afghan one.

For NATO countries, there are looming issues closer to home that will increasingly dominate their attention. On the day after the Manley report was published, a news story from *The Times* of London headlined: "Russia puts on flashy display of military might. War games show biggest of its kind since Soviet times." Where was this flashy display? Not east of Poland, but off the coasts of France and Spain. The story goes on to state that "the war games, held close to two NATO member-states, were the most forceful reminder to date of President Vladimir Putin's determination to flex Russia's military muscles as relations with the West have deteriorated."

So, when NATO leaders show up in Bucharest in April to pool their collective wisdom, the idea that Canadian problems in Kandahar will dominate their thinking is as farfetched as this year's orange crop in Newfoundland. Rather, NATO leaders, conscious of years to come for Mr. Putin in Moscow with his burgeoning military and his cold Russian hand on European energy supplies, will be looking for ways to disengage in Afghanistan as soon as possible.

They will dress this up, but their first priority will be to re-establish the original purpose of NATO – to keep the Americans in, and the Russians out. The Afghan adventure will stand as a reminder for all military alliances that countries must watch the home fires first.

Embassy

The Bully General
February 23, 2008

THE GOOD BUT CHEAP PEOPLE OF HAMELIN HAD ONE AND IT SEEMS we now have a Pied Piper as well, in the person of the Chief of Defence Staff, General Rick Hillier.

The piping has been going on since his appointment by the previous Prime Minister, Paul Martin, in early 2005. In the intervening years his tunes have beguiled many Canadians. In the absence of any honesty on Afghanistan on the part of all leaders, he has gained a reputation as a straight talker – one that Canadians can turn to for "telling it like it is."

His most recent tune, played late last week before an adoring audience of the Conference of Defence Associations, was to tell members of Canada's Parliament that he needs their "overwhelming" support for the Afghan military mission. Proving to be the piper that he is, he warned that if that support is not forthcoming, the Taliban enemy is watching and, in a style Joe McCarthy would have been proud of, went on to say, "the longer we go without that clarity, with the issue in doubt, the more the Taliban will target us as a perceived weak link." Even more demagogic, "I'm not going to stand here and tell you that the suicide bombings of this past week have been related to the debate back here in Canada. But I also cannot stand here and say that they are not."

General Hillier's words were a direct attack on the Liberal opposition, as it is evident that the compliant Harper government is prepared to give him anything he asks for. The Liberals, ever since they lost their public-policy way, are dithering more on Afghanistan than they are on whether or not to defeat the government. This is ironic, since it was the "dithering" Paul Martin who appointed the Chief – and then went on to approve his plan for Canada's war in Afghanistan.

The General's plan, as presented to the Prime Minister in March 2005, was a comprehensive one for Kandahar: more JTF2 special forces, command for nine months of the regional multinational headquarters, an 800-1000 person combat-ready task force, a Provincial Reconstruction Team, and, in Kabul, the Strategic Advisory Team. The General was steadfast in his view that the combat component in Kandahar would only be there from February 2006 to February 2007.

As Bill Schiller reported in the *Toronto Star* (and Stein and Lang in *The Unexpected War)*, Martin was no pushover. He wanted "unequivocal assurances" that the Afghan package would not prevent Canadian military contributions for possible international actions in Dafur, Haiti or the Middle East. Schiller reported that the Prime Minister did not want "any 'Yes, Minister' business." And, in the fatuous, modern way of policy verification, Martin "looked Hillier squarely in the eye and demanded his commitment. He got it."

Since then, a lot of blood and ink have been spilled. But throughout, the General and the government have been steadfast in the belief that, with more time and now with more troops, the enemy can be defeated – and the Chief of Defence Staff's policy vindicated. First there was a need for a two-year extension for the combat task force to 2009, and today we are in the process of extending it for a further twenty-nine months to July 2011. As well, the numbers game continues to inflate. The Manley Panel talked of a further 1000 troops, but, on February 22, the deputy commander of Canada's battle group publicly stated that 5,000 additional combat troops are needed in Kandahar.

The General has instinctively known it was more important to have support in North Bay than it was on the banks of the Rideau. From the very first days he has targeted a metaphorical North Bay

– or perhaps Little Hearts' Ease – as the source of his support in the political system, and his early descriptions of the enemy ("ball of snakes" and "detestable murderers and scumbags") have coloured the political landscape. His support by the huckster for patented cold medicine on Saturday-night hockey has proven that honouring the casualties is less important than their exploitation.

Even the Manley Panel was taken in by the General's optimistic views on the possibility of victory in Afghanistan. The Panel would not put a finite time on such a possibility, saying "no end date makes sense at this point" – and in doing so supported Hillier's ultimate game plan. The Panel in a Machiavellian touch suggested that the extra troops needed should come from our reluctant allies and, if not, then Canada should wind down the mission. However, with an eye towards North Bay, it enigmatically went on to say the "sacrifices made there, by Canadians and their families, must be respected."

Throughout this period the General has been less the leader of the Canadian military than another politician – of whom we have more than enough. As a result he has been deficient in his main responsibility to provide Canadian troops with appropriate equipment needed to fight the war and limit casualties.

Central to the war – and to the inordinate number of Canadian casualties – has been the quality of armed personnel carriers, mine-detection equipment and helicopters.

Peter Pigott in his book *Canada in Afghanistan* writes of the sorry and deadly experience with APCs, and equally with the efforts to deploy unmanned aerial vehicles. Mr Pigott details the experience with "the Iltis ("battlefield taxis"), BV-206 AMV, the G-Wagon ("an SUV with armour panels"), the LAV III ("unreliable in rough country"), the Coyote, and the Nyala ("vulnerable to IEDs"). All six Sperwer UAVs crashed due to Afghan "wind shears and turbulence." And, most importantly, we are still scrounging the international community for helicopters which in the view of the Manley Panel would better ensure "the safety and effectiveness of the Canadian contingent."

The Conservative government was quick to fire a senior public servant when the potential for deaths arose from a shortage of medical isotopes. In Afghanistan we are dealing with actual deaths and the maladroit performance of the Chief of Defence Staff should attract similar consideration. However, a bad policy that has the government's full support is not about to be abandoned, and it is apparent that the government needs the General more than he needs the government.
The Citizen

Book Reviews
April 2008

War at the Top of the World: The Struggle for Afghanistan, Kashmir, and Tibet, by Eric S. Margolis. Key Porter Books, 330 pp, 1999 revised and updated, pp. 330, 2007, $24.95.

Canada in Afghanistan: The War So Far, by Peter Pigott. Dundurn Press, pp. 224, 2007, $35.00.

Fifteen Days: Stories of Bravery, Friendship, Life and Death from Inside the New Canadian Army, by Christie Blatchford. Doubleday Canada, pp. 370, 2007, $34.95.

Outside the Wire: The War in Afghanistan in the Words of Its Participants. Edited by Kevin Patterson and Jane Warren. Random House Canada, pp. 294, 2007, $32.00.

The Unexpected War: Canada in Kandahar, by Janice Gross Stein and Eugene Lang. Viking Canada , pp. 332, 2007, $35.00.

[Final Report of the Independent Panel on Canada's Future Role in Afghanistan. pp. 90, January 2008. http://www.independent-panel-independant.ca/reportViewer-eng.asp?selMenu=1](http://www.independent-panel-independant.ca/reportViewer-eng.asp?selMenu=1)

HARPER'S MAGAZINE IN ITS MONTHLY INDEX OF NUMBERS, A FEW weeks ago, reported that there had been 835 books published in the United States about the war in Iraq and 32 of that number were books for children. I have searched the various indexes and could only find five books that deal exclusively (or in the case of the Margolis book substantially) with Canada's war in Afghanistan. Fortunately, none is meant for children.

While quantity is no measure of substance there are many aspects of Canada's role in Afghanistan that are not covered by these five books; we can only hope that there are works in the writing that will add to the understanding of Canadians concerning how we got where we are today – and what we are about. One major lacuna is that there are no books written by military personnel (except for brief accounts sent home of battles in *Outside the Wire*) either from those with Afghan mud on their boots or by those who could add some measure of insight to Canadian insurgency tactics and why such an inordinate number of NCO soldiers have died. To assume that Foreign Service and CIDA development personnel might be preparing their own books would be an unexpected blessing.

Nevertheless, these five books, all published in 2007, do constitute a valuable shelf of work for Canadians on things Afghan. I am not aware of another circumstance where there has been such a timely and valuable contribution for Canadians in providing information and understanding to one of our most troublesome public-policy issues. There is a minimum of overlap between the books, and each in its unique perspective contributes to our understanding of what Afghanistan was and is today.

Eric Margolis is the only non-Canadian, but his frequent appearances in the Canadian media over the years have been such that his views are familiar to many. He has been a peripatetic traveller in central and south Asia for the past three decades (after serving in the American Army in Vietnam) and is on a first-name basis with many of the key players in the politics of the countries in the region.

His "top of the world" metaphor is an appropriate one, given the geography of the area – and his overview.

Few can match his experience and knowledge, and this 1999 book, updated in 2007, is a useful starting point for those seeking some measure of understanding of the broader contexts in which the Afghanistan conundrum must be viewed. India and Pakistan, India, Pakistan and China, India and Russia and the bit parts played by Nepal, Tibet, Sikkim, Bhutan, Burma, Aksai Chin and the "stan" countries are all appropriately covered. The description of his trek with the Pakistani army to the battlefield on the Siachen Glacier is worth the price of the book. It illustrates in chilling, bone-jarring language the nature of the battlefields in this part of the world, and the unfinished business they represent. While Mr Margolis can be seen as a constant forecaster of large political disasters, and he is not shy in this book, it is by no means inappropriate to suggest that the seeds of several larger conflicts are present in this part of the world. Four (with an aspiring fifth) out of the nine acknowledged nuclear-weapon states have common borders in the region, and the best that can be said so far is that they have all been sane and sensible in the role that these weapons play.

The background information on Afghanistan and the personal relationships arising from his numerous visits since the late 1970s give this book a value that cannot be found elsewhere. Importantly, he makes little distinction between those who were mujahedin for one war and Taliban for another – as he sees them on an Afghan continuum rather than through the changing eyes of Westerners. The fascination of these medieval warriors with modern weapons to the restless and rootless in the Middle East and elsewhere is equally documented.

His relationship with the Pakistani military is also documented and, despite his often-laudatory tones, he provides ample background on why this military has played such an enormous role in everything that has happened in south Asia since the British rolled up their tents sixty years ago. Given recent events in Pakistan, Mr

Margolis' comment that, "The military was the only Pakistani institution that managed to avoid being fouled in the national swamp of corruption and chicanery, or that succeeded in holding popular respect in a country steeped in poisonous cynicism" may seem over the top. At the same time, when viewed a few years into the future, he may be more correct than we are prepared to acknowledge today. However, for anyone looking for some degree of balance on the India-Pakistan disputes, this is not the place to look. He has an animus towards India and Indians that in many respects undermines the value of his central thesis on the importance of this region.

Peter Pigott, a former employee of Foreign Affairs, is an author who has given life to Canada's aviation story (with side trips to Hong Kong) and his book *Canada in Afghanistan* is a significant departure. It is two books in one: the first is a fast-paced, sixty-page summary of Afghan history, ranging from the Sumerians to Karzai. As an entry point for readers, it is one of the best I have seen and for those who believe that all history is prologue it is the sort of introduction to a complex area that is seldom available. It is the second part of the book that brings things up to date with the first entry of Canadian troops into Afghanistan in late 2001, and the subsequent efforts to forge a policy and military deployments that made sense in that changing environment. It is a sympathetic account and makes few judgements on the results.

However, in the last chapter of the book, Mr Pigott documents the sorry effort to provide the troops with equipment appropriate to the task and the seeming ease with which the Taliban has parried the Western thrust with appropriate cheap counter tactics and weapons. Quoting Churchill's experience in the same area over a hundred years ago, the author suggests that supply will never meet the demand – or more correctly the need. While readers may disagree with his pejorative-laden descriptions of the enemy in Afghanistan, he does detail their greatest strength. Quoting Gwynne Dyer about how the Afghans have affected foreign conquerors, he writes: "Eventually they will cut their losses and go home."

The author details the sad litany of armed personnel carriers (APCs) in Afghanistan. Ranging from the Iltis ("battlefield taxis") to BV-206 AMV, the G-Wagon ("an SUV with armour panels"), the LAV III ("unreliable in rough country"), the Coyote, and the Nyala ("vulnerable to IEDs"), this one piece of equipment has been the source of more Canadian casualties than any other in Afghanistan. Recent reports and deaths suggest that matters have not improved.

The story of unmanned aerial vehicles (UAV) is equally troublesome. Rushed into fulfilling the need for "over-the-hill" tactical intelligence, the decision was made to purchase the Sperwer UAV which had been designed for the European theatre. In Afghanistan, the Sperwer was a total disaster. The author quotes a military officer: "By the first week of December, we were just about to be fully operational. About this time we also had our first crash." Five crashes later (there were only six vehicles), it was determined that Afghan "wind shears and turbulence" were too much for the equipment. However, the Canadian content, snowmobile engines from Bombardier, worked well. And we are still looking for helicopters.

Two of the books, *Fifteen Days* and *Outside the Wire*, tell the stories of mainly Canadian military personnel, often in their own words. In Christie Blatchford's *Fifteen Days* there is the jaundiced eye of an experienced and self-depreciating journalist who has seen much and knows much about the human condition. (Her story of loose bowels while under fire is a classic.) I was not prepared to like the book, as Ms Blatchford in her daily writings in Canada has a tendency towards the "sob" or Mary Sunshine. But here she rises well above such a tendency and gives the reader a tight, ground-level account of what it means to be a soldier in Afghanistan. This is combined with accounts of grieving and fearful relatives in Canada.

Outside the Wire on the other hand is a compilation of journal entries and accounts of a range of persons who have worked in Afghanistan since 2002. Soldiers, medics, doctors, psychiatrists and aid workers are all jumbled together and the quality of the writing, while weak at times, is compensated by its diversity and uniqueness.

The story "Mascara" by Marija Dumancic, a CBC journalist, stands out particularly. She was assigned to northern Afghanistan to help female journalists develop an all-woman radio station. CBC/Canadian ethics and one Afghan reporter clashed when it turned out she wanted to interview her sister who was running for election. In good Canadian fashion:

> *The staff had a meeting, and although it was tense at times, we all had our say. Finally we agreed that another reporter would do the whole interview again. . . . But I still went to Tajikistan. These ladies needed makeup.*

Many of the same people appear in both books and the value of this is the different slant that Ms Blatchford provides on a set of circumstances from that given in their own words in *Outside the Wire*. Lieutenant-Colonel Ian Hope provides a first-hand account of Task Force Orion in Helmand province which he commanded. The Canadian Task Force was located to the west of Kandahar province, despite the fact that the area was mainly the responsibility of the British military. Following an engagement in and around Heyderabad, in support of an American platoon, Col. Hope was ordered to take his Task Force to Nawa and Garmser to the south, as both of those towns had just fallen to the Taliban. Upon receiving these orders and asked if he had any questions, the Colonel laconically replied: "Where are Nawa and Garmser?"

The directions were found and Colonel Hope and the Task Force went off to do battle. Both towns were captured (or at least the centre of Garmser) and a few days later both were handed over to British and Afghan forces.

Christie Blatchford devotes a chapter to this battle and her account matches that of Col. Hope up to the end. However, her account of the outcome is more troublesome. She reports that the British military decided they would not defend the two towns and would follow the Canadians out. Major Kirk Gallinger, one of the Canadian commanders, is quoted as follows:

Book Reviews | 59

> *They [British] were such a light force. I can understand their CO not wanting to get his soldiers decisively engaged. Nobody else in Afghanistan had that wherewithal and had that ability, that operational tactical ability to manoeuvre, like we did. And quite honestly, no one else was willing to take those types of risks to be able to support the Afghan government like we were."*

The Unexpected War takes us back to the beginning. Janice Stein and Eugene Lang have provided a unique and, in Ottawa terms, as much of an insider book on Afghanistan as we are likely to see for some time. It is a depressing book – even for one who has chased more Ottawa sheep than is healthy. As someone remarked, those who like sausages should not view their making; the making of Canadian Afghan policy from 2001 onwards is no prettier. The motto for the exercise should be the frequently quoted Dr Ken Calder, assistant deputy minister of policy for DND, who in 2003 said: "We don't know anything about this country." But, as the book and recent events demonstrate, Canada's Afghan policy has little if anything to do with Afghanistan.

Stein and Lang in clear and sharp language provide a policy-element-by-policy-element portrait of the road on which we are still walking. The initiating event was the decision in October 2001 to join the Americans in their dash to get rid of the Taliban and the subsequent rush of self-congratulatory euphoria – as everyone was taken in by how easy it was. But the worms of poor planning soon appeared when The *Globe and Mail* in late December published a picture showing Canadian soldiers with prisoners and the Minister of Defence did not know what was going on. A blip maybe, but the issue of prisoners continues to dog Canadian policy to this day.

Surprisingly, in the aftermath of the defeat of the Taliban in late 2001 and their decision to go south to lick their wounds and regroup in the comfort of Pakistan, Canadian policy followed its traditional approach. Again Stein and Lang methodically detail the careful measuring of each decision against military capacity, meeting American expectations (which were surprisingly low) and, importantly, taking decisions that carried finite time constraints. This approach took Canada to Kabul, continued naval involvement in the Persian Gulf – even with nominal Canadian command of ships associated with the Iraq war – and a year-long deployment to then relatively peaceful Kandahar. This strategy of a "little-bit-for-everyone, everywhere" while messy to outsiders (especially with respect to Iraq) worked well – and would have continued to work well except that there was a new Prime Minister and shortly thereafter a new Chief of Defence Staff.

The new Martin government came into office in late 2003. The new defence minister, David Pratt – who only lasted eight months – in comments to the authors is quoted as saying that, "Afghanistan wasn't a priority during my tenure. I was focussing on procurement, defence policy, NORAD and BMD and the Proliferation Security Initiative." This while there were two-thousand Canadian troops in Kabul and General Rick Hillier was in command of the ISAF. As with all Canadian elections, foreign and defence policy rarely rose to any level of concern among the electorate, and that of 2004 was no different. During the election and after, note the authors, Mr Martin and the Liberals made noises about where Canada should "contribute meaningfully to peace and nation-building around the world. Afghanistan, again, was not in his sights; Haiti, the Middle East and Dafur were."

Shortly after, there began one of the strangest periods of Canadian policy formation that the country has ever seen. "Conflict prevention was going to be critical to our foreign policy going forward," the Prime Minister is quoted as saying, and the word went out for an International Policy Statement (IPS). It was to be a "defining feature of the Martin government, one of the prime minister's top priorities, an attempt to redefine and transform Canada's role in the world." Foreign Affairs was given the coordination pen and International Trade, National Defence and the Canadian International Development Agency were expected to drop their traditional vertical views of the world and move to a "horizontal" approach in order to give the Prime Minister his "transformational" policy.

Of course the issue bogged and the Prime Minister's Office took control of the process, but "it soon became apparent that neither the PCO nor the PMO had the expertise or institutional horsepower to give shape to a document that was the product of endless compromises." In desperation, the PMO decided that Jennifer Welsh, a Canadian Oxford don, was their saviour for the policy statement and, over the howls of the traditionally minded, she was given the "pen." Not surprisingly, this did not work much better – as what the Prime Minister naively wanted consisted of pushing an imaginary rock up an imaginary hill and describing it in sufficient detail to provide focus for those charged with its implementation.

Over at National Defence, General Rick Hillier had returned from Kabul and was the new Chief of Defence Staff. Hillier understood more than most that what the Prime Minister wanted was a differentiating concept that would separate his government from that of his predecessor and, at the same time, made sense of a changing and troublesome international environment. Illustrating how deficient the policy process had been, Hillier simply combined the concepts "of failed and failing states" and the "emergence of global terrorism," added the American concept of the "Three-Block War," and suddenly there was something that the Prime Minister could accept – proving once again that old wine in new bottles still sells. "The Defence Review saved the IPS. Hillier's contribution was the outstanding contribution to that effort," the authors quote the former Prime Minister as saying.

Hillier, in addition to being a "soldier, a field commander, and an 'operator,'" was also a Pied Piper. He could lead and could charm the dollars out of the tightest tight wad at Treasury Board. The first test of the new policy was, of course, Afghanistan – since Dafur and Haiti were not seen as being amenable to significant Canadian intervention. Before long, Hillier was promoting a five-element package for Afghanistan – a PRT in Kandahar; a renewed deployment of JTF2 Special Forces in the same region; lead and command for nine months of the Kandahar region multinational headquarters; and, the icing on the cake for any foot soldier, the deployment for one year, beginning in February 2006, of a combat-infantry task force of about eight-hundred to one-thousand troops to "conduct stabilization and combat operations throughout Kandahar province." The fifth element was the creation of a 15-member team, called a Strategic Advisory Team that would work with important ministries and advise the Afghan government on public administration.

Surprisingly, there was little debate within the government on the bold plan. The Prime Minister convened a meeting with Bill Graham, Hillier and others to discuss the plan, but apart from a desultory examination of the other priorities of the Prime Minister – Dafur, Haiti and the Middle East – it would appear from the authors' comments the Hillier plan was considered a slam dunk. "Hillier gave the prime minister unequivocal assurances that the complete package that he recommended in Afghanistan would not inhibit the Canadian forces from contributing significantly to an international force for Dafur (or Haiti or the Middle East), beginning early 2007." The *Toronto Star* subsequently reported, "Martin made it plain . . . that he didn't want to be patronized . . . He didn't want any 'Yes, Minister' business. He looked Hillier squarely in the eye and demanded his commitment. He got it."

Associated with the Afghan plan was Hillier's far-reaching plan to transform the Canadian military, and it was from that transformation he expected the flexibility to mount a second mission to another part of the world. Subsequently, the Finance Minister queried the total cost of the Afghan mission ($1.2 billion; now estimated to be in excess of $6 billion) and suggested that the multilateral-headquarters component be eliminated. Not to be outdone Hillier decided that element could be funded out of DND's existing budget and the full package was approved by Cabinet. Dafur was still of importance to the Prime Minister and he pressed for something to be done. Ever the wily soldier, Hillier met the demand by donating 110 clapped-up, aging, Grizzly armoured personnel carriers to the African Union peacekeeping force. They were shipped via Senegal – and it is not clear whether they made it to Dafur or were of any use.

In the summer of 2005 Bill Graham and the CDS spoke publicly about the Afghan plan and, while Graham talked of a complex plan with a complex message, Hillier, on the other hand, started his love affair with the Canadian media and public with speeches that sounded like pep talks before a hockey game. The CDS got the headlines, but it "buried the more sophisticated nuanced message that Graham was trying to communicate, a message that more accurately described the purposes the government had approved."

A few months later there was a new Conservative government, a new Prime Minister and the first troublesome casualties from Kandahar. Surprisingly, Prime Minister Harper decided to make the Liberal Afghan policy his own and before long, through Parliamentary-sharp practise, obtained a two-year extension for the combat role in Kandahar. Today the Prime Minister is trying to engineer another two-year extension for the combat role in Kandahar that would take it to 2011.

The Manley Panel was the strategy the Prime Minister used to gain support for the second extension. The Panel report released in early 2008 is a document meant to beguile Canadians into believing that, with time and patience, the current Afghan strategy of the government and NATO will work. Unlike John McCain in the United States who has honestly suggested that American policy in Iraq might take a hundred years, here the reasoned tone is one that "no end date makes sense at this point." The Panel details the importance of the mission to Canada and the world, and then establishes a series of near-miracles for success to occur. At the same time the Panel then suggests that, if the miracles do not occur, then Canada would be justified in quitting the Afghan plains. This has provided the government with a wide road on which to operate and, if it does not succeed in making the miracles happen, it can place the blame on others – especially some European members of NATO who have not risen to the occasion.

If nothing else, war should teach, and the issue for Canada and Canadians is whether or not we have learned anything over the past seven years. Certainly there is little indication that our leaders have learned much. We have had seven defence ministers, six foreign ministers, three prime ministers, a host of ministers and presidents at CIDA and an Independent Panel. In all that time and with all of those eminent Canadians, not more than fifty per cent of Canadians, and often there is much less, are convinced that either NATO or Canada can succeed in the changing and difficult environment of Afghanistan. Importantly, there are few signs that the Afghans themselves are prepared to even come close to meeting the reasonable expectations that its Western friends have made. Perhaps it is time that the next vote in Parliament should be one of confidence on Afghanistan – and the opposition, for once, should give Canadians an opportunity to make their voices heard on the matter. It is time that the manipulation by the infernal, internal Ottawa game players should come to an end. (February 20, 2008)

bout de papier, Vol. 23, No. 3.

Over There
July 2, 2008

THE HILLIER COMET HAS NOW FADED FROM OUR CANADIAN SKIES. IT was a comet of some brilliance and its afterglow will be with us for some time to come. For many, General Hillier's presence for the past three years as Chief of the Defence Staff has taken on an almost messianic colouration – of things military and the importance of the Canadian soldier. Temporarily at least, he created a closer bond and understanding between Canadians and their military.

Afghanistan is General Hillier's war. While efforts have been made to label it Martin's and/or Harper's war, because of the Kandahar deployment now stretching into 2011 – with serious talk that it needs to extend well into the next decade – it was General Hillier who, more than anyone else, put together the Canadian Afghan plan in 2005.

As such, in no small measure the General's historical legacy is intimately tied to that war and its eventual outcome. The associated policies of the transformation of the Armed Forces (which was to produce resources for other military deployments) and massive equipment purchases are bogged down in the normal Ottawa morass, and will do nothing for the General's long-term image.

Every commentator, political and military leader who has spoken in recent weeks has concluded that Afghanistan is worse today than it was in 2005. This is not only in the south but also in the east (attacks up 40 per cent over the same time last year) and expectations are rife that it will include the northwest in the coming months. Even the Pentagon, not known for its pessimism on military matters, recently reported to Congress that there are no short-term or easy answers in

Afghanistan, and gloomily reported that the Taliban has "coalesced into a resilient insurgency." The Senlis Council, an international drug-policy think tank, in its usual breathless style, is now telling us that there are too many young men in Afghanistan!

For all of those committed to the current military strategy, the only corrective action is for thousands of additional foreign troops – and pushing further into the future the date when all of this will produce a peaceful Afghanistan. The American commander who has come recently to Afghanistan is now asking for more than 10,000 additional troops. Lyndon Johnston must be cursin' in his grave.

In the meantime the spectre of the tribal areas of Pakistan providing support, sanctuary and militants for the Taliban has become more real with each passing day. The Pakistani Taliban has emerged from the shadows and is in open revolt against Islamabad, and there are attacks in and near Peshawar. Pakistan's fledgling democracy – with large expectations from the people and stubborn opposition from the military – is in no condition to effectively control matters or direct the future.

Rather it will stumble along with an effort to wean the Tribals from the dual dangers of deepening fundamentalism and closer ties with the Afghan militants. In the meantime, with weak governments in both Kabul and Islamabad, their relations will become more acrimonious. Loose talk by Western politicians for military action inside Pakistan will not help.

One can only hope that the West and NATO are learning a fundamental lesson in this debacle. NATO's ability to coordinate military action in Afghanistan is non-existent. Afghanistan is far too removed, and the dangers it may have represented a few years ago no longer course through our bodies politic. Rather, other issues have come to the fore and there is a need to rethink how to deal with places like Afghanistan – which will remain a regional trouble spot for decades to come. It no longer represents a danger to significant Western interests and the sooner this manifests itself into a coherent non-interventionist military strategy the sooner we can end the ramp ceremonies at Trenton.

When the Afghan mission was open for discussion in 2005, Prime Minister Martin and his colleagues did not exercise due diligence; the discussion – to the extent that it is known – was not about Afghanistan, but rather whether it might pre-empt other initiatives by the government in such places as Dafur, the Middle East or Haiti.

Even when, a year later, Prime Minister Harper wrapped himself and his government in the Hillier plan, there was no significant public discussion or careful consideration by either the Prime Minister or his ministers. When a further extension of the mandate was considered necessary, John Manley and his panellists rounded the edges and dulled the debate, ensuring that the Liberals and Conservatives merged their slight differences. In the middle of all of this, the one person with direct military experience around the Cabinet table, who could tell the difference between an Ilitis and colitis, was unceremoniously moved to Veterans Affairs.

The surprising element is that the debates and discussions in Canada have had very little to do with Afghanistan. Instead, they have had much to do about Canada and Canadians – and their never-ending willingness to see themselves as they would like to be seen rather than how others may see us. Mr Manley and his panel unintentionally expressed it best when they wrote: "Canada's participation in the outcomes will directly affect Canada's security, our reputation in the world, and our future ability to engage the international community in achieving objectives of peace, security and shared prosperity."

Modern local wars rarely provide desired outcomes or create conditions that we think are important to our well-being. As with drunken drivers, there are no straight lines. As we approach the eighth year of the Afghan war there are no signs that the outcome will add to the historical legacy of General Hillier. Rather, there will be proof that when you are smarter than the politicians who surround you, you need to do the thinking for both.

The Citizen

Eyeless in Gaza
January 9, 2009

FOR A TINY PART OF THE WORLD, IT IS ALMOST EIGHT TIMES SMALLER than Ottawa, Gaza has had a large grasp on our attention. Earlier, sightless Sampson is reputed to have destroyed a temple there. In the intervening years from the time of the Philistines, who gave us the modern name Palestine, it has had more incarnations than Madonna. The emergence of the state of Israel is but the latest chapter in its challenging and bloody history.

Today's nasty war reflects the seemingly impossibility of moving the Israelis and the Palestinians into some measure of accommodation if not peace. While the Canadian government and many Canadians can with some measure of conviction assign blame and pick sides, many others have decided there is sufficient reason to assign blame equally.

This has been a long time coming from the days when many saw the emergence of Israel out of the ashes of the Second World War as a justifiable imposition on the Palestinians and one legitimized by a vote in the United Nations. Those who win wars generally get to write the first version of history and Israel has been the most successful regional military power since the days Caesar crossed the Rubicon. However, history has a way of catching up with those, again as with Caesar, who win wars but are unable put in place a peace to eliminate the need for future wars.

No one would argue that the environment in which the Israelis have lived and fought since the tough, bloody war of 1947-48 was easy or one in which the Israelis were in complete control. However, the sorrowful record of wars, insurgencies, invasions, terrorism and bloody mindedness on both sides strongly supports the idea blame is more than divisible, it is essential if there is any expectation some sort of acceptable accommodation can be achieved.

The existence of Israel is a fact of today's international life. At the same time the need for a Palestinian state is equally a fact of today's international life. Even the 1917 Balfour Declaration, the initial source in some measure of the creation of the state of Israel, in additional to calling for a "national home for the Jewish people" also stressed that "nothing should be done which might prejudice the civil and religious rights of the existing non-Jewish communities in Palestine." Unfortunately, the achievement of the second part of the Declaration has not happened in the intervening years.

The Palestinians have not created either the political institutions nor the leadership to help them navigate the shark infested waters of their daily existence. While comparisons are generally odious, the Jews in late 19th century Europe were able to establish a focussed international political structure which lead to the Balfour Declaration and ultimately international acceptance of the state of Israel.

Today it is fair to say Israeli leadership has at times been just as obdurate and suicidal as that of the Palestinians. Even the current caretaker Prime Minister has been moved to say they have "spent 40 years refusing to look with our eyes open." Tragically for thousands, war is the default position of the Israeli political system, as the current war in Gaza demonstrates, and in doing so it seeks to drag the rest of the world along with it.

In spite of these weak leaderships, we should not lose sight of the vast progress that has occurred since the 1967 and 1974 wars. Notwithstanding the Gaza war, the equation for accommodation is in place and there can be some optimism that it can be further in the coming months. The peace agreements with Egypt and Jordan, the Oslo Accords and the establishment of the Palestinian Authority, the 2006 Israeli withdrawal from Gaza, the makings of an agreement with Syria, the static standoff with Lebanon and, importantly, the acceptance of Israel by most of the states of the Middle East and North Africa are achievements of considerable importance.

One of the legacies of the Bush Administration is the idea that by labelling groups as terrorists we solve difficult problems. Even the United Nations has "bent to his empty mind" in its willingness to see labelling without differentiation as an important achievement. It is not accidental the world has not been able to obtain an acceptable definition of terrorism despite some fifty years of effort. Labelling may bring some comfort to governments which have not made the efforts to resolve long festering sores but it does nothing for world peace for other governments to stand and salute such nonsense.

The international community has invested an inordinate amount of good will, skill and resources to creating an equitable solution. There is every sign that the Obama Administration will not delay in trying to put the final touches on an agreement that will see the emergence of the state of Palestine. The rest of the world can only hope that it is successful but in the meantime all countries, including Canada, have an obligation to be balanced in its comments and policies.

The issue is not who is right or wrong on the current war but rather whether the situation created by this war can be parlayed into an agreement which leaves Israel more secure in the south and to make the beginning of a rapprochement between the contending Palestinian factions. This is a tall order and for Canada to simple state that it is with Israel right or wrong does absolutely nothing to assist in the heavy lifting that needs to be done.

A Nasty Little Middle Eastern War Brings More Evacuations
January 14, 2009

ANOTHER CRISIS. ANOTHER EVACUATION.

There have been few months in the past several years when there has not been a need for countries to evacuate their citizens from dangers in foreign countries. Indonesia, the United States, Thailand, east Africa, Sri Lanka and the mother of all evacuations, Lebanon, have claimed public attention

To some extent, Canadians appear almost surprised by these developments wondering why there are Canadians in the midst of such disasters.

There is no understandable reason for such surprise. Since the closing dayof the Second World War, millions of people have migrated to Canada from all parts of the world.

To the millions from Europe there are millions more from the four corners of the world, ranging from the Falklands (the Malvinas to our Argentinean Canadians) to those who came of age in Samoa.

These new Canadians are unlike our earlier ancestors.

Previous migrations to Canada, including those of our Aboriginals (only around 15,000 years ago, according to recent research) were one-way affairs. There were no return tickets and there was no expectation of a return home, or even communication with family and friends left behind.

Rather, Canada was home and those who faced the perils of the North Atlantic were not willing to do so again no matter how daunting the new land.

The post-war global migration coincided with the globalization of two technologies. The first was aviation, centered on the jet engine. Today, everywhere in the world is within 24 hours of everywhere else. Airlines even record passengers against a special category called visiting family and friends or VFF.

Associated with inexpensive worldwide travel was the ever broadening and cheapening of world-wide communications. Cellular technology and the Internet put the remotest parts of the world in direct contact with downtown Moose Jaw.

And in good company with these migrants returning to previous countries of residence are other Canadians who, like their compatriots skiing and skidooing on the edges of potential avalanches, want to visit the four corners of the world in search of exotic adventures.

While the figures are difficult to establish, it is not out of range to suggest that upwards of five million Canadians are outside of Canada for part of any given year. Despite the ups and downs of the economy, Canadians form an important component in the four to six per cent annual growth in international travel.

Gaza is therefore no exception. Palestinians now wander the world, not unlike the Jews of earlier centuries, looking for safety and succour while millions remain in the holy lands trying to put together a state in an environment that is not only hostile but engages the interests of most of the world¹s important countries. And they do return to the Palestinian territories after arriving and setting up in Canada.

As evacuations go, the one from Gaza last week went reasonably well. A bit slower than some in armchairs here would have liked, but nasty little wars have a tendency to do that If there was a surprise, it was there were so few Canadians that needed evacuation. For the past number of years there have been regular evacuations of Canadians from Gaza and occasionally from the West Bank, largely due to Israeli controls.

There are really no surprises in that these territories are very dangerousplaces and there can be no expectation that will change anytime soon. Rather, Canadians with families and close friends there will continue to travel in order help their elderly parents, their children and others.

Yet while the evacuation may have gone fairly smoothly, the positions adopted by both the Canadian government and the Liberal leader of the opposition with regards to the fighting in Gaza are anything but.

Support for Israel, irrespective of its wisdom or practicality, is now the default position of the Canadian government. It is clearly evident in the statements of the government.

Both parties have adopted a position that in its simplicity is more obdurate than the position of the government of Israel and most other countries that have an interest in limiting the damage now being done in Gaza and beyond.

If Canadians need an independent view on the war then they could do no better than read a recent statement issued the International Committee of the Red Cross (ICRC). The ICRC, the most reticent and judicious organization in the world, does not rush to judgment nor does it often inform the world of its views.

However, last week the ICRC stated it believed the Israeli military failed to meet its obligations under international humanitarian law to care for and evacuate the wounded. This was accompanied by a statement by a senior official of the UN that there was a need to investigate whether or not war crimes were an element in this war.

In voicing de facto support for Israeli actions in Gaza, our leading political parties have lumbered Canadians with a policy that puts a higher value on domestic vote-getting then the tragedy of today's Gaza. We deserve better.

Embassy

Afghanistan: Beginning Again?
March 15, 2009

PHASE THREE OF THE WAR IN AFGHANISTAN IS NOW UNDERWAY. THE decision made in the last months of the Bush administration to increase troop levels and the confirmation of that decision by President Obama will see a dramatic escalation of the war and significant changes to the Canadian role.

The first additional American units will be arriving in country in the coming days and, based on announcements out of Washington, it would appear that they will be deployed around Kabul, as well as assisting beleaguered American troops in the eastern provinces where the bulk of existing forces are located. Before the year is out, an anticipated 20 to 30,000 additional American troops will be deployed to Afghanistan. The numbers remain vague as, to a considerable extent, the Afghan deployments are conditional on the speed of the drawdown of American forces in Iraq.

There have not been any official announcements, but there are suggestions that before the year has ended there will also be significant American troops in both Kandahar and Helmand provinces in the south. With the arrival of the Americans there will be a significant change in the Canadian role. One suggestion is that it will consist of policing the city of Kandahar and the continued training of Afghan forces.

Even if 30,000 additional American troops are deployed, most observers do not believe that will be sufficient to counter the resurgent Taliban. The Americans have already begun their arm-twisting of NATO and other coalition countries to increase their existing contribution, or at a minimum to discourage a drawdown of the 37,000 non-American forces now in the country. Already, the administration has signaled that it is "hoping for more from the Afghan government, we're hoping for more from our allies, but also prepared to do more as it relates to military and non-military resources." No doubt the Canadian decision to withdraw from combat operations in mid-2011 will be at the top of the American agenda during the February 19 Presidential visit.

The second element, and the most important, in the new American policy was the appointment of Richard Holbrooke as special envoy for Afghanistan and Pakistan. Holbrooke has had a long career in American diplomacy and is remembered for his role in the Dayton Accords on the Balkans. He picked up the sobriquet "the Bulldozer" for his negotiating style and was once quoted as saying that he had no hesitation in "negotiating with people who do immoral things." In the end, even Slobodan Milosevic was no match for his willingness to use every means to bring the Balkan wars to an end.

Mr. Holbrooke's appointment, along with the apparent willingness of the Obama administration to broaden the policy options in Afghanistan, should see in the coming months an opening of the political options beyond the expectation that there can be a military solution.

Late last month the American Secretary of Defense, Robert Gates, gave early notice of the changed policy environment. In testimony before Congress, Mr Gates said: "If we set ourselves the objective of creating some sort of Central Asian Valhalla over there, we will lose." He went on to say that the previous American goals for Afghanistan had been "too broad and too far into the future" and that today there was not enough "time, patience or money" to pursue overly ambitious goals. The Secretary concluded that the Afghan war was "our greatest military challenge."

These statements completely undercut what has been American and NATO policy, including Canada, in Afghanistan. The basic policy, ever since the Taliban was driven from power in early 2002, was to create, in the words of the former American Secretary of Defense, a "Central Asian Valhalla." Nearing the end of eight years of war with no possibility of an effective end to the Taliban in sight and a broadening of the war into Pakistan, it is refreshing if not late to see at this time some measure of realism about Afghanistan and Pakistan creeping into our policies.

The American government is still in the process of reviewing and elaborating the elements of its new policy. However, with the announcements concerning increased troop levels and the appointment of the Presidential envoy, the coming months will see a full-court press with the following elements:

> Military action to limit the spread of the insurgency and to push back in areas where the Taliban now dominate. There will be significant civilian and military casualties.

> The Karzai government will be pressured to improve its performance, especially in the quality of its own armed and police forces and to reduce corruption. It is likely the Americans will push to see Mr Karzai replaced in the coming months, beginning the march to doom that accompanied similar American actions in South Vietnam.

> More overt and comprehensive efforts will be made to divide the Taliban and to bring some into the Kabul government.

In neighboring Pakistan there will be a harder push by American forces to interdict Taliban forces before they cross into Afghanistan. Equally, there will be increased pressure on the government of Pakistan to increase and improve its own interdiction efforts in the Tribal Areas. More likely than not, the first casualty of these efforts will be the newly minted Pakistan government which is already on life support.

In so many ways there is not a lot that is significantly different in what the new administration will do. A bulldozer is only a bulldozer no matter how good the driver, and for the next year or two Afghanistan will be much the same that it has been for the last two – many, many casualties and very little change in the enigma that is Afghanistan.

Embasy

Book Review
March 2009

The Gamble: General David Petraeus and the American Military Adventure in Iraq, 2006-2008, by Thomas E. Ricks. New York, The Penguin Press, 2009, 394 pp., $31.00.

BOOKS DEALING WITH MILITARY STRATEGY OR EVEN MILITARY tactics are usually the work of retired generals who in the softly glowing afterlife from the battlefields update the records and correct historical judgements. These form their own literary genre and library shelves groan from their weight and importance. Even the ancient Rigveda, without dates, documents the military strategy employed in the Battle of the Ten Kings in today's Punjab. Innumerable writers ever since have added to the tradition and their views, ranging from Sun Tzu to Caesar to Mahan to Clausewitz, continue to influence those charged with the most important of state functions. All too often the old aphorism "generals are always fighting the last war" has greater currency than warfare requires. Field Marshal Sir Douglas Haig, even after the disastrous Battle of the Somme, continued for years to emphasize the value of the horse. Today, there are those who believe he was right, giving new meaning to "hagiography."

It is not surprising in the age of 24-hour news and the interconnectivity of global security that waiting for such "afterlives" is not tolerable, and there is a need for greater instance. Nowhere is that need more evident than in Iraq and now in Afghanistan. Much has been written about the errors of American military strategy in the first phase of the Iraq war. Thomas Ricks, the Pentagon correspondent for the *Washington Post,* in an earlier book (*Fiasco: The American Military Adventure in Iraq)* had much to say on the matter, and now in his new book, *The Gamble,* he returns, starting when the fiasco was at its most profound.

In his opening paragraph "Things Fall Apart (Fall 2005)" Ricks details the killing of Iraqi civilians by American Marines in Haditha, and out of that disaster he creates the point around which the book revolves. It is Ricks' conviction that the disaster at Haditha was a product of the American strategy and assumptions underpinning the war – and forced serious generals and commentators to accept that they were on the road to perdition unless changes were made. Ricks writes:

> "What happened that day in Haditha was the disturbing but logical culmination of the short-sighted and misguided approach the U. S. Military took in invading and occupying Iraq from 2003 to 2006: Protect yourself at all costs, focus on attaching the enemy, and treat the Iraqi civilians as the playing field on which the contest occurs."

He goes on quoting in part a counterinsurgency expert:

> "Marines were "chasing the insurgents around the Euphrates Valley while leaving the population unguarded and exposed to insurgent terrorism and coercion." This bankrupt approach was rooted in the dominant American military tradition that tends to view war only as battles between conventional forces of different states. The American tradition also tends to neglect the lesson, learned repeatedly in dozens of twentieth century wars, that the way to defeat an insurgency campaign is not to attack the enemy but instead to protect and win over the people."

These quotes from *The Gamble* provide the central thesis of the book and for the remaining pages Mr Ricks recounts the story in great detail of how a few retired generals and General David

Petraeus, specifically, took on the daunting task of changing the political assumptions underpinning the American invasion, thus rewriting the American military orthodoxy on how to fight counterinsurgency wars. The retired generals, some of whom had served in Iraq, were the sparks that began the legitimatization of the questioning of the ideologues around President Bush, including the Secretary of Defence, Donald Rumsfeld. Ricks, in detailing these sparks, demonstrates that the existing uniformed leadership of the military were clearly out of their depth and were unprepared to counter the paucity of knowledge and sagacity among the ideologues that formed the civilian leadership and directed the war.

The media offensive by retired officers began in March 2006 and was initially ignored or downplayed by the civilian leadership. Rumsfeld and the President were the dumb rocks against which the criticism deflected. Both were intensely and ideologically wedded to the existing approach and were incapable of recognizing that they were swimming in a whirlpool. In one telling anecdote by a participant in a meeting with the President, Ricks reports:

> "The president would say, 'Get this done,' and leave the room," he recalled. "And then Rumsfeld would start squabbling with Condi – 'We're not gonna secure your PRT!'" – a reference to the State Department-led Provincial Reconstruction Teams that were at the heart of the strategy of rebuilding the economy of Iraq from the bottom up in order to improve security and so eventually reduce the American military presence. His [the participant] thought on Rumsfeld at that point, he said, was, "Well, you fucking idiot, that's your ticket out of Iraq."

As for the President, when asked about Rumsfeld, he gave his standard Brownian response, "He's doing a fine job." He then picks up on another of his own psychological crutches, "... I'm the decider, and I decide what is best. And what's best is for Don Rumsfeld to remain as the secretary of defense." Ricks' comment is that Rumsfeld lasted another seven months in office. However, the author does not mention that it was not his discredited strategy which ended his time in office but the Republican disaster in the 2006 Congressional elections.

The bulk of Ricks' book details the work General Petraeus directed in rewriting American military doctrine in counterinsurgency wars and his assumption of command of American forces in Iraq. Petraeus, earlier, was commander of the 101st Airborne in Iraq and later (after another tour in Iraq) was appointed commander of the American Command and General Staff College in Leavenworth, Kansas. It was not an assignment he welcomed, but "Under his command, Leavenworth would become the starting point for a new approach in the war that would involve making peace with the tribes of Iraq."

Petraeus is frequently described as an "intellectual" and, in the best tradition of the word, he surrounded himself with a rich brew of advisers. Early in his Leavenworth command he convened a meeting not only of military officers "but also representatives from the CIA and the State Department, academics, human rights advocates, even a select group of high profile journalists." As Ricks comments, "It was instantly clear that his wasn't going to be the standard Army manual written by two tired majors laboring in a basement somewhere in Fort Leavenworth." Ottawa's recent efforts to craft foreign policy might take a page from Petraeus' book.

Central to his advisors were a trio of outsiders who would normally not be allowed within sight of a manual-rewriting exercise. First was a "quirky" Australian infantryman with a Ph.D. in the anthropology of Islamic extremism, Lt. Col. David Kilcullen, who had earlier written an essay, "Twenty-Eight Articles: Fundamentals of Company-Level Counterinsurgency." It was a breezy take-off on the "Twenty-Seven Articles" written in 1917 by Lawrence of Arabia on how to fight in the Middle East. A second outsider was Emma Sky, an anti-military Brit with deep expertise and experience on the Middle East. The third was a Mennonite-educated Palestinian pacifist, Sadi Othman. They and numerous others who subscribed to Petraeus' approach fundamentally rewrote American counterinsurgency doctrine.

The new doctrine was published towards the end of 2006 and had "two striking aspects: It was both a devastating critique of the conduct of the Iraq war and an outline of the approach Petraeus might take there if ever given the chance. In political terms, it amounted to a party platform, the party in this case being the dissidents who thought the Army was on the path to defeat in Iraq if it didn't change its approach." It was those things, but in its basic content it was largely an orthodox document, reflecting the experience of others over the past fifty years in fighting insurgencies in all parts of the world. Its main points were:

- "An operation that kills five insurgents is counter-productive if collateral damage leads to the recruitment of fifty more insurgents."
- "If military forces remain in their compounds they lose touch with the people, appear to be running scared, and cede the initiative to the insurgents."
- "Often insurgents carry out a terrorist act or guerrilla raid with the primary purpose of enticing counterinsurgents to overreact."
- "Treat detainees professionally and publicize their treatment."
- "At no time can Soldiers and Marines detain family members or close associates to compel suspected insurgents to surrender or provide information."
- "Have local forces mirror the enemy, not U. S. Forces."
- "Remember, small is beautiful."

The new doctrine found widespread support within the military leadership, largely due to the endorsement of the new Secretary of Defence, Robert Gates, and the ultimate accolade of appointing Petraeus as the new American commander in Iraq with responsibility for its implementation. The most public manifestation of these far-reaching changes was the debate about increasing American troop levels – the Surge – to support the change in strategy.

In large measure the changing of the strategy and increasing the crew were helped by a very significant development in Iraq that Ricks argues was very much an American initiative. The jury is still out on the origins of the initiative, but there is no doubt that the decision by a majority of the Sunni tribes in Anbar province to switch sides and support the Americans was a stroke of fortitudinous circumstance. These changes in tribal affiliations as much as the changes in strategy led to the steep decline in American casualties and the level of overall violence – and for the first time since the start of the war provided a large measure of hope for a better future.

The long-term significance of the Sunni tribal affiliation changes is unknown. However, what is known is that these tribes, which were central to Saddam's power, were not inconsequential players and their, initially, self-imposed withdrawal from Iraqi politics was an aberration. Their decision to re-engage, supported by millions of American dollars and the creation of the Awakening Councils and associated militias, could be an event where the law of unintended consequence will have opportunity to flower. While the Shia-dominated government in Baghdad understands full well that these militias are a counter to their own; while past confessional/ethnic negotiations were difficult, an army of over 100,000 Sunnis will ensure even greater difficulty in the future.

Ricks is completely right to end his book on a pessimistic note. American military strategy is important, but only in a temporal sense. While the war to date can be classified as a counterinsurgency it does not presage the future course of events. Ricks' inventory of issues in Iraq – Muqtada al-Sadr, the well-armed Shia leader, the role of Iran, the Shia-dominated military, the Awakening militias, the Kurds – is more than enough to give the wise pause. In the words of a former American ambassador, " I think [what is going to happen in Iraq] is going to be determined much more by what happens from now on than what's happened up to now."

In this telling of the American war in Iraq very little is said about Afghanistan. However, the portents are already there. General Petraeus is now the commander of Central Command which includes Afghanistan; the Afghan insurgency is as intense today as the war in Iraq was in 2005-2006 and the surge in additional troops (mainly American) is underway. There are signs that the war in Afghanistan will be waged on the basis of the recent experience in Iraq, irrespective of the fit. Generals and the fighting of the last war is a syndrome that is not easily overcome. At this time (March 2009) there is no reason to believe Afghanistan will yield to even the temporary respite that is now evident in Iraq, based on a change in strategy and the increase in troops. Alexander, Kipling and the Russians in the end understood, but it will take a few more years for the Americans, NATO and Canadians to learn the bitter lesson again.

bout de papier, Vol. 24, No. 2.

Afghanistan: The Hole Gets Deeper
October 14, 2009

THERE IS SAD IRONY IN THAT AMERICAN COMMANDERS IN Afghanistan are now seeking more than 25,000 additional troops. Over 2300 years ago, another invader from the west, Alexander – before history called him the Great – mired in a struggle he was not winning, sent messengers back to his Macedonian headquarters ordering another 25,000 Greek troops into Bactria, as the region was then called. In the end they made little difference and two years later Alexander ran for safety in western Persia, leaving many of his troops behind to become Bactrians over time.

Not all history is relevant to today. However, Afghan history in its distain for invaders should be instructive if not didactic for all concerned Western leaders. History teaches, as one academic recently observed, that there have been only two exit strategies in Afghanistan. The first is to retreat as did the British and Soviets, with staggering losses, while the second is to leave a large army of occupation.

It is a variation of the army of occupation that is the one around which Western expectations in Afghanistan now revolve. Western forces are to stay long enough to create a stable, centralized Afghan security force that will be able to deal with the Taliban in all of its manifestations. Muted are the earlier Western objectives of social change through development and democracy.

American military strategy, and that is the only one that matters, now emphasises protection for the Afghans from the excesses of the Taliban. This copies what they believe they did in Iraq over the past two years. The earlier Afghan strategy was all about seizing and holding territory, irrespective of the cost in Afghan lives. In reality there is little difference between the two – and the switch certainly will not dramatically alter the current situation. An inordinate number of Afghan civilians are being killed and the Taliban has extended its influence to nearly all regions of the country.

Today's continuing slide into chaos confirms that there can be little expectation the current strategy will succeed any more than those of the past. The demand for more troops, even before the first Obama surge of 21,000 American troops are fully deployed, demonstrates the desperation of the situation. General Stanley McChrystal's deeply pessimistic request for more troops only describes a situation that has been evident for more than two years.

The fiasco of the recent election with its proven fraudulent excesses suggests that the Afghans up to and including President Karzai have learned little in the Democracy 101 classroom, touted by those who never take off their rose-coloured glasses. As matters now stand it is likely that President Karzai will be declared the winner, based on slightly more than a 50 per cent majority of an electorate consisting of about 30 per cent of the Afghan population. Afghanistan does not need more divisions – and it is already clear the elections have created additional ones within the small Afghan pro-Western camp.

There are equally signs that in this imbroglio the Americans are tempted to fall back on a tactic it used in South Vietnam with disastrous results. These signs suggest they will attempt to dump President Karzai and install someone they believe will be more amenable to their will. The press reports of the recent meeting between Richard Holbrooke, the American special envoy, and President Karzai reflect Mr Holbrooke's earlier sobriquet as being the "bulldozer." Lest Canadians take exception to such an approach, it should be remembered that a Canadian foreign minister a year or so ago tried the same tactic with respect to the governor of Kandahar.

These developments support the conclusion that the mission is in serious trouble, if not in its death throes. Of equal concern is the continuing disarray within NATO. While there have been public statements by Britain, Germany and France of their continued support for the mission, Afghanistan is deeply unpopular in these countries, as it is in most others. The results of the looming elections in Germany could well be influenced. Already, German Chancellor Angela Merkel, in cooperation with Britain and France, has called for an international conference that would try and put more responsibility on the Afghan government for its own security.

British Prime Minister Gordon Brown has deepened the rifts in NATO by reopening the unequal- burden-sharing debate. The Netherlands will withdraw next year and it remains the expressed policy of the Canadian government that its combat forces will withdraw by July 2011. Uncharacteristically, the new Secretary General of NATO publicly scolded only Canada for its decision.

In the United States the Obama administration is caught in the crossfire of its earlier rhetoric of Afghanistan being "a war of necessity" and the intractable problems it represents. The Democrats are already divided on health reform and many of Obama's supporters believe the Afghan war undermines prospects for further significant domestic social and economic reforms. The anti-war movement which has been quiescent since the departure of Mr Bush is planning to be much more active this fall on Afghanistan.

The next two years will be difficult and troublesome for Canada. There will be casualties at a rate that was not seen in the previous eight years, and the belief will increase that the deaths are meaningless. Canada will be on the sidelines and this will become an American war. To the extent that there will be a role for other Western countries, this will involve major European NATO partners only. Sacrifice has a very short shelf life in the affairs of the world.

Embassy

Book Reviews
November 16, 2009

A Soldier First: Bullets, Bureaucrats and the Politics of War, by General Rick Hillier. Harper Collins Publishers Ltd., 2009, 509 pp., $34.99.

Lessons in Disaster: McGeorge Bundy and the Path to War in Vietnam, by Gordon M. Goldstein. Holt Paperbacks, 2008, 300pp., $20.50.

IT IS RARE IN PUBLIC LIFE TO SEE A SUBSTANTIVE BOOK WRITTEN within a year of a senior officer leaving office offering a detailed and provocative description of military life overlapping life in Ottawa's fast lane. And there is much more: It also offers penetrating prescriptions for the many potholes that mar the Ottawa fast lane, the problems with peacekeeping and the misnamed peacemaking in a variety of dangerous places, and the failures of NATO and the United Nations in organizing the international community in such matters. General Rick Hillier has done exactly that and, while news reports have already cherry-picked the book of some of its provocative views as well as its descriptions of many around Ottawa and its arcane processes, the book has not been examined in any detail, nor have its various conclusions been tested against the world as seen by others.

It is worth emphasizing what an unusual event this book represents. General Hillier is the first Chief of the Defence Staff to write a book upon his retirement since the time General Jacques Dextraze did so in 1977. Only Dextraze (although it has not been possible to find a reference to the Dextraze's book) and Hillier have recounted their unique contributions in the service of Canadians since the position of Chief of the Defence Staff was established in 1964. There have been fifteen such Chiefs since then. Equally, there are few others in the military at Hillier's rank who have written such works. General Lew MacKenzie is a singular exception.

In Foreign Affairs there are a few books in recent memory that provide the public with an examination of its work in some detail. Alan Gottlieb detailed his many years in Washington in such a way as to make it a classic for any Canadian involved with the Americans and Nick Couglin wrote of his insightful wanderings in Colombia and the Sudan. Derek Burney's *Getting It Done: A Memoir* offers a direct comparison to Hillier's book in that it describes in great detail the practicalities of a life in the Foreign Service. Lester Pearson did much the same in *Mike,* detailing the central role played by the department in shaping and delivering public policy. Unfortunately the soil is barren in other parts of the public service. One needs only to look south to see and understand the value of such books for an informed citizenry and a consequential public debate on defence and foreign policy.

Hillier's book is a breezy romp through the life of a dedicated soldier with two important overarching themes. First, Canada and Canadians have consciously devalued both the importance and the role of the military in achieving national goals. He writes: "I'm not sure that the CF [Canadian Forces] ever had a significant relationship with the people of Canada. Since the Second World War, our military was never really regarded as the armed forces of Canada by Canadians themselves; Canadians never took ownership of the military."

The second theme of the book emphasizes the fact that the role Canada plays in today's world is more tied to having a well-trained, well-led and well-equipped military than any other factor. Not for Hillier the idea of "soft power" as the road for Canadians when they confront nasty and dangerous states sliding towards failure. In the view of the General, ". . . for many years our political landscape had been dominated by a select group in Canadian society, self-proclaimed opinion leaders who I prefer to think of as snake-oil salesmen, who had been allowed to create the impression that Canadians were very sensitive, would advocate only "soft power" and would support their military only in the role of peacekeepers." He goes on to state with the assurance of snake-oil salesmen everywhere that, "To the contrary, Canadians, in enormous numbers, understand the sheer lunacy of "soft power" and that really, in life, there is just power, soft or hard, and that the levers of influence always work both ways."

In his view, what the "vast majority of Canadians" wanted was "more information on the Afghanistan mission – they were starved . . . on why we were there, what our national interests were, what activities our troops were involved in and what else we were doing on the ground to support those activities." Hillier writes that he gave a lot of speeches and public presentations and validated the value of his words by comparing shows of hands by audiences before and after of their support for his position. "At every speech I gave, the audience would start out at about 50-50 in their support for our presence in Afghanistan. By the time I wrapped, that support would be at 75 to 80 percent or higher in favour."

Hillier's description of what Canadians needed by way of information is correct. Unfortunately, there is little evidence to support, apart from the afterglow of his speeches, that Canadians were significantly changed by his public endeavours in their opinion on the war. In June 2006, a year after General Hillier was appointed Chief of Defence Staff, polling reported 59 percent of Canadians supported the combat mission in Afghanistan; in October, 2009, more than a year after he retired, the same pollsters reported less than fifty per cent support. In the same period, Liberal and Conservative politicians who read the national tea leaves better than most came together and voted a parliamentary deadline on the mission for mid-2011. There are many reasons for this change in public support for the mission, but it can be said with some certainty that the efforts of the General to explain the war did not have the effect he claims in his autobiography. His outreach to the paparazzi of the sports and entertainment world appears to have been seen by many Canadians for what it was – warm words without serious content. The description of Don Cherry in one photo caption as a "Canadian philosopher" may be accurate for some, but it has little to do with explaining a complex war in central Asia.

One of the amazing dark holes in the General's account of the war in Afghanistan is how and why the decision was made to deploy a Canadian combat mission to Kandahar in 2005. At the time General Hillier had just been appointed (February 2005) Chief of the Defence Staff and Paul Martin was Prime Minister. There was a vacuum in Ottawa on both defence and foreign policy and the Prime Minister was looking for policies that would be "transformational" in both areas, or at least policies that would sharply differentiate his government from that of Prime Minister Chrétien. Nowhere was there a cogent explanation of just what the transformation would entail and for many months officials in Foreign Affairs, Defence and the PCO/PMO laboured to satisfy the Prime Minister. Even the hiring of a professor from Oxford failed to put meat on what the Prime Minister had in mind.

General Hillier skates around his role in this debate and the success he ultimately had (and surprisingly does not claim) in obtaining agreement for the five elements that became our Afghan policy in 2005. Other writers give General Hillier pride of place in developing, selling and carrying out the Kandahar policy. Paul Martin in his 2008 autobiography *Hell or High Water* writes that the "burden of my message to General Hillier was that our commitment in Afghanistan had to be shaped in the context not only of other current commitments but potential new ones. He assured me that he understood, and that whatever the next stage might be in our Afghanistan mission, it would not preclude our capacity to deploy elsewhere." In Mr Martin's mind the "potential new ones" included Dafur, the Middle East and Haiti.

Mr Martin also writes that he was impressed by General Hillier's advocacy of what was called "the three block war" as the basis for

Canadian combat operations in Afghanistan. The concept originated with an American General who in the late 1990s used it to describe the various challenges faced by soldiers on the modern battlefield. These challenges could within a three- block-area range from full-scale military action, peacekeeping in the traditional sense and at the same time organizing humanitarian assistance. The war in Mogadishu, Somalia, in the early 1990s used the concept, but its future utility was undermined once two American Blackhawk helicopters were shot down with a significant loss of life. However, Mr Martin spends some time explaining that his agreement for the deployment to Kandahar was a limited one, as he did not want to be locked into an open-ended commitment. "We did not have the capacity to do everything we wanted to do militarily in the world.... And it was important that our military commitment in Afghanistan not crowd out every other mission we might choose to undertake," Martin writes.

Mr Martin's account of the Kandahar deployment is supported in large part by Janice Stein and Eugene Lang's 2007 book *The Unexpected War: Canada in Kandahar*. Both carried out extensive interviews with the principal participants in the Kandahar deployment debate and Mr Lang was chief of staff to the defence minister at the time. As such there is high credibility for their account of the debate – and it is all the more surprising in light of these public accounts of General Hillier's role that he underplays his involvement throughout his book. One would have hoped *A Soldier First* would have contained a detailed firsthand account of why Canada became a participant in its first ground war since Korea. General Hillier spends more time detailing his activities while head of the ISAF in Kabul, starting in December 2003, than he does in his role in Ottawa in 2005.

Of equal note is the lack of any reference in the book to a detailed examination or intelligence assessment of what the deployment in Kandahar would involve. Mr Martin's description of what he understood would be the environment in Kandahar is worth recording:

> The plan General Hillier presented to me was based on Provincial Reconstruction Teams, meaning the gradual restoration of order by the military in expanding circles, with reconstruction intimately linked and immediately underway once the area was secured. . . . In my time as Prime Minister, we never envisaged a broad military campaign that would make reconstruction efforts more difficult, if not impossible, as we bit off more than we could chew. In my view, the change in strategy under the subsequent government was unfortunate. I don't think anyone, including me, expected the Taliban resurgence that Canadian troops encountered when they moved to Kandahar. I do believe, however, that the virtual abandonment of reconstruction efforts in the first year or so of the new government was a mistake.

By 2005 there was ample evidence that the Taliban resurgence was well underway in both the south and east of Afghanistan. The lack of any understanding or apparent willingness to assess what would be encountered in Kandahar province borders on folly on the part of those, including General Hillier, who put together the Kandahar plan. This lack of assessment or even some measure of the risks led to an under-manned, under-equipped and in some measure under-led Canadian force on the ground in Kandahar – and that has continued to this day. The willingness of the Harper government to continue with the folly based on little more than hope remains as one of the great mistakes of any Canadian government.

General Hillier does not offer any reflections on this sad outcome for his efforts. For him the rehabilitation of the Canadian Armed Forces, their reconnection with Canadians and such ephemeral events as the Highway of Heroes are more important than providing his successors and others with signposts and recommendations for the future. Towards the end of the book he writes, "If anybody had told me that we were going to go into intense combat operations, sustain total casualties of over 100 soldiers killed and about 400 wounded, and suffer all these losses within three years and that Canadians would still support the mission, I would not have believed them." The jury is still out on the depth of that support – and one would hope that in the future the General would offer advice and help as Canadians grapple with ongoing casualties, the possible exit from Afghanistan and what will be the next overseas operation for the new Canadian army. Unfortunately, the new Chief of the Defence Staff seems to have taken a vow of silence and as such is unlikely to offer Canadians any advice on these issues.

Instructive for Canadians on how a country should examine the conditions under which soldiers should be sent abroad to die is the debate in the United States on increasing its troop levels in Afghanistan. Already history's judgement on American policy in Afghanistan will be that it is solely responsible for the present disaster. Not only is Afghanistan on the verge of implosion without significant numbers of additional foreign troops, but equally the spillover of the war into large parts of Pakistan adds a dimension that is downright scary. The world can live with a failed Afghan state, but it cannot live with a failed Pakistan.

It is these mutually supporting disasters that the administration is now facing as it seeks to come up with a policy that does not dominate the last three years of President Obama's first term. It is likely that there will be a decision to send significant numbers of additional American troops to Afghanistan, but in making that decision the administration is looking for "off-ramps" where it can start to withdraw troops without precipitating a faster slide to failure there. As many others have learned there are no risk-averse military operations and Afghanistan will not become an exception to that rule.

It is the squaring of these concerns that has given importance and prominence to Gordon M Goldstein's book of 2008 *Lessons in Disaster: McGeorge Bundy and the Path to the War in Vietnam.* Professor Goldstein examines the discussions and actions in the Kennedy administration through the eyes of McGeorge Bundy, national security adviser to both Kennedy and Johnson. After leaving Washington in 1966 Bundy was troubled by the role he played in the American disaster in Vietnam, and these are seriously explored and analyzed along with the parallels they offer in the debate over Afghanistan today. He gives very high marks to the role Kennedy played in looking down the road farther than any of his advisers; fresh from the disaster at the Bay of Pigs, the President did not see his military advisers as providing either impartial or even sound advice.

Lessons in Disaster has become essential reading in today's White House, although there is more than just time separating 1962 and 2009. However, political leadership is one element that can save us from disasters on the scale of both Vietnam and Afghanistan. Military advisers, including Chiefs of the Defence Staff, have large roles to play in the decision-making associated with wars in foreign places. However, as Professor Goldstein emphasizes, Prime Ministers and Presidents, actually decide – and in doing so there is a need for greater wisdom and foresight than we have seen so far on Afghanistan. There is not much time left for Afghanistan or for Pakistan and *Lessons in Disaster* more so than *A Soldier First* should be the required reading for those involved.

General Hillier was a unique star that flashed across the Canadian skies and it would be wrong to suggest that there was no impact on Canadians. At a time when there is little faith or trust in current leaders and governments generally, there is ample evidence that General Hillier did connect with many Canadians. For many, he represented values and attributes not seen in most of our leaders. A letter by Monique Kok in the *Ottawa Citizen* recently reflected the legacy of the General for many Canadians:

> *A year ago when I read that Gen. Rick Hillier, then Chief of Defence Staff, was retiring, I surprised myself by bursting into tears. I'm not the type of person to cry about this sort of thing, having no family members in the Canadian Forces. To my shame, I'm not sure I can even name the current chief of defence staff.*

But when I read that Gen. Hillier was retiring, I felt a tremendous sense of loss. . . . Hillier's guileless and frank reports made it seem as if one of us – albeit the one with the best vantage point – was reporting faithfully back to us.

bout de papier, November 16, 2009

Colvin is Just Doing His Job
November 28, 2009

POOR RICHARD COLVIN. SWIFT BOATED BY DEFENCE MINISTER PETER MacKay as "not credible" and a mouthpiece of the Taliban, now the Attorney General of Canada is on his back, threatening prosecution if he dares to answer a parliamentary committee's request to see documents he wrote about detainee abuse and torture in Afghanistan.

The character assassination and bullying are nonsense of course – the same government that slandered Colvin also promoted him to an intelligence job with top-secret clearance in Canada's Washington embassy – but if one can set aside the revulsion, what does the Colvin affair teach about the duties of public servants to tell the truth? As a law professor and a retired diplomat (who once held Colvin's job in Washington), there are four lessons we think every civil servant in Ottawa should know.

One lesson is that the conventional wisdom – that Colvin is a whistleblower who is now being punished – is an attractive Hollywood story, but a distant relative of the truth. Colvin was sent to Afghanistan with a job to do, which was to gather observations on political issues related to Canada's mission. His notes are the focus of everyone's interest, not because he did his job poorly but because he did it well. He also did well when, sensing imminent government interference because he was summoned as a witness before the Military Police Complaints Commission, he invoked a Treasury Board policy that entitles civil servants to an independent lawyer on request.

Nor did he transgress his job by accepting Parliament's invitation to testify last week, even if it infuriated the Harper government and sycophantic civil servants above him. For, like all civil servants, Colvin owes a duty of loyalty to the Government of Canada – including Parliament.

This explains why, for all their loathing of Colvin, Peter MacKay and other cabinet ministers mutter that he won't be fired – because he can't be. Since they can't fire, they bully; it's all they have.

The second lesson is that many, perhaps most, civil servants do not truly understand the duty of loyalty placed upon them. Ignorance suits the Harper government; it relishes control, and the uninformed err safely on the side of excess loyalty. Too much loyalty, however, means too little innovation or constructive criticism at best, or exploitation and job dissatisfaction at worst. It is better, for Canada and for civil servants themselves, to know truly where the limits of loyalty lie.

The Supreme Court of Canada wrote the final word on the duty of loyalty in 1985:

"The loyalty owed is to the Government of Canada, not the political party in power at any one time. A public servant need not vote for the governing party. Nor need he or she publicly espouse its policies. And indeed, in some circumstances a public servant may actively and publicly express opposition to the policies of a government. This would be appropriate if, for example, the Government were engaged in illegal acts, or if its policies jeopardized the life, health or safety of the public servant or others, or if the public servant's criticism had no impact on his or her ability to perform effectively the duties of a public servant or on the public perception of that ability."

Note what the Supreme Court's analysis does not require. Civil servants owe loyalty to the government of Canada – the Crown, if you will – but not the governing party. In public, no civil servant need agree with party policy. Civil servants can dissent from government of Canada policy in public, within limits, such as when the government is "engaged in illegal acts, or if its policies jeopardized the life, health or safety of ... others."

Seen that way – the legally correct way because the Supreme Court says so – Colvin did not violate his duty of loyalty to the government of Canada. Complicity in torture is highly illegal – a war crime. Government policies or mistakes that lead to torture are ruinous to life, health or safety. Colvin was not just legally correct but supremely ethical to disclose about torture and the detainee transfer policy – no matter what the political aftershocks. That he did so with dignity in Parliament, after notifying his superiors, gives him additional protection under the Public Servants Disclosure Protection Act.

The third lesson is that dissent has to be done carefully. Going directly to the media with a counterpunch or leaked document is not as safe as it should be. That is not because journalists are dishonourable – only the rarest scoundrels don't protect sources – but because the lower courts seem resistant to the Supreme Court's direction when disclosures are journalistic. The lower courts are probably wrong, but their error is a reality.

The best way for would-be disclosers is to see a lawyer. This is because confidential information and instructions given to a lawyer are protected by the iron rule of solicitor-client privilege. The information normally cannot be forcibly discovered, not even by police, and is inadmissible in court. Whether the information is unprotected or top secret is immaterial, and the privilege exists to foster free, frank discussion with the lawyer.

Thus Colvin disclosed to his lawyer, and his lawyer cleverly arranged disclosing to the world. The lawyer proved her worth by picking a path through hazards both real and imagined – for a favourite government tactic is to intimidate civil servants into secrecy without actually having a legal basis. Section 38 of the Canada Evidence Act, which the Attorney General overuses to gag persons who possess national security or international relations information, is one such questionable threat because the law does not provide any criminal penalty for ignoring section 38 secrecy per se. The government also exaggerates the Security of Information

Act: Much of that law was struck down as unconstitutional by the courts three years ago.

In short, the tigers the government uses to enforce secrecy often are toothless, or can be safely defanged by a lawyer, particularly if he or she is an expert in public law.

Technology also makes safe disclosure possible without a lawyer. Wikileaks (wikileaks.org) is an ultra-secure, totally anonymous website that accepts documents from around the world. No source has ever been exposed through Wikileaks, although it has been used over a million times. Think of it as the web's brown envelope, which not even China's notorious Internet spies have cracked.

The final lesson is of course one of ethics. When Peter MacKay taunted and laughed at reporters questioning how retired general Rick Hillier saw secret documents ahead of testifying in Parliament – the very same secret documents that the government has threatened Colvin not to let Parliament see – he demonstrated reprehensible ethics (search for it at cbc.ca/video).

Making an ethical disclosure means never personally sinking to MacKay's level; it means lifting the full weight of Canada's democracy above it. The Canadians who lost their lives in Afghanistan, and the many more maimed, sacrificed in defence of ideals – including transparency and parliamentary democracy. Civil servants let them down when assisting a government that, confronted with its responsibilities under Canadian and international law, such as avoiding torture, ducks, bobs, weaves and shoots messengers in its tortuous path.

They even let down their fellow civil servants, like Colvin. Of the many bureaucrats he copied on his reports, not one has disclosed those documents so that Canadians might independently decide whether Colvin or the government is the more truthful. They have left him undefended – even when, as just explained, disclosure can be lawful, safe and ethical. It is a course, frankly, chosen of fear and ignorance.

We recommend this course: Civil servants and diplomats are privileged to be some of the best educated Canadians, and have an ethical responsibility to help other Canadians understand government's complexity. Techniques exist to disclose safely, without becoming an unemployed martyr. Our government's involvement in Afghanistan is tremendously complex, and the civic interest depends on Canadians understanding it, even – perhaps especially – when the truth is hard, such as torture. The same is true for other complex subjects ringed in secrecy when the Supreme Court's criteria come into play: the H1N1 flu, for example.

If civil servants comport themselves with such honour in Canada, as is more often done in America (think Daniel Ellsberg) or Britain (think Katharine Gun), Canada will be a stronger country. Never doubt it.

With Amir Attaran/The Citizen

Speech

January 26, 2010

AFGHANISTAN: PUBLIC POLICY IN A TIME OF WAR

USUALLY WHEN STARTING REMARKS SUCH AS THESE THERE IS THE ritual of opening with appropriate light comments. Unfortunately there is very little that is amusing when the subject is Afghanistan and the torturous path of Canadian policy over the last eight years. The best that can be said remains Kipling's still perceptive words about war in the region. In the *British Soldier*, he wrote:

> *As you lie wounded on the Afghan plains*
> *And the women come out to slice up you remains*
> *Pick up your gun and blow out your brains*
> *And die like a soldier on the Afghan plains.*

Or even more prophetic are his words in *The White Man's Burden*:

> *Take up the White Man's burden-*
> *The Savage wars of peace –*
> *Fill full the mouth of famine*
> *And bid the sickness cease;*
> *And when your goal is nearest*
> *The end for others sought,*
> *Watch Sloth and heathen Folly*
> *Bring all your hopes to nought.*

Kipling, of course, writing over a hundred years ago, continues to be relevant on war in distant places but he remains controversial. For many he was the voice of imperialism, especially British imperialism. However, for many more, his was a more subtle, complex voice, especially on matters of war. The death of his son John in France in 1915 illustrates this aspect of his writings. Shortly after his son's death he wrote **My Boy Jack.** This poem remains evocative of the deep divide between the battlefields and the fields of home when young people die. It is today an often performed stage play as well as a movie. The lines, in the voice of John, state a well worn message that reaches out to us today:

If any question why we died
Tell them, because our fathers lied.

It was Christmas 2001 when Afghanistan intruded on Canadian consciousness. Then a picture appeared in the Globe and Mail showing Canadian soldiers with Afghan detainees. The Minister of National Defence of the day, Art Eggleton, when questioned on the matter gave the impression this was news to him and no explanation was offered of what these Canadian soldiers were doing in Afghanistan with prisoners.

To a lesser or greater degree the role of Canadian ministers, both prime and otherwise, on the Afghan issue has not improved since Mr Eggleton's poor performance. Today, the mantra from the Chief of the Defence Staff is that all Canadian troops will be withdrawn as of July 2011 while the Prime Minister and the Minister of National Defence make somewhat less definitive statements, or perhaps I should say less believable ones, suggesting that there will be a role for the Canadian military in Afghanistan after the July 2011 date. Fudge has been a common factor in government explanations of things Afghan.

In some ways Afghanistan was a war where the imperative to participate was overwhelming for Canada. The global impact of the attack on the United States by al Qaeda on September 11, 2001 was such that Canada as the closest neighbour and as an alliance partner of the United States through NATO and NORAD demanded that we had to play a large role in support of the United States.

At all levels of Canadian society there was outrage following the attacks. The death of 26 Canadians in the collapse of the World Trade Centre added a very personal Canadian dimension and for months afterwards there was strong and widespread support for the decisions of the Canadian government.

It was a Saturday, October 7, 2001 when the call came advising that the Deputy Minister required a group of us to meet that afternoon in his office. Once convened he advised that President Bush had spoken to the Prime Minister that morning and informed him that the United States was going to invade Afghanistan to take out Al Qaeda bases and bring about a change in the government of Afghanistan itself. In the notification was the expectation of Canadian participation. Regime change had its first airing.

Subsequently we were to learn that the United States, earlier, had been in direct contact with the government of Afghanistan and demanded that the al Qaeda leadership in Afghanistan be detained and turned over to the United States for trial. The Afghan government refused with the result that the United States decided to invade.

Concomitant with the strong Canadian support for the United States during this period was the concern that the border remained as open as possible for the free flow of goods and services. Americans have never regarded the border in the same way as Canadians and there were many Americans who saw it as being a very soft point of access for terrorists bent on entering the United States. Within hours of the 911 attack there were reports that most of the hijackers had entered the United States from Canada; a canard that still has life today. Of course, the 1999 entry of Ahmed Ressam into the United States with bomb making materials with the intention of bombing Los Angeles airport offer unfortunate but accurate indications that Canadian security arrangements did have serious problems.

Long lines of trucks carrying the life blood of the Canadian economy were constant and prominent features of the reporting of the period. The urgent cries of help from Canadian industrial and business leaders focussed attention in Ottawa that not only was there a major security issue but an equally pressing economic one as well.

John Manley in the intervening years reflected both the security issues as well as the economic ones. On September 12, 2001, the day after 911 Mr Manley, the then Foreign Minister established the first edge of Canadian policy in this new world.

> *"Canada has soldiers that are buried all over Europe because we fought in defence of liberty and we're not about to back away from a challenge now because we think somebody might be hurt."*

Art Eggleton, the then Defence Minister echoed Manley's robust talk saying that Canada "will play a major role" but ever conscious of the limitations of the armed forces added that the government had to ensure that the Forces "got the resources" they needed to do the job. And in language depicting the naivety of the times went on to say that we will "stand with our allies in weeding out the perpetrators, in destroying the organizations, wherever they may be."

This was the language of September 2001. However, by November a more subtle and cautious approach was evident in the remarks of then Prime Minister Chrétien on the 20th:

> *"The principal role that we hope they [the Canadian Forces] will have if whenever and if they go there [Afghanistan] – because there is no final conclusion – will be to make sure aid gets to the people who need it. Of course, we don't want to have a big fight there. We want to bring peace and happiness as much as possible."*

[Mr Chrétien's grasp of things Afghan has been open to question. In his autobiography published in 2007 he refers to the Afghanis. This of course is the unit of the Afghan currency and is the equivalent of referring to Canadians as dollars.]

These statements first by the Foreign and Defence Ministers and then by the Prime Minister established the parameters of the decision making on Afghanistan between 2001 and late 2005. As one commentator put it, it was "early in, early out."

In shaping Canadian policy in such simplistic terms there was little understanding of what were the risks in Afghanistan and most importantly there was no understanding of the dynamics that were to drive the Bush Administration in the following years. It was an attempt to not pay the piper but yet be part of the claque that applauded when necessary and to be included in the small group that put boots on the ground.

Afghanistan in 2001, in some measure, was starting to recover from the predations of the Soviet occupation which ended more than ten years earlier. Refugees were returning and political leaders were learning that there was more to governing than quoting the Koran. It was a client state of Pakistan which since 1947 has regarded Afghanistan, as the British did earlier, as an essential part of its own security.

However, reflecting the abyss Afghanistan had fallen into following the defeat of the Soviets, only Pakistan and Saudi Arabia recognizing its Taliban government that emerged in the mid 90s. In its biggest mistake the new Taliban government provided a welcome to Osama bin Laden when he was forced out of the Sudan by American pressure in the mid '90s. While bin Laden wanted to return to Saudi Arabia, Saudi Arabia wanted him as far away as possible in order to protect its own fragile security situation.

Up until this time the Taliban was largely concerned with increasing its own domination throughout Afghanistan and external issues rarely intervened. Occasional long range missile strikes by the Americans in retaliation for terrorist's attacks in East Africa and elsewhere were the only intrusions of foreign realities.

During the fall of 2001 there was little effort to share with Canadians the intentions of the government on Afghanistan. If there was one overriding factor it was the impact of American security measures on the Canadian economy. As such there was deep seated concern that Canada had to stay closely attuned to American policy irrespective of the cost.

There were few statements about Afghanistan itself and for the most part, there was a reluctance to accept the difficulty that the country represented for outside armies. The defeat of the Soviets had faded and the nastiness of the Taliban government towards its own people and the destruction of the giant Buddha statutes in the Bamyian valley added to the convenient idea that Afghanistan represented an evil force in that region and the world.

So it was in this atmosphere that the government decided to use the military. In some measure the decision was made easy by Article 5 of the NATO treaty. It is the "all for one, one for all" clause whereby an attack on one member of NATO was to be considered an attack on all. It was the first time in the history of NATO that Article 5 was invoked and it provides fodder for historians to come as to its legitimacy. The NATO treaty is concerned with war between sovereign states. There is some legitimacy for the view that an attack by a non-state actor such as al Qaeda could be a trigger for the activation of the 1949 treaty. Equally there is doubt whether or not the attack by al Qaeda constitutes an "armed attack" as defined in the treaty.

At the time these were considered to be nit picking and within a few days of the American decision to invade, members of Canada's JTF2 were in Afghanistan. It was members of the Joint Task Force that appeared in the photographs in December with the Afghan prisoners. Early in 2002, eight hundred members of the Princess Patricia's Canadian Light Infantry were on the ground in Kandahar. In one form or another Canadian soldiers, diplomats and aid workers have been in Afghanistan ever since. The Canadian debate has ebbed and flowed since but the high point of Canadian support for the invasion was mainly in its early days.

Since those early days of the war there have been three prime ministers, seven ministers of defence, eight ministers of Foreign Affairs, three Chiefs of the Defence Staff, and six ministers at CIDA. In addition, there have been two resolutions in the House of

Commons and the report of an Independent Panel under the direction of John Manley.

Throughout these eight years of war, Canadians have been less than impressed with the leadership surrounding the decision making associated with the war. Even the appointment of General Hillier and his bellicosity did little to change the basic hesitation of many Canadians however much they enjoyed his fresh style. Polling today suggests, at best, less than fifty percent of Canadians support the war. Even the Manley Commission was critical of the government in its inability to talk to Canadians about the reasons for the war.

Essentially there has not been an articulated and sound rational for the Canadian policy for the war in Afghanistan that Canadians have found convincing. As such there has been deep scepticism on the part of many Canadians. When the Manley panel was appointed in 2006 there was an opportunity to engage Canadians in a debate but that did not happen. The Panel heard from a wide-variety of experts both from within and without government but this was all done in private. There were no public hearings and it subsequent report was soon forgotten. However it had one important result. It allowed the Liberals in the House of Commons to join with the government in extending the life of the combat mission in Afghanistan to mid 2011.

The lack of deep thinking about the war by the Manley Panel is illustrated by two of its recommendations. One called for an increase of a thousand more combat troops in Kandahar to assist the Canadians. The second was that we should watch closely developments in Pakistan. In light of developments in the past two years both recommendations reflect naivety if not deception about the war.

It is that factor – the rationale for the war – more than any other factor that has lead Canadians to their deeply and continuing felt reservations. Over the past eight years Liberal and Conservative governments have offered the following rationales for the war and why Canadians are there. The explanations have changed over time but it is possible to detect six different rationales:

> First there was the argument that if we did not fight them over there, we would have to fight them here. It was not long before attacks in London, Madrid, Amman, Bali and arrests in Toronto and elsewhere undermined that argument.
>
> Then there was the most Machiavellian idea which had underground currency, that by fighting in Afghanistan we could avoid having to make commitments in Iraq. This argument was used in support of the decision to send the combat unit to Kandahar in late 2005.
>
> Later there was the idea suggested by the defence minister of the day that the mission was all about retribution for the Canadians who died in 911. This was reinforced in the minds of many, by the comments of the then Chief of the Defence Staff that we were fighting "detestable scumbags and murderers."
>
> More recently there have been efforts to sell the war on the basis that a struggling democratic government had to be supported and in doing so there would be emancipation for Afghan women, schools and hospitals would be built and opium production eliminated. That idea died with the corruption associated with the last presidential elections and the postponement of those for the national assembly.
>
> Today, the central theme is that we need to buy time to train an Afghan army and national police force so that they can take over security responsibilities for the country.
>
> And more recent still is the idea that Canada must stay until mid 2011 to fulfill our commitments even though there is no

expectation there is anything magic about the departure date. No one expects that by mid 2011 there will be any significant changes in the security situation in Afghanistan even with the surge of American troops.

All of these ideas and rationales in their own way have some validity. However the constant searching and changing of the rationale based on the hope that one or more of them may find traction among Canadians have caused confusion and cynicism.

Throughout this period there was also the Bush factor or more politely, Canadians had difficulty in accepting much or the rhetoric that was associated with American policy both in Afghanistan, in Iraq and elsewhere. As I mentioned earlier Canadians strongly supported the Americans in dealing with the 911 tragedy. It was in that sense the initial Canadian deployments to Afghanistan took place. The fact the UN Security Council voted for the invasion and there was surface unanimity within NATO on the matter caused most Canadians to support Canadian involvement.

Equally, the decision by the Americans in 2005 to turn over responsibility for Afghanistan to NATO troops, once Iraq became the overwhelming challenge for the Americans, also found support among Canadians. Importantly, the casualty rate for Canadians during this period was relatively light. Only eight Canadians died during the period 2002 to 2005 and four of them were as a result of American friendly fire when a F-16 dropped a laser-guided bomb on the Canadians who were training at Tarnak Farm to the south of Kandahar. In comparison, in 2006, when the war resumed with a vengeance, 37 Canadians died including diplomat Glyn Berry.

But the easy initial victory in Afghanistan in 2001 and the subsequent American decision to invade Iraq completely inverted the equation. Prime Minister Chrétien was not leading Canadian public opinion when he looked for ways to avoid making Canadian military commitments in Iraq. Canadians were already uneasy about that adventure. That unease deepened in the following months and years but ironically the Iraq unease contributed to the willingness to increase the Canadian military commitment in Afghanistan.

By the time Paul Martin became Prime Minister in 2004, and the obvious need for greater NATO combat forces in Afghanistan, the issue in some measure from mid-2005 onwards was one of managing the relationship with the Americans. The decision not to engage militarily in Iraq and the decision not to participate in the American ballistic missile defence program contributed to an erosion in the American relationship. For some in Ottawa the decision to put a combat force into Afghanistan in 2005 was seen as a way to improve relations with the United States.

I should emphasize that all decisions in government involve a balancing of sometime unrelated issues. The decision for a combat unit for Kandahar was seen at the time as a low cost one but one that could provide benefits in the larger concern of maintaining access to the American market for Canadians goods and services.

At the time as well there was a new Chief of the Defence Staff. Paul Martin on the advice of his Defence Minister, Bill Graham, appointed General Rick Hillier in February 2005. General Hillier, as most will concede, did not come out of the same mould as all of his fourteen predecessors since 1964. General Hillier as his recent autobiography states was "A Soldier First" and his subtitle goes on to provide further editorial comment by writing "Bullets, Bureaucrats and the Politics of War."

Equally it was an unusual time in Ottawa. Paul Martin was relatively new as Prime Minister and he had one objective and that was to distinguish his administration from that of the scandal-ridden Jean Chretien. Martin's overriding theme was one of transformation, in that he wanted new policies on both defence and foreign affairs that would distinguish his government from that of Chrétien.

Unfortunately as with all such political slogans there was little content as to what the transformation would entail. While Foreign Affairs, Defence and the PCO laboured to satisfy the Prime Minister, even going so far as to hire a professor from Oxford, they had little success in meeting the undefined needs of the new Prime Minister. In large measure the exercise was one of pushing an imaginary boulder up an imaginary hill with success coming on reaching the top and enjoying the view.

General Hillier has much to say about his life in the Canadian army, but one of the greatest holes in his book is that he skates around his involvement in the Ottawa debate about the role Canadians should play in Afghanistan from 2005 onwards. Others have been less reticent. Janice Stein and Eugene Lang in their book, "The Unexpected War – Canada in Kandahar" gives full credit to the General in focussing the debate in Ottawa and detailing his five elements that should constitute Canada's Afghan policy from 2005 onwards.

Paul Martin in his 2008 Autobiography "Hell and High Water" writes that the "burden of my message to General Hillier was that our commitment in Afghanistan had to be shaped in the context not only of other current commitments but potential new ones. He [Hillier] assured me that he understood and that whatever the next stage might be in our Afghanistan mission, it would not preclude our capacity to deploy elsewhere." In Mr Martin's mind the "potential new ones" included Dafur, the Middle East and presciently, Haiti.

I should emphasize that Canadians in a number of ways have not turned their backs on the soldiers and their families who personally bear the brunt of the war. Rather Canadians, in a sophisticated way, have separated those who have loyally carried the burden from those who made the decisions to go to war in the first place. Canadians soldiers have distinguished themselves in Afghanistan and for the most part have done so independent of an articulated policy in Ottawa. Unfortunately, all too often this has confused the debate and interfered with an appropriate national debate on the war and the associated issues. Both the Liberals and Conservatives are content with this state of affairs and to not have Afghanistan cluttering their agendas. In the last election Afghanistan hardly registered as an issue.

General Hillier had his way and Paul Martin agreed to his five point plan for Canada in Afghanistan. The five elements were

A Provincial Reconstruction Team in Kandahar

A renewed deployment for the JTF2 Special forces in the same region

Lead and command for nine months for the NATO headquarters in Kandahar

The fourth element was the creation of a 15-member team, called a Strategic Advisory team that would work with key ministries and advise the Afghan government on public administration. This was the result of a specific request from President Karzai to General Hillier when the latter commanded NATO forces in the Kabul region.

And central to these elements was the deployment for one year, beginning in February 2006, of a combat infantry expeditionary force of about 800 to 1000 troops to "conduct stabilization and combat operations throughout Kandahar province."

Surprisingly, there was little debate within the government, parliament or the country on the bold plan. The Prime Minister convened a meeting with Bill Graham and Hillier and others to discuss the plan but apart from a cursory examination of the other priorities of the Prime Minister – Dafur, Haiti and the Middle East –there was little examination of the plan.

Stein and Lang comments in their book that "Hillier gave the prime minister unequivocal assurances that the complete package that he recommended in Afghanistan would not inhibit the Canadian forces from contributing significantly to an international force in Dafur (or Haiti or the Middle East), beginning early 2007." The Toronto Star subsequently reported, "Martin made it plain . . . that he didn't want to be patronized. He didn't want any "Yes, Minister" business. He looked Hillier squarely in the eye and demanded his commitment. He got it."

In late 2005, Dafur was still of importance to the Prime Minister and he pressed for something to be done. Ever the wily soldier, Hillier met the demand by donating 110 aging Grizzly armoured personnel carriers to the African Union peacekeeping force. They were shipped via Senegal in West Africa with few if any road connections to the Sudan in east Africa. It is not clear whether they made it to Dafur and if so were of any use. Not surprisingly, the BBC hit TV series from the seventies "Yes Minister" is still being watched in Ottawa.

Associated with the Afghan plan was Hillier's far reaching plan to transform the Canadian military and it was from that transformation he expected the flexibility to mount a second mission to another part of the world. Subsequently, the Finance Minister queried the total cost of the Afghan mission. At the time DND estimate was for $1.2 billion. Today it is now estimated the cost will push $20 billion and no one is prepared to take that number to any bank.

The Finance Minister still thought that the cost was far too high and suggested that the multilateral headquarters component be eliminated. Not to be outdone, Hillier decided that element could be funded out of DND's existing funds and consequently the full package was approved by Cabinet.

Both Bill Graham and General Hillier spoke publicly about the Afghan plan. Graham the careful and effective minister spoke of a complex plan with a complex message. Hillier on the other hand, started his love affair with the Canadian media and public with speeches that sounded like pep talks before a hockey game. The CDS got the headlines but in the words of one commentator, "it buried the more sophisticated nuanced message that Graham was trying to communicate, a message [that] more accurately described the purposes the government had approved."

In all of this it is important to remember that Hillier was doing a lot more than just trying to sell his Afghan plan. As he makes clear in his autobiography, he was out to create a military in which Canadians would support and appreciate. Hillier was of the view that over the years, Canada and Canadians consciously devalued both the importance and the role of the military in achieving national goals. He wrote in his autobiography "I'm not sure that the CF [Canadian Forces] ever had a significant relationship with the people of Canada. Since the Second World War, our military was never really regarded as the armed forces of Canada by Canadians themselves; Canadians never took ownership of the military."

Hillier's second theme in his speeches during this period in late 2005 and onwards was to demonstrate that the role Canada's plays in today's world is tied to having a well trained, well led and well equipped military than to any other factor.

Hillier was no fan of the idea of "soft power" as the road for Canadians when they confront nasty and dangerous states sliding towards failure. In the view of the General ". . . for many years our political landscape had been dominated by a select group in Canadian society, self-proclaimed opinion leaders who I prefer to think of a snake-oil salesmen, who had been allowed to create the impression that Canadians were very sensitive, would advocate only "soft power" and would support their military only in the role of peacekeepers." He went on to state with the assurances of a snake oil salesman himself, that "To the contrary, Canadians, in enormous numbers understand the sheer lunacy of "soft power" and that really, in life, there is just power, soft or hard, and that the levers of influence always work both ways." Take that Lloyd Axworthy.

A few months later Mr Martin was no longer the prime minister and the Conservatives with a minority swept into government. Ever since the new government has been knocking the Liberal label of as many aspects of government as they could find. However, the one they did not touch was the liberal Afghan policy. The Prime Minister decided to make that policy his own and before long through parliamentary sharp-practises obtained a two-year extension for the combat role in Kandahar. Two years later he engineered a further two year extension using the Manley Panel report to coop the Liberal opposition.

There is some sense of relief in Ottawa now on Afghan policy. Even though there is some scepticism that our military role or even combat role will end in 2011, there is some expecttion that the long Afghan adventure is coming to an end. Even the disaster in Haiti provides a bit of a silver lining. Many Canadians believe Canadians troops in Haiti are a better fit then being half way around the world dodging IEDs with absolutely nothing to show.

It is relatively easy to detail the problems of the Afghan deployment. And I have not even gotten into the issues associated with the provision to equipment appropriate to the mission. The lack of heavy lift helicopters until mid last year, in the minds of many directly contributed to Canadian casualties. The same can be said about the constant problems with adequate armed personnel carriers. And the issue still has life. Late last week a former Chief of the Defence Staff publicly questioned why Canada's aging CF-18 have not been sent to Afghanistan. Of course this former CDS is ex air force. As one person said at a time of frustration with the equipment issue, the only thing that has not been sent to Afghanistan are the submarines bought a few years ago from the British.

Many would argue that these issues are normal for a deployment of this complexity and in such a difficult and unforgiving environment. Anyone familiar with military history will remember that one of our longest living euphemisms -SNAFU – was probably used by Roman troops as that tried to keep the Scots at bay across Hadrian's Wall; during the Second World War it became a motto for American troops. But there is more to the problems in Afghanistan than just normal military inefficiency.

The war in Afghanistan is today and has been since early 2005, a high-level insurgency where an ounce of insurgency can counter tons of counter insurgency. There are many parts of Afghanistan where there is some measure of normalcy to daily life. However, these places are becoming fewer and fewer. We hear about these places largely on the basis that they are areas where the Germans, the Italians and other NATO members have hung out their flags. These are the areas where the Tajiks, the Uzbeks, Hazaras and the Turkmen live.

These groups represent close to 50% of the population and have traditionally been in opposition to the Pashtuns who dominate the south and east of the country. These are the Pathans as they were called by the British and they are the dominant group in the country. They fought the British and they fought the Russians and today they fight the west while at the same time they dominate the pro western government in Kabul. Equally, there are more Pathans in Pakistan than there are in Afghanistan, the result of the border that the British imposed in the late 19th century.

These deep historical differences have little to do with Islam. All are Muslim and there is no threat. Where there is dispute it is because some claim to be more Islamic than others – hence the Taliban – and Islamic fundamentalism. However, Afghans were always more fundamentalist – or perhaps traditionalist is a better word - in comparison to other Moslem countries. In some measure the coups of 1973 and 1974, the removal of the King and the subsequent invasion by the Soviets in support of their fellow travellers were all part of an effort to "modernize" Afghans. The extensive economic and social reforms by Afghan governments from 1973 onwards, make NATO's modernizing efforts pale in comparison.

The central issue in the coming months is not whether the Taliban can be eliminated from Afghan life. That is not possible. As General Stanley McChrystal, the American commander in Afghanistan recently said: "You can kill Taliban forever because they are not a finite number." Ultimately, the war in Afghanistan today is whether the pro western government can be given a sufficient edge in the fighting so that there is some willingness on the part of the Taliban or on parts of the Taliban to enter negotiations. Even on that there are very few signs that this is happening or will happen in any time frame that is acceptable to western governments. The Americans remain central on that issue but as all will have seen, the Obama government is not one that is in for the long haul on Afghanistan. Twenty five Americans have already died this month in Afghanistan and that is before the surge gets underway.

For Canada, our Afghan policy has had very little to do with Afghanistan. From its inception in 2001 it was based on commonality with the Americans first and them commonality with our European allies, who like us, thought Afghanistan an easier decision than Iraq. Added to this were the machinations of a very effective Chief of the Defence Staff who saw the war as the means by which the Canadian military could emerge from its "decades of darkness.

In between we sought to give the mission some "Canadian" ideals with our ephemeral pleas that we should be liberating the women of Afghanistan, and opening hospitals and schools. These ideas are today part of the dust of a very complex and ancient country. Today our policy is to soldier on until 2011 in the hope that the prime minister can be taken at his word and that we will leave our combat role in Afghanistan. If the tea leaves of the past can be believed that may be more hope than reason talking.

Our Afghan policy can best be described in the words of an illustrative former American Senator, Patrick Moynihan. Senator Moynihan when faced by policy where hope outdistanced reason was wont to say that there was a "leakage of reality." On Afghanistan as with many aspect of our foreign and defence policy there has been a constant leakage of reality. Today with ramp ceremonies at Trenton and overpasses on the 401 crowded with Canadians, our leakages have caught up with us in a most tragic way. We can only hope that Afghanistan has more to teach us than we have taught the Afghans. Thank you.

Public Sector Executive Network, Conference Board of Canada

Peter Kent goes to War
February 23, 2010

THE DECISION BY A COUNTRY TO GO TO WAR OR TO ASSUME OBLIGAtions of mutual defence are fundamental and far-reaching. History is replete with examples of the care and circumspection most countries give these life and death decisions. Even in the early days of the Second World War, the government of the day in Ottawa took careful measure of its obligations, consulted Parliament and, more than a week after war had erupted in Europe, declared war on Germany.

Canada's war in Afghanistan was less direct in its declaration. Then, there was a decision by the Security Council and the activation by our NATO allies of the requirement for mutual defence in Article 5 of the NATO Treaty. As such, Canada again went to war in accordance with well understood rules and international agreements and to some extent with the agreement of Canadians.

While some have questioned the application of Article 5 of the NATO Treaty to the attacks by al-Qaeda, a non-state actor, on the United States, no one has seriously questioned the legality of our involvement in the Afghan war.

Nevertheless, the questions raised are important as there could well be future wars in which Canadian involvement is triggered through our obligations under the mutual defence provisions of the NATO Treaty.

So it was amazing when the press recently reported that the Minister of State of Foreign Affairs (Americas), Peter Kent, declared that "an attack on Israel would be considered an attack on Canada." Then, realizing that he was in the land of quicksand, he immediately appealed to a higher authority, going on to say "Prime Minister Harper has made it quite clear for some time now and has regularly stated that an attack on Israel would be considered an attack on Canada."

A curious and unprecedented manner in which to create a political obligation to go to war.

What prompted these comments at this time? Is there a higher risk of war in the Middle East today than in the past? Is there an expectation Iran with its burgeoning long-range missile and nuclear weapons programs is poised or able to attack Israel? Has there been a request from Israel for such a statement by Canadian leaders? Has there been a request from Israel for a mutual defence arrangement, which is what Kent's statement implies? Would a third Palestinian intifada be sufficient to trigger such a commitment? Or would an attack on Israel automatically trigger a declaration of war by Canada on the presumed aggressor?

The questions are many and serious. A follow-up interview in the Globe and Mail and a statement from the Prime Minister's Office did little to clarify Kent's comments. In the absence of Parliament, Canadians remain in the dark as to why a junior minister of the government can casually make announcements on such a fundamental and dangerous matter.

There is no ambiguity in the government's unwavering support for Israel. The willingness in 2006 to support Israel during its invasion of Lebanon and its more recent incursion into Gaza placed Canada alone in the world in its unquestioned support for the aggressive actions of the government of Israel.

Canada throughout the long Middle East debate and a series of wars in the region had previously concluded that the creation of a Palestinian state was both equitable and workable. The outline of a two-state solution is already evident, with one exception. This is the unwillingness of the government of Israel to stop the construction of new settlements on Palestinian land that the Israelis call "disputed territories." While some progress has been made on the matter, the intransigence of the Israeli government in order to safeguard its current governing coalition remains the major obstacle to a comprehensive agreement.

The fractiousness, fragility and martyr-obsessed preoccupation of the Palestinians does not make compromise easier.

All of the countries of the world, including the United States and probably a majority of Israelis, accept that it will be through satisfaction of Palestinian requirements for a homeland that we will see a reduction in the tension and violence that has characterized the area now for over 60 years. The region does not need outsiders adding fuel to the flames by reckless and unwarranted assertions of military alliances and mutual defence.

Some have suggested that the statements by the junior foreign minister and backed by various actions of the Canadian government have more to do with Canadian politics than with the Middle East. If that is the case, then all Canadians should hang their collective heads in shame that their government would play such games in the world's most dangerous area. Perhaps it is time for ministers of the government to read Middle East history beyond that in the Book of Chronicles of the Old Testament.

Ottawa Citizen

Afghanistan: The Quagmire Gets Deeper
September 29, 2010

IN A FEW MONTHS IT WILL BE TEN YEARS SINCE WESTERN TROOPS invaded Afghanistan. The Soviets stayed for a similar period, but eventually the futility of their war eroded the power structure in Moscow and before long destroyed the seventy-two-year-old experiment in Marxist-Leninism. The British stayed much longer, some 105 years, and, while they lost three wars, they kept the Afghans under some measure of control through skirmishes and fighting from the bordering hills. With the independence of neighbouring Pakistan in 1947, the British gratefully left, leaving it to the dark arts of Pakistani intrigue and subterfuge to calm the region. Alexander, the smartest of all invaders, realized the futility of his efforts and ran for the Indian Ocean, escaping back to Persia after only two years or so in the region.

History rarely forecasts the future, but it does provide some touch with reality in places such as Afghanistan. When outsiders decide that their interests can only be protected through thousands of boots on the ground, supported by technology, history is useful in suggesting that there are often more powerful forces at work than military might and tactics. Clearly, we have arrived at that point in the Afghan war – and it is time greater effort was made to end the bloodshed and ineptness that have characterized the war for the past nine years. There is now, more than ever, a need to look to other precedents, even historical ones, to remove this bloody and expensive albatross from our collective necks.

The past twenty months since the election victory of Barack Obama in November 2008 have been momentous ones for

Afghanistan. There was some expectation that the new President and his advisers would bring a clearer vision to the failed war for the first time since the heady days of late 2001 when northern Afghans united and, assisted by irregular American troops, overturned the Taliban government in Kabul – and drove its remnants into the mountains of Pakistan. In some measure the unexpected luck in Iraq, following a surge of troops and a collective decision by the Iraqi Sunni leadership to withdraw support from al Qaeda in Iraq, provided both political and military space for the new administration to fundamentally rethink the Afghan war.

In many ways this was attempted. Bob Woodward's recent book *Obama's Wars* details just how earnest that effort was, and yet at the same time how lumbered the American policy process is when there is a complete lack of understanding of places like Afghanistan and its neighbours. Obama, with the success of his rhetorical flourishes during the election, circumscribed his efforts from the very beginning by declaring that the war in Afghanistan was one of necessity. No one is free from history and Mr Obama with his unique opposition to the war in Iraq was attempting to create some measure of political support for the war in Afghanistan in order to bring the war in Iraq to a conclusion.

By 2008 and early 2009 it was evident that the war in Iraq was effectively over. It had entered a phase where the Americans were tired; the Iraqi political process had taken over and the Iraqi military was sufficiently coherent and effective to assume the heavy lifting. Unfortunately, the new administration in Washington was not quick-footed or sufficiently hard-headed in its assessments to take this into account when it started on its determination of what to do in Afghanistan. Economic turmoil in the United States was partly to blame, but Obama's view of Afghanistan being a war of necessity clearly influenced his unwillingness to cut through the lack of understanding of what had happened in Afghanistan in the years since the successes of late 2001.

By 2002 the Afghan boat had sailed well beyond the ability of the Americans to change its course. The Americans, accompanied by largely, unwilling allies co-opted by a misuse of Article 5 of the NATO treaty, were a crew without access to the Afghan bridge.

Every commentator with any measure of understanding of what happened in the United States in 2002 and the beginning of the war in Iraq in the spring of 2003 now identifies that war as one of unmitigated disaster. If Barbara Tuchman were writing today she would have no trouble in including that war into her *March of Folly*, an examination of when governments make decisions that are well within the bounds of lunacy.

The Taliban leadership, freed from the pressure of fighting in Afghanistan and safely within the bosom of their brothers in Pakistan, quickly demonstrated to the Americans and the rest of us that we have much to learn about Afghans and the manner in which they fight. Our understanding of how the Afghans defeated the Soviets with well over 110,000 troops on the ground has been coloured by the romance that has been associated with American and Saudi assistance during that period. It undervalues the bravery of the hundreds of thousands of Afghans who refused to yield in the face of Soviet military might and brutality. Despite efforts to characterize some Afghans as scumbags and murderers, we have learned at the cost of tens of thousands of lives, including thousands from the invading forces, that the insurgency is made up of Afghans who are not going anywhere. Change when it comes in Afghanistan will only occur when the Afghans deem it necessary. It will not be on the basis of the need for greater security in New York or the emancipation of the Afghan people.

President Obama and his advisers, when they began their efforts in early 2009 to give direction to the war in Afghanistan, fell immediately into the troop-happy trap. (The one exception was Vice-President Joe Biden who resisted to the end any increase in troop strength). Despite eight years of war with every setback blamed on the lack of troops, the new efforts were immediately circumscribed by having only one policy option from American military leaders – more troops and the possibility of a counterinsurgency strategy that emphasized protection of the Afghan people from the depredations of the Taliban. It was the same back in the late 1960s when failure in Vietnam was misdiagnosed as a lack of troops. President Johnson and his advisers should have known better and "with the clear light of retrospect" most have said so.

In early 2009 the same misdiagnosis was offered for Afghanistan, and the new inexperienced President succumbed to the blandishments of his military and agreed to send 30,000 more troops – but with the caveat that reductions of force levels would begin in July 2011. Even worse, while the military wanted 40,000 troops "to do the job," he reduced the number and already the failure will be Obama's in the writings that are underway because he did not provide sufficient troops.

The opportunity for a new approach on Afghanistan has now passed and, while forecasting in such circumstances is hazardous, there can be no hope that by July 2011 conditions in Afghanistan will support the beginning of the drawdown of American troops.

Many from the early days of the war in Afghanistan identified it as of secondary importance in the region. Of greater importance was Pakistan and the events of the intervening years have confirmed those assessments. While Afghanistan provided comfort to Osama bin Laden and his associates and recruits prior to 2001, there is ample evidence that is no longer the case; rather the danger has slide-stepped into Pakistan. In the process, al Qaeda's mixture of militant Islam and anti-Western ideology has flourished, creating large dangers for Pakistan itself and the world.

These developments, coupled with a weak civilian government still lacking legitimacy and more water than Noah had to deal with, have resulted in a Pakistan teetering on the edge of implosion or a return to military rule. Today's news stories (October 1) of the death of three Pakistani troops and many civilians at the hands of NATO forces inside Pakistan, the closing of supply routes into Afghanistan and the destruction of over two dozen oil-tankers at the Pakistan-Afghanistan border give graphic evidence of the fragility of the situation. The Pakistan Interior Minister is quoted as saying "We will have to see whether we are allies or enemies" in reference to the United States. Meanwhile, President Hamid Karzai legitimately fumes in Kabul about American officials being quoted that he has been diagnosed as a "manic depressive" and was on medication and "had severe mood swings." Perhaps this is openness in government, but more likely American officials trying to gild the first version of history of this tragic policy.

On November 29, 2009 President Obama issued "Final Orders" for the Afghanistan-Pakistan strategy. Unfortunately, these orders, which are still operational, stated that "reversing the Taliban's momentum" was the main of six operational objectives. "Preventing al Qaeda from gaining sanctuary in Afghanistan" was number three. This confusion of priorities has been evident from the beginning of the war in Afghanistan and will continue to detract from any ability to achieve some measure of success in the region.

Reversing the momentum of the Taliban should not be our main objective; rather the main objective should be containing the ability of al Qaeda to organize and carry out attacks on targets outside of the region. Most observers accept that al Qaeda is no longer active in Afghanistan, but continues with its efforts in Pakistan. Equally, there is good evidence that the continuation of the war in Afghanistan provides increasing support for al Qaeda – and the longer the war the more likely that support will increase and become more widespread. Some of the participants in the uncovered terrorist plots in Canada have cited the Afghan war as their motivation. Other countries have reported the same.

Of course Taliban success in Afghanistan does suggest that al Qaeda would once again be welcomed in that country. However, that would not significantly alter the present situation. Instead, it should provide an opportunity to put in place a policy of containment for al Qaeda which is now undermined by the failing effort to keep the Taliban out of Kabul. The security of Canada, the United States and Europe has not been helped one iota by a continuation of the war, nor would it increase with some lacklustre measure of its success.

Ten years of war and with the promise of more to come should be sufficient motivation to rethink central Asia. The possibility that the current strategy will undermine the existence of Pakistan in its current form should provide sufficient worry on an order much higher than a Taliban success in Afghanistan would entail. It is time for the United States and its allies to accept the fact that the Afghan war is lost, as painful as that will be. Not to do so soon will only ensure that the pain of doing so in the future will be much greater.

Prism

Afghanistan: Canadian Sunset
October 31, 2010

THE CANADIAN OFFICER WHO, A FEW YEARS AGO, POETICALLY NAMED the Canadian staging base in the United Arab Emirates, Camp Mirage, knew more than was acknowledged at the time. Today the Camp, like all mirages, has disappeared. Equally, mirage-like will be an appropriate epithet to apply to the fast-disappearing Canadian combat mission in Afghanistan. Before long, all that will remain of our ten years of combat and associated operations will be the tragic and sad ceremonies adding the names of our dead soldiers to cenotaphs across the country. As with the dead of past wars, these deaths will continue to darken the lives of their families for generations to come. As well, if the treatment of the physically and mentally wounded is not improved by officialdom, it will be another reminder of the price paid by a few.

Canada's involvement in Afghanistan will be a decade old when the withdrawal of our combat units is completed late next year. It is the longest military mission in our history. The ten years have been both momentous and sadly flawed. The early euphoria of going off to war in step with the United States and our European allies and seeing the Taliban quickly driven from power provided all of us with justifiable pride. But, in strange places of which there is little understanding or knowledge, there are always big worms in the bitten apple. Even before the self-congratulating had finished, there were signs that only a small battle had been won.

Within a few months the Taliban demonstrated that, while they lost a battle, there was a war looming – and it would be a war that would be fought on their terms. Their success in out-fighting, out-manoeuvring and out-politicking NATO and American forces will be added to the historical legends of the Afghans. Hopefully, for military schools around the world, it will provide another example of how to defeat ambition when it exceeds capability. More than anything else, it must be a salutary lesson for Western powers when there is an expectation that the intervention of modern military power can overcome insurgencies based on deep- seated cultural and religious forces.

In retrospect, the euphoria of the early months of the Afghanistan invasion should have been a warning. Nothing is ever that perfect in real life. The shadowy opening battles spearheaded by the Northern Alliance, American bombing from 30,000 feet and special-operations troops, including Canada's own JTF2, were the stuff of theatre. While an accurate account of that period is yet to be written, at the time it met the expectations of many that those who were responsible for the destruction of the Trade Centre towers had to be punished. The hope was struck that a new era was about to begin in Afghanistan for the first time in more than thirty years, overcoming centuries of obscurantism, tribalism and the meddling of outsiders.

The worms of defeat became evident when in December 2001 The *Globe and Mail* published a picture of Canadian troops with Afghan prisoners. The governmental response suggested that it did not know what was going on. There was uncertainty in the response even to the point where there was some doubt that the Minister of National Defence knew there were Canadian soldiers in Afghanistan. As well, the picture was the first illustration of the lack of preparation in Ottawa for war; for the first time it raised the issue of what to do with persons captured by Canadian troops, an issue that still shadows our involvement in the war and will last long after the withdrawal of Canadian combat units.

Canadian participation in Afghanistan was one of muddle. Even before Afghanistan was considered a "war of necessity," planners in the Department of National Defence warned that it was a place well beyond our capabilities. In a report in the late '90s these planners wrote that there were two places in the world where we should avoid military engagement. The first was the Caucasus and the second was Afghanistan. The planners at that time knew their history and knew the capabilities of the Canadian armed forces – but knowledge and understanding are never barriers when the force of political fever dictates otherwise.

The overwhelming need to keep the Canada-United States trade routes open in the aftermath of 9/11 foreclosed any possibility that the problems of going to war in Afghanistan would receive serious attention. The United States was angry and not prone to accept advice, and so Canadian troops were sent into battle without any careful thought about the consequences.

In the early years of the war there were opportunities for careful assessment and the exercise of some measure of judgement. The first Canadian deployments were finite and task specific. Yet throughout that period there was no analysis, no effort to establish command unity, nor was there any serious attempt to create some measure of regional support to safeguard the ouster of the Taliban and make it permanent. Before the year 2001 was out, the importance of Pakistan to the survival of the Taliban was evident, yet it was years before this was recognized as the central factor in the future of Afghanistan.

Equally, the outside forces sought to create in Afghanistan a new political system with a highly centralized government and administration, contrary to the long history of Afghanistan. Canada was a willing partner in these developments and the self-congratulations that surrounded the selection of Hamid Karzai as the new President which, in the minds of many, sealed the future of a new liberal democracy in central Asia. Today, he is dismissingly referred to as the mayor of Kabul.

The seriousness of the war became overwhelmingly evident in 2005, when American forces were stuck in an Iraqi dead-end tunnel; NATO was called upon to provide muscle for countering a resurgent Taliban. Canada, with a new Chief of Defence Staff in Rick Hillier, who wanted to replace forty years of neglect of the

Canadian military, found a compliant minority government unable and unwilling to ask tough questions. For reasons not entirely clear to this day, Canada assumed responsibility for Kandahar province, one of two centres of concentration for the Taliban. Other NATO countries assumed responsibility for other provinces and, while there was a nominal NATO general in charge in Kabul, his authority was shredded by having to operate through each of the national capitals. There was no unity of command and, rather than acting as an effective force against the Taliban, the new NATO forces provided a fertile environment for the continued growth of the Taliban and their dominance over the battlefields.

In the meantime, increasing Canadian casualties and growing opposition in the country prompted the Harper government to create an Independent Panel on Canada's Future Role in Afghanistan. If the Panel had been created five years earlier, it might have had relevance. However, being appointed in 2007 well after successive Canadian governments had committed to a combat role, its relevance was marginal and, not surprisingly, it merely confirmed the wisdom of the decisions of previous governments. It did detail the "ifs" that stood in the way of success in Afghanistan, but resolutely supported the flagging Western military efforts. The words of the Prime Minister that Canadians "did not cut and run" were central to the report of the Panel.

Throughout the past nine years of the involvement of the Canadian military in Afghanistan, one issue more than any other demonstrated how unprepared the Canadian armed forces were to fight a war halfway around the world. This was equipment. As we know from a recent report by the Auditor General Canadian, military procurement practices have never found their way into textbooks as examples of sound financial planning. Nearly every day of Canadian involvement in Afghanistan saw illustrations of how unprepared the military was to fight a war in a difficult and unknown environment.

The stories are legendary: combat uniforms unsuited for the

Afghan environment; personnel carriers that initially and for a number of years would have been unsafe in downtown Toronto; dependency on other governments for in-country air transport; the initial deployment of drones that could not withstand Afghan winds; and for a number of years, the lack of heavy-lift, long-haul air transport into Afghanistan. One day the military wanted to sell its battle tanks; a short while later they were being shipped to Afghanistan. In the midst of these deficiencies, there were two outstanding pluses. One was the quality of Canadian soldiers that was, unfortunately, eroded by the lack of numbers; and two the quality of the medical care that wounded soldiers received at the hospital in Kandahar. The latter being an essential response to the deficiencies.

With less than a year left in the life of the Canadian combat deployment, there is already speculation about Canadian defence and military policy in the aftermath of the withdrawal from Afghanistan. Canadian opinion has been plumbed and, not surprisingly, Canadians are against another military mission like Afghanistan, and there is nostalgia for a return to blue- helmet peacekeeping – as if these are polar opposites in today's world. Polls also show that most Canadians would rather spend the money necessary to maintain and equip the military on non-military things closer to home, and forgo the messy glory dreams of some generals and politicians. These polling-based preferences resemble those after the fall of the Soviet empire with the expectation of a "peace dividend" that would see ploughshares and economic and social development dominating the new age of ever-brightening skies.

Our experience in Afghanistan should disabuse all of such self-centric illusions. Reality in all its messy, phantasmagorical essences bubbles to the surface and the structured world of the Cold War and east-west simplicity is gone forever. The history of Afghanistan is worth remembering before we mount new horses for the ride into the future. Not to do so will saddle another generation with ramp ceremonies and the need for the very best of medical rehabilitation.

Prism

Book Reviews
April 15, 2011

The Longest War: The Enduring Conflict Between America and Al-Qaeda, by Peter L. Bergen. Free Press, New York, 2011, 473 pp., $32.00. (I put in the order you review, but not necessary!)

The Wrong War: Grit, Strategy, and the Way Out of Afghanistan, by Bing West. Random House, New York, 2011, 302 pp., $33.00.

FUTURE HISTORIANS WILL WITHOUT DOUBT LABEL THE FIRST DECADE of the 21st millennium as one of war and violence, global in its scope and effect. The 2001 attacks within the United States in both New York and northern Virginia and the sadly flawed response both by the Americans and their world-wide supporters will be added to the list of historical "follies" that were documented so well by Barbara Tuchman some years ago. The books under review – *The Wrong War* and *The Longest War* – while different in intent, deal with the same set of issues. The war in Afghanistan and the war with Al-Qaeda are part of the same tapestry and, as both books demonstrate, the failure of one war has meant the failure of the other.

It has now been almost ten years since those searing pictures of aircraft slamming into the twin towers of the World Trade Centre in New York and the disappearance of one side of the Pentagon in fire, smoke, injury and death. The subsequent collapse of both towers will stand for all time as iconic depictions of the birth of the new millennium. The crash of the fourth aircraft in the fields of central Pennsylvania was only marginally less searing in comparison with the immediacy of the other events. The decision by some of the passengers on the fourth aircraft to attack the hijackers, knowing that sure death would follow, in some ways presaged consequential American policies. As both of these books demonstrate, those American policies prolonged the tragedy, saw the deaths of tens of thousands, only a few of which could be directly associated with the 9/11 tragedy, and cost trillions of dollars. Today, with no success in sight, these policies continue to drain American resources – ethically, spiritually and financially – to the point where the firmament of the "City upon a Hill" is in danger of sliding into irrelevancy.

These are American-centric books. Canada and other allies of the Americans in both of these wars are not included, even incidentally. They are books reflecting the fact that these are American wars and, while allies have paid significantly in lives and money for their involvement, central to both books is the knowledge that the United States sets the stage, directs all actors and will decide when these wars come to an end and on what terms. Allies are bit players, expected to play roles until such time as Washington concludes that continuing the wars will not further American aims, either domestic or foreign. These books demonstrate that there are times when it is wiser and, certainly, less costly to stay out of American adventures, as we did in 2003 in Iraq.

There are no indications that the two authors, Bing West and Peter Bergen, collaborated or knew of the other's work as they wrote their books. It is one of those serendipitous and fortitudinous events that within weeks of each other these books were published. Bergen, an experienced print and television journalist, has long been on the terrorism trail, being one of the first Western journalists to interview Osama bin Laden back in 1997. Early in his narrative he makes the central point of his book that not only were the policies of the Americans wrong in the aftermath of 9/11 but we have been lucky in that al-Qaeda has been equally ham-fisted. Its efforts for regime change in the Middle East, to get Western troops and influence out of the region, and the expectation that attacks on the "far enemy," the United States, will cause the U. S.-backed Arab regimes – the "near enemy" – to crumble have been abject failures as well.

While both books were written before the current turmoil in the region, it is safe to say that these events have little to do with the exhortations of Osama bin Laden. It is equally appropriate to say that we do not know where this struggle for the heart and soul of the Middle East will lead in the coming years. The only thing certain is that justice, civility and neighbourly friendliness will not be its main features.

Bergen details bin Laden's belief that the United States was a "paper tiger" on earlier American decisions to withdraw from Lebanon in 1983, Somalia a decade later, and the unwillingness to stay the course in Vietnam even earlier. As with acolytes everywhere there were those around bin Laden who confirmed "his delusions." Even the failure of the Soviet Union a decade or so earlier and its defeat in Afghanistan fed into bin Laden's belief that the United States, like the Soviet Union, was weak and ripe for attack. In his cosmology an attack on the United States would remove the one prop ensuring the survival of his "near enemies," especially Saudi Arabia, in the Middle East.

Bergen equally tracks the fact that bin Laden had his detractors in the movement who at the time understood the folly of a large-scale attack on the United States. Some understood that such an attack would provide the motivation for a strong American response while others saw it as undermining the comfortable and safe relationship that had been established with Mullah Omar, the Taliban leader. However, no one foresaw the swiftness of the American response with its invasion of Afghanistan within a month of the airplane attacks in the United States.

Partly on the basis of religion, bin Laden was able to convince Mullah Omar, who styled himself as "Commander of the Faithful," to provide protection. Even after the 9/11 attack, Mullah Omar, when asked about turning bin Laden over to the Americans, was compelled to say in "cosmic" terms: "We cannot do that. If we did, it means we are not Muslims; that Islam is finished."

Bergen writes that bin Laden, through subterfuge, was able to keep his planning for the 9/11 attacks secret. As well, bin Laden and his followers were able to give Mullah Omar the one person who stood in the way of the Taliban's complete dominance over Afghanistan. This was Ahmad Shah Massoud, the leader of the coalition of anti-Taliban groups known as the Northern Alliance. Al Qaeda, two days before the 9/11 attacks, successfully assassinated Massoud. Ironically, the assassination provided the Americans with firm allies in the north, once it was decided in early October, 2001 to invade Afghanistan and begin the process of defeating the Taliban and driving al Qaeda into hiding in Pakistan.

Bergen approvingly quotes Napoleon's advice, "Never interrupt your enemy when he is making a mistake" and in the subsequent decade the Taliban, al Qaeda and the Americans were guilty of ignoring such advice. For the Americans, there were two major blunders. The first was its inability or unwillingness to provide sufficient force to capture bin Laden in the Tora Bora area of eastern Afghanistan. At the time, November-December 2001, bin Laden and many of his supporters had narrowly escaped from Kabul and were only a few days and even hours ahead of American troops. The American military commander General Tommy Franks subsequently explained his refusal to send in more troops when there was good evidence that bin Laden was in the region.

> My decision not to add American troops to the Tora Bora region was influenced . . . by several factors: The comparative light footprint of coalition troops in theatre, and the fact that these troops were committed to operations ongoing across Afghanistan; the amount of time it would take to deploy additional troops would likely create a 'tactical pause' which would run the risk of losing the momentum our forces were enjoying across Afghanistan [and] uncertainty as to whether bin Laden was in fact in Tora Bora. Intelligence suggested that he was, but conflicting intelligence also reported that he was in Kashmir; at

a recreational lake NW of Kandahar [and] at a stronghold on the Iranian border."

General Frank's decision, no matter how appropriate in military terms it might have been, set the stage for the failure of the major reason for the war in Afghanistan – to decapitate al Qaeda and eliminate it as the inspirational force for terrorism in many parts of the world. Bergen disagrees with General Frank and details the various troops that were available to quickly deploy into the Tora Bora region; he highlights this as one of the earliest blunders of the fight against terrorism, but equally of the war against the Taliban. Dejectedly, Bergen notes that at the end there were "probably more journalists at Tora Bora than there were Western soldiers."

The second blunder during this period related to the decision to take the American "eye" off al Qaeda and the war in Afghanistan and begin the process for the invasion of Iraq four months later. Bergen records, in late November 2001, Defense Secretary Donald Rumsfeld told General Franks that President Bush "wants us to look for options in Iraq." Bergen notes, and others have confirmed, that this distracted enormously and tragically from fighting the war in Afghanistan. The Western euphoria following the early successes in Afghanistan, despite the escape of bin Laden to safety in Pakistan, was overwhelming and misplaced in Washington and, while it took two-plus years for the Taliban to rejuvenate, it did so in an environment where there were few if any constraints. Bin Laden's retreat into the wilds of tribal Pakistan was as cataclysmic for the Americans as it was for the Taliban, but at the time he was only forty-four years and the nature of his organization and his appeal throughout the world became stronger after his escape from Tora Bora than it had been before.

Half-defeated enemies are the worse kind, as the world has come to know. Both the war in Afghanistan and the war against terrorism continue to live on in a half-lighted world where original objectives have disappeared and been replaced by the need for exit strategies.

Subsequent to these events of ten years ago, today the Americans have come to realize once again that wars are easy to start, but satisfactory conclusions are increasingly elusive when fifty dollars of explosives can decimate a million-dollar machine and maim lives. As well there is now the realization that there is more danger to the welfare of your citizens from your own bankers than from religious fanatics in a distant corner of the world.

Bergen's book is a worthy addendum to Lawrence Wright's 2006 Pulitzer Prize winning book *The Looming Tower: Al-Qaeda and the Road to 9/11*. He picks up and finishes the story that Wright so magnificently wrote of the beginnings of our modern age of terrorism, largely associated with the Middle East. Bergen writes with knowledge and understanding of the past decade's war against terrorism and is not shy in identifying the policy faults of the American government. Al-Qaeda has been successful, or perhaps it has less to do with success than with the attraction of its message, in many parts of the world. While it has been severely weakened in the past decade and it may only be a matter of time before bin Laden is captured or killed, its "franchises" in Southeast Asia, the Middle East and North Africa, along with "home grown" terrorists in many Western countries, mean that this war will remain a prominent and serious feature of our world. Bergen concludes: "Bin Laden's ideas have circulated widely and will continue to attract adherents for years to come. Arresting people is generally a relatively simple matter. Arresting ideas is another thing entirely. . . . The Longest War continues."

Bing West is a rare writer. He writes about war and especially insurgencies based on extensive military (Marine) experience both on the ground and from within the Pentagon where, during the Reagan administration, he was an Assistant Secretary of Defense. His latest book, *The Wrong War*, reflects numerous visits to Afghanistan where he was embedded with military units in the middle of some of the fiercest fighting American troops have experienced. His reflections on the Afghan war are those of the grunts on the ground (West has been called "the grunt's Homer") and his conclusions are those of a man who has thought deeply about war in our age, especially when the objectives are more than war itself can deliver.

Central to West's conclusions is the failure of American strategy in Afghanistan from the early days down to the present. As Peter Bergen demonstrated, the failure to capture Osama bin Laden and the inability to do anything to affect the rebuilding of the Taliban in tribal Pakistan were such foreboding events that the failure of the military mission in Afghanistan was, if not consequential, ordained. The failure of the strategy did not become apparent until after 2005 when the Taliban had reorganized, along with the failure to establish an Afghan government in Kabul whose writ ran further than the suburbs of that city.

West was embedded with American troops in two of the "most violent provinces – Konar in the northeast, and Helmand in the south . . . where more coalition troops were killed . . . than anywhere else." Central to the book's success is the easy manner in which West tracks American strategy over the ten years of war and especially the on-again-off-again idea that counterinsurgency (COIN) was central to victory. There were six American commanders between 2002 and 2009, who, in West's view, "followed no single strategy." Early on, the "emphasis was upon chasing down al Qaeda fighters" followed by two years of counterinsurgency with an emphasis on convincing "village elders to support the occasional forays of Afghan officials into the countryside." When this failed there were vain efforts urging "Karzai to adopt reforms rather than assigning provincial posts based on tribal and crony patronage." The Taliban came back with a vengeance in 2006 and Western troops "shifted back to raids and gunfights" as the Taliban "assumed shadow control because they hadn't been defeated in 2001."

By 2008 the American chairman of the Joint Chiefs of Staff was worried enough to say publicly that "I'm not convinced we're winning in Afghanistan. I am convinced we can. That is why I . . . am looking at a new, more comprehensive strategy for the region."

West comments: "Seven years of failure before looking at a new strategy was an indictment of military as well as political leadership. By the time Bush left office, the Taliban resurgence had spread widely." President Obama, while clear-headed on his thinking about the war in Iraq, was from the beginning less so on Afghanistan. As others have written (see Bob Woodward's *Obama's Wars*), Obama succumbed to the standard advice of his military advisers who saw "more boots on the ground" as the road to success in Afghanistan. To disguise the fact that this was only milk in new bottles, there were numerous reports that the additional troops would be able to focus on counterinsurgency – conveniently forgetting that it had been tried a few years earlier.

West extensively examines the application of counterinsurgency ideas in Afghanistan. He compares its application there to "the 'old' counterinsurgency theory" as applied in the Philippines, Malaya, Algeria and Vietnam, stressing that in those countries military activities were "focused against the enemy." In comparison, the "new" counterinsurgency, in both Afghanistan and Iraq, "stressed services and protection to the people, while downgrading killing or capturing the enemy." West emphasises that "beating the Taliban" was no longer part of the American lexicon. Secretary of Defense Gates in a speech at the National Defense University in 2006 declared that, "Where possible, kinetic [force] operations should be subordinate to measures to promote better governance, economic programs to spur development, and efforts to address the grievances among the discontented."

In the same year a new COIN manual (its production had been supervised by General David Petraeus) was released, where it was stressed that "revolutionary war was 80 percent political and 20 percent military . . . Political factors have primacy in COIN." The turnabout could not be more dramatic as, in the previous manual written in the aftermath of the war in Vietnam, the strategy was "Concentrate on destruction or neutralization of the enemy force, not on terrain."

The war in Afghanistan is today a lesson in how to negotiate out of a bad situation with little expectation that it can become better The conflict became one where the central concept of counterinsurgency was to "clear, hold and build" in the contested areas. None has been achievable over any reasonable period, with many military personnel sarcastically describing their activities as "mowing grass." Today the American military has added a fourth element to its counterinsurgency strategy – "transition." This addition to the counterinsurgency doctrine in Afghanistan may be the initial step in disengagement and negotiation; it reflects comments by Vice-President Joe Biden, "the president has made something exquisitely clear to each of the generals: He said, 'Do not occupy any portion of that country that you are not confident within 18 months you're going to be able to turn over to the Afghans.' " Already, transitions have been announced in three provinces where the insurgency has had little impact. However, it does reflect the fact that the American timetable in Afghanistan is little influenced by Afghans. Rather the presidential election next year demands that the Americans start withdrawing soon. Secretary Gates in 2009 stated that "If we set ourselves the objective of creating some sort of central Asian 'Valhalla' over there, we will lose, because nobody in the word has that kind of time, patience and money." President Obama, the same year, is quoted as saying that Afghanistan would not become a "Jeffersonian democracy."

West's descriptions of the problems with the war in Afghanistan are nuanced, based on experience and knowledge that only a thoughtful soldier would have. Unfortunately, his prescriptions are flawed by those same factors. He sees the answer as staying in Afghanistan with less conventional forces by building "an adviser task force." He suggests that the American military should hand off "nation building" to the State Department and de-emphasize population protection. West, ever the warrior, sees present policy as enfeebling "our warrior ethos and has not led to victory."

As others have found over the years a "warrior ethos" has little to do with winning wars in complex places, and where foreigners are given a wary eye. Despite the national pain that will follow, the Americans now need another "Vietnam" moment when disengagement and withdrawal is more honourable than soldiering on in a place where, as Kipling wrote over a hundred years ago, "the arithmetic of the frontier" is insurmountable.

Bout de papier

Afghanistan: Is the War Still Necessary?
May 4, 2011

AN UNSETTLING AND UNSETTLED INSURGENCY IN LIBYA, ACCOMPAnied by regime-changing civil unrest throughout the Middle East, Thais and Khmers wandering far from the Middle Path, royal weddings and especially a national election have pushed Afghanistan into the background. Ironically, this may be more helpful in the long term for Afghans than what has been achieved by Western forces which have laboured so tragically and costly for the past decade.

The demands of the 2012 presidential-election campaign will ensure that the Americans will withdraw some of their forces in the coming months, no matter how meagre. Other members of the NATO-based coalition have increasingly marginalized their role and events in the Middle East will cause Afghanistan to drop further in their priorities. Canada, which has soldiered in Afghanistan since the fall of 2001 and borne the brunt of the fighting in Kandahar province for the past five years, is now on the cusp of ending its combat role. By early fall, the 2800-person expeditionary force will be replaced by the 950-member Canadian training team.

The new Canadian training deployment, named Operation Attention, will be based in Kabul but will have a medical-training unit of some 100 persons in Mazar-i-Sharif in the north and an approximately 30-person unit at the regional military-training centre in Herat in the west. All three areas have been relatively peaceful in Afghan terms, but that is not saying much about the future in a country where, even after ten years of war, the Taliban can still deliver bloody and sophisticated surprises to Western forces. The

Taliban has once again proven the durability of local insurgencies in countering outside combatants.

The most recent surprise was a reiteration of the earlier Taliban "get out of jail early program" for a prison in Kandahar. On April 25, close to five-hundred prisoners, mostly Taliban members, easily escaped from Sarposa Prison through a thousand-foot tunnel that was built over a five- month period.

Several of the escapees have been recaptured and the head of the prison has been symbolically arrested on suspicion that there was inside support for the escape. This reaction gives new meaning to locking doors after the fact. Sarposa, of course, is not new to the "get out of jail early program" of the Taliban. In June 2008, a Taliban team organized the jailbreak of some 800 prisoners by attacking the prison's main entrance. In the aftermath of that breakout, the Canadian government made the rebuilding of the prison and the training of staff one of its "signature" projects in Afghanistan. More than four-million dollars was spent and it became the poster project for visiting Canadian dignitaries.

The war in Afghanistan is littered with such examples of what is wrong with Western policy. At the beginning, the focus was on the elimination of al Qaeda and the use of Afghanistan as a base for world-wide terrorist operations. In some measure these objectives would have been more achievable through diplomatic and police operations than by a military invasion. The invasion, even with its early success, energized the opposition and, over time, with the degrading stalemate for coalition forces, the presence of the West created an even larger problem for the world, especially in neighbouring Pakistan.

From the very early days the coalition's policy focus was alien to most Afghans. Thus, the early euphoria of seeing the Taliban driven from government was short-lived. The cost in lives of the new policies – the winning of hearts and minds in support of Western objectives, elections, the creation of a centralized administration and government, bringing social change to a still medieval society – and the inability of an imposed Afghan government in Kabul to become national created a dysfunctional system that was only sustained by the billions in foreign money that flowed into the country.

Many of these policies should have been long-term ones for Afghans themselves to achieve. Unfortunately they became the basis on which coalition governments legitimized the Afghan war to their own people. While progress was made on some of them, this was not enough to create widespread support in Afghanistan or among Western countries.

The failure to capture Osama bin Laden in November 2001 and his escape to Pakistan should have been the point at which the large Western invasion into South Asia ended; the death of bin Laden on May 1 at the hands of American Special Forces in Pakistan has now ended one of the main reasons for the war. There are many who will continue to seek personal and political liberation through violence, but the mystique that bin Laden added will disappear over time. As such he will follow the paths of other self-proclaimed "madhis" who have emerged from the deserts seeking domination with sword, word and personal charisma.

However, the growth of al Qaeda franchises in North and East Africa, Yemen and elsewhere continues to demonstrate the sway that bin Laden had over the disaffected in many parts of the world. Today, in Afghanistan, the Western invasion has been reduced from one of eliminating terrorist threats to Western countries to one of chasing disaffected Afghans around their own country.

Small events such as the prison breaks and the killing of Western military personnel by recruits to the Afghan police and army have eroded the limited objectives and replaced them with large ill-defined and largely unachievable ones. In such circumstances failure was not an acceptable option and so today there are over a hundred-thousand foreign troops still in Afghanistan. The scope of the operation has much to do with Pakistan and any solution will see a return of the Taliban to full power in Afghanistan.

Afghanistan is an example of where we see the application of political and military policy in its full light – after it has been tested on the battlefields. Failure is never acknowledged and it is only when there is a replacement policy that there is some awareness that what went on before was found wanting. The new policy overshadows the failure of the previous policy and, before long, there will be new, artificially manufactured optimism for the success of the new one. Of course it takes a brave leader in a Western democracy who has ordered soldiers to their death to acknowledge failure and begin the process of disengagement that unwinnable wars require.

A limited example of this was Prime Minister Harper's reaction to the recent jailbreak at Sarposa. Admittedly, the comments were made during an election campaign, but they do illustrate the mindset of leaders when confronted with something as defining as the failure of policy. "Obviously we're disappointed with this particular failure there. But you know, this is a long learning experience and we'll continue to plug away and continue to work with the Afghan authorities to make progress on these issues," the Prime Minister said. "To plug away" might well become the motto for Canada's engagement in Afghanistan. Certainly, no one in Ottawa is examining the failure or offering informed advice on how this first war of the 21st century might be brought to an end.

The current Western policy in Afghanistan is uniquely American with the rest of the coalition largely lending flags to demonstrate Alliance solidarity. In the next few months there will be a complete change in the American officials directly in charge of the war. General David Petraeus, the military commander in Afghanistan and the author of the current counter- insurgency strategy (less killing of insurgents, more peaceful engagements), will become the Director of the Central Intelligence Agency and Leon Panetta, the current CIA director, will replace Defense Secretary Robert Gates. Petraeus will be replaced by General John Allen who has been credited with enlisting Sunni tribal leaders on the side of the Americans in Iraq. Ryan Crocker, an experienced American diplomat, will become the new American ambassador in Kabul.

All of these appointees are seasoned Washington insiders and a common characteristic is their association with the creation of the conditions leading to the American withdrawal from Iraq. It can be assumed that President Obama does not want to start 2012 with a worsening war in Afghanistan on his hands, and part of the new American policy will be the start of serious force reductions. The central plank in a force-reduction plan for the Americans and the rest of the coalition will be the continued rapid expansion of Afghan military and national police forces. This has been underway for some time and it is the only element in the policy that supports the transfer of the responsibility for national security to the Afghan government. The transfer of such responsibility two months ago in three relatively peaceful provinces will provide the pattern for future action.

The death of bin Laden contributes positively to American disengagement and withdrawal pressures. He was the rationale for the invasion in 2001 and, as long as he was alive, provided the rationale for the "war of necessity" in American eyes. That necessity is no longer evident and Americans, in the face of more serious domestic problems and looming elections, will regard the spending of two-billion dollars a week in Central Asia as neither necessary nor appropriate.

From the American perspective, it does not matter if the Afghan indigenization policy works in the long term. Rather, with the death of bin Laden, there is a need for some measure of short-term success that will permit significant American disengagement and allow others to take responsibility for the mess in Afghanistan. That means Pakistan. Pakistan will now assume its historical role of suzerainty over Afghanistan. As has been evident for some time, the American-Pakistan relationship is getting worse with each passing day. It is the billions of dollars each year of American assistance to the Pakistani military that has kept the relationship operational. The frequent use of drones by the Americans against the tribal areas of Pakistan has sunk relations to new lows, and the raid that led to the death of bin Laden inside Pakistan without their knowledge will add further tensions. Already the Americans have been forced to move one of their drone bases from Baluchistan to Afghanistan.

The recent visit of Pakistani Prime Minister Yousuf Raza Gilani to Kabul on April 16 suggests that a Pakistan-Afghanistan rapprochement may be in the works. One press report suggested that Gilani urged Karzai, whose own relations with the Americans are fractious at best, to "ally Afghanistan with Pakistan and China." Gilani is reported to have said the Americans had failed both countries and Afghanistan "should forget about allowing a long-term U. S. military presence in the country." The world has much to gain from such a rapprochement and it would add to the pressure in Washington to cut and run from what is no longer a "war of necessity."

Prism

Afghanistan: An Unnecessary War
May 4, 2011

THREE YEARS AGO THEN PRESIDENTIAL CANDIDATE BARACK OBAMA described the war in Afghanistan as one of "necessity." He largely did so because Osama bin Laden was still roaming the area, providing inspirational and organizational leadership to terrorist and insurgent forces. As well Mr Obama was making a distinction with the war in Iraq, which in comparison was not one of "necessity" for the United States.

In the months since, he has successfully engineered the end of American involvement in Iraq. American forces have now withdrawn to strategic bases and are no longer playing a significant role in the security of the country. By the end of the year there will be very few American troops left. In ending the Iraq war, President Obama has done so without creating significant political opposition.

The death of Osama bin Laden at the hands of American Special Forces on May 1 eliminated one of the main props for the Afghan war being one of necessity and now provides the President with an opportunity to recast many aspects of American foreign and security policy in the region. When the President authorized the latest surge of American troops into Afghanistan in early 2010, bringing the total to more than 100,000 along with 30,000 more from coalition countries, it was a desperate attempt to create conditions in which a withdrawal of American forces could be seriously contemplated.

The surge was also accompanied by a change of American commanders and renewed emphasis on a new counterinsurgency doctrine. Conventional counterinsurgency doctrines emphasized the killing of insurgents. The new policy sought to use military force to create political, economic and social conditions that would undermine popular support for the Taliban. That did not happen and today the Taliban is as strong as ever while the Karzai government is as weak as ever – and the net effect of American and Western policy is the creation of new adherents to the doctrine of international terrorism.

American policy in 2010 represented both carrots and sticks and, as with all such ambiguity, it was more "Hail Mary" than realistic. In some measure it did not even reflect the inclinations of either the President or the Secretary of Defence, Robert Gates. Gates, in 2009, said that "if we set ourselves the objective of creating some sort of central Asian "Valhalla" over there, we will lose, because nobody in the world has that kind of time, patience and money." President Obama was very much on the same wavelength when he remarked that Afghanistan would not become a "Jeffersonian democracy."

Fundamental Western interests in Afghanistan were always tied to the use of the country by al Qaeda as a launching pad for terrorist attacks in Western countries. The failure to capture bin Laden in late 2001 and the return of the Taliban in 2005 from its sanctuaries in Pakistan required a new Western script – hence the objective of transforming Afghan society into something approaching "Jeffersonian democracy." It was and is not an achievable objective. As Secretary Gates suggested there is not the time, patience or money in Western countries for that to happen.

The death of Osama bin Laden does not end his charismatic effect on millions. His ideas have travelled the world and have attracted disciples not only in Muslim countries but equally among Muslims in Western countries. That will continue, but, with his death and no one in the wings to play the role he played, his ideas will join those of others who have emerged from the deserts of the Middle East in the expectation that the sword can end the continuum of history. This has been evident for some time, but invading Western soldiers in Muslim countries are poor instruments in countering bin Laden's ideas. Rather, as has been the case with other phases of international terrorism arising from the Middle East, concerted cooperation among targeted countries has been and will continue to be the best and most successful response.

In Washington, there is serious unease that the current policy has failed and, importantly, with a cost of over two-billion dollars a week, there are dual reasons for the administration to act. The first step in that process is already underway with the intensification of the training programs for Afghan military and police. While this may not produce national army and police forces it will provide the training and weapons for traditional non-Pashtun groups in Afghanistan to hold their own against the Taliban. A few weeks ago the Afghan government assumed responsibility for security in three provinces, albeit provinces with little Taliban activity. Nevertheless, the idea is to provide an alternative script against which a withdrawal policy can be implemented.

The dysfunctional American relationship with Pakistan provides another reason for the withdrawal of Western troops from the region. Pakistan has no reason to believe that Western staying power is of any significance and the American tilt towards India on nuclear matters has undermined its legitimacy among most Pakistanis. As such, a return to a situation in which local forces are dominant is in longer-term Western interest, as well as that of other regional powers. Benign neglect is a harsh conclusion to reach in the history of the tragedy of Afghanistan for the last several decades. A return to traditional Pakistani suzerainty over Afghanistan will do more to bring opportunities for peace in the region than with the continued presence of tens of thousands of Western troops.

Embassy

An Unnecessary War
June 10, 2011

A FEW DAYS AGO PRIME MINISTER HARPER CASUALLY DECLARED THAT Afghanistan was no longer a threat to the world and there was no need for Canadian combat troops to remain. Unfortunately, the Prime Minister was several years late in coming to these conclusions. In the intervening years more than one-hundred-and-fifty Canadians were killed, hundreds more severely wounded, and billions were spent in support of a cause that was doomed from its very inception. Largely ignored have been the tens of thousands of Afghans who have died in the fog of this unnecessary war.

The war in Afghanistan was born in the panic and bravado following the 9/11 attacks on the United States. The initial successes of seeing the Taliban routed and, along with al Qaeda, driven into the tribal areas of Pakistan led to premature conclusions that the war was over. It also led to erroneous conclusions regarding the nature of Afghan society, its symbiotic relationship with Pakistan and Pakistani strategic interests in the region.

Equally, following the 9/11 attacks, there was an over-characterization and over-reaction to the threat al Qaeda presented to the West. Al Qaeda and its leader Osama bin Laden were elevated to a supra-evil state level. In part this was to create an enemy worthy of the attention of a superpower but equally to attract international support for the war on terror – and increase toleration in Western societies and elsewhere for the suppression of human rights and the use of torture. As for Afghanistan, Western leaders perpetuated the idea that the nature of the war on terror was such that it had to be fought over there in order to avoid having to fight it at home.

In Canada, neither the political nor the military leadership nor people generally gave serious thought to actually going to war. However, as history has repeatedly demonstrated, serious thought *is* needed before doing battle. By October 6, 2001, Canadian soldiers were in Afghanistan – and the first public notice was hesitation or lack of knowledge by the Minister of National Defence at the end of the year as to what they were doing. In the intervening years Canadian troops have remained in Afghanistan and, if recent announcements have any currency, they will be there until at least 2014.

Canadian involvement in the war was justified on the grounds of NATO Alliance solidarity with the United States. There were self-justifying statements on the threat al Qaeda represented to Canada and there was almost unanimity in the country that going to war in Afghanistan was both legitimate and appropriate. The unanimity was reinforced by the ease of the early victories and, with these, thoughts were given to ideas, programs and projects that would see Afghanistan converted from a medieval state into one where social justice would abound.

In the meantime, Afghanistan dropped from centre stage with the American invasion of Iraq and the lack of success in tracking bin Laden. A new government in Ottawa and a new Chief of Defence Staff blindly accepted military responsibility for Kandahar province and, before 2006 ended, Canadian casualties increased dramatically and the Canadian public realized that an actual war was underway.

Instead of dealing with the important issues associated with the war, Ottawa decided that the issue was one of ensuring there was continuing public support for the troops fighting and dying. An overdressed, inarticulate sports commentator, the Chief of Defence Staff and a variety of public personalities entered the fray and sought to convince Canadians that it was unpatriotic to question the war, and that victory was just around the corner. A panel of experts was appointed to add gravitas, but the reality of the war and the factually well-based perception that it was an unwinnable quickly undermined the earlier boosterism.

Meanwhile, it was becoming apparent that Pakistan was not the ally as had been assumed at the beginning. The arbitrary border with Afghanistan did not divide people, but rather established a common cause against the Western invaders. Islamabad was neither capable nor prepared to mount a significant counterinsurgency campaign within its own boundaries and its border regions remained at the centre of the war in Afghanistan. Strategically, when the United States decided to legitimize the Indian nuclear-weapon program in 2007, without offering to do the same for Pakistan, the prospects of Pakistani cooperation on Afghanistan eroded even further.

In the 2008 presidential campaign, President Obama juxtaposed the conflict in Afghanistan as one of necessity in comparison to the war in Iraq. In the succeeding months the war in Iraq was effectively ended, but to maintain his political credentials, President Obama dramatically increased American troop levels in Afghanistan. These increased levels only partly offset the withdrawals by NATO countries, and today there are few signs that there is any measurable success.

The death of bin Laden a few weeks ago provided Washington with an opportunity to reassess the situation in Afghanistan and there are now signs the United States will increase the pace of its troop withdrawals. Some withdrawals had already been promised for later this year, but the realization has now reached Washington that the war in Afghanistan was as unnecessary as that in Iraq. With the 2012 presidential-election campaign already underway and the need for enormous cuts in expenditures, it could be that the Western war in Afghanistan will begin its fade into oblivion.

The war was not really about Afghanistan. It was an unfocussed, badly planned adventure that in the end had little to do with that country, and the best that can be expected in the coming years is that the Afghans will be able to come to some conclusions about how they want to be governed. Before that day arrives, many more

Afghans will die and regrettably it will be Afghans killing Afghans. Perhaps out of that chaos, outsiders without their armies will be able to help.

The Citizen

Tone Deaf Foreign Policy on Israel
August 3, 2011

FOREIGN AFFAIRS CANADA ISSUES A LOT OF PRESS RELEASES. LAST year there was more than one per day. For the most part, these were innocuous, offering congratulations on national days, regrets over disasters, condolences on deaths or Canadian views and advice on foreign policy issues – the daily routine of a department of government following the events of a busy world.

It was not surprising then, when on May 28 Foreign Minister John Baird decided Canadians needed specific advice on "participation in Gaza Flotillas" and as a result decided to issue a press release. The release came just a few days before the first anniversary of the May 31, 2010 flotilla in which six ships, carrying humanitarian aid to the people of Gaza, were intercepted by Israeli commandos in international waters. The long-vaunted skills of the Israeli armed forces were not evident that day, as nine civilians were killed and seven Israeli commandos injured. A few days after the incident one Israeli newspaper headlined a story "Gaza Flotilla Drives Israel into a Sea of Stupidity."

The surprise in the Foreign Affairs press release was its content and not that it was issued - it attracted little or no attention in the media. The content was such that it could have been issued by the Foreign Ministry of Israel without changes. The only thing missing was a background chorus of Hava Nigala.

The release "urged" Canadians wishing to deliver humanitarian goods to the Gaza Strip to do so through "established channels," stressing that the use of unauthorized efforts was provocative and "ultimately unhelpful to the people of Gaza." The release went on to say that "Canada recognizes Israel's legitimate security concerns" and the right to protect itself and its residents from attacks by Hamas, and that there are "legitimate and constructive ways to help the people of Gaza," including through the International Committee of the Red Cross/Red Crescent." Unrelated, the release then calls for the immediate return of Israeli soldier, Gilad Shalit, "held by Hamas for almost five years."

This year's flotilla had none of the drama of 2010. Except for one boat, the flotilla was effectively blocked in Greek ports. Greece cooperated since Turkey was no longer the favoured nation of Israel in the eastern Mediterranean. Some of the protesters, diverted from the boats, tried to crowd Israel's air-arrival facilities which the Israeli authorities easily countered. This year's political theatre played farce.

There is considerable historical irony in the policy of the Israeli government in its blockade of Gaza. In mid-1947, more than 4500 Jewish refugees, survivors of the concentration camps, boarded a derelict ship, the Exodus, in France and headed for the shores of Palestine. The British denied access to the coast, boarded the ship and two refugees and one crew member were killed. The British first attempted to have the refugees returned to France, but there was little cooperation from the French authorities. Instead the refuges were returned to Hamburg, which was then part of the British zone of occupation in Germany.

The May 28 press release overlapped with another incident in which an Israeli newspaper reported that Prime Minister Harper coordinated his actions at the G8 with the Prime Minister of Israel on the eve of the Summit. According to the paper, Mr Harper was carrying Israeli water when he prevented any reference to the 1967 borders for Israel in the Summit Communiqué. Afterwards both governments acknowledged that Mr Harper and Mr Netanyahu spoke prior to the Summit, but denied that the conversation dealt with the 1967 borders; instead, according to respective spokespersons, they spoke only of the G8 Meeting – a distinction that can only be parsed by the cognoscenti of spin.

These are not unique events in Mr Harper's unwavering and uncritical support for Israel. In 2006 there was support for Israel in its invasion of Lebanon and in its 2008 incursion into Gaza. In that support Canada was unique in the international community. More disturbing were statements in 2010 by Peter Kent, then the junior minister in Foreign Affairs, that "an attack on Israel would be considered an attack on Canada." He went on to include the Prime Minister as his authority by stating, "Prime Minister Harper has made it quite clear for some time now and has regularly stated that an attack on Israel would be considered an attack on Canada."

In the years of Mr Harper's prime ministership there has been no comprehensive explanation of the government's blinkered support for Israel. The only reason offered was that Israel was the only democracy in the Middle East – thin and specious reasoning, and becoming more so.

Some commentators have noted that one of Mr Harper's political passions is to bury the Liberal Party of Canada. The last election provides some measure of his success on that score. Perhaps historical Canadian foreign policy is an element in Mr Harper's motivation on Israel. It can be argued that Canadian foreign policy, as inherited by Mr Harper, was a creation of the Liberal governments of the last sixty or so years. In the aftermath of the Second World War, it was Liberal governments, and especially Lester Pearson, which urged Canadians to use their sacrifices, new wealth and confidence to become part of the emerging world order.

Nowhere in those early days was this more manifest than in the Middle East where Canada supported the creation of the State of Israel. When Britain, France and Israel, in a pique of madness, invaded Egypt in 1956, Mr Pearson and the government of Canada of the day crafted an international intervention that avoided deep rupture to the Western Alliance and provided a decade of peace in the Middle East.

Sadly, the decisions of the Harper government to blindly support Israel are not in the interest of either country. For a government that uses public relations as a key tool in its foreign policy, it was over the top for Mr Baird to characterize the Palestinian campaign to win recognition at the UN in September as a public-relations move. Perhaps the Palestinians are taking a page out of Mr Baird's own song book and, for a people with few options on the international stage, public relations is all that is left. For Israel to try and defeat the effort by the Palestinians to obtain broad international recognition through the United Nations is to deny the Palestinians access to the very process that legitimized the creation of the State of Israel.

For the past twenty years, a variety of Israel's leaders, supported by a majority of Israelis, have sought to create conditions for a lasting peace with their neighbours. In recent years, tortuously, the shape of that future peace has emerged. Unfortunately, recent Israeli electoral machinations have altered the placement of the goal line. As a result, Israeli intransigence more than Palestinian unwillingness for compromise has prevented a peace agreement.

Canadian moral and political support for Israel is unique in the world; unfortunately it contributes absolutely nothing to solving the deep problems of the region. In the meantime the complexities grow and history will not be kind to the-tone deaf role Canada is playing.

Prism

How Peace Came to Paradise
January 15, 2012

IT WAS A PRISON-WORN MANUEL ANTONIO NORIEGA WHO STEPPED off a plane in Panama City on December 11. The former Maximum Leader of National Liberation was finally back home, only a month shy of 22 years of imprisonment in the United States and France. His return concluded the questionable legal processes of those years, but the beginning of a new era that will be entirely legitimate in the minds of most Panamanians.

I was a party to those events in late 1989 when American marines invaded Panama in the early hours of January 20. The marines easily overcame resistance by the Panamanian army and forced Noriega to seek sanctuary in the embassy of the Vatican. There, according to more lore than fact, he surrendered on January 3, 1990 to the Americans, after being bombarded with loud hard-rock music. He was quickly flown to the United States, completing one of the most expensive extraditions in modern history.

In the previous September, I had arrived in Central America as ambassador to Costa Rica, El Salvador, Honduras, Nicaragua and Panama. The region was at war. There was a nasty, brutal insurgency in El Salvador where American forces supported an extreme right-wing government willing to kill priests, nuns and anyone else who got in its way. Next door in Nicaragua the Americans financed and supplied a ragtag group of Contras, guerrillas largely based in Honduras.

Early in the morning of January 20, after a lengthy office Christmas party the night before, my telephone rang and it was the Foreign Minister, Joe Clark, seeking information on what was going on in Panama. He reported that there were news reports that the Americans had invaded Panama and the cabinet would be meeting in the next few hours to discuss the Canadian reaction. At that point I had never been to Panama, as it had been decided that I would not present credentials because of the nefarious activities of the regime.

However, Canada did have a long-time honorary consul in Panama City, Ruth Denton, a former resident of Montreal and daughter of a doctor who had spent considerable time in Newfoundland working for the Grenfell Mission in St. Anthony. I called Denton, surprisingly the telephone system was working, and she, from her apartment overlooking Panama Bay, provided a vivid picture of the invasion and particularly the battle for the nearby airport. A quick call to Canadian Press in Toronto provided additional information on the invasion from American reports and within the hour I was able to call Clark back and provide an "in depth" report of what was going on in Panama.

Within a few days, Noriega was in an American prison, and the winner of the May 1989 elections, Guillermo Endara, was sworn in as president. A few days later I flew into Panama City, was picked up by the American military in a Hummer vehicle (this was the first use of the Hummer by the Americans during a war) and taken downtown.

The next day, accompanied by Peter Boehm, the political officer from the embassy in San Jose, I went to the presidential palace to present my credentials to the new President. There was no electricity and, upon climbing the stairs, I was met by a young woman with a baby in her arms. She introduced herself as the daughter of the President and wanted me to know that as a teenager she had attended school in Hamilton and thoroughly enjoyed the time spent there. President Endara was gracious in welcoming me to Panama as the first ambassador to present credentials to him and looked forward to working with Canada in the coming months to improve the relationship.

Panama was the first large event of my three years in Central America. In neighbouring Nicaragua, the left-wing Sandinista government of Daniel Ortega battled the Contras. Costa Rica, under President Oscar Arias, was slowly being squeezed by the United States into these wars and was seeking an internationally supported settlement for the various conflicts. Earlier, in co-operation with other Latin American leaders, Arias began a deftly managed process known as Contadora, named after the Panamanian island were early peace discussions took place. For his efforts Arias was awarded the Nobel Peace Prize in 1987.

By 1989, the supporting winds from Washington for the wars in Central America were ebbing, following the retirement of Ronald Reagan to his California ranch and the start of the pragmatic presidency of George H.W. Bush. The Americans under Bush began to rethink American involvement, following the exposure of American illegality under the Iran-Contra scandal and increasing domestic opposition to the nastiness of the wars in El Salvador and Nicaragua.

There was, however, one piece of unfinished business that the Americans were determined to carry out and that was to see Manuel Noriega eliminated as Panamanian leader. In the previous few years Noriega had moved from a steadfast American ally and paid CIA agent to being a minor thorn in American plans for the region. Fuelling American concern was of course the future of the Panama Canal. President Jimmy Carter in 1977 had negotiated a treaty in which ownership of the waterway would be transferred to Panama at the end of 1999.

The removal of Noriega from the scene gave Washington the freedom to participate in the Arias peace process in which Canada was already a participant. In October of 1989, even before the removal of Noriega, Prime Minister Brian Mulroney and Foreign Minister Joe Clark engineered Canada's full membership in the Organization of American States. Canada's aloofness from the organization had always been a piece of false Canadian conceit and full membership, which took place at its annual meeting in San Jose,

Costa Rica, was full recognition that Canadian foreign policy in the Western Hemisphere had finally come of age.

The peace process was already well underway, and the defeat of Daniel Ortega by Dona Violeta Chamorro in the Nicaraguan presidential elections of February 1990 was a promising early development. Chamorro, the widow of a Nicaraguan journalist assassinated during the earlier Somoza regime, provided a popular rallying point for the non-Sandinistas – and became both a symbol for the rest of the region and a vindication of the idea that fundamental change was possible through elections.

Change in El Salvador was a more difficult achievement, but eventually negotiations led to agreement with the Farabundo Marti Liberation Front (FMLN), the main insurgency group, to forgo armed struggle and participate in electoral politics. In this process the United States ended its support for the Contras in Honduras and, in subsequent years, peace efforts were concentrated on Guatemala. However, reflecting the racial nature of the conflict, little fundamental progress has been made there and the indigenous people remain much the way South Africa was prior to 1994.

Throughout these years Canada played a large role in seeking a negotiated settlement to the various wars. Ironically one of the United Nations' most successful peacekeeping initiatives, which is rarely acknowledged, was organized in late 1989 to provide outside verification and control for the various agreements that were to come into effect. In today's bellicose world, peacekeeping has lost some of its lustre, but now relatively peaceful Central America owes a very large debt to international peacekeeping. Canada played the largest role of any country in those activities and two distinguished Canadian generals, Ian Douglas and Lew McKenzie, won early recognition for the skill and patience they brought to the process.

Today it is difficult to imagine the level of turmoil and bloodshed in Central America, prior to 1989. It was at the centre of all international reporting and hundreds of Canadian organizations made it the focus of their activities. They were backed by the Mulroney government, although there were heated debates on overall Canadian policy.

The region now, apart from Guatemala, remains an example of the value of international backing for regional peacekeeping initiatives. Oscar Arias recently retired from a second term as President of Costa Rica and, in Nicaragua, Daniel Ortega is back as President. In Panama, the wisdom of Jimmy Carter's foresight in negotiating an end to American suzerainty over the Panama Canal is more evident than ever. The canal, under Panamanian leadership, is under-going its first large expansion since its opening by Teddy Roosevelt in 1914.

The Citizen

Book Review
April 12, 2014

Return of a King: The Battle for Afghanistan, by William Dalrymple. 2013, Bloomsbury Publishing, London, 568 pp., $22.00.

RARELY DOES ONE READ A BOOK DEALING WITH EVENTS NEARLY two-hundred years ago and find it is not only a fascinating and rollicking journey but enormously relevant for today. Such is William Dalrymple's *Return of a King*. It is an exhaustive examination of the British invasion of Afghanistan in 1839 with new, original material from contemporaneous Afghans. As if mocked by today's events, the British also wanted to bring about and perpetuate regime change in Kabul.

Living in New Delhi much of his adult life, Dalrymple has long mined the history and art of central and south Asia. His latest book explores an area and a war which many have written about before, but no one can match him in turning that rich, prescient ore into works that are difficult to put down. Equally, his work carries relevance for today as we cope with intra- and inter-religious struggles, security pivots and emerged and emerging economies.

Scottish-born Dalrymple's father was a cousin of Virginia Woolf; literary talent seems to have been in the air. His first book, published in 1989, was *In Xanadu*, a "travel" narrative of Marco Polo's trek from Jerusalem to Shandu, the seasonal home of Kubla Khan. Dalrymple was only twenty-two at the time and the book – rich in the history of the lands travelled and people observed – established him as a major writer.

Central Asia and the Indian sub-continent were more interconnected and politically over-lapping historically than is understood today. Those of us raised on a history of a world with oceans as the only road in the spread of culture, people and trade need to appreciate the history of long-distance travel by land across the Euro-Asian-Indian land mass. As Dalrymple has shown in earlier works, the route between Europe and Asia – the "Silk Road" – is as relevant today as it was a thousand years ago.

The significance of this vast area, especially for human migration, was given new emphasis earlier this year. DNA analysis found genetic markers linking peoples living in the Russian Republic of Altai with the indigenous populations of North America. Altai is a small, remote area of Russia, surrounded by Mongolia, China and Kazakhstan. Although its population today is just over 200,000, its history as a European-Asian crossroad suggests that some Turks, Mongols, Yeniseians, Tocharians, Persians or Uralic peoples crossing its lands may have made it all the way to the southern reaches of the Americas.

Perhaps we should not be surprised that in the late 18th century British and East Indian Company officials in London and Calcutta were exercised by word that the Russians were eyeing Central Asia. For many, Russian interest, coupled with Napoleon's earlier determination to separate the British from their large involvement in the Indian subcontinent and possibly further east, was enough to convert possible Russian intent into overt intentions.

Dalrymple traces these developments throughout the early years of the 19th century in the context of changes in Persia, competing dynasties in Afghanistan and the rise of the Sikh kingdom of Raja Ranjit Singh on the western edges of the East India Company's lands. He reminds us that the Battle of the Nile between the French and British navies in August 1798 was part of Napoleon's longer-term goal of driving the British out of India. The total defeat of the French navy by Rear Admiral Horatio Nelson put an end to Napoleon's plans for a sea route to India, but throughout the rest of his reign he harboured dreams of disrupting the British in India.

Having used "General Winter" (and defense in depth) to rout Napoleon's eastward thrust in 1812, the Russians were looking south. Before long they "had moved their frontier south and eastwards almost as fast as Wellesley [East India Company's Governor-General in Calcutta] had moved that of the Company north and westwards, and it was becoming increasingly evident – at least to the armchair strategists in London – that the two empires would at some point come into collision in central Asia." Wellesley (the older brother of the Duke of Wellington) regarded Afghanistan as the key asset in central Asia in blocking Russian expansionist moves into the region. He and his successors began a series of manoeuvres, including the expansion of British control over Afghanistan.

Dalrymple's description of Afghanistan (or Khurasan, as Afghans called it) during the two millennia before the 19th century is still relevant. It "had had but a few hours of political or administrative unity. Far more often it had been 'the places in between' the fractured and disputed stretch of mountains, flood plains and deserts separating its more orderly neighbours." Adding to the lack of geographic cohesion were the "different tribal, ethnic and linguistic fissures fragmenting Afghan society." Without changing a word, his historical fissures describe today's Afghanistan – "the rivalry between the Tajiks, Uzbeks, Hazaras and the Durrani and Ghilzai Pashtuns; the schism between Sunni and Shia; the endemic factionalism within clans and tribes, and especially the blood feuds within closely related lineages."

In the early part of the 19th century, sitting at the top of these fragmenting fissures, was Shah Shuja from the Sadozais part of the Durrani clan. In 1805 he was overthrown by Dost Mohammad Khan of the Barakzai side in the Ghilzai clan. While both were Pashtun, often there was less love between them than with the Tajiks and Uzbeks who made pragmatic alliances based on their own interests. (Former President Hamid Karzai is from the same sub-tribe as

Shah Shuja while Mullah Omar, the head of the Taliban, is from the Ghilzai clan.) Once overthrown by Dost Mohammad, Shah Shuja was allowed to go to India where he was supported and protected by the East India Company, and available to return to the throne when the British invaded in 1839.

While the Russians made small intelligence forays into the lands in between, Dost Mohammad was king and sought to keep intact the traditional lands of the Afghans. He was amenable to the Russian moves as a counter to feints by the remnants of the Persian Empire into western Afghanistan, especially around Herat. Pressure also came from the south where the Sikhs under Raja Ranjit Singh had ended profitable raids by the Afghans across the Indus River. Throughout this period Afghanistan included Peshawar and the lands stretching to the Indus River.

The British, working through the East India Company and sitting in imperial splendour in Calcutta, were growing alarmed. They saw Dost Mohammad's activities to keep his kingdom reasonably intact as inimical to their own position east of the Indus. "The tournament of shadows", as the "Great Game" was seen by many, was encouraged by a variety of off-stage actors in London and St Petersburg who saw their respective expansion of empires as intersecting and conflicting in the lands of the Afghans. Various embassies (travelling diplomatic missions in those days) travelled vast distances. "Intelligencers" – British spies – recruited agents throughout the region and the British in India decided on the need for regime change in Kabul to ensure the safety of their regime throughout most of India.

Dalrymple tracks this "tournament of shadows" through committees of British officials in London and Calcutta who were required to describe the proverbial camel without having seen one. This, despite the fact they had a first-rate official in Kabul – Alexander Burnes – whose understanding of the Afghans still offers valuable insights and conclusions. Not surprisingly Burnes' value was undermined by Claude Wade, the "keeper" of Shah Shuja (keen to regain the throne).

Dalrymple captures the nature of the Calcutta regime in his description of the first visit out of Bengal by George Eden, Governor General Lord Auckland. Eden was the ancestor of another Eden who in 1956 thought that he could overturn Egyptian nationalism under Nasser. Quoting an eye witness, Dalrymple records that the former Eden left Calcutta with "850 camels, 140 elephants, several hundred horses, the Body Guard, the regiment that escorts us, and the camp followers. They are about 12,000 in all."

At the time, the oddness of Auckland's role was noted by his nephew, Captain William Osborne: "A private English gentleman and the servant of a joint stock company [that is, the East India Company], during the brief period of his government [he] is the deputed sovereign of the greatest empire in the world; the ruler of a hundred million men. There is nothing in history analogous to this position..."

The British eventually accepted Wade's views on the need for regime change in Kabul and pulled together an army that marched out of British India, 60,000 strong, crossing the Indus in two places. It entered Afghanistan through the Khyber Pass and through the Bolan Pass (south of Quetta) leading to Kandahar. On August 7, 1839, eight months after it had assembled, the invasion force entered Kabul. Dost Mohammad had fled three days earlier. Shah Shuja was placed on the throne he had lost three decades earlier.

A prominent tribal leader of the time, Mehrab Khan, is quoted by Dalrymple as warning "You have brought an army into the country, but how do you propose to take it out again." A sentiment echoed through Afghan history. One-and-one-half years later the British had their answer. Shah Shuja found little popular support. Before long he was deserted by tribal leaders and was seen by most Afghans as "a servant of the Kafir infidels." As one poet wrote at the time:

> But in this land you were doomed
> Here your death was certain.

The British garrison was besieged on all sides. After several months and the death of many of the British leaders, including Burnes, it was decided to withdraw from Kabul down the Kabul Gorge. On January 6, 1842 thirteen thousand left Kabul with the temperature "considerably below zero point." Attacked from the hills along what is the most inhospitable fighting ground in the world, only one, a medical doctor, arrived in Jalalabad. Correcting a historical myth, Dalrymple details that over the following weeks many hundreds more were to escape from Afghanistan and make it back to British India.

British leadership, both political and military, in London and Calcutta was responsible for this – the greatest debacle in British colonial history. As in all such cases the reaction was for revenge. Before long an Army of Retribution under Major-General George Pollock was created. By early April 1842 it had relieved the siege of British troops at Jalalabad. A few days later the army arrived in Kabul and burned it to the ground. Having learned its lesson, the army quickly departed Afghanistan. It was almost four decades before another British army ventured beyond Peshawar.

The 1880 invasion also was prompted by possible Russian involvement in Afghanistan; this time the British stay was even shorter than that of 1839. Again, thousands of British troops died and in the words of one historian British "Forward Policy" had failed. The conclusion, long in coming, was that "if the Russians went into Afghanistan, they would have the same problems or worse."

An overwhelming regret is that Dalrymple's book was not available thirteen years ago when the United States and several cooperating countries, including Canada, invaded Afghanistan and, like Britain in 1839, hoped to bring about regime change. Even the futile Soviet invasion of 1979 created no caution in the minds of those who enthusiastically supported and participated in the 2001 invasion.

Today, after years of war, tens of thousands dead and national treasuries badly dented, another invasion of Afghanistan is coming to an end as foreign troops depart. The debate in Canada as elsewhere is over what was achieved. Various positive social indicators have been promoted in support of the invasion, elections have been held, but fundamentally little seems to have changed. The Taliban control large swaths of the country. The newly created and Western- trained Afghan National Army, touted as the bulwark against the insurgency, has met with little success. The description of Afghanistan as "the places in between" still applies. Kabul seems doomed to remain a temporary resting place for short-lived regimes. The Taliban and its power base, the Pashtun Ghilzai clan, seem destined to return to power and Western-oriented leaders may be lucky to escape with their shoes on. Like Shah Shuja, they likely will carry the curse of being "a servant of the Kafir infidels."

Dalrymple's memorialization of a war more than one-hundred years ago will do nothing to ease the suffering of Canada's war wounded returning from Afghanistan or the pain of so many Canadian lives lost there. But it powerfully underscores the need to be far better prepared before undertaking such commitments, to better consider the decision against the weight of history, and to accept full responsibility for the needs of those who pay the price. The 21st century badly needs to learn from the 19th.

bout de papier, Vol. 28, No. 2.

The futility of war
February 25, 2015

IT IS TO BE REGRETTED THAT HISTORIAN BARBARA TUCHMAN IS NO longer with us. If she was, there is some certainty she would add the "war on terror" and its offshoots to her catalogue of political follies she intelligently identified in her book The March of Folly.

The book has been described as "meditation on the historical recurrence of governments pursuing policies evidently contrary to their own interests." As Western powers stumble around the battlefields of the Middle East and Central Asia, there is overwhelming evidence supporting the conclusion that today's policies are contrary to their own interests.

Since the start of our third millennium, the back-to-back wars against so-called terrorism are really wars against ourselves. Bill C-51, the Security of Canada Information Sharing Act, is but the latest misdirected attempt by the government to fight a war it wants it to be, not the one we read about each morning.

In the last half of the previous century the scourge of terrorism was as serious as it is today. To board a flight often provided the opportunity to see Algiers or Havana. Nevertheless our sense of self-interest did not lead to misguided attempts to treat terrorism as wars that could be won through the use of Western military forces in places of which they had little understanding and were not less welcomed.

Rather the Western reaction largely was to deal with terrorism as a product of overwhelming frustration created by imposed colonial-era gerrymandering of borders and imposed political arrangements. There was general agreement the external manifestations of these frustrations had to be contained and to some extent there was currency for the concept of international terrorism, as compared to the terrors contained by national boundaries. The one over-reaction was the attempt to have American forces intervene in Lebanon. The bombing of their barracks in Beirut soon put an end to the folly of that adventure.

In turn this prompted the international community to create a body on international containment treaties aimed at protecting the larger world from hijackings, attacks on diplomats, aid and humanitarian workers and businesspeople and travel by those who would do us harm.

This provided a thick forest of containment measures such as the Tokyo, Hague and Montreal Conventions dealing with air travel and the Convention on the Prevention and Punishment of Crimes against Internationally Protected Persons. Such measures combined with increased screening of travelers, domestic police and security enhancements, international police co-operation and efforts to solve underlying political and economic issues largely contained the scourge of violence outside of national boundaries.

Today we are living with the legacy of the American over-reaction to the events of 9/11. Then, the tragic failure of American security agencies to identify an internal attack led to a lashing out and the October 2001 military interventions in Afghanistan and, two years later, in Iraq.Over a decade later, these interventions are seen as the follies they were. In Iraq we are now dealing with the consequences.

Another military intervention in which Canada is a willing participant will do nothing to quell the forces at work there and in neighbouring Syria.Another few months will likely see an Afghanistan similar to what it was prior to the American invasion of 2001. Last year in Afghanistan, the UN reported the highest level of civilian casualties in five years.

If more proof of the folly of such interventions is needed we need only to look at today's Libya, only three years after the West declared "mission accomplished" there.

Most tragically these Western military interventions have accentuated the forces at work in our own countries where a few native born and recent immigrants see some measure of commonality with the local forces in the invaded countries.

The increasing numbers of violent reactions—Madrid, London, Glasgow, Texas, Stockholm, Frankfurt, Toulouse, Boston, Brussels, Saint-Jean-sur-Richelieu, Ottawa, Sydney, Paris and Copenhagen—are graphic. But in the cool light of retrospect these are manifestations of a disparate lot influenced more by inner demons than a massive conversion externally directed.

Western political leaders singularly see the invasion of another country as an easy short term policy rather than coping with the complexities the violence represents. Certainly all see such invasions as providing short term domestic political support. There is no evidence to suggest, despite its repeated use, that Canadians understand the political manipulation that is underway.

The disparity between the folly of today's wars and serious effort to resolve the political problems inherited from the Western colonial era continues to grow as political leaders fuel the flames of racial and religious mistrust among their own citizens. Nowhere is this more evident than here in Canada, where we have a prime minister who has not seen a war he did not like.

Indeed, Prime Minister Stephen Harper actively seeks out wars in which Canadians can be engaged. His legacy will be as a warmonger, rather than his imagined "values."

Embassy

Bibi Goes to Washington
March 11, 2015

IT IS UNUSUAL IF NOT UNIQUE TO USE IRONY AND CHUTZPAH TO describe the same situation. But in their own way they describe the policy of the Israeli government under Prime Minister Benjamin Netanyahu, in its efforts to prevent the international community from reaching an agreement with Iran on its nuclear program.

Israel has nuclear weapons. Since the early days of the creation of the country through the division of Palestine in a UN General Assembly vote in 1947, Israel has secretly used its science and technological abilities to build a full arsenal of nuclear weapons. Today it has nuclear weapons numbering in the hundreds with associated air, land and sea delivery systems.

Israel was nuclear weapons power number six after the five permanent members of the Security Council—the United States, Russia, United Kingdom, France and China. Israel's nuclear weapons status was before that of India and Pakistan which had used Canadian technology and material to produce its first weapons.

Subsequently only North Korea has joined the nuclear weapons club, although South Africa, Iraq, Syria and Libya have tried. There is speculation that Saudi Arabia—an ally on Israel in its anti-Iran policy—and/or one or two Gulf States may attempt to cross the nuclear weapons bar.

Israel created its nuclear weapons largely on its own except for early assistance from France. It did so possibly without testing. The only possibility of a test was the non-attributable nuclear explosion in the southern reaches of the Indian Ocean in September 1979.

Speculation surrounding the explosion at the time was that it was Israeli or South African.

Israel has never admitted that it has nuclear weapons but with a deadly smile it cloyingly asserts it will not be the first country to introduce such weapons into the Middle East.

The Iran nuclear program has been more episodic interrupted and slowed by war, revolution, sabotage and sanctions. Nevertheless, today it is substantive, but some months away from having a nuclear weapons component. Iranian officials maintain with a smile as cloyingly as that of the Israelis that its nuclear program is intended for peaceful energy purposes only.

That requires a suspension of disbelief, as there are elements of the program, especially uranium enrichment and delivery systems, strongly supporting the view that Iran has a nuclear program nearing the ability to produce nuclear weapons.

Of the nuclear weapons states, only Israel, India and Pakistan have refused to sign the world's premier treaty against the spread of nuclear weapons—the Treaty on the Non-Proliferation of Nuclear Weapons, or NPT. North Korea was a signatory but withdrew in 2003. Iran remains a signatory country and uses NPT provisions for the peaceful use of nuclear energy to justify its nuclear activities.

Ironically, it is the efforts of the five initial nuclear weapons states plus Germany (P5 + 1) that united in 2006 to try and reign in Iran's nuclear activities and ensure they are limited to peaceful uses.Limiting nuclear activities to peaceful uses only is, of course, a political decision, not a scientific one.

As Canada painfully learned several decades ago after the transfer of nuclear technology to India and Pakistan, scientific knowledge is not divisible into neat compartments, one peaceful, the other weapons. The two countries professing peaceful intentions at the time to a willing Canadian audience today are nuclear weapons states.

The world is a wiser place today, but the overwhelming need to contain the spread of nuclear weapons is greater now than ever before. North Korea with nuclear weapons and a young untested leader should send all of us to our backyard, shovels in hand, to dig our fallout shelters. Countries such as Israel and Iran, both under internal and external threats, should cause a similar reaction. IS terrorism, in comparison, is nothing more than a lone mosquito on a northern July breeze.

And yet the one state, Israel, with the greatest concern for the outcome of the negotiations between the P5 + 1 and Iran is the skunk in the elevator. A willingness to go to Washington and intervene in the American political system demonstrates recklessness bordering on madness. It was not as if Israeli Prime Minister Benjamin Netanyahu had anything to say or could offer alternatives to the negotiations represented by the work of P5+1. Rather it was an opportunity to harangue United States President Barack Obama and the laudable efforts to put controls on the Iranian nuclear program.

Prime Minister Netanyahu apparently believes the only answer to Israeli security problems is war. Three years ago he appeared ready to go to war with Iran on the nuclear issue and it was only with firm and consistent pressure from those who understood the folly of such action that he hesitated.

Prime Minister Netanyahu understands the American political system as well as he understands his own. The deep fissures within that political system allow him to strut upon its stage knowing there are those who see him as a valuable ally in the looming elections. The United States has been captured by the prime minister and by doing so he has a free hand to do very much what he wants to do in the Middle East.

He has captured the Canadian government as well. In the celebrations in Washington last week, the ghost of a former Canadian foreign minister past wandered around the edges throwing his own spitballs at the administration. It seemed it was August 1914 when mass hysteria and madness paraded as policy. As with 100 years ago, there will be an enormous price to pay if adults do not intervene.

Embassy

Perpetual Wars
March 28, 2015

THERE IS A DEADLY SENSE OF DÉJÀ VU AS LEADERS GO ABOUT EXTENDing and expanding the Canadian military presence in Iraq and now into Syria. There is considerable passion and there are few aspects of the decision that have not been spun for an interested public.

Deter, degrade and defeat flow from our leaders tongues with the ease of salesman selling a new mouthwash; "precision" bombing is discussed as if this was equivalent to tossing curling stones in down town Moose Jaw; training by foreign troops of local forces are accepted as if this was a woodworking class in the local trades school; recovery of downed pilots from Islamic State controlled territory is glossed over with the suggestion that the Americans will handle this nasty possibility; and the legality of extending the war to Syria is justified by parsing sections of the United Nations Charter by the chief lawyer for the Canadian military, hardly an unbiased observer.

And now the "philosophers" of our military mission have weighed in. The Foreign Minister has concluded the whole operation is a matter of "moral clarity," words not dissimilar to those used to gen the medieval public for the crusades; the Defence Minister, on the other hand, sees the war as an enormous humanitarian exercise, leaving many scratching their heads. The cartoons will be underway soon; a large bomb falls on Tikrit and a child says to another "Don't worry it's a Canadian humanitarian bomb."

Unfortunately there is one aspect of the war that is being ignored and as with most moderns wars it is the most important. No one especially the militaries involved have offered any assessment of success in understandable terms of what this war will achieve. Most will only say that a conclusion is years away which in today's world is no answer whatsoever.

We have dressed for a ball that we do not understand, invited ourselves, knowing we have no capability of influencing the outcome. Instead, leaders who should know better see the war as means of scratching a small itch in the national body politic – fear of an imprecise national security threat. In response they send our soldiers to die and this even before they have satisfactorily deal with the wounded of the last.

We do not have to go back to the Vietnam War for a detailed understanding of the futility of fighting forces on their own land. Eleven years of fighting the Afghans with overwhelming forces and money, the creation of comprehensive new security and military forces, the fostering of civilian political measures of electoral politics and the holding of elections and the creation of a hot house corrupted economy based on foreign money have done absolutely nothing to change anything of any significance in that ancient land.

The Afghans are just not interested in nor amenable to western forces that invaded with one purpose in mind – getting rid of a non-indigenous terrorist organization – and then, carried away with the early ease, deciding that ancient ways of government be updated as if they were dealing with a mechanistic complex. The bones of others who tried whiten the sands. Today Afghanistan resembles a three legged camel trying to climb a mountain.

And this failure led to others. Iraq where most of the current war is being fought is a classic example of going to war for the wrong reasons and then leaving knowing that the place had been damaged beyond redemption. And then there was Libya. A post-colonial patchwork of a country held together by a man who talked to the stars and beguiled western leaders with the enormity of his wealth. He died in a sewer and his country died with him. Today we have to go back to the Punic Wars to understand the forces that now contend there.

And we are now on the edge of another disaster in the Yemen. There another post-colonial patchwork of a country has lived longer than its religious and regional divides could sustain. As many have suggested, Yemen may be the most dangerous of all the wars as it may well engage the forces of the Sunni majority of the Middle East against those of the Shia and their main protector, Iran. Already the Sunni forces are coalescing around Saudi Arabia and Egypt both countries lacking a cohesive national purpose beyond the end of a gun.

It is not alarmist to suggest that while western forces have large interests at stake in these modern wars, they have no hope of protecting those interests through the use of incapable and limited military forces. They are in fact making matters worse and in doing so ensuring that their own interests will be trampled in the process.

War is not diplomacy through other means. In today's world it has become a convenient policy option for political leaders who are not willing to invest in actions that attempt to build down the contending forces.

The inclination to send in the troops, or if these matters were not so dire, send in the clowns is the more appropriate phrase, reflects a nasty streak in our body politic. It is ironic that as we near our 150th Anniversary as a country we have become one of the world's war mongers. And all for the edification of a small group of leaders including the Prime Minister who for the past ten years have more than any other government in the history of the country decided that the tearing down of what has gone before is more important than building for the future.

> ... [A]s we know, there are known knowns; there are things we know we know. We also know there are known unknowns; that is to say we know there are some things we do not know. But there are also unknown unknowns – the ones we don't know we don't know. And if one looks throughout the history of our country and other free countries, it is the latter category that tend to be the difficult ones.
>
> —Donald Rumsfeld, United States Secretary of Defence for the invasions of Afghanistan (2001) and Iraq (2003)"

2. Inside the Shadows – The Quest for National Security

THE MODERN CONCEPT OF NATIONAL SECURITY REACHES BACK TO the wars of 17th century Europe and the foundational peace treaties of Westphalia. Along with the emergence of the nation state came the idea that such states needed the wherewithal for survival that was dependent not on the good will of others but on its own preparedness. It was an age when national survival was built on the adage of Vegetius - **Si vis pacem, para bellum** – If you wanted peace, prepare for war. So it was and hopefully, not ever will be. But it has been an ingrained concept among most of the world leaders ever since. More troubling is that in its modern manifestation national security has been expanded by leaders in a variety of places and times to include just about any troublesome issue that requires more than a sound bite or longer term planning.

Originally the concept centred on the military preparedness of a state to meet invaders intent on domination. Since, the threats have become more diverse and to a great extent more difficult to defend. As well, the diversity of modern nation states ensures that threats can come from within, probably with greater certainty, than those from without. Canada in the 60s and 70s of the last century and with lingering elements down to the present provides an example that is fairly normal in global terms. Perhaps only Iceland and Japan retain the norm of internal cohesiveness inherent in the early concept of the nation state. Otherwise, all nation states include divisions and fissures of language, religion, race, culture and historical conflicts that from time mar the surface of national unity and trouble those with responsibility for the security of the state.

Many states have been successful in dealing with issues of national unity; largely resulting from political patience in coping with the rights of minorities, wise and moderate counsel in dealing with associated violence, political leadership and the exploitation of fractures within the offended group. The standard against which success can be measured was the American Civil War which reflected the transformation of an agrarian society into an industrial one. The central issue of race was decided but as is readily evident today it remains a large and troublesome matter that still roils the body politic.

Of equal interest and in terms of involving a greater number of people is the Hispanization of the United States. The impasse in the American political system with the associated issue of immigration (or more accurately, migration) from the south into the United States provides an example for all countries with large immigrant population. Many countries with large recent incoming migration from the south have not been particularly wise or practical in coping with the associated issues of integration especially of those with manifestations of daily life that differ significantly from the national mainstream or in the language of the streets, not like us.

It is this issue that is particularly current in national unity and national security debates throughout the world. There is some irony that the people of the colonial powers of Europe went south in their "civilizing" missions, but more accurately in search of new riches and today having to cope with many people from those "civilized" lands coming north. Today the migration northward is equally economic but also, in large measure, there is a search for personal security from the conflicts generated in the gerrymandered lands left behind by departing colonial powers. The conflicts in those lands, not surprisingly, attract the interest of these recent migrants and there is a few who resort to violence in order to provide support to their co-religionists or national groupings back home. Confusingly, into this mix there are a few who decide that violence offers an answer to their personal demons.

The locations of the associated violence in recent years illustrates the scope of the national security issue – Madrid, London, Glasgow, Texas, Stockholm, Frankfurt, Toulouse, Boston, Brussels, St-Jean-sur-Richelieu, Ottawa, Sydney, Paris and Copenhagen. Not surprisingly the spread and scope of such violence is in direct proportion to the willingness of Western leaders to send their military into the conflicts of other countries. Most see immediate domestic political advantage in doing so and there is often consequential increased support at home, and often, from within, participating alliances. As all of the 21st century foreign military adventures (and earlier ones) have demonstrated there are also consequential costs in lives and resources and the certainty that they will fail with large unintended consequences. The political and security environment in all invaded countries are today worse than they were before such invasions.

One of the serious "unintended consequences" of foreign military adventures is the widespread discrete acts of violence throughout the world. A direct consequence of this violence is the rush by Western governments to try and change the balance between the institutions of national security and its citizens. There is not a security institution (and intelligence ones can be included as well) that when faced with a significant act of violence do not rush to their political masters and seek new powers of intervention. And in many instances political master are already ahead of these institutions in announcing additional and new interventionist policies and laws that significantly alter the balance with citizens. More often than not, like the rush to war, there is no consideration of whether or not changes in the balance will provide greater security for the citizen.

In the aftermath of 911 on September 11, 2001, as with so many other matters, the clamour for altering the balance between security institutions and the citizen, as well as the rush to war, knew few bounds. Sadly voices of caution were ignored or denounced as those of persons who lacked the needed patriotic fervour that such situations demanded. The USA Patriot Act, or to give it its full name – "Uniting and Strengthening America by Providing Appropriate Tools Required to Intercept and Obstruct Terrorism Act of 2001" – illustrates three aspects of such laws. The first was the speed with which law makers are prepared to give legal effect to a wide variety of measures that alter the balance with citizens – the Patriot Act was enacted in a little more than six weeks after 911; the second is the willingness of law makers to fundamentally erode long established legal protections inherent in a democratic system; and three the unwillingness of leaders to ensure that there are new and substantial oversight and review mechanism capable to dealing with these new measures that affect the balance with citizens.

The Canadian government was not much behind the United States in rushing new legislation through Parliament in response to the threat of terrorism. The Canadian Anti-Terrorism Act was introduced by the Liberal Government of the day in the House of Commons on October 15, 2001 and received Royal Assent on December 18, 2001. The Act expanded security and surveillance powers, pre-emptive detention and trials hidden from public view. However, the most fundamental aspect of the new law was the creation of new crimes related to terrorism which then required the RCMP to re-enter the area of national security, an area from which they were largely excluded by the creation of the Canadian Security Intelligence Service in 1984. To say the RCMP was unprepared for this new role is to stretch "understated" to new limits.

Commissions of inquiry five years later conclusively demonstrated that the RCMP was overwhelmed by these new responsibilities. Serious injury was inflicted on many Canadians some whose imprisonment in the Middle East was occasioned by RCMP inability to distinguish between terrorism activities and daily living. Justice for some came through these Commissions. For others the government has decided to out wait and out-money their efforts in the courts. Many of their situations are deal with in the following articles.

The murder of two Canadian military persons in October of last year has now occasioned another attempt by the government to expand the powers of our security institutions. As with the 2001 Act this new draft legislation expands the powers of our security institutions but there are no arrangements for sunset provisions nor is there any willingness to expand the authority of existing weak and incapable oversight organizations. There are two certainties in this sad state of affairs – there will be more acts of terrorism and innocent Canadians will be seriously affected in the response. Retired

Supreme Court justices should not get rid of their black robes yet; they will be required for the expected investigations.

Some of the articles included in this section on National Security deal with Canadians in trouble in foreign countries. Normally such articles would be included in the next section of the book dealing with Canadians Abroad but since their problems are largely the result of or involve the work of Canadian police and security organizations they are included in this section on National Security. [April 25, 2015]

Bush's Power has Limits
July 30, 2006

PRESIDENT GEORGE BUSH TODAY IS PROBABLY CONSIDERING THE advice the conspirators, "the filth and scum of Kent," gave themselves in Shakespeare's Henry the Fourth. Before they began their rebellion against the King, Shakespeare had Dick the Butcher utter the immortal words of persons who plan large "crimes" that "the first thing we do, let's kill all the lawyers."

There is no doubt today that for those who abide by the supreme rule of democratic society – the rule of law – the Supremes of the United States Supreme Court have rendered a sobering and, hopefully, conclusive judgement on the limits of Presidential power. It does not matter whether you believe American hegemony is benevolent or malevolent, the decision of the Court, the first such decision since 2001, is a ringing endorsement of the resilience and depth of American democracy. [The full decision can be found at http://www.supremecourtus.gov/opinions/05pdf/05-184.pdf].

Over the last several years there has been legitimate concern that some of the elements in President Bush's "War on Terror" were seriously at odds with fundamental principles of American jurisprudence. Renditions, extraordinary and otherwise, secret detention centres, snatch and grab operations on the streets of European cities, and the use of abusive and disingenuous interrogation and punishment techniques have all undermined the legitimate security concerns of the United States and its allies. Equally, the use of such instruments has created additional and even larger security concerns in other parts of the world.

The most significant of these elements in the "War on Terror," however, was the creation of the detention facility at Guantanamo Bay, Cuba. Right from its beginning in early 2002 there were legitimate concerns expressed as to its legitimacy under the Geneva Conventions of 1949 which codified the "Rules of War." The United States was a signatory to these conventions and successfully used them when not followed by other states. Equally, the decision to create Military Commissions instead of using existing tribunal to establish guilt or innocence of detainees created an environment that cried out for redress. It also demanded that there be some balancing between the legitimate security concerns of the state and the rights of detainees to certain fundamental elements of fairness.

Many countries face the same dilemma. A British court on June 28 decided that control orders on suspected Iraqi terrorists were so severe that they were in contravention of Article 5 of the European Convention on Human Rights. Article 5 prohibits detention without trial and the judge, in effect, ruled that the restrictions on the suspected terrorists were such that they amounted to imprisonment without trial. This decision followed on an earlier decision by the British courts that detention of suspected terrorists without trial was illegal.

Some of these same issues concerning the use of Security Certificates and preventive detention are now before the Canadian Supreme Court. It is expected to rule in the fall. One comment in the United States Supreme Court decision may be of interest to the Canadian Supremes as they debate the issues. The American court stated: "*Even assuming that Hamden is a dangerous individual who would cause great harm or death to innocent civilians given the opportunity, the Executive nevertheless must comply with the prevailing rule of law in undertaking to try him and subject him to criminal punishment.*"

The issues before the Supreme Court of the United States were significantly different than those in Canada and the United Kingdom. There the case revolved around Salim Ahmed Hamdan, a Yemeni national who was captured by militia forces in Afghanistan in November 2001, turned over to American forces and subsequently transported to Guantanamo Bay. In 2003, the American authorities deemed him eligible for trial by Military Commission and in 2004 he was charged with one count of conspiracy "to commit . . . offences trialable by military commission." The issues before the American Supreme Court were threefold: the legitimacy of the charge of "conspiracy," the legitimacy of the Military Commissions and the legitimacy of the procedures used by the Military Commissions.

On all three matters a majority (five to three) of the Supreme Court ruled that the American government was acting contrary to both its own laws and those of the Geneva Conventions. On the use of "conspiracy" the Court ruled that Mr Hamdan was not charged with an "offence . . . that by the rule of war may be tried by military commission."

The Supreme Court, on the procedures used by the military commissions, boldly stated that *"the procedures adopted to try Hamdan deviate from those governing courts-martial in ways not justified by practical need, and thus fail to afford the requisite guarantees.*

. . . [A]n accused must, absent disruptive conduct or consent, be present at all stages of a criminal trial or to address the validity of the conspiracy charge . . . ." More pointedly still the Court stated that the "rules specified for Hamden's commission trial are illegal." On the validity of the Commission itself, the Court rules that it *"lacks the power to proceed because its structure and procedures violate both the UCMJ [American Unified Code of Military Justice] and the four Geneva Conventions signed in 1949."*

The clarity and boldness of this decision puts paid to the many Cassandras who bought hand wringing to a new level during the appointment process of the new chief justice, John Roberts and associate judge Samuel Alito. Many saw the balance of court being permanently altered by these appointments so that the executive arm of American government would find greater support and succour. Even if Chief Justice Roberts had taken part in the consideration and decision of the case, which he did not, the present majority would have still carried the day on the matter.

The decision is equally important in the political sphere. The American Congress has demonstrated an abysmal lack of effectiveness and courage in carrying out its constitutional responsibility of being a balance and a check on the Presidential arm of the American government during times of intense national troubles. The Supreme Court's decision could well provide a rallying point for other legitimate concerns arising from the "War on Terror." It will certainly add to the volume of foreign criticism of many of the aspects of that War.

The importance of the decision for the case of Omar Khadr, the teenage Canadian who has been charged under the same process as that for Mr Hamdan, is uncertain. In the case of Mr Khadr the charge is murder and not "conspiracy" which the Supreme Court ruled was not covered by the rule of war. Equally, a murder charge, given its specificity and the likelihood that the evidence could be given in a more open environment than that envisaged by the Military Commissions could lead the Americans to try a different mechanism for Mr Khadr.

In all of this, it is unlikely that the American authorities will empty Guantanamo anytime soon. More likely the pressure will increase for other countries to accept their nationals, with suitable guarantees on subsequent treatment; or for third countries to take the many that were in the wrong place at the wrong time and ended up in the Caribbean. Equally, there will be an effort to structure a legal process that meets the strictures imposed by the decision of the Supreme Court and a few will still face a day in a court. Some, however, will just remain as prisoners at Guantanamo.

Guantanamo and the "War on Terror" will be with us for some time to come.

The Citizen

The Same Old Mounties
September 23, 2006

IT DOES NOT HAVE THE SAME RING AS THE CHINESE ANNUAL ANIMAL zodiac names but for Canadians these are the years of the inquiry. First Justice Gomery, in his inimical theatrical style, provided Canadians with a sorry and squalid account of malfeasance and misappropriation. Now Justice O'Connor in the quiet demeanour of a wise and intelligent man has provided a comprehensive and devastating account of the tragedy of Maher Arar.

Next week former Supreme Court justice John Major will begin public hearings on Air India Flight 182. There is also the possibility of another inquiry if the government accepts Justice O'Conner's recommendations concerning Messrs. Almalki, El Maati and Nureddin.

These inquiries largely or will focus on the actions of public officials below the level of ministers and their aides. In the case of O'Connor and Major the investigations are or will be concerned with officials who work on security and law enforcement.

It would be comforting to believe by this time in our evolution into a country where most Canadians expect civility, fairness and tolerance to dominate their public institutions, the role and responsibilities of public official, especially those in security and law enforcement, would have been settled.

There is also the expectation there would be an existing, independent authority available to adjudicate public complaints, to redress grievances and to provide compensation when citizens are wrongly or illegally served. As Justice O'Connor mentions, he was surprised that a Commission of Inquiry was necessary for this to happen in the case of Mr Arar.

Why and how this state of affairs exists was only a part of Justice O'Connor remit. His first report provides a clinical analysis of what happened to Mr Arar and the shortcomings of the involved institutions and their officials. Where information and evidence was lacking on important points Justice O'Connor readily draws conclusions and makes inferences that are learned and stands the test of common sense.

A second report will be available in a few months and will assess the need for an oversight body for RCMP national security investigations.

It is unfortunate that the terms of reference were not broader on this. It is long been evident that there are serious problems with the existing review body. The RCMP Public Complaints Commission has been in existence for a number of years. Its previous chair has provided public testimony of the need for an overhaul of its mandate. By limiting Justice O'Conner's role to the "national security" activities of the RCMP, a valuable opportunity was lost.

The fundamental problem with the Arar Commission first report is that it provides little historical context or policy prescriptions for the issues associated with policing in Canada. Its specific recommendations, laudable as they all are, do not (and perhaps could not given Justice O'Conner's mandate) address any of the serious structural, policy and political oversight issues that have plagued policing and security matters in Canada for a large number of years.

These issues are not new. Twenty-five years ago the MacDonald Commission of Inquiry looked at many of these questions and provided comprehensive recommendations to the Trudeau government in 1981. As a result the Canadian Security Intelligence Service (CSIS) was established along with an independent oversight body called Security Intelligence Review Commission (SIRC). The RCMP was stripped of responsibility for national security matters, although the staffing for the new CSIS was made up of former members of the RCMP.

There were even earlier reports on these matters. The Taschereau Commission concerning the defection of Igor Gouzenko as long ago as 1947 highlighted some of these issues. Twenty years later in 1968 it was necessary to again look at some of the same problems and the Mackenzie Royal Commission again made recommendations.

The Macdonald Commission report details the negative attitude of the RCMP to change especially on issues of national security. The Report noted dryly that Prime Minister Trudeau in making a public announcement of changes to the RCMP wanted to say ". . . with the full agreement and understanding of the Force. . ." simply announced ". . . with the full understanding of the Force".

A reading of the MacDonald report provides a sense of déjà vu when compared to what Justice O'Conner has to say. Many of the same issues are covered and given the record of the RCMP it will bob and weave on Justice O'Conner's recommendations. However, little will change and it is with some certainty it can be said that some years down the road there will yet be another distressing set of events involving the RCMP and there will be yet another commission of inquiry.

It does not have to be that way. The government should take advantage of this opportunity to make fundamental changes to the structure of policing in Canada. There are more fundamental issues at stake than simply oversight, coordination, training, supervision and policy guidance, important as these things are, within the Force.

The government in deciding on the changes that are necessary to provide a nimble and flexible national police force should go well beyond the specific recommendations of Justice O'Conner. The need to do so has long been evident and Justice O'Conner's report provides ample evidence that changes are long overdue.

The RCMP is a complex and amorphous police organization. More than a century of tradition and occasionally tinkering has resulted in a police force incapable of or slow in adjusting to today's complex national and international policing issues and in that it is not alone among the police forces of most countries.

The RCMP, among other things, is the national police force; it is the provincial/territorial police force in eight provinces and three territories and in over two hundred communities ranging from the high arctic to the American border (often referred to as contract policing); it is the police force on many reservations; and when the Prime Minister (and many other VIP including visitors to Canada) go to sleep at night, the RCMP are near at hand

It should not be a surprise then when in December 2001 the government decided the RCMP would again have responsibilities on some national security matters, the Force stumbled badly.

Other governments are making significant changes to their national police forces and for Canada there are two major changes the government should make to avoid the mistakes of the past. First and foremost the scope of RCMP responsibilities should be reduced. The Force should be divested of its responsibility for contract policing across the country and the function given to a separate organization. As part of this move responsibility for policing on reservations and protection policing should be given to the new organization.

The second major change should be in the role of the minister responsible for the RCMP. The creation of the Department of Public Security, replacing the Office of the Solicitor General, has not provided sufficient or effective political oversight of the national police force.

The historical separation between politics and policing needs to be maintained but many of the issues that a modern national police force has to content invariably involves significant and complex political issues. While structural and legal changes are needed, more attention must be given to the qualities of the person appointed minister. Many of the past ministers never lost their training wheels.

The Citizen

The Commissioner Takes Us on a Musical Ride
September 30, 2006

THE ONLY THINGS MISSING FROM PARLIAMENT HILL ON THURSDAY morning were the Musical Ride and Jeanette MacDonald and Nelson Eddy doing a chorus from *Rosemarie*.

The Head of the GCI, that is the Great Canadian Institution (now that the Hudson Bay Company is a post-office box in Delaware and the Toronto Maple Leafs continue to wave their sticks as aimlessly as falling autumn leaves, the RCMP is the only GCI left) "appeared" before a Commons Committee and spoke about the work of the Force concerning Maher Arar and its reaction to the comments made by Justice Dennis O'Connor.

It was an appearance even William Hutt playing Lear in Stratford would be proud of. The Commissioner did not give sworn testimony and it was fortunate that he did not as the comments made and the answers given left a lot unsaid. The Committee format amply supported the giving of non-answers and the cross currents among its members made the Straights of Juan de Fuca seem as a millpond.

The Commissioner put a lot of emphasis on the effort by the Force to correct the information that had been given to the Americans in 2002. The information was contained on three computer discs and in later written communications, the description of Maher Arar and Monia Mazigh was given as being "Islamic extremists suspected of being linked to the al-Qaeda movement." As well, according to the O'Connor Report, Mr Arar was described in writing to the Americans as a "suspect", "a principal subject of its investigation", "a person with an 'important' connection to Mr Almalki", "a person directly linked to Mr Almalki in a diagram titled "Bin Laden's

Associates: Al Qaeda Organization in Ottawa", and "a business associate or a close associate of Mr Almalki."

And what did the RCMP corrective "effort" involve? As Justice O'Connor's Report shows, the corrections were largely incidental communications that had other purposes than an attempt to correct the serious mistakes that had been made in earlier exchanged material. After Mr Arar had been detained by the Americans on September 26, 2002 Mr Arar was then described as a "witness" and that the Force was unable to indicate that "Mr Arar had links to al-Qaeda." This is bailing Bonavista Bay with a sieve.

More flawed were the Commissioner's comments on that over used cliché of TV investigations: "What did he know and when did he know it?"

The Commissioner stated that he was fully aware of the matter shortly after Mr Arar was detained by the Americans or at the time he was sent to Syria. Full marks. The seriousness of the matter required that he be informed and that he was suggests someone in the Force understood that.

In his press conference comments following his appearance before the Commons Committee, the Commissioner was pushed hard on this issue by journalists. His responses, which mirrored those before the Committee, made the following points:

- The RCMP did not know what information the Americans had and the Commissioner avoided any comment on why the RCMP was unable to obtain details on what the Americans had, despite the fact that these were "open book" investigations involving both countries. The refusal of the Americans not to appear before the O'Connor Commission is no excuse for this.

- The Commissioner did not answer in any direct way, questions as to why he did not take action to correct the public record concerning Mr Arar especially when the leaks started to occur.

- In his responses on this the Commissioner retreated behind a wall of bureaucratic bafflegab. In his own words from the press conference. "So we started to brief up, to provide information literally days after it became public knowledge.

- And a whole process went into place which took a considerable amount of time given the amount of information and documents that existed in various parts of the country and indeed in the possession of many departments because a number of departments were clearly involved. . . . So that took a considerable amount of time."

> And when pushed by a reporter: "Well, I think Justice O'Connor does deal with that, in that he does state and I accept that there was less than, you know, perfect correlation between what information was in the possession what department but, remember, this was – it became a Canadian position, a government position which required the coordination and bringing together of all the departments so that we could have a Canadian position because it wasn't just the RCMP's position that was important . . ."

The Commissioner does not say and no one asked him why it was that by mid-June, 2003, eight to nine months after Mr Arar had been detained and the Commissioner's awareness that a "nightmare" had been created for Mr Arar, the RCMP opposed a coordinated government position as represented by the "one voice" letter that Foreign Affairs had flogged for some six weeks. The written response of both the RCMP and CSIS at the time was to escalate their concerns; Mr Arar was no longer a "witness" or a "person of interest" but was now the subject of a "national security investigation."

The Commissioner did little better on the issue of the leaks. The sternness of his delivery made up for the lack of content. "The leaks took place. Justice O'Connor clearly states he does not know – we have not been able yet to determine where the leaks have coming from. We initiated on our own, the RCMP did – we weren't asked or told to do it. We did it because we believe, as I said, it is a deplorable thing to leak information of this nature especially when it attacks the character and reputation of any individual."

Earlier the Commissioner took refuge behind the problems raised by the judicial appeals on the validity of the search warrants against the Citizen and its reporter. He also took some comfort in the fact that even Justice O'Connor could not determine the source of the leaks. However, if the information in the leaks suggests anything it is that they were from persons who were directly involved in the investigations. If the evidence was as strong against Mr Arar as this, then he would still be in prison.

The Commissioner was outstanding on the great balm of our modern age – the apology. It was delivered up front and, not being cynical, bought a small lump to the throat. The skill with which it was done was again reminiscent of William Hutt. Unlike at Mr Hutt's stage appearances, however, there should be no applause for this thoroughly unsatisfactory and incomplete performance.

I mentioned at the beginning one of the things missing from Parliament Hill on Thursday morning was the Musical Ride. In light of what went on, that comment needs to be modified. At least the rear ends of the horses were there and they were seated around the Committee table.

The Citizen

Another RCMP Report for the Pile
December 27, 2007

IT WAS 1949 WHEN I MET MY FIRST MOUNTIE. CPL. EARL ROSE HAD arrived in Gander as part of the new colonial power to ensure that the forces of mayhem were kept in check while the airport town emerged as the crossroads of the air world.

A few years later, in then Frobisher Bay, I occasionally flew with Sgt. Lorne Fletcher of the RCMP air-services arm, as he provided essential and life-saving search, rescue and supply flights in the eastern Arctic – and took outstanding pictures of that wonderful land. And in 1967 I arrived in Ottawa and for the next 36 years often worked closely with members of the force both at their headquarters and in several embassies, as they provided police-liaison services to foreign governments. I took them to meetings and I carried them out of bars.

Over most of those 50-plus years there was easy camaraderie and professional respect with a wide variety of officers. A characteristic of these members was the extensive expertise and experience that most accumulated – from the first days in Regina to when ceremonial spurs were hung on the walls of the retirement rec room.

The list of responsibilities is a long one and like the universe still expands: a lone officer in an isolated Baffin Island community, policing on reserves and in innumerable small towns, expertise in drugs, money laundering, intimidation in new ethnic communities, terrorism, the ever-expanding Criminal Code, the occasional transgressions emanating from the federal and provincial political systems and demands from political leaders to overcome the forces of disunity and external threats.

It's is a long way from the paramilitary force that Sir John A. sent to the northwest to quell secession and, as the most recent report stated, "arguably the most complex law enforcement agency in the world today."

Not surprisingly there were large and small stumbles along the way. The last 60 years are littered with the reports of commissioners of inquiry who did little to assist the force to adapt to the complex world of Canadian policing. Kellock-Taschereau, Mackenzie, McDonald, Morin-Hughes and O'Connor are largely footnotes of history in terms of their effect on the ever- wending RCMP stream. And, yet to come is the wisdom of Major and Iacobucci.

The most recent report comes from David Brown, a Toronto lawyer and former chair of the Ontario Securities Commission, along with four others – including a former commissioner of the force – who formed a task force on governance and cultural change in the RCMP.

The task force was grievously hobbled right from the beginning. As it stated in its report, "it would not be unreasonable to argue that some or all of the solution to issues confronting the force rests in breaking it up. Such a consideration would require a much broader public policy debate as to the policing model which best suits Canada and best serves Canadians. Such a debate is not within the mandate of this task force."

That mistake has been at the centre of every commission and task force that has been issued terms of reference to examine the force. They have all looked at the horse manure, but not the horse. And today, all we see are more shovels.

The task force did recommend the creation of a new independent commission for public complaints and oversight. The RCMP is probably the only major police organization in the world that does not have such an effective body, and at least that will go some way in providing members of the public with a means of having complaints addressed.

However, there is a long way between the recommendation and implementing legislation, and it will be tempting for a government to limit the effectiveness of the new oversight commission – as it did with the existing one.

Another recommendation of the task force is largely Ottawa and MBA mumbo jumbo. It is to establish the RCMP "as a separate entity from government," but at the same time it would remain "ultimately accountable to the minister – and through the minister to Parliament." We will need Dumbledore to make that one improve the world of policing.

An essential problem with all modern-day policing is either not enough political direction or the wrong kind. Most of the past ministers responsible for the RCMP have been singularly incompetent – the weakest members around the cabinet table. Most were incapable of establishing a balance, and most often there was no direction.

At the same time, prime ministers, when large issues of public policy required effective policing, were prepared to intervene – often by way of a nod and a wink. They would push the RCMP into areas in which it had little competence or experience or, most regrettably, to potentially engage in dirty tricks or the breaking of the law. John Diefenbaker tried to do it; Pierre Trudeau and Jean Chrétien did it. When it went badly, prime ministers largely offloaded their responsibility to members of the force or other officials, and called commissions of inquiry with limited mandates.

The recommendation for a new civilian board of management might ensure that RCMP members will get paid for overtime or might have a regular working day. However, it will do little to steer the force into the requirements of modern-day policing. The board, as is the case with most appointed by transitory politicians, will be a mile wide and less than an inch deep. It will, however, be available to help share the blame with the commissioner when things go wrong again.

As Canadians go into the 141st year of Confederation and the RCMP into its 135th year, it should be time that we gave ourselves an exclusive national police force, and all of the provinces accepted their responsibilities for their own policing. Recent history has demonstrated that that is what we need and, in terms of the world around us, what the future requires. Unfortunately, the performances of all governments, past and present, offer little hope that this will happen.

The Citizen

National Security Wonderland
April 9, 2008

GEORGE ORWELL IS OFTEN QUOTED TO THE EFFECT THAT POLITICAL euphemisms exist in order to make "murder respectable." In today's speak, the government misuses UN resolutions and national security concerns to make respectable the denial of the return of a Canadian citizen to Canada.

Mr Abdelrazik, a Canadian citizen, has spent the last six or so years in a maze constructed and maintained by the government of Canada. It is a maze that had an entry point but, every time there is a slight glimmer of an exit, the government builds a new wall.

Various official documents released to Mr Abdelrazik's Canadian lawyer, Yaver Hameed, and to the media detail the ever-changing position of the government. First and foremost, however, the documents provide an early confirmation that Mr Abdelrazik's maze crawling began with a request from the government of Canada that he be detained by the Sudanese authorities in 2003.

CSIS has denied this, but its denials are neither definitive nor convincing. To give verisimilitude to its denial, it has asked its oversight committee to review the evidence. Given the lack of transparency in CSIS oversight, this is akin to asking the Vatican to rule on the authenticity of the Turin shroud.

CSIS's actions in 2003 regarding Mr Abdelrazik are eerily similar to actions it and the RCMP carried out in 2002 and 2003 with respect to Maher Arar, Ahmad El Maati and Abdullah Almalki. In the intervening years the O'Connor and Iacobucci Commissions detailed the deadly amateurism of both the RCMP and CSIS. Those details echoed their ineptness of twenty-five years ago in the prelude to the bombing of Air India 182.

The cornerstone of the government's position resides in a UN-Security-Council resolution blocking assets of suspected international terrorists and an associated international no-fly list. Inclusion on both lists is at the request of national governments. There are no provisions for independent standards or the vetting of information provided by these governments.

Not surprisingly, as with domestic no-fly lists, there is great scope for error, misrepresentation and outright deception. If the Americans could not keep Senator Ted Kennedy off their no-fly lists, it is not difficult to understand that a mistake could be made for a person named Abousfian Abdelrazik. For many, unfortunately, in this age of paranoia on national security, the name screams for inclusion on someone's list!

There is also the matter of the sources for such information. All governments and the American government in particular have not been particularly fastidious in the means such information is collected, and in its subsequent assessment and use. Harsh and illegal interrogations, including torture, and the drawing of large conclusions by inexperienced and ignorant police and security officials – under great pressure not to make a mistake – have been the source of many of the suspicions leading to such listings. In the blackness that backstops national-security issues there is little scope for concerned citizens to exercise independent judgement.

Not surprisingly, a lack of trust, suspicion and doubt surround government decisions in such matters. Even a senior legal official with CSIS had difficulty in understanding what information could be used when speaking to a Parliamentary Committee. In the last few days, the Foreign Minister and lawyers for the government appearing before the Federal Court misconstrued the provisions of the applicable UN resolution. Demonstrating how out-of-touch the government is, it argued before the Federal Court that such matters are ones of "Crown prerogative."

More surprising is the expectation by the government that its position on Mr Abdelrazik meets the smell and duck tests of common sense. First, the government expects us to believe that Mr Abdelrazik is such a security risk that it is best to leave him in Sudan – a country that provided a home for Osama bin Laden from which he went to Afghanistan and began his worldwide terrorist campaign. It says little about Canadian counter-terrorism capabilities if Mr Abdelrazik's return to Canada could not be supervised and monitored here, thus lessening any risk he may represent. As was suggested in testimony before the O'Connor Commission the cost of such supervision may be an element in such decisions.

A second and even more preposterous tenet of the government's position is that Mr Abdelrazik be provided shelter and succour within the Canadian embassy in Khartoum. Canadian Foreign Service officers are a versatile lot, but it beggars the mind to have them act as custodians of a security risk who has been denied a Canadian passport for national-security reasons.

In the United States the days of reckoning for those who created and perpetuated gross crimes against the principles on which the Republic was founded are about to begin. Numerous lawyers and other officials in various parts of the American government, in the coming months, will have to publicly account for their actions and, while some exempt former President Bush from this accounting, the same cannot be said for his Vice-President.

Many in the US Congress and beyond believe public accounting for ignoring or fictionalizing long-standing domestic and international legal principles has to be made. These principles concerning torture, secret interrogation sites in third countries, the prison at Guantanamo and the invasion of the privacy of American citizens are issues that will provide fodder for Congressional investigations.

In Canada we have had some measure of public accounting through the O'Connor Commission and somewhat less so through that of Iacobucci. In the aftermath of this national breast-beating, there was every expectation that we could look forward to significant changes in the way in which our police and security organizations operate. It is a national shame that nothing has been done and, from the way Mr Abdelrazik is being treated, there can be little expectation this will change.

Arar Blame Game Continues
September 10, 2008

FORMER RCMP COMMISSIONER GIULIANO ZACCARDELLI RETURNED to public attention this past week with a pathetic explanation of his understanding of the events surrounding Maher Arar. With bravado bordering on bathos, the former Commissioner sidestepped any personal responsibility for what happened. Instead he off-loaded responsibility to the Americans and indirectly suggested that CSIS was equally to blame. And to show that epiphanies can be as real today as they were two-thousand years ago, the former Commissioner came down against the use of tasers by the national police force.

Mr Zaccardelli, speaking from the comfort of his post-retirement job with INTERPOL in Lyon, France, staged his public re-manifestation in an interview with CBC's Peter Mansbridge. Mr Mansbridge, with more gravitas than the Pope, gently questioned Mr Zaccardelli, providing a cosy forum in which he attempted to muddle the issues involved more thoroughly than he was able to do during his testimony before a Commons committee in September and December 2006. It was that misleading and erroneous testimony that prompted his early resignation and retirement.

The role of the media is one of the most troublesome and unsettling issues in the tragedy of Maher Arar. To see the national broadcaster being used in this way today demonstrates that six years later very little has been learned and very little has been accomplished.

As well, a few days ago the RCMP let it be known that they were winding down their investigation into the related leaks, as they were unable to come to any conclusions as to who was responsible. It was these disastrous leaks that surrounded Mr Arar while he was in a Syrian prison and continued to be made long after he returned to Canada.

It is also likely that soon the RCMP will wind down a second investigation into whether or not Canadian officials were criminally responsible in any way for his treatment at the hands of the Syrians. If ever there was a case of the cats investigating the mice, it was these two investigations by the RCMP. They offer no confidence whatsoever that the results are to be believed or trusted – or that the investigations were assiduously done.

In the meantime the former Commissioner, without being effectively challenged by Mr Mansbridge, promoted the ideas that Mr Arar was only a "person of interest" to the RCMP; that the Americans may have had additional information of their own; that the Americans were unique in "throwing away the rule book" and, by innuendo, that CSIS was part of the problem due to the "clear friction and disagreement" with the RCMP.

There is no evidence to support such ideas either in the O'Connor report or in the thousands of pages of testimony on which it was based. Their repetition two years after the fact is an exercise in rewriting history in a manner that even the Soviets in their heyday would have taken some pride.

Mr Arar may have been a person of interest because of his association with others, but, during the early days of the RCMP investigation and during the year he was in Syria, he was also described officially by the Force as being part of "a group of Islamic Extremist individuals suspected of being linked to the Al Queda terrorist movement" – and that description was provided to the Americans. It was these words that found their way into the American deportation document – without the qualifier that he was "suspected." Equally erroneously, Dr Monia Mazigh was similarly labelled both to Canadian customs and to the Americans.

Later in June of 2003 the RCMP (and CSIS) stated that "Mr Arar was a subject of a national security investigation." As Justice

O'Connor succinctly wrote: "He was not." For Mr Zaccardelli to state that he was only "a person of interest" is completely contrary to detailed and documented evidence.

There is no evidence that the Americans had information concerning Mr Arar other than what was provided by the RCMP. In April 2001 Mr Arar travelled to the United States and subsequently the American renewed his permission to work in that country. It would have been highly unlikely that the Americans would have done so if there had been any suspicion of him dating from the eighteen months he worked in Boston. In the aftermath of the O'Connor inquiry, no less a person than the minister of public safety stated that he had seen the American file on Mr Arar – and there was nothing that supported the way he had been treated by them.

Mr Zaccardelli's emphasis that the Americans were unique in throwing away the rule book does not stand up to close scrutiny either. There is ample evidence in the O'Connor report to conclude that the rule book was also jettisoned by the RCMP. Unfortunately they were abetted by political leaders of both major parties – who were perfectly willing to see the erosion of fundamental safeguards in the fictitious war on terrorism and to provide both the RCMP and CSIS with new powers that diminished the protections available to individuals.

Mr Zaccardelli's comments concerning CSIS have a large déjà vu component. Not so many years ago when CSIS was formed from the body of the RCMP Security Service, there were years of acrimony and tension between the two institutions. The commissioner at the time along with other senior officers went out of their way to undermine and diminish the new security organization, and it is not a stretch as others have noted to suggest that this contributed to the bombing of Air India 182 and the death of 229 persons.

Throughout the years of the Arar tragedy, Mr Zaccardelli was the Commissioner of the RCMP. As reports and inquiries have consistently stated, there are serious and fundamental issues and problems with policing and security work in Canada, and it is evident that Mr

Zaccardelli did little to improve matters during his six years in office. His recent efforts to place the blame on others must be ignored. Already there is an emerging script that there is little that needs to change. Unfortunately, with that approach it will not be long before we have another disaster within the Canadian body politic.

The Citizen

Iacobucci's Failure to Live Up to His Own Standard
October 29, 2008

THE SECOND PHASE OF THE INQUIRY INTO THE TORTURE OF FOUR Canadians in Syrian and Egyptian prisons ended last week when former Supreme Court Justice Frank Iacobucci released a report on his findings which included a number of recommendations.

His report followed that of Justice Dennis O'Connor, who investigated the case of Maher Arar. In September 2006 Justice O'Connor also provided recommendations to the government for a new review mechanism relating to national-security activities of the RCMP.

There the similarities end. While Justice O'Connor conducted a public inquiry in every sense of those words, Commissioner Iacobucci was directed by his terms of reference from the government to conduct an "internal inquiry." This meant, in plain language, a secret inquiry, and that, adapting language from his own report, "indirectly" resulted in a secret trial of those officials who provided testimony to the commission. (In the interest of full disclosure, I gave testimony before the commission and my testimony is discussed in the report.)

Commissioner Iacobucci and the lead counsel for the commission, John Larkin, have emphasized in the report and in public comment that the terms of reference for the commission precluded a more open inquiry.

These comments have been taken at face value, but there is little evidence to support that view. While the terms of reference describe it as an "internal inquiry," there are elements in those terms that would have allowed the commission, if so inclined, to conduct some of its evidentiary phase in public – as Justice O'Connor did

– without doing damage to that great veil of governmental protection, "national security confidential." As it was, only administrative and procedural matters were discussed in public sessions by Justice Iacobucci.

In defending his decision to keep the evidentiary phase of the inquiry secret, the commissioner ignored a section of his mandate which gave permission "to conduct specific portions of the Inquiry in public if he is satisfied that it is essential to ensure the effective conduct of the Inquiry." The commissioner did not see fit to comment on this authority and instead relied on the hoary standby of acting under orders when defending his decision.

Unlike Justice O'Connor, Commissioner Iacobucci interpreted his mandate in a narrow and limiting way and, in doing so, added to the injustices that were under investigation. The mandate given to Justice O'Connor was for a public inquiry with some limitations, but, even so, Justice O'Connor had a strong sense that as much evidence as possible should be heard in public – and Canadians given an opportunity to form opinions about that evidence. Justice O'Connor went to the Federal Court twice to try and defeat governmental efforts to curb his work and curtail information in his public report. When not satisfied with the results, he clearly indicated in his public report where the government censored.

This issue goes to the very essence of inquiries: independent commissioners who are willing to maintain and fight governmental attempts to hobble. This essence was stated in Commissioner Iacobucci's mandate. The first paragraph emphasized that the review "should be done through an independent and credible process that is able to address the integrated nature of the underlying investigations and inspires public confidence in the outcome." This essence was missing in Commissioner Iacobucci's approach to his mandate and his work.

Two issues in the report relating to consular matters need comment, as they are at the centre of the commissioner's criticism. The report sets out an interpretation of the Vienna Convention on Consular Relations that does not bear any relationship to the wording in the convention. Importantly, the convention does not offer any direction with respect to persons who have dual citizenship, including that of the arresting state.

To the extent that there is international law on the issue, it unambiguously proclaims: "A State may not afford diplomatic protection to one of its nationals against a State whose nationality such person also possesses." While Canada denounced this treaty in 1996, it remains an important consideration for many other countries.

These issues are at the heart of the matters examined by Justice O'Connor and Commissioner Iacobucci. They find careful examination by Justice O'Connor, but much less so and, as noted, erroneously so by Commissioner Iacobucci. These issues increasingly dominate many of the difficult situations with which consular and diplomatic officers contend. As such, the "magic-wand" approach that has predominated for Canadians does little to see them successfully resolved.

Commissioner Iacobucci, in his report, wrote of "means and ends" in public administration, and went on to stress that a "democracy ... must justify the means to any end – including in this case, its response to terrorism." He stressed that officials must "exercise their best judgement to try to attain the delicate balance that both protects our democracy and preserves and enhances our fundamental freedoms."

It is unfortunate that, by conducting a secret trial – anathema to the "fundamental freedoms" – the commissioner did not live up to his own standard. Perhaps he found the standard more difficult to observe during the reflective aftermath of the events examined than it was for the officials who were on the firing line.

Embassy

The media aren't always a help
November 11, 2008

ALL CANADIANS ARE GRATIFIED THAT CBC REPORTER MELLISSA FUNG has been released by her captors and is now safe. For four weeks she endured unspeakable psychological and physical dangers. Experience with several other Canadians who have endured much longer abductions in equally dangerous situations suggests Ms Fung will need time to gain equilibrium in her life, despite her plucky answers to reporters following her release.

An important element in her release was the news blackout CBC and other news organizations maintained during her 28 days of captivity. CBC News publisher John Cruickshank, speaking following Ms Fung's release, stated: "In the interest of Mellissa's safety and that of other working journalists in the region, on the advice of security experts, we made the decision to ask media colleagues not to publish news of her abduction."

An intelligent and appropriate position. However, it would be more acceptable if the media were to follow that policy more widely and not only when one of their own was in danger.

There have been numerous Canadians kidnapped over the years and often in conditions as dangerous and volatile as that found in Afghanistan today. I was directly involved in most of those kidnappings, managing the actions of the Canadian government in seeking their release. In Colombia, Ecuador, Brazil, Nigeria, South Africa, Iraq, Mexico and Lebanon, Canadians have been abducted and suffered physical and psychological mistreatment for months and years. Fortunately, in only one, a criminal kidnapping in South Africa, was the Canadian killed.

Another case involved the abduction of seven Canadian pipeline workers in Ecuador in 1999. Every effort to obtain their release over several months was dogged by reporting both erroneous and accurate. But none of the reporting helped in the negotiations and most likely increased the price that had to be paid before they were released. At the time there was no introspection on the part of the media on the impact of the reporting. For most, the story was more important than the well-being of those being force-marched through the Ecuadorian and possibly the Colombian jungles.

In many of these situations publicity, in addition to money, was one of the important ingredients motivating such abductions. Equally, in many of them, publicity in Canada and elsewhere was a constant worry for those involved, knowing that such media action did nothing to help – and not infrequently interrupted and slowed efforts to negotiate releases.

In those cases there was little co-operation on the part of the media to accept advice from government officials. More often than not, the media were antagonistic, and there was a view that the officials were hiding behind the no-publicity pleas in order to cover up mistakes and inaction.

The media are neither monolithic nor malevolent. But there is a fundamental urge to see reporting in situations where Canadian lives are in danger as serving some greater good and the playing out of the proper role of media in democratic societies. To accept direction from governments is not something that comes naturally or willingly to journalists.

Even court decisions are no longer willingly accepted when they infringe on the self-proclaimed prerogatives of the media. While in most instances the courts are final arbiters, the media have taken every opportunity to press their interests, which many do not see as differing from the interest of the public.

In the aftermath of the passage of the Anti-Terrorism Act in December 2001, the media played an important role when governments tried to elude and ignore responsibility behind the modern

Orwellian concept of "national security confidential." These were dangerous times when lives were destroyed and reputations tarnished with no expectation that the evidence, issues and claims would be adjudicated in an open court.

But there is another face to the media in this environment and it is apparent in their treatment of Maher Arar. Many journalists were supportive, but several were not. While they may not have been malicious in the stories they published, it would not be mistaken to state that the impact of their reporting did violence to Mr. Arar. Damaging stories were created on nothing more than leaks from persons who had a vested interest in doing harm. Some of these stories were printed while Mr. Arar was still in prison in Syria – and did play a role in the time it took to have him released.

Perhaps it is time, now that the actions of governmental officials have been closely examined, that the profession of journalism were to examine its own role in these tragic matters and establish guidelines for handling them in the future.

In the meantime, Ms Fung is now out of danger and the decision of the media to stay silent on her 28-day kidnapping is to be applauded. However, the applause would be louder if the media were to accept that such actions are equally appropriate when the victim is not a journalist.

The Citizen

Book Reviews
November 24, 2008

Guantanamo's Child: The Untold Story of Omar Khadr, by Michelle Shephard. Toronto, John Wiley & Sons Canada, Inc., 2008, 270 pp., $29.95.

Dark Days: The Story of Four Canadians Tortured in the Name of Fighting Terror, by Kerry Pither. Toronto, Penguin Group, 2008, 460 pp., $35.00.

WE ARE NOW SEVEN YEARS ON FROM THE WORLD-CHANGING EVENTS of September 11, 2001 and the consequential "war on terror" launched by President George W Bush and his coterie of over-reaching, hubristic associates. His administration is shambling to the end of its shameful existence and it will be some time before revisionist historians will put lipstick on that pig. Unfortunately the countervailing forces of reason, decency and prudence have been slow to emerge, and it is only now that some of the inadvertent casualties of that war are being identified.

It was only a few months after 911 that some of the elements of the dark side of the war on terror began to appear in the mainstream media. In December 2002 Dana Priest and her colleagues at the *Washington Post* reported on the phenomenon of extraordinary rendition at the same time that Guantanamo became part of the public lexicon as a place beyond the rule of law. And it was not many months before the evils and terrors of "Black Prisons" and of Abu Ghraib illustrated the lack of morality and decency within some elements of the American policy and security agencies and armed forces. Except for a few soldiers, no one of rank has been held legally or morally accountable for these indelible stains on the "City upon a Hill."

In Canada, with high dudgeon, we have stood aloof from the moral and legal failures of our neighbour. We stumbled into the open-ended war in Afghanistan and chameleon-like we sidestepped Iraq. However, time increasingly demonstrates that in the dark side of the war on terror our own hands have stains – and these should not be allowed to fade with the passage of time.

These two books, Michelle Shephard's insightful and unique look into the first family of Canadian terror and Kerry Pither's authoritative and sad chronicling of the four Canadians who were ensnared by the webs created by our out-of-their-depth and untrained security and police organizations illustrate the Canadian casualties. The books should stand for some time as examples for those both in and out of government of how six decades of "reform" of our security and police organizations have failed. Equally, the books provide stark reminders of how thin the protection is for citizens when the rule of law and reason are dumped or circumscribed in order to give the illusion of security.

Michelle Shephard's *Guantanamo's Child* tells the story of the Khadr family and its troubled journey from Egypt to Canada to Pakistan, and ultimately to death in Afghanistan. It is a rare story and, despite media attention going back over a decade, it is only in Ms Shephard's superb telling that there is any sense of understanding and comprehension. It is the first book that relies on the cooperation of members of the Khadr family and particularly the willingness of Omar's sister, Zaynab, to speak openly and, from my knowledge, honestly of a dysfunctional and migratory clan searching for certainty in an uncertain world. As Ms Shephard writes, "The Khadr family is endlessly fascinating, infuriating, belligerent, simple, and yet complicated, sometimes naïve, sometimes savvy."

The patriarch was Ahmed Said Khadr, a professional engineer from a reasonably well-off Egyptian family who, against the wishes of his family, migrated to Canada. In so many ways there are strong echoes in his life to those of several other Egyptians – particularly Ayman al-Zawahiri, the founder of Islamic Jihad and later deputy to Osama bin Laden, who became a close friend of Ahmad – of his generation who, frustrated with the lack of political and economic change in Egypt, sought change through violence based on their twisted understanding of Islam. (Lawrence Wright's *The Looming Tower: Al-Qaeda and the Road to 9/11* provide an outstanding account of the evolution of al-Zawahiri and the Islamic Jihad of Egypt into Al Qaeda).

Mr Khadr was one of thousands of Egyptians who came to Canada during this period and there were few signs then of the course the rest of his life would take. However, the Soviet invasion of Afghanistan in late 1979 provided a "rallying call for the world's Muslims" and Ahmed was no exception. For most, the war had little to do with the historical role, irrespective of religion, Afghans played in central Asia. Rather the war was now "a war against Islam."

Within a few years (1983) Ahmed made his first visit to Afghanistan and was among the very first of thousands who followed, and this, in some ways, was not significantly different from what happened in Spain in the second half of the 1930s. Before long his family was with him in Peshawar and they began their fateful, deadly journey – and their close association with Osama bin Laden and Al-Qaeda. It lead to the death of Ahmed and one son, the serious wounding of another, the disaffection of another son who for a while became a CIA agent and the capture of Omar and his imprisonment in Guantanamo.

Lest we forget, these were the years when the Afghan mujahedin were the poster boys of the world in their heroic, bloody struggle against the Soviet invaders. Washington and Riyadh were united in a common, secret struggle and poured billions of dollars into the Afghan resistance – with much sticking to Pakistani fingers – and promoted the idea this was jihad at its very finest. (George Crile's *Charlie Wilson's War* tells this story and its blowback of unintended consequences from the perspective of today's world).

Ms Shephard's focus is Omar and she provides a sympathetic story of a person caught up in a global maelstrom he did not understand, as well as being a member of a family that will provide psychologists and sociologists with fertile ground to till for years to come. However, as Ms Shephard constantly reminds us, this was a child (at the time he was captured by the Americans in 2002, he was fifteen) who deserves if not our sympathy then our understanding and a willingness to apply the moral standards of a just and tolerant society.

Previous governments both Liberal and Conservative have escaped serious criticism of their unwillingness to accept responsibility for Omar. Many other governments, ranging from the United Kingdom and Sweden to Saudi Arabia and Yemen, have accepted responsibility for their citizens with some more serious blots. However, there are still no signs that the government of Canada has begun serious discussions with the Americans to have him returned to our shores. Canadian governments have hidden behind the sins of the father, the words and dress habits of his mother and sister – and the hilarious idea that there is a justice system at Guantanamo. And in the meantime, as Ms Shephard ably documents, there are now serious doubts that Omar threw the grenade that led to the death of an American medic. More ominously, he is being judged within a system which "has no rules" and against which the United States Supreme Court on four separate occasions has found serious and substantial fault.

The story of Omar Khadr reflects largely on the sins of omission by Canada. The subjects of *Dark Days* by Kerry Pither cut more closely to Canadian bone and our sins there are ones of commission. These sins are based on the ignorance and stupidity of our security and police organizations and their inability to either understand a complex threat or, on the part of the public, to even understand the threat that badly conceived policy represents for all of us.

Ms Pither begins her account of the harsh treatment of four Canadians at the hands of their own government and media with the plea that they "have the right to be presumed innocent." At the end of her book there can be no doubt they are innocent victims of over-zealous, uninformed, ignorant and in some instances malicious police and security organizations.

These organizations were helped by a media that were willing to use unverified and inaccurate leaked information and, most troublesome of all, a media that were willing to be used for a "scoop" or to sensationalize. None of the news organizations involved has seen fit to provide an accounting of its misdeeds and mistakes. Ms Pither's book details all of these flaws and for that alone her work performs a valuable public service, since it is a sign of our time that societies quickly forget the evils that are perpetrated in their name.

Dark Days tells the stories of Maher Arar (he provides the foreword for the book), Ahmad El Maati, Abdullah Almalki and Muayyed Nureddin. She relies on the four for firsthand accounts but as well uses the thousands of pages of testimony and conclusions from the O'Connor Commission of Inquiry to cross reference and verify. In this she is assiduous in her attention to detail. The book was published in late August and so far there has not been one instance where exception has been taken to her facts or her conclusions.

The melding of four complex experiences to provide a coherent story is worthy of commendation. At the same time to create an easy-to-read account of that complexity is rare, especially in a first book. Ms Pither's experience with the Arar team (she did press relations for Monia Mazigh from early 2003 onwards) and her penchant for lists and chronologies results in a book that will remain the definitive work on this troublesome and disturbing matter.

Maher Arar is quoted in the book: "In our society, to be labelled with this 't-word' is worse, unfortunately, than a serial killer" and this theme correctly fills the book. Suspicion, underhanded accusation and malicious leaking, and not the courts, are the vehicles that were used to darken the reputation of the four men. This inexorably led to their imprisonment in foreign countries and their torture at the hands at some of the world's most adept torturers. Ms Pither does not hide from either the nastiness nor the banality of the violence visited on the four men – and for those who are sceptical of such firsthand accounts it can be stated with some finality that there is nothing in these accounts that cannot be verified by contemporaneous and third-party accounts.

The shame is not in the telling but in the willingness of Canadian political leaders to rush to erode our rights and protection under law, as they did with the Anti-Terrorism Act of December 2001. These changes were made in the willing blindness not to realize that these would be abused. History has shown that our security and national police have been incapable of meeting new threats to national security. That history demonstrates that first the RCMP and more recently CSIS do not have the moral or legal foundations to either police themselves or to adjudicate mistakes or to provide competent leadership during periods of national crisis.

Kellock-Taschereau, Mackenzie, McDonald, Morin-Hughes have all tilted at that windmill with less effect than Quixote and Panza. More recently Justice Dennis O'Connor and Dennis Brown have tilted as well. Former Supreme Court Justice Iacobucci's report, while detailing the tragedy of four Canadians, by mandate was not asked to look at remedies – a conscious omission by the government. And we are awaiting the wisdom of former Supreme Court Justice Major with respect to Air India.

After 911, as with previous periods of national concern, the RCMP developed a passion for the new mission of Sunni-based terrorism urged on by politicians and the media who should have exhibited greater balance and oversight. Ms Pither also documents the failure of the RCMP and CSIS three years earlier in dealing with Ahmed Ressam who was captured by the Americans before he was able to bomb Los Angeles Airport – adding to the willingness of police and security officials and national politicians to cut corners and throw kerosene on what was in reality a small Canadian fire.

These two books in conjunction with the report of Justice Dennis O'Connor are the only documents which provide Canadians with the opportunity to stand back once again and see the failures of their elected representatives and their willing agents in the RCMP and

CSIS. The nature of these failures has been constant in the Canadian body politic since the post-war years when Igor Gouzenko wandered around Ottawa with documents exposing Soviet spying in Canada. Roughly every two decades these failures have been examined and dissected by eminent jurists. But another constant of our body politic has been our inability to create institutions in which we can have some measure of confidence, if not trust. Ms Shephard and Ms Pither demonstrate once again how much we have failed.

bout de papier, Vol. 24, No. 1.

Cannon's Misinformed Response to Guantanamo
December 3, 2008

AN ANCIENT AXIOM SUGGESTS THAT ONCE YOU FIND YOURSELF IN A hole you put down your shovel and start looking for a ladder. Obviously, the advisers to the new Foreign Minister Lawrence Cannon missed this bit of wisdom; he was reported to have told the press a few days ago that any change in the government's policy concerning Omar Khadr was "premature." He went on to say legal proceedings were still in progress and "it's our government's intention to follow and respect the process."

There are no shortages of ladders on things Guantanamo today. The festering sore that was a centrepiece of the Bush War on Terror is in tatters, and it is only a matter of time before President-elect Obama puts a stake through its heart.

From its very inception, the prison facility at Guantanamo was attacked by those who saw it as representing the basest of the many questionable policies of the Bush administration's multifaceted war. The facility represented the denial of over 800 years of legal protections going back to the Magna Carta. These protections – namely *habeas corpus* and public trials – have been at the very centre of our fundamental protection against overreaching governments who use temporal difficulties to justify such egregious actions.

Fundamental to the establishment of the prison camp at Guantanamo was the effort by the Bush administration to posit that prisoners there were beyond the legal protections available to persons within the 50 states of the Union. This was extraterritoriality of the worse kind. Unfortunately, the United States Congress went along with this bit of legal fiction to the point that it attempted through legislation to give effect to the administration canard.

Fortunately, the third wheel of the American system of government, the judiciary up to and including the Supreme Court, refused to be swayed by this legal gerrymandering. In a decision (Boumediene v. Bush) last June the Supreme Court ruled detainees had a constitutional right to seek redress though the federal courts.

In doing so the Court destroyed the legal fiction so carefully crafted by the Bush administration and Congress. Since then, a Federal Court judge in Washington, Judge Richard Leon, ruled last month that five Algerians, held at Guantanamo for nearly seven years, were held unlawfully – confirming *habeas corpus* remained at the centre of all American jurisprudence. Demonstrating how thin is the legal veneer for Guantanamo, Judge Leon had been appointed by President Bush and in 2005 ruled that such persons had no *habeas corpus* rights.

Guantanamo is also a euphemism for torture. This is the more pernicious and perhaps the longer-lasting legacy of the prison. The sadism of Abu Ghraib has disappeared over time, but that associated with Guantanamo has been filtered by a shameful legal process unbecoming of a "City upon a Hill." It has become symbolic of "American Exceptionalism"—a policy that precipitated the frightening decline of American global influence.

It is against this backdrop that President-elect Obama has to come to grips with the legacy of the Bush administration. During the campaign he committed to closing the prison, ending the military-commission system of trials and the trying of detainees in American courts.

There is no reason to suspect that the President-elect has altered his views. Unfortunately the Harper government intention "to follow and respect the process" at Guantanamo, instituted by President Bush and now declared illegal by the American courts, represents a sad and ignoble response.

Every other involved country in the world has sought to have its citizens, and in some cases non-citizens, removed from the vagaries and now-illegal processes of Guantanamo. Even Saudi Arabia has weighed in on behalf of many of its citizens, going as far as establishing a centre for the rehabilitation of citizens who engaged in terrorism.

Revenge, punishment, retribution and ideological blindness are not ideas which Canadians support as foundations for public policy. Canadians have greater expectations from their governments than meanness of spirit and blindness to action. These attributes are all the more in play when they are attached to the far-from-proven actions of a 15-year-old in the wilds and confusion of Afghanistan seven years ago.

A new Canadian foreign minister who has direct and legal responsibility for consular policy and a new environment in the United States provide an opportunity to seek the early release of Mr Khadr. Why it will not do so is one of the abiding mysteries of this government. Perhaps it was an inadvertent and uninformed first step by Mr Cannon; if so there is ample justification for a quick turnaround, as there is no reason to be "eyeless in Gaza" on a matter of this fundamental importance – from which the Americans and the world are moving on.

Embassy

Dangerous Work
December 16, 2008

THE REPUBLIC OF NIGER IS NOT VERY HIGH ON OUR LIST OF FAMILIAR countries. It piqued our interest a few years ago when it was alleged that Saddam Hussein was seeking uranium ore for his nuclear-weapons program there – and formed part of the house of cards constructed to justify the American invasion of Iraq. An "outed" senior official at the CIA and the obstruction and perjury criminal convictions of the chief of staff of the American Vice-President put an end to that story.

With the disappearance of two dedicated and respected Canadian public servants, it is back in the news. Robert Fowler and Louis Guay along with a driver went missing on Sunday when they failed to return to Niamey following a trip up country. Their vehicle was found, but so far there is little information available as to what may have happened.

There was a web posting by a faction of the Niger Movement for Justice (MNJ) stating they were kidnapped for unspecified reasons, although one of its leaders later recanted.

Niger is one of the poorest countries in the world. Landlocked, it is at or near the bottom of all the development indices used by the United Nations. Its 13-million people eke a meagre existence out of the sands of the Sahara, except for an area in the southwest where the Niger River provides some respite before wending its way to the Gulf of Guinea through Nigeria.

In the nearly fifty years of independence from France, its political history has been equally bleak. Military and single-party rule have dominated; however, in recent years there has been steady progress to representative democracy. Last year an elected president resigned when he lost a vote of confidence in the National Assembly.

Ethnically and culturally, Niger resembles several of its neighbours in this region of Africa. Along their northern borders with Algeria and Libya there are the nomadic Berbers and Arabs, generally known as Tuaregs. Farther south are people of sub-Saharan Africa; in Niger these are largely Hausa, a group that is also found in northern Nigeria. Nearly all are Muslim.

Not surprisingly, the cultural divide is greater than the superficial religious unity. The nomadic Tuaregs, less than 10 per cent of the population, have been in some measure of revolt, under the umbrella of the MNJ, against the Hausa-dominated government in Niamey. A low-level insurgency has been evident for several years and, in the best tradition of the United Nations, Secretary General Ban Ki-moon appointed Mr Fowler to go to Niger as his special emissary and report on what the international community could do.

Mr Fowler was an ideal choice. For more than a decade he has been one of a select few of international officials who have laboured to assist and support Africa on many of its myriad problems. Civil war, racial violence, blood diamonds, development have all been areas of concern for him, and in every sense of the word he was the strongest advocate for Africa within the government of Canada. Mr Guay has equally impressive credentials on Africa.

These are not easy days for those who labour in the search for peaceful solutions or provide humanitarian assistance, or who seek to bring news of these events to Canada and the world. Many who resort to violence do not share the view that such persons are working in their interests, and they are prepared to violently impede and intercept.

It is early days in this matter; facts are very few. It is essential to stand back and forgo speculation that might well increase the harm to Mr Fowler and Mr Guay. The United Nations, appropriately, has the lead in establishing the facts of the matter and with an extensive team in Niger is in the best position to conduct the delicate work that will lead to their safe return. The role of Foreign Affairs is to ensure that the safe return of Mr Fowler and Mr Guay is not sacrificed in any way on the altar of other interests.

Recently, Canadians learned the value of quiet diplomacy carried out by professionals who only have the safety of the victim in mind. CBC reporter Mellissa Fung is alive and well due in great measure to the total world-wide news blackout that was voluntarily accepted by all media organizations.

Such a blackout is not possible in this disappearance. Some of the horses are already out of the barn. What is needed is a deep sense of responsibility to eliminate unwarranted speculation and the reporting of unverified information.

Some have suggested that the nature of the work by Mr Fowler and Mr Guay creates a different story line than that surrounding Ms Fung. That is sophistry of the worse kind. In an age when good people willingly put themselves in harm's way for a greater good, these are opportunities for the media to restore the word "responsible" to journalism.

The Citizen

The Duty of Fairness
March 23, 2009

ONE OF THE FEW CONSTANTS OF THE HARPER GOVERNMENT HAS been its dedication to the concept of law and order. The economy may be going south faster than Canadians to Mexico; the wheels on the Quebec electoral bus flattening and the sombre ramp ceremonies are a reminder of an unwinnable war in Afghanistan, but in the midst of such troubles the government returns to what it believes as one of its core verities.

No matter the other difficulties, goes the litany, new law-and-order proposals find broad support within the Canadian body politic. Last week further proposals emerged and even Myron Thompson, our only living Neanderthal, emerged from deep retirement to rattle his chains and remind us of the evils that lurk among the dust balls under our beds.

Today the emphasis is on longer and higher minimum sentences for certain crimes, but other initiatives remain in the hope that, through the accidents of minority government, they can receive the force of law. Imbedded in the Harper-Conservative approach is the desire for retribution and revenge, irrespective of cost or result. In the midst of this, Canadians rank among the highest in the world in terms of personal security. It is increasingly clear that there has been less "law" in some of these efforts than most Canadians expect. As the watchdog of the government's efforts, the Federal Court of Canada has twice, in less than a year, been highly critical.

The latest highly critical decision was on March 4 when Justice Robert L. Barnes released his decision concerning the government's policy shift in the fall of 2006 to withdraw support for the clemency plea of Ronald Smith, a Canadian under sentence of death in Montana. In doing so, the government overturned a policy supported by previous Liberal and Conservative governments, along with the courts, to seek clemency for Canadians sentenced to death in foreign jurisdictions. The earlier policy was based on the reality that all judicial systems create injustices – and none were more final or egregious than those affecting prisoners sentenced to death.

Ronald Smith was no charmer when he and two accomplices murdered two Americans in the wilds of Montana in August 1982. Mr Smith ultimately pleaded guilty and asked that the death penalty be imposed. The Montana courts obliged, but in the intervening years he appealed his sentence and his case is still before the courts. Should the courts maintain the death penalty sentence, it will be an executive decision by the governor of Montana as to whether or not the sentence will be imposed. However, the Montana legislature, reflecting an increasing American-wide rejection of the death penalty, is on the verge of eliminating the death penalty from its laws in favour of life imprisonment.

Throughout these almost three decades Mr Smith has been supported by the government of Canada, not because of any belief he was innocent of the crime but rather as part of the wide-spread belief of Canadians that the death penalty has no legitimacy in the laws of civilized, democratic countries.

No distinction was made in the previous policy in relation to where Canadians faced execution. The United States was treated the same as Vietnam or Saudi Arabia, and in doing so there was an elemental fairness towards all Canadians. This was based on the evidence that there was as much chance for judicial error in the United States as there was in Vietnam.

Justice Barnes in his March 4 decision did not in any way undercut the right of any federal government to change policy. But, as in so many Federal Court decisions, the justice did insist that there be procedural fairness in the process through which policy changes were made. The unfairness of the means – it would be unfair to describe it as a process – in which the government changed its policy was apparent at the time.

In late October 2006 a newspaper story highlighted Mr Smith's situation and the support he was receiving from the government of Canada. Initially, Foreign Affairs responded that the clemency policy of the government had not changed. Within a few days there was a new policy that, in the words of Justice Barnes, was "made very quickly and without any widespread or considered consultation." In the coming days various government ministers sought to give substance to the policy, but it never emerged as anything more than "the back of the envelope" tack it was.

In court, the government argued that its new clemency policy was "fundamentally a matter involving political and morality-based choices lacking a sufficient legal component to allow for judicial review." Justice Barnes disagreed. Mr Smith was owed "a clear duty of fairness" and there was "no evidence of a consensus or of a policy decision being taken by anyone." He went on to describe the policy-change process as "amorphous," "unaccountable" and "inconsistent" – and not one made on "broad grounds of public policy."

This was the second Federal Court decision in less than a year that was highly critical of the government's effort to redraft policies affecting Canadians in trouble in foreign countries. Last August Justice Michael Kelen took then Public Safety Minister Stockwell Day to task for his "wholly unreasonable" decision to deny transfer of a Canadian citizen from an American to a Canadian prison. In his decision Justice Kelen noted that it was normal for judges to give "significant deference" to ministerial decision. It is fortuitous for Canadians in difficulty overseas that deference is not always an element in the decisions of the Federal Court.

The Citizen

Missing the Target
September 29, 2009

IT IS NOT OFTEN CHIEF JUSTICE BEVERLEY MCLACHLIN SPEAKS outside the precedents of the Supreme Court. She did so last week before an Ottawa audience and she had something serious to convey. What she said has needed saying for some years.

Terrorism — and its associate, the war on terrorism — have been used to justify torture and other ignoble acts. It has led the world into two nasty, prolonged wars, the infringement and curtailment of civil, political and human rights, and the labelling of communities in our diverse society with some measure of responsibility for the problems created far from our shores.

Most egregious are the "security certificates," which, on the signatures of the ministers of immigration and public security, provide for the indefinite preventive detention of resident non-Canadians – with none of the attendant procedural safeguards available to Canadian citizens. As such these certificates have created a class of Canadian residents who are far from equal before the law.

A few years ago the Supreme Court tried to do away with some of the excesses of these certificates, but not all. These measures are being justified in the name of an illusory and overstated need for national security, often founded on a desire to dampen paranoia in the United States.

Based on these misdirected and unnecessary activities, Canadians have died overseas in numbers not seen since the war in Korea – and more will die in the next two years before our combat commitment in Afghanistan ends. Residents of Canada have been detained for prolonged periods and been subjected to harsh and intrusive control measures. Canadian governments have collaborated with nasty foreign governments in having Canadians detained, and have used the fruits of such detentions as justification for their action. It was only when forced by the power of the courts that governments have reluctantly taken corrective action.

Not surprisingly, the nation's top jurist has not been a blind bystander to these troublesome aberrations. Chief Justice McLachlin, in her September 23 speech before the Women's Canadian Club of Ottawa, pointed her finger at the simple truth underlying many of the government's actions: "The fear and anger that terrorism produces may cause leaders to make war on targets that may or may not be connected with the terrorist incident."

In an understatement of what has happened, she added, "Or perhaps it may lead governments to curtail civil liberties and seek recourse in tactics they might otherwise deplore ... that may not, in the clearer light of retrospect, be necessary or defensible."

Canadian history is filled with the actions of governments that the "clearer light of retrospect" has judged harshly. Discriminatory aboriginal policies and residential schools, the forced migration of Inuit from the shores of Hudson Bay to the High Arctic, the detention of Ukrainians and other Canadians of east European origins, a racially based immigration system, and the detention of Canadians of Japanese ancestry are but the most easily recognizable. Chief Justice McLachlin is perceptive in adding governmental policies and actions concerning terrorism to this sad litany of the terrible failures of governance.

Coincidentally, a few days before the Chief Justice spoke, a Federal Court judge eliminated some of the stringent conditions that have dominated the life of Mohamed Harkat for the past three years. Harkat was detained under a security certificate when it was alleged that he was a "sleeper" al-Qaeda agent. A few days later a Federal Court in Montreal freed Adil Charkaoui who had been monitored under conditions similar to those of Harkat.

These two judicial decisions followed actions by CSIS and lawyers for the Crown which failed to meet the requirements of the Court for more information in order to justify the legal restrictions. Outrageously, CSIS and Crown lawyers decided to be their own arbiters of these matters and withdrew from the fray. This after Harkat and Charkaoui spent years in prison and years under stringent monitoring. The question needs to be asked: Since when do executive arms of the government decide what judicial decisions they are going to ignore?

A second question is the security one. For the past six years or so, ministers and senior officials have sworn outside and inside courtrooms that Harkat and Charkaoui represented serious national security threats. The recent action by CSIS suggests they still are, but nevertheless CSIS has been prepared to walk away in order to defend its "methodologies and investigative techniques" from public scrutiny.

CSIS cannot have it both ways. If these men are threats to the safety of Canadians then CSIS had an obligation under law to stay the course and seek solutions through the courts.

Or perhaps the Chief Justice was right; CSIS and the government may have made "war on targets that may or may not be connected with the terrorist incident." Her comments were ex cathedra in their freshness on a matter that has become the backdrop to our times. Her message was simple and reflected the conclusions of a forgotten child from years ago — the emperor has no clothes.

The Citizen

The Biggest "But" in Canadian Judicial History
January 29, 2010

THE SUPREME COURT HAS SPOKEN ITS LAST WORDS ON OMAR KHADR. Regrettably it is a political decision and one that has little to do with justice, fundamental or temporal. Surprisingly all nine justices joined in the decision which gave pre-eminence to the government's absolute power over foreign affairs. There is no joy for Khadr whatsoever in this decision and, equally important, there is no joy for any Canadians who encounter serious difficulty in foreign countries.

Khadr's future is now left to the mercies of the federal government which has not demonstrated either mercy or compassion.

Sadly his future is also now in the hands of the vicissitudes of the U.S. government which, since the Obama administration came into office, has talked the good talk for the inmates of Guantanamo; however, it has lost its way on its plans for corrective action. Fundamental justice for the victims of Guantanamo is part of the wreckage of America's ineffective strategies in correcting the horrors of previous American policies on terrorism.

Khadr has been no stranger to the Canadian courts, having now been the subject of four earlier cases in the Federal Court of Canada. In all of the previous cases, the courts have risen above the narrow parochial security and foreign policy issues and have provided Khadr and Canadians with ringing endorsements of the rule of law and the importance of the person in our society.

As many have made clear since the Khadr family broke into Canadian consciousness in the mid-'90s, it is a family that has had a troublesome history and a troublesome impact on what most understand to be matters directly inimical to Canadian interests and to Canadians. It is lamentable, however, that the country's ire has descended onto the shoulders of a person who was a minor when his alleged crimes took place.

The Supreme Court in its decision did give recognition to the principle that was inherent in the earlier Federal Court decisions. It stated that Khadr's "Charter rights were violated" by federal officials. It also said, "We conclude that Canadian conduct in connection with Mr. Khadr's case did not conform to the principles of fundamental justice."

In the biggest "but" in Canadian judicial history, the Court went on to state that "It would not be appropriate for the court to give direction as to the diplomatic steps necessary to address the breaches of Mr. Khadr's Charter rights." Cynically, the Court's decision even reminds us of what Section 7 of the Charter of Rights and Freedom has to say:

7. Everyone has the right to life, liberty and security of the person and the right not to be deprived thereof except in accordance with the principles of fundamental justice.

Only four months ago, the Chief Justice, Beverley McLachlin, speaking outside the Court was much more perceptive and open on the issues surrounding cases such as that of Khadr. Addressing an Ottawa audience, the Chief Justice forthrightly detailed the serious injustices inherent in government actions dealing with terrorism. Then she said: "The fear and anger that terrorism produces may cause leaders to make war on targets that may or may not be connected with the terrorist incident."

Even more fundamental was her observation: "Or perhaps it may lead governments to curtail civil liberties and seek recourse in tactics they might otherwise deplore ... that may not, in the clearer light of retrospect, be necessary or defensible."

It is unfortunate that the Chief Justice and her colleagues did not apply her wisdom of last September to the matter of Omar Khadr. Instead she and her colleagues gave absolute precedence to the "powers under the royal prerogative" available to the federal government in the conduct of foreign affairs. The Court in its decision stated "it is for the executive and not the courts to decide whether and how to exercise its power" and then in words that the most hidebound bureaucrat would accept went on to say that "the government must have flexibility in deciding how its duties under the power (foreign affairs) are to be discharged."

This judicial gerrymandering means that while the Court has agreed that Khadr's Charter rights have been violated by the government, it refuses to provide him with a remedy. In this curious world that the Supreme Court has constructed, a violation of the most central element in our written constitution – the right to life, liberty and security of the person – is trumped by a hoary tradition of the Royal prerogative over foreign affairs.

Curiously, the decision of the Supreme Court complains of the inadequacy of the information available to it with respect to Khadr. However, it then observes that while Khadr "has not been moved from Guantanamo Bay in over seven years, his legal predicament continues to evolve."

This is a sad comment by our supreme jurists.

The only option now available to Khadr is to have a trial under a U.S. Military Commission which can be compared to courts in Iran. Friday was a sad day in the history of the Supreme Court of Canada, and we can only hope that, in the earlier words of the Chief Justice, "the clearer light of retrospect" will correct this injustice.

The Citizen

The Sad Reality of the Iacobucci Report
March 3, 2010

LAST WEEK, FORMER SUPREME COURT JUSTICE FRANK IACOBUCCI completed his report on his "internal" investigation into the torture of three Canadians in Syrian and Egyptian prisons in the early years of the decade. As with the earlier O'Connor report concerning Maher Arar, the Iacobucci report focussed on the actions of Canadian officials prior to and during their detentions. The three Canadians – Abdullah Almalki, Ahmad Abou-Elmaati and Muayyed Nureddin – have all since returned to Canada, but press reports state that the torture in Syrian and Egyptian jails ended any possibility of resuming normal lives.

The February 23 supplement to Iacobucci October 2008 report became necessary when the government refused permission for the Commissioner to publish certain information that it argued was prohibited under Section 38 of the Canada Evidence Act. This is the catch-all section of the Evidence Act that allows the government to censor information on the basis that it would be injurious "to international relations, national defence or national security."

Commissioner Iacobucci, in his main report, wrote that he applied the "national security" rules with a view to "providing the public with as complete as possible an account of the Canadian officials and my findings in respect of those actions." Even with that objective the government took issue with several sections of the report and it took over a year for the government and the Commissioner to reach an agreement. It should be noted that Justice O'Connor encountered the same problem and, when he appealed to the Federal Court, Justice Simon Noël in his decision sought to apply some measure of reason and consistency to the position of the government.

It is important to stress that the O'Connor and Iacobucci reports are intimately interrelated. O'Connor, whose mandate only covered Maher Arar, in his report recommended that the circumstances surrounding government action concerning the other three men be subject to an inquiry.

The reports cover a period when the RCMP and CSIS were directed both in law and by political instructions to investigate terrorism, especially terrorism associated with al Qaeda, and dealt with it either through disruption or prosecution. It was a time also, in the aftermath of the passing of the Anti-Terrorism Act of 2001, when the RCMP was again given responsibility for dealing with acts of terrorism. Up until that time and since the creation of CSIS in 1984, the RCMP assiduously avoided being involved in national-security matters – both by inclination and the territoriality of CSIS. Its experience with the Air India investigation lent support for the view that the Force had little ability when faced with major crimes involving Canada's ethnic communities.

As such the RCMP was less than prepared to re-enter this complicated field and the O'Connor report in particular detailed the lack of experience and competence. Both reports, however, emphasized the legitimacy of the various investigations that led to the interest of both the RCMP and CSIS in the four men. Interest, however, does not permit sloppy investigations, over-wrought characterizations – or investigative actions initiated with foreign-security organizations in the hope that torture or harsh imprisonment will provide justification for the initial interest. Clearly, the passion for the mission overwhelmed any genuine knowledge of the people investigated, as well as fairness or sound judgement on the implications of the investigative tools.

Both reports concluded that the men were tortured while imprisoned in Syria and Egypt. One of the main issues associated with the torture was whether actions by Canadian officials either contributed to or may have led to the torture. On the second part of that question, there is less than compelling evidence. Both Syria and Egypt have long been identified with the use of torture and to enter their prisons, especially those associated with their security services, is to know that torture is a favourite tool of investigation. Unfortunately, many Canadians, like many others throughout the world, accept that or, even worse, are prepared to argue that torture, when associated with identifying potential acts of terrorism, is both necessary and legitimate.

It is, however, the question of whether or not actions by Canadian officials contributed to torture once the three men were imprisoned in Syria and Egypt. This is the main focus of Commissioner Iacobucci's supplement to his main report. From the new information released in that report it is easy to see why the government fought to keep these details secret. It is not so much that the new information is "injurious" to national security. Rather, as with so many of these matters when the government hides behind "national security" concerns, the issue is clearly one of embarrassment – and a complete lack of control and judgement when security officials operate without any regard or understanding for the implications of their actions.

The substance of Commissioner Iacobucci's supplement is only five pages, about 1500 words; but they are five pages that all Canadians should read and remember. The essence of these words is that CSIS, without considering the impact of their actions on the well-being and welfare of Ahmad Abou-Elmaati, wrote to Egyptian security officials, prepared questions to be asked and travelled to Egypt to obtain information. The Commissioner emphasized that this was done without consultation with Foreign Affairs and this "likely contributed indirectly to Mr Elmaati's mistreatment in Egypt."

In the precise language of a former Supreme Court justice, the Commissioner went on to write:

> While the evidence is not conclusive, it is in my view reasonable to infer on all of the evidence available to me ... Mr Elmaati suffered mistreatment of some form as a consequence of the Service's [CSIS] interaction with Egyptian authorities.

The Commissioner goes on:

> I find that the Service's June 2002 interaction with Egyptian authorities ... was deficient in the circumstance ....

> The Service did not consider what effect its actions might have on the Egyptian authorities' position towards Mr Elmaati and the manner in which he might be treated.

And in a chilling comment Commissioner Iacobucci reports that:

> *Several witnesses, from both CSIS and the RCMP, told the Inquiry that it was not the responsibility of intelligence or law enforcement officials to be concerned about the human rights of a Canadian detainee, which were for DFAIT alone to consider. This approach is not in my opinion satisfactory.*

Hopefully, and on this there is little concrete evidence, this mindset, now that it has been exposed, has been corrected. However, the contrary information is strong. The history of the work by the RCMP and CSIS associated with national security provides little encouragement that anything has or will change. While public exposure is of some temporal value, our political leadership demonstrates little inclination to putting the rights of individual Canadians ahead of misidentified and misunderstood security threats. Unfortunately, Commissioner Iacobucci's work and words will soon be forgotten.

Embassy

Torture and Public Policy
April 2, 2010

TORTURE IS NOT A COUNTRY-SPECIFIC PHENOMENON. IT IS FAR TOO comfortable to say that Syria or China or Saudi Arabia or Cuba or Bulgaria can be labelled as states that use torture routinely as part of their national policies. As recent history has demonstrated, the fellow travellers on the torture road are numerous, and found in the best of nations. Today, of course, we are far wiser than we were years ago when torture, like a deranged relative, was relegated to the attic and not discussed in polite company.

The attacks of 9/11 are often used as the seminal date for the resort to torture by the government of the United States on the argument of necessity; they were also used to justify our collective slide into hysteria and madness. Large enemies, and particularly successful ones, have always occasioned the lowering of standards by democratic governments and societies.

Equally in the face of large enemies, there is the assertion of the belief that citizens of democracies must forgo some of their basic rights in order to ensure collective security. There has been no shortage of leaders who, when faced with enemies they little understand, see the diminution of their own citizens' rights and freedoms as the answer. Unfortunately, again as we have seen, that approach finds considerable support among the people affected.

Relating to this, I would argue that torture in all its manifestations in places like Canada is not a policy in and of itself. Rather it is a consequence of other policies and decisions which, when combined, lead to a lowering of our morality, and our political and human-rights standards. It reflects a willingness to use means to achieve a political objective, irrespective of whether or not these means are either appropriate or workable.

But most importantly, torture in any of its manifestations, corrodes the very basic premises of our societies. In our efforts to stamp out torture in our modern world, all too often we concentrate on those who carry out the acts themselves, in the shadows as the former American Vice-President was often quoted as saying. All too often we ignore the political leadership that is behind its use – those who give it political legitimacy.

In the United States, in the aftermath of the September 11, 2001 attacks, the American executive arm of government, with the cooperation of Congress and, for a period, the courts, created, sanctioned, and permitted the use of torture with the elusive objective of obtaining information to prevent future attacks. Equally, it was a demonstration by a government that nothing was sacrosanct in its "war on terrorism."

Most will have seen the photographs from the kindergarten class in Florida on the morning of September 11, 2001 where President Bush was meeting with children. The entry of an aide and the whispering into the ear of the President of information on the attacks provide a historical image that will live on forever. The television camera is unrelenting in reporting the bewilderment on the face of the President and, for many of us who saw those pictures, there was a small gasp of understanding that the American world had dramatically changed. As commentators constantly remind us, when the world of the United States dramatically changes, we are all affected by every twitch and sense of outrage.

We are only now beginning to understand how significant those changes were. Central to them was the willingness of the United States government to remove torture from the shadows and place it at the centre of American policy. The creation of Guantanamo; the construction of its equivalent at Bagram air-force base, north of Kabul; the use of "black prison sites" in Poland, Romania, Lithuania, Bulgaria and other countries still to be identified; the kidnappings on the streets of foreign cities by the CIA; and the off-loading through renditions, extraordinary and otherwise, of interrogations to Jordan, Egypt, Morocco, Syria and Saudi Arabia were all manifestations of the use of torture.

And this by a country that, throughout the last two-hundred years, provided the world with a unwavering beacon of liberty, freedom and the primacy of the rule of law. It was no longer the "City upon the Hill" but rather the purveyor of political darkness that is still with us. It should be stressed that, sadly, there was no shortage of allies for the United States in these nefarious activities.

Canada was not immune to these forces. We were never a place where political and human rights trumped our collective needs. "Peace, order and good government" remains a mainstay of our daily lives, in spite of the Charter of Rights and Freedom and various other initiatives to give the citizen some measure of protection against the overweening powers of the state.

The recent decision by the Supreme Court on Omar Khadr provides sad evidence of how little progress has been made in Canada. Then, the Supreme Court bowed to the archaic and illiberal authority of Crown prerogative for foreign affairs, rather than redress a Section VII Charter violation of Mr Khadr's rights. If ever a Canadian court, and especially the Supreme Court, bowed to the will of the executive, this was it. And surprisingly, there was little, if any, moral or legal outrage. The sins of the father when visited on his son finds modern acceptance within our Supreme Court and the country at large.

Equally outrageous is the continued use of preventative detention by the Canadian government and its sanction by the courts. It is a modern reflection of our willingness to inter Ukrainian Canadians during the First World War and Japanese Canadians during the Second. Today, even more pernicious, if that is possible, the victims of our preventative detention law are non- Canadians with their imprisonment based on the secret testimony of security officials

– whose judgement and knowledge has been found impaired by at least three commissions of inquiry and numerous court decisions.

What is particularly egregious about this security certificate law is that it classified residents of Canada into two categories: one for citizens and another for non-citizens. Yet most Canadians find that distinction completely acceptable. Not so many years ago, similar detentions were made in their thousands in the United States, based on little more than place of birth. Subsequent information found that none were charged or found to be involved in any aspect of terrorism.

I mention these two examples because they are the handmaidens of torture. They create in the minds of many the belief that, in times of crisis, it is appropriate to use discriminatory tools of secret information, to deny rights long understood to belong to all and to create a climate in which harsh interrogations in foreign countries are acceptable. Justice in the best of times is an elusive objective. In times of crisis it, along with truth, is a very early casualty. Unfortunately, many of our citizens find that acceptable, and there is little inclination for change by governments.

The inquiries of Justice Dennis O'Connor and Justice Frank Iacobucci detail the willingness of Canadian police and security organizations to sanction torture in order to obtain information. Also, in the reports from the O'Connor and Iacobucci inquiries, there is ample evidence of the transgressions of both the RCMP and CSIS. But what is not made clear in these reports is the fact that political direction and oversight of the two organizations was completely absent.

Reading the two reports is to assume that both organizations operated in a time and space in which there was no one willing to stand out or up against the hidden powers available to our security and police organizations. There was no one who would say that it was morally wrong or contrary to the laws of Canada. Since 2001 there have been six different ministers in charge of the RCMP and CSIS, and from the reports it is clear that none of them exercised any sense of direction or involvement in the work of these organizations. Equally, prior to 2001 there was a steady stream of inept ministers in charge of this area of government which in many countries is considered one of the most important and significant.

It was this laissez-faire atmosphere that made it impossible to obtain a consensus within government when there was a sense or understanding that torture or the possibility of torture was evident from the treatment of a Canadian in a foreign prison. Both CSIS and the RCMP, with support from the PCO, were not prepared to engage in collective action in support of the detained Canadians. This was amply demonstrated by Justice O'Connor in his report dealing with the attempt to author a "one voice" letter to the Syrian government in support of Maher Arar. Rather, both CSIS and the RCMP tried with malice aforethought to deride this effort by changing their characterization of Mr Arar. Once the letter-writing initiative was underway, they stated that he was the subject of a national-security investigation. As Justice O'Connor succinctly wrote: "He was not."

Even more telling of this atmosphere are the contents of Justice Iacobucci's supplementary report issued three weeks ago. The need for a supplementary report was occasioned when the government refused permission for certain information to be published in his main report which was released in October 2008. The government argued that the information in question was injurious "to international relations, national defence or national security" in accordance with Section 38 of the Canada Evidence Act.

What was this "injurious" information? Interrogation and investigatory techniques? Personal details? Not at all. The information was nothing more than an assertion by members of the RCMP and CSIS that "[i]t was not the responsibility of intelligence or law enforcement officials to be concerned about human rights of a Canadian detainee." There are many problems with the main Iacobucci report, but his ability to fight to get this assertion on the public record mitigates some of those problems. For our security and law-enforcement officials to ignore concerns about the human rights of Canadians in foreign detention should be regarded as one of the most chilling admissions by officials of one of our most important institutions of government.

One aspect of the torture issue that is overlooked is the role of lawyers representing the government. We are all familiar with Shakespeare's ringing phrase "Kill all the lawyers." But as with many such quotations, a very important preamble is dropped. The original phrase, from Henry VI, Part 2, is "If you plan large crimes, first kill all the lawyers." If he wrote today, Shakespeare might be inclined to say that you must "first co-opt the lawyers."

Unfortunately, large crimes and serious policy errors have occurred in recent years and lawyers for governments have been co-opted in the circumvention of the rights of citizens. Some of us who have laboured in government during these years have witnessed the role played by lawyers – and some have been their victims. Unfortunately, in Canada there has not been an examination of the role of lawyers in this capacity, nor are there examples of when lawyers for the government have exercised collective morality when they played a central role in such activities.

Lawyers have a preferred and honourable role in our societies. Their profession is self- regulated and, more than other employees of the state, there are norms of behaviour and activity that support a large measure of independence. However, in the passion to find the terrorists in our midst, independence of thought and action by lawyers acting for the government has been foregone. In 1985 the Supreme Court of Canada had something to say about independence of thought by employees of the government of Canada. It has special relevance for those who are charged with the application of the laws of Canada:

> "*In some circumstances a public servant may actively and publicly express opposition to the policies of a government. This would be appropriate if, for example, the Government were engaged in illegal acts, of it its policies jeopardized the life, health or safety of*

> *public servants or others, of it the public servant's criticism had no impact on his or her ability to perform effectively the duties of a public servant or on the public perception of that ability."*

These are wise words anytime, but particularly so when there are unfounded concerns of the presence of large enemies.

In the United States this issue has received much attention. Jay S Bybee and John C Yoo, both lawyers in the Department of Justice, were the authors of an opinion in 2002 that gave legal authority for the aggressive interrogation of Abu Zubaydah, suspected of being an operative for al Qaeda. In a subsequent report lawyers in the Office of Professional Responsibility concluded that both Bybee and Yoo had demonstrated "professional misconduct." A more recent report by a Department of Justice lawyer rejected that conclusion. Rather, the new report stated that there was only "flawed legal reasoning," but the two lawyers were not guilty of "professional misconduct." The reasoning for this new conclusion - "difficulties in assessing these memos now over seven years after their issuance is that the context is lost."

The legacy of Nuremberg sacrificed on the altars of urgency and necessity. Lest anyone think that is the end of the story, it should be noted that Mr Bybee is today a federal judge and Mr Yoo is a professor of law at the University of California in Berkeley.

In all of this, it is easy to take the easy road of condemnation and outrage when torture is discussed. Saudi Arabia and Syria are easy to condemn. But today the enemies of political and national morality are closer to home and in the words of Pogo, the great philosopher from the last century, "we have met the enemy and he is us."

Prism. From a speech at the Law School, University of Windsor

Iacobucci Appointment: Another Document Delay Tactic
April 4, 2010

FORMER SUPREME COURT JUSTICE FRANK IACOBUCCI IS A BUSY MAN. No sooner had he released an addendum to his inquiry report on the treatment of three Canadians in Syria than he was appointed by the government to evaluate what documents might be divulged to members of parliament relevant to their examination of the transfer of prisoners in Afghanistan.

The government, recognizing when there is a skunk in the room, has been trying to hold its collective nose from the stink associated with its handling of the detainee issue. First there was an effort to circumscribe the investigation by the Military Police Complaints Commission; then, when attempts at shooting the messenger, Richard Colvin, backfired and when a lengthy prorogation of parliament was not sufficient for the stink to evaporate, it turned to a former Supreme Court Justice to look at nine years of documents associated with Canadian involvement in Afghanistan since 2001.

In the meantime, the government has released 8800 pages relating to the detainee issue. However, between the dark holes of the yet-to-be-known, these pages appear only to illustrate the mindless trivia that characterize internal governmental communications.

The performance of the government on the matter to date provides no confidence that the appointment of Mr Iacobucci is anything more than a delaying tactic. The credibility of the government on the matter is so ragged that some of that negative reputation must now be associated with Mr Iacobucci and his willingness to accept the Queen's coin as part of the government's effort to dodge accountability. Delay, which is inevitable with Mr Iacobucci's work, will provide the government with sufficient cover for several months, if not years, and prolong accountability to some future date when the issue may have lost its present currency and public attention.

The appointment of prominent jurists to investigate matters for governments has had a long and honourable tradition in Canada. Canadians have been well served by the process and one does not have to go back very far to find evidence of this. Gomery, O'Connor and Mr Iacobucci himself have performed well on matters that needed the cool headedness of the judicial mind and experience. In doing so they have surmounted the seedy handling of the issues that gave rise to their appointments and, for the most part, they brought some measure of honour to the independent inquiry business.

But such appointments are not for all times and for all seasons. Commonality and misuse are the enemies of quality in such matters. The appointment of Mr Iacobucci to provide advice on the release of information to parliamentarians on the Afghan detainee issue is a misuse of such assignments. This is not simply a matter within the executive or within our judicial system. Rather it represents a fundamental conflict between the elected representatives of Canadians and the executive arm of government.

Over the past several months the Conservative executive arm has demonstrated that it is determined to prevent Canadians from having detailed information on whether or not Canada is in default of fundamental international obligations, as detailed in the Geneva Convention on War and the Convention against Torture. As these Conventions find full reflection in the Canadian Criminal Code, the enforcement of Canadian law is involved as well.

These are not minor conventions and laws. They are the major bulwarks constructed by the international and national community in order to maintain some measure of civility and protection when countries descend into the madness of war and the indecency of torture. In the language of lawyers, the provisions of these

Conventions provide for *jus cogens* or global jurisdiction for the crimes committed and is binding on all states.

For the Canadian government to bob and weave in order to avoid prompt and open investigations of such matters allows the possibility for such crimes to go unpunished – and the identification of Canada as a defaulting state.

Canadians can be proud of the role Canada has played for many decades in developing under law an international system that provides hope in places where the lights have been extinguished. Most Canadians do not want their government subverting for questionable national-security concerns these established and essential principles which for many around the world remain as a beacon of promises to come.

There are few details available as to how Mr Iacobucci will perform his task. It should be remembered that it took him sixteen months to obtain governmental permission for a few- hundred-word addendum to his 2008 report. The words in question had nothing to do with national security, only the observation by Commissioner Iacobucci that members of the RCMP and CSIS did not accept responsibility for what happens to Canadians when they are being tortured in the prisons of Syria and Egypt.

We can only hope that Mr Iacobucci might find the fortitude to declare an aversion for the task he has been asked to perform. The bad work that is being undertaken here should not be made good by the quality of the worker. If there are legitimate legal issues involved, then the appropriate mechanism is for the government to reference the matter to the Supreme Court for its views. It is not a matter that should be hidden from the people of Canada through the work of one individual toiling in the shadows.

The Citizen

Flimflam and Keeping Canadians Safe Act
April 25, 2010

FLIMFLAM HAS LONG BEEN A TOOL FOR THOSE WHO WISH TO DECEIVE or mislead. Governments everywhere use it at will. Here, it is an element in the Harper government's efforts to convince us that there is a serious law-and-order problem – requiring laws to be changed to provide for longer sentences and less judicial discretion in sentencing.

Disturbingly, there have also been calls for the appointment of "law and order" judges. More recently, at a time when there are great fiscal pressures, money has been found for additional prisons. The Parliamentary Budget Officer is about to release a report on the billions that these unnecessary changes will cost.

In many ways this is an agenda that Californians, in much worse circumstances, signed onto twenty-five years ago. Before long, they were spending nearly as much on prisons as they were on education. Today, on the verge of state bankruptcy, tens of thousands of prisoners are being released in order to ease the self-imposed fiscal pain.

There is ample and convincing evidence that this is a policy chasing a chimera, a fantastic and grotesque product of fevered imaginations. There is no "law and order" deficit in Canada. Rather we are the envy of the world, with a continuing decline in both the number of crimes reported to the police and their severity.

However, as with flimflam artists the world over, there is a need to continue feeding the beast and to keep imaginations fevered and bothered.

The latest item in this chase was the announcement a month ago by the Minister of Public Safety to reintroduce amendments to the

International Transfer of Offenders Act. This Act came into being in the second half of the 1970s, following initiatives by Canada and others to obtain agreement for the transfer of convicted persons to their country of citizenship to serve sentences. It was an idea that had great merit, as it provided the opportunity for such persons to serve their sentences close to family and friends and in the familiar culture of home and language.

Equally important, it overcame the problem associated with the return of such persons to Canada once a sentence had been served in a foreign prison. These persons have an absolute right to return to Canada and, in such circumstances, there had been no opportunity for appropriate authorities to make personal assessments on such matters as the likelihood of reoffending, and to put in place programs that would help the peaceful reintegration of such citizens into Canadian society.

The existing International Transfer of Offenders Act provides a sensible, pragmatic response to these issues which are legitimate public-policy concerns. The Act permits Canadians convicted in a foreign country to apply to return to Canada and serve their sentences in Canadian prisons. Here, they can be assessed by correctional officials on such issues as the likelihood of reoffending, their danger to other Canadians and for the provision of programs that would assist in reintegration. Over the years nearly 2000 Canadians have been transferred to Canada under the provisions of the Act and Canadians have been well served by its underlying concerns for their safety and security.

However, the Harper government in 2006 decided that this approach did not meet its illogical philosophy on issues of law and order and began denying many Canadians permission to transfer to a Canadian prison. The rejection discretion available under the Act is limited and the government's early use of it was disallowed by the Federal Court in two instances. As a result there is now an effort to amend the Act in order to provide greater discretion to the minister in rejecting applications for transfer from Canadians imprisoned abroad.

The flimflam of the government's position starts with its legislative title for the amendments. It is called "Keeping Canadians Safe (International Transfer of Offenders Act)." It does no such thing. Canadians will not be safer if these amendments are passed by Parliament. Rather they will be less safe, bearing in mind that anyone rejected for transfer by the minister will return to Canada at the end of their foreign sentence without being subjected to supervision by either prison, parole or police officials. In many cases these officials may know nothing about the crimes committed in the other country – or the dangers such persons represent to Canadians.

In his announcement of the intention to amend the Act, the Minister of Public Safety gave four factors that would govern his decisions on transfers. These include the endangerment of public safety and the safety of children, the likelihood of the continuation of criminal activities, and whether there has been participation in rehabilitation programs. The amendment to the Act also provides the minister with the discretion to use "any other factor" considered relevant.

These are all important factors, but their use prior to transfer creates only an illusion of keeping Canadians safe. All persons transferred under the existing Act enter a Canadian prison. There, assessments can be made by professionals of the threat such persons present to the safety of Canadians before being released through the parole system – a reasonable approach to a law- and-order problem.

Instead, the government would rather take a chance that a Canadian who has been denied transfer and who has spent years in a foreign prison will return to Canada rehabilitated – and will automatically become a productive member of society. Flimflammery.

Embassy

Khadr Saga is Far From Over
October 16, 2010

OMAR KHADR IS THE PROVERBIAL POOR RELATIVE. HE HAS BEEN AN edgy reminder for the past eight years that our Canadian family includes persons who regularly represent our larger obligations to others and to ourselves. While many Canadians have closed their minds to Mr Khadr's tribulations, punishing him for the sins of his father and the outrageous behaviour of other members of his family, he has grown in stature and importance – as he emerged into adulthood in the awful prisons that the evil minds of American officials created.

Mr Khadr has done so in an environment that would have defeated many – a chatteled childhood, torture at the hands of his American captors in Afghanistan, a kangaroo judicial process in Guantanamo Bay that will remain for years to come a blot on the landscape of the rule of law and human rights, and the denial of any measure of assistance from his own government which, before the intervention of the Federal Court of Canada, showed a willingness to cooperate with his American jailors.

Even more egregious was the smarmy unwillingness of the Supreme Court to order the Canadian government to seek his release.

Today there is emerging evidence that his ordeal at the hands of the American government may come to an end. However, there should be no expectation that his mistreatment by his own government will be over. Sadly, the process that is now underway is not "a get out of jail free card" for Mr Khadr, nor, as some have claimed, a trial.

The flurry of media reports over the past few days, none of which are particularly authoritative or attributed, suggests that the American government through its Military Commission in Guantanamo Bay may be prepared to agree to a plea bargain with Mr Khadr that would bring his trial to an end. There was a similar effort last summer, but the American offer did not significantly reduce what his sentence might have been if the trial continued to its normal conclusion.

News reports today suggest that the new American offer would be an improvement on what was on offer previously. Central to the American offer is that Mr Khadr would have to voluntarily plead guilty to one or more of the charges that have been at the centre of the case presented by American prosecutors at the Military Commission. These include murder, attempted murder, conspiracy and material support for terrorism.

Also mentioned in various press reports is the fact that the guilty plea would result in a prison sentence of approximately ten years. However, it is not clear whether or not the prison sentence would be additional to the eight years Mr Khadr has already spent in American custody.

There have been reports as well that the Americans would agree to Mr Khadr's transfer to a Canadian prison to serve part of his prison sentence. For such a transfer to take place Mr Khadr would have to request the transfer; the Americans would then formally present the request to the government of Canada and then the Canadian government would have to give its consent. As part of the consideration of the transfer request by the government of Canada, it would have to be assured that all legal processes involving Mr Khadr in the United States were at an end. This could be part of the plea bargain agreed to by Mr Khadr – that he would not undertake legal action against the United States.

Equally important, the Canadian government would have to convert Mr Khadr's American sentence to an equivalent Canadian sentence based on the crimes for which he had pleaded guilty. The main question here would be whether the government would assess Mr Khadr's sentence under the Youth Offenders Act or the Criminal Code. Needless to say, an assessment under the Youth Offenders Act would result in a Canadian sentence much less than under the Criminal Code.

There should be no assumption that the government of Canada would agree to Mr Khadr's transfer. Since 2006 this government has rejected a considerable number of transfer requests from Canadians convicted in other countries. Such rejections overturned a long-standing Canadian practise of approving such transfers. The previous practise was based on the understanding that in order to protect Canadians it was wiser to have our own officials assess convicted persons before they were let loose among us. Not to transfer such persons would mean that, at the end of their foreign imprisonment, they could return to Canada without any impediments to their freedom, and more likely than not without any effort for rehabilitation.

Before all of these intricate and complex issues come into play, Mr Khadr is facing a very tough decision on October 25 when his trial reconvenes in Guantanamo. Does he accept the advice of his lawyers and agree to plead guilty which could mean a sentence of possibly another decade in prison in addition to the eight he has already served? The alternative is to take his chances before the Military Commission, knowing that it is a completely unfair and unjust process and the likelihood of winning being close to zero.

In the coming days we will have a chance to see the quality of Mr Khadr's fortitude and strength. No matter what he decides, Canadians are assured that Mr Khadr will be part of our daily lives for some considerable time to come.

The Citizen

Ghosts of the Past Still Scare Today
February 28, 2011

TOMMY DOUGLAS WAS LARGER THAN LIFE WHEN HE WAS STILL WITH us. So it should be no surprise that, from the beyond, he continues to provide rocks for tossing at the straw houses of national security. His latest is the effort to have the courts force the government to release surveillance reports which the then Security Service of the RCMP laboriously collected on him during the days of his public life, from 1939 to the mid 1980s. No doubt it would bring a lopsided smile to his face to know that he outlived the Security Service.

It is depressing to read the Security Service reports that have been released so far. These reports, even with extensive redactions, illustrate the narrow single-mindedness of the Mounties of the day, as they went about their work tracking Mr Douglas' eclectic activities. Reflecting the paranoia of the times, Mr Douglas' activities were deemed to be communist and a danger to Canada.

In a submission to the Federal Court, Paul Champ, the lawyer representing Jim Bronskill, the Canadian Press reporter seeking the release of the Douglas records, wrote: "For over 40 years, Mounties surreptitiously scrutinized his speeches and articles, attended his political conventions, monitored his associations, infiltrated private meetings at which he spoke, and eavesdropped on his private conversations."

There is only one apparent indication that someone questioned these activities. On the margins of one report, which indicated that Mr Douglas was critical of the Liberal Party of Canada, a RCMP analyst without apparent irony asked "What has this got to do with subversive activity?" Such questions were rare and even Mr Douglas singing "We Shall Overcome" rated inclusion in the file. Even when he retired in 1978 at the age of 74 the Security Service was not convinced of his bona fides, with one analyst noting that the file should be kept active since "There is much we do not know about DOUGLAS."

What were the activities that so concerned the Security Service that more than eleven-hundred pages of documents were collected? At least it might be legitimately expected that there was some evidence of spying, plans for bombings, acting on behalf of a foreign power or even the advocacy of violence. Nothing of the sort emerges from these reports.

Rather, Mr Douglas advocated nuclear disarmament (which later was promoted by Ronald Reagan), opposed the wars in Korea and Vietnam, supported the civil-rights movement in the United States, opposed apartheid in South Africa, supported political prisoners in Portugal and Spain and Jews imprisoned in the Soviet Union. All very stirring stuff, unique only in that Mr Douglas was years ahead of many of his fellow citizens in advancing views that today would create no controversy whatsoever.

These documents, however, demonstrate a larger and scarier truth. The doofusness of the forces of Canadian security forty years ago was not unique to that time and place. Today the re-involvement of the RCMP in national-security matters, as a result of the 2001 Anti Terrorism Act, and the successor to the Security Service, CSIS, display the same shallowness of thought and complete lack of supervision. The targets are different, reflecting the mindlessness of the illogical "war on terrorism" and the assumption that thousands of Canadians because of religion or national backgrounds have moved over to the dark side. In doing so, both the RCMP and CSIS skulk around meetings and monitor conversations and emails in order to identify Canadians – who can expect knocks on their doors from RCMP officers and CSIS agents. There is little to distinguish today's skulkers from those who hid in the shadows around Tommy Douglas.

It has taken the perspective of jurists urged on by a small band of lawyers to force the cold, dead hands of government from most historical records. In doing so, with those of Tommy Douglas, we are provided with a rare understanding of the inanities of our security services in their inability to understand their own societies. Today the "cold, dead hands" of government's control of all documents and the excessive use of national-security confidentiality ensure that Canadians have little to no accounting of this essential area of our democracy. It is perhaps understandable the government does so but for us to understand the present, we need to know the past.

A retired RCMP inspector from the period Tommy Douglas walked the land was quoted as saying "We were looking at people who we thought were trying to overthrow the government – through working with the Communists, or the anarchists, the Trotskyists, the whole crew." The retired inspector went on to comment that this work was "pretty broad brush" but that today we had to bear in mind "the instructions we had from the government were limited."

Now, thanks to the ubiquitous cell-phone camera, Canadians can often see for themselves the public transgressions of our minders. But the private transgressions are deeply hidden and governments are loath to admit that there are any. When there are allegations, the full power of the national-security state is brought to bear, and the public, in complete ignorance, moves on – trusting the benignity of our minders.

Two commissions of inquiry peeled back the curtain somewhat from today's "benignity." There is not much revealed, but we learned of the willingness of the RCMP and CSIS to manufacture evidence, over-characterize innocent behaviour and take extra-legal action. A year-long fight in the courts by one Commissioner resulted in the release of a few lines from one fiercely protected document. Again, the document contained no national secrets; instead it reported that officials from the RCMP and CSIS believed they had no responsibility for Canadians in difficulty in foreign countries.

It is again time to remember the wise words of Chief Justice Beverley McLachin who in 2009 spoke: "The fear and anger that terrorism produces may cause leaders to make war on targets that may or may not be connected with a terrorist incident. . . . Or perhaps it may lead governments to curtail liberties and seek recourse in tactics they might otherwise deplore . . . that may not, in the clear light of retrospect, be necessary or defensible." Tommy Douglas would approve.

Prism

The Politics of Geographic Perimeters
April 20, 2011

NEXT YEAR THERE ARE PLANS TO COMMEMORATE THE BICENTENNIAL of the War of 1812. There will be re-enactments of famous battles and most likely the Laura Secords of today will provide the sweetness needed to lessen the angst that some Americans may still feel with the chasing of Dolly Madison from her home and the burning of the White House behind her. Andrew Jackson notwithstanding, it was a successful campaign for the Empire. The War cemented the southern borders of present-day Quebec and Ontario and provided the starting point for the political creation of Canada some fifty-odd years later.

In the intervening years Canada's relationship with the United States has been a constant and overwhelming factor in our daily lives. National elections have been won and lost on issues associated with this relationship, and it is a rare Canadian leader who has not had to deal with some issue where Washington was the addressee. Trade and economic issues have dominated, and a succession of treaties and understandings stretching from 1855 down to the present have sought to give form and legality to the movement of goods, services and investments. Parallel with these trade and economic agreements have been hundreds of other treaties and understandings, both national and sub-national, dealing with issues of foreign policy, defence, security, migration, and crime. In addition to the millions of professional and personal relationships across the border, they reflect one of the world's most complex bilateral relationships.

One of the few surprises in this election is how little foreign policy, and especially Canada's relations with the United States, is an issue of debate and difference. This is all the more surprising since, only a few weeks before the election was called, Prime Minister Harper and President Obama signed one of the most far-reaching documents affecting the relationship since the War of 1812.

The joint declaration signed on February 4th in Washington was titled *Beyond the Border: A Shared Vision for Perimeter Security and Economic Competitiveness.* In the words of the declaration, both countries intend to "pursue a perimeter approach to security, working together within, at, and away from borders of our two countries to enhance our security and accelerate the legitimate flow of people, goods, and services between our two countries."

The declaration has received little public or political attention in the few weeks since it was signed. It may, as its self-description states, be a "vision" and is so far into the future that there is no need for concern now – hence the "glazing of eyes" on the part of Canadians. That is a serious mistake.

There are two constants in Canada's management of its relationship with the United States. The first is that Canadian leaders have avoided large, across-the-spectrum agreements with the United States where the "gives and takes" would be balanced beyond specific Canadian objectives.

The second constant is that the smaller the scope of an agreement the more likely it will attract the necessary political support in the United States required for it to succeed in the constantly boiling pot of conflicting American interests. The larger or more complex the agreement the more likely different interests in the United States will be engaged, and in doing so cancel each other. This constant also applies to Canadians. The scope of the Free Trade Agreements of 1988 and 1994 engaged the interests of millions of Canadians and as such created large-scale ferment, debate and opposition.

Contrary to these constants, the February joint declaration establishes an enormous, complex agenda for bilateral cooperation, coordination and concertation. There is particular emphasis on the "next generation" of integrated cross-border law-enforcement operations, the pursuit of joint national-security and transnational crime investigations, and improvements in the sharing of information in the area of critical infrastructure and cyber security. There are other "visions" in the declaration as well, including the verification of the "identities of travellers," their screening "at the earliest possible opportunity," and the establishment of an "integrated Canada-United States entry-exit system."

These may be legitimate objectives. The declaration also includes words concerning respect for "our separate constitutional and legal frameworks that protect privacy, civil liberties, and human rights." It also speaks of "the sovereign right of each country to act independently in its own interest and in accordance with its laws."

Nevertheless, the joint document is an enormous deception. Since 9/11 the common border has become less common, with the United States employing control procedures that have slowed the flow of goods and services in order to pretend that it is enhancing its national security. The frequent iteration by senior American officials that Canada represents a threat to their security and well-being has become a significant element in the speed at which 77 per cent of Canadian exports cross the border.

The Canadian urge for far-reaching agreements on crime and security along with common pre-travel screening of individuals entering Canada, the United States or crossing the border is a disguised effort to allay American security fears. The Americans will change nothing in respect to their current policies, procedures and laws. Canada, however, will have to change much that is part of the face that we show the rest of the world. In exchange, the Canadian promoters of this "vision" expect that American barriers to entry of Canadian goods and services can be lessened. In doing so there is a danger, if not a certainty, that Canadians will become the *castrati* to the American tenors.

Rideau Institute

Peace, Order and Windy Government
August 29, 2011

CHUTZPAH IS ONE OF THOSE WONDERFUL HEBREW WORDS THAT have wandered into the English lexicon and found constant expression both in literature and popular idiom. It is a synonym for audacity but, in the way of all wandering words, has come to be used almost-exclusively negatively when gall, arrogance, insolence and impertinence need to be described in understandable terms.

Chutzpah came readily to mind in past weeks as the public announcements of Public Safety Minister Vic Toews took on an air of unreality and unbelievability.

Mr Toews is responsible for the activities of one of the most important, sensitive and coherent ministries of government. Within his control is the RCMP, CSIS, the Border Security Agency, Corrections Canada, the Parole Board and numerous other functions, all relating to the security and well-being of Canadians.

No other minister of the Crown has such onerous and important responsibilities. His dour countenance, where a smile is as rare as a politician in Ottawa in August, is an appropriate one as he takes initiatives to free the streets of Canada of war criminals, dodging deportees and smoke smugglers.

Many would assume that with the many levers of law enforcement at his control there would be some evidence of a plan to deal with these long-evident problems of public policy. Unfortunately there is no such evidence.

For nearly fifty years successive Canadian governments have spoken loudly of dealing with the small number of alleged war criminals that have entered the country. Unfortunately these same governments have not accompanied their words with a big stick or even a little one. Over those fifty years there were two successful prosecutions of Rwandans for war crimes, and three persons – originally Hungarian, Dutch and Lithuanian – were stripped of their citizenship for activities during the Second World War (the Lithuanian was only eight years old when the war ended). These three left the country.

A commission of inquiry on war crimes in 1987 suggested that there might be over 1000 war criminals in Canada and urged prompt legal action given the aging of this population. Since then there have been numerous conflicts around the world where there have been serious allegations of genocide, war crimes and crimes against humanity. This strongly suggests the number of potential war criminals has increased significantly and there is evidence that some have entered Canada.

Mr Toews announced in July that the government is looking for thirty of these potential war criminals and posted their photographs electronically. The hope was to enlist the public in the work of his responsibilities, so that the alleged criminals might be located and deported.

All of the thirty have citizenship in countries where the possibility of investigation and prosecution is as close to zero as you can get without using negative numbers. This in spite of the constantly repeated fact that their alleged crimes are crimes in the Canadian Criminal Code and Canada has willingly assumed responsibility for their prosecution under international law.

There are few ideas in the Canadian political system that, no matter how irrelevant to an issue, cannot be used again. So later in July, Mr Toews was again before the cameras promoting another initiative.

This time he announced the posting of the personal details of another thirty individuals on the country's computers; individuals who had been ordered deported. Again he appealed for the help of Canadians to do the work of his department. Clearly, he had hopes that the success of his earlier initiative when seven individuals had been located could be repeated.

Here the numbers are truly astounding and Mr Toews' actions had all the relevance of sticking his finger into the air of Ottawa and convincing us he could forecast rain in Jakarta. In 2008 the Auditor General wrote that there were over 40,000 persons who had been ordered deported, but could not be located. Since then, thousands more have been added and, on the other side of the ledger, a relative few have been located and deported. There can be every expectation that today there are more people subject to deportation than there were in 2008.

Being the Minister of Public Safety, it could be expected that Mr Toews would not be prone to recommending actions to Canadians that would undermine their safety. But chutzpah knows few limits.

A week or so ago the Minister was visiting Canadians in the region where Ontario, Quebec and New York State have a common border. It is an area that has long been troubled by ineffective policing in the face of brazen tobacco and drug smugglers. Canadians in the area suggested to the Minister that their safety was on a par with living in northwest Pakistan. The Minister in response suggested that they might wish to take advantage of prospective changes in Canadian law on self-defence; the *Ottawa Citizen* on August 20 quoted him as saying "I'm not advocating that people use [guns] but if there's a legitimate..."

Now that takes chutzpah to a level Canadians have not seen for some time – the Minister responsible for their safety telling them to take up a gun. Even Rick Perry, a candidate for the Republican nomination, did not outdo Mr Toews when he suggested that, should the Chairman of the Federal Reserve dare to increase the American money supply and then visit Texas, he would be treated appropriately. Texas has the highest execution rate in the United States.

Even the ancients who put together the Hebrew language would shake their heads over the extreme to which their friendly word chutzpah has been taken.

Prism

Criminal Justice Without Reason
November 9, 2011

CENTRAL TO THE SUCCESS OF ALL DEMOCRATIC SOCIETIES ARE THE laws which regulate the daily interactions of citizens and the associated mechanisms through which transgressors are judged and punished. Throughout history, the laws societies give themselves have evolved on the basis of reason; in the process, they have shed those elements of law that found foundation in faith, myth and emphasis on retribution and revenge for transgressors.

Aristotle, as he did on so many other aspects of democratic societies, wrote some 2300 years ago that "law is reason free from passion." While his words have been ignored and debated ever since, his pithy aphorism has emerged as the solid rock on which democratic societies have been able to accept justice for all as their most sacred principle. The hesitations and advances over the years are illustrated by the apocryphal Moses story, when he answered his grumbling wanderers that he was able to get God to reduce his commandments to ten – but adultery was still in.

Aristotle's aphorism has seen both increased adherence and digressions in the past century in Western societies. There has been both an emphasis on laws designed to spread the equality of justice while at the same time there are shrill cries to increase the safety of citizens. "Wars" on crime and drugs and being "tough on crime" are common rallying cries from political populists, most of whom see little comfort and real dangers in moving away from the exhortations of the Hebrew bible of an "eye for an eye" for those who transgressed.

Sadly, in spite of overwhelming evidence to the contrary, they see simplistic solutions for one of the constants in human evolution – the willingness of some to go outside societal boundaries.

It is a reasonable judgment that, for the past 50 or so years, Canada has followed Aristotelian direction as it has gone about shedding its laws and regulations of historical baggage associated with faith, myth and Old Testament urgings based on small, less-complex societies. The ending of the death penalty and harsh, cruel imprisonment conditions were signposts along the road of the emergence of Canadian law based on reason, where the modern ideas of equality, restorative justice and rehabilitation became central.

No one would argue that the present system is perfect and not in need of ongoing examination and change. The flux of our society as thousands from vastly different environments come to our shores each year, the restless needs of our aboriginal peoples for long-incoming social, economic and political justice, and the inability of our local and national police forces to understand and meet these associated oncoming challenges requires skilled and intelligent responses from our political system.

What these large changes do not need are responses based on unreason and unbridled passion, based on a dimly perceived past in which injustice and inhumanity dominated.

Since 2006, the present government has promoted the view that there are serious problems with our criminal-justice system and in recent weeks has assembled a number of new laws that are under debate in Parliament. Central to these new laws is the view that the discretion of the judiciary is not to be trusted, and rehabilitation and restorative measures inherent in our prison system are inconsistent with our need to protect ourselves from the predations of criminals.

As many have detailed elsewhere, these measures fundamentally alter the careful calibration of criminal laws over the past half-century, and when fully implemented will fundamentally alter our system of justice and add billions of dollars to its cost.

Yet surprisingly, Canadians have exhibited a blissful ignorance on these issues and odds are that these measures will pass Parliament in the coming weeks. Two provinces, Ontario and Quebec, have raised objections to the measures, but only Quebec has attacked them on the basis that they represent a fundamental reordering of our judicial principles.

It is ironic that the United States, which has experimented with these sorts of changes over the past several decades, is slowly coming to the realization of their costs and lack of effectiveness in dealing with crime and its enforcement. A recent book by a former professor of law at Harvard University, William J. Stuntz, titled, *The Collapse of American Criminal Justice*, deals with these same issues.

The book's title summarizes his views on the effectiveness of populist measures associated with "tough on crime" policies, even during a period of then-rising crime rates in the United States. The country, for both the lack of effectiveness and cost, is abandoning such measures and is seeking answers with measures that were at the core of Canadian policy in years past.

In Canada, of course, there is ample evidence of the wisdom of our earlier approach, with crime rates falling to the lowest level in our history, demonstrating that there are no problems to be fixed in this area – or justification for a "tough on crime" agenda. Even the justice minister in recent days has had difficulty in justifying the wisdom of these laws. He was reduced to the banality of saying that "Canadians gave us a mandate to go after criminals in this country and that is exactly what we are going to do." Reason has exited the criminal-justice system.

Embassy

No job for the Mounties
November 17, 2011

ROBERT FOWLER, IN A MOST CREDIBLE AND READABLE ACCOUNT OF his 130-day kidnapping, *A Season in Hell*, writes that his survival was "a near run thing." That judgment brings home to all of us the near-death experiences these kidnappings are. In writing he provides an enormous public service to those of us who observe such events from a distance and grope for solutions that we hope do less harm than good.

For Fowler and Louis Guay, the hourly uncertainties accompanied by the knowledge of what has happened to others in similar circumstance provided roiling emotions that were not comforted by the austere Saharan landscape where there are more shadows than light.

Such kidnappings are surrounded by shibboleths that have taken on the aura of received texts by governments. The most prominent, of course, is that these crimes are the scourge of all and that governments will not pay ransoms. This defensive stratagem became a consensus with G7 governments in the mid-'70s and remains the most frequently stated untruth when such events occur.

It is repeated by media outlets without serious questioning or wondering as to what are the alternatives. As well, the media are a contributor to the dangers involved for the victims when they succumb to the urge to replace fact with speculation, and offer speculation as the basis for government action. The one exception to this in recent years has been a willingness by some media to minimize reporting on such crimes when their own employees are the victims. Both the CBC and *New York Times* have done so, but there are few signs that other victims are covered by such a laudatory and, so far, self-serving approach.

Fowler's book does much more than provide an account of his and Guay's personal experiences. It is also a searing indictment of how the Canadian government handles kidnappings and the need for change before we awake some morning and find someone has been killed in similar circumstances.

It is not as if such events are uncommon. Before I retired from the Foreign Service in 2003, I was involved in more than 100 kidnappings of Canadians in all parts of the world. With one exception (in South Africa, where the victim was killed shortly after being captured), all were resolved with the release of the victims and their early return to Canada. Since then there have been numerous others, again with fortunate outcomes for the victims.

However, as Fowler has stated, these are indeed "near run" things and there are serious problems with Canadian government policy. He is right to detail his concerns and in doing so prompt changes in how the victims and their families are treated by their own government.

The central issue is, of course, the willingness of governments to pay ransoms. Needless to say, that policy has seen as many exceptions as there are black flies in northern Canada in June.

All countries involved in such negotiations have paid ransoms, despite public affirmations of fidelity to the "no-ransom policy." Even the United States and Israel, two of the foremost proponents of the policy, have within the last month paid ransoms to obtain the return of citizens. Since 1970, Israel has released nearly 2,700 prisoners in exchange for the return of seven of its citizens and five bodies. The Americans paid the granddaddy of all ransom payments; this when they provided weapons to Iran for the release of their diplomats in Tehran in the 1980s. The Israelis handled the transaction and the money earned paid for a civil war in Nicaragua.

Other countries, including Canada, have done the same and the only debate is how it is done and the willingness of those involved to distort the facts. The prime minister may be technically correct in stating that no government ransom was paid for the release of Fowler and Guay. However, Fowler's telling comment that he was not released because of his "blue eyes" points accurately at the underlying reality, and to ransom arrangement being made by intermediaries.

Fowler also paints a dismaying picture of the role played by the RCMP during the kidnapping. Starting in the late 1990s the RCMP began to promote a role for its officers in these international kidnappings. The arguments were that these were crimes and its mandate required involvement. These arguments ignored the reality that the Force had no mandate to enforce Canadian law outside the borders of Canada. Equally, it was apparent to all of us involved that the Force had neither the knowledge nor the experience to support its involvement. The comments in Fowler's book fully support that earlier conclusion.

Fowler's comments on the actions of the Force throughout the kidnapping add to the large pile of evidence that this is an organization that no longer serves the best interests of Canadians.

It is time the Canadian government accepted the conclusion that the RCMP today is too large to succeed. The size of the Force, with nearly 30,000 employees and growing, the diversity of its responsibilities, the lack of internal leadership, and no political or independent oversight all contribute to the conclusion that it is a stumbling giant living on its own historical myths. No other country has required a single police force to do so much for so many over such a large territory.

The government has announced the name of the latest victim who will take on the title of commissioner, Bob Paulson, who was coincidentally quoted in Fowler's book as the senior RCMP officer who angrily told Fowler's wife that "not one red cent is going to be paid to release a couple of high muckety mucks." Paulson admits it was him, but said that he had been "professional, cordial and respectful" in the meeting.

Paulson will do no better than the last commissioner, a hapless civilian who was used to the non-lethal wars of the Privy Council Office and was grievously wounded by the bureaucratic "sensitivities" of senior RCMP officers. The government should make clear that this will be the last appointment of a new commissioner until there is a restructuring of the Force.

Contract policing for the provinces and territories should be the first line of the restructuring.

The Citizen

Lacking in Justice
April 29, 2013

IT IS A STORY THAT CHARLES DICKENS COULD EASILY HAVE INCLUDED in *Bleak House,* his magnificent story of children and justice. To begin, it was in the first half of the 1970s when a number of early-teen boys were sexually abused in a small town in Cape Breton. Twenty or so years after the events, several of the abused children, now adults, came forward and provided the RCMP with sworn testimony of what happened – and the man who was responsible.

The first of the victims provided his account to the RCMP in British Columbia in January 1995 and they in turn forwarded the matter to the RCMP in Port Hawkesbury, Nova Scotia. Following an investigation, the RCMP charged Mr Ernest Fenwick MacIntosh on December 4, 1995 with a variety of sexual-abuse crimes, involving children; two months later, on February 21, 1996, they issued a Canada-wide warrant for his arrest.

It became known shortly thereafter that Mr MacIntosh was no longer in Canada and was living and working in New Delhi, India. As a result one of the complainants (their names are still protected by court order) called Foreign Affairs in Ottawa enquiring what could be done to have Mr MacIntosh returned to Canada to face trial. The information provided was verified, including confirmation from the RCMP of the Canada-wide warrant. The Passport Office was informed in a letter dated August 10, 1997, with the request to have Mr MacIntosh's passport revoked in accordance with appropriate provisions of the Canada Passport Order.

The Passport Office concluded that there was an appropriate basis under its Regulations to revoke the passport. A letter to that effect dated September 22, 1997 was delivered to Mr MacIntosh in New Delhi. Mr MacIntosh decided to appeal the revocation order by the Passport Office and on January 20, 1998 the matter was heard by Justice P. Rouleau of the Federal Court of Canada (Trial Division).

Justice Rouleau in his decision dated January 21, 1998 stated that there was "a serious issue to be tried," but found the Crown did not provide the Court with enough evidence to support the revocation, saying that the "only material submitted by counsel for the Minister was her interpretation of the facts, unsupported by any affidavit or documents." He went on to order the suspension of the revocation (stay) of Mr MacIntosh's passport until May 26, 1998.

The Court file does not indicate any further action until April 20, 1998 when lawyers for Mr MacIntosh and the Crown filed a Notice of Discontinuance and Consent, ending the judicial action. The revocation order by the Passport Office was effectively cancelled and Mr MacIntosh kept his passport. Surprisingly, the Federal Court public records do not contain the January 21, 1998 decision by Judge Rouleau, nor the April 20, 1998 Notice of Discontinuance and Consent.

In the meantime, on June 17, 1997 the Chief Crown Attorney for Cape Breton recommended that the extradition of Mr MacIntosh from India be pursued, but it was almost six months later that it was approved by the Deputy Director of Public Prosecutions for Nova Scotia and it was eight months later, on August 14, 1998, that a formal request was made to the International Assistance Group of the Department of Justice in Ottawa.

Governments can be slow and judicial systems even slower, but it was not until July 2006 – almost eight years from the decision to seek extradition – that the extradition request was forwarded to the government of India. Justice Beveridge of the Nova Scotia Court of Appeal laconically wrote in August 2011: "No explanation was ever offered, then or now, for why it took so long to proceed with the extradition request, or for the three years between when it was admittedly ready for submission and action."

The government of India and especially its judicial system has a reputation of using the fullness of time to its extreme boundaries. However, in this case, it acted with unusual speed. Mr MacIntosh was arrested on April 5, 2007 and a little over a year later he appeared in Provincial Court in Port Hawkesbury, Nova Scotia on June 8, 2007.

Mr MacIntosh initially appealed the validity of the charges filed in the Nova Scotia Supreme Court of 36 counts – 18 of indecent assault and 18 of gross indecency – involving six complainants. His appeal was dismissed on March 19, 2010 and two sequential trials (the original charges were severed into two) were held. The first was on July 5-9, 2010 and resulted in Mr MacIntosh being convicted and sentenced to four years imprisonment.

The conviction was appealed to the Nova Scotia Court of Appeal and, in a decision dated August 11, 2011, Justice Beveridge, writing for the majority, declared that the "delay was unreasonable" and the right of Mr MacIntosh to be tried "within a reasonable period of time was infringed." He went on to "quash the convictions and enter a stay on all of the charges."

The Attorney General for Nova Scotia supported by the Attorney General of Canada appealed this decision to the Supreme Court. In a ruling issued on April 22 it decided that the "right of the accused to be tried within a reasonable time was violated" and dismissed the appeal, ending a case that for the victims went back more than thirty-seven years and for the justice system eighteen years.

The Supreme Court has yet to release the written reasons for its decision, but no doubt they will mirror the reasoning of the Nova Scotia Court of Appeal. The victims and their supporters who attended the April 22 Supreme Court hearing came away less than impressed with the manner in which the seven Justices conducted the hearing, and their decorum. The hearing was short, approximately ninety minutes, largely consumed by the presentations of the two governments and close questioning by the Justices. The judges adjourned for fifteen minutes and then returned with their dismissal decision.

In the words of one victim the Justices were "laughing" during the proceedings and overall were "disrespectful" of the victims. "They turned things into a joke." He went on to say that "being molested by MacIntosh was no laughing matter for myself or his other victims. Our Legal 'Unjust' System failed ALL children and ALL Canadians."

Legally, the matter is dead, but the Supreme Court Justices should review their own behaviour on April 22; after all, decorum on both sides of the bench is an essential element of all judicial procedures. If the judges want to make a statement against the government's fixation on victims, then there are better ways of doing so.

Equally the conduct of the Crowns, both in Nova Scotia and Ottawa, should be independently examined. The great failure of this matter was the lack of reasonable timely action in these jurisdictions. The second failure is any explanation of why the Crown in Ottawa failed to present the Federal Court with the available information to revoke Mr MacIntosh's passport in 1998. Nova Scotia has indicated that it will be examining the action of its officials. Ottawa can do no less.

Canada's Preventative Detention Scheme Akin to Internment Camps
June 18, 2014

THE DUST IS NOW SETTLING AROUND THE MANUFACTURED CRISIS BY Prime Minister Harper on the appointment of Justice Marc Nadon of the Federal Court of Appeal to the Supreme Court.

Lost in this latest governmental slippage on its own banana peel is any effort to look at the substance of recent Supreme Court decisions. Instead, the tendency has been to keep a scorecard of the wins and losses by the government, as if this was a sporting event rather than large commentaries on the future of our country.

Many of the recent decisions by the Court have dealt with cases involving the government's law-and-order agenda, which fundamentally puts more Canadians in prison and for longer periods. For the most part the Court has chipped away at peripheral aspects of the new laws, but has refused to deal with the fundamental social and legal arguments that the government has used to buttress its attempts to undermine Canada's long-standing policies regarding the incarceration of its citizens.

Proportionality, judicial discretion and rehabilitation as central elements in sentencing have been thrown overboard and replaced by a primeval urge for punishment and societal and personal revenge. This, in a country with one of the least and declining criminality records in the world.

The recent Supreme Court decisions will do little to push the government off its illusionary railroad, leading to new prisons and overcrowded ones – taking us back to the last century.

The recently announced response of the government to the earlier Supreme Court decision on the unconstitutionality of existing prostitution laws illustrates the matter. The government's response is to avoid dealing with the social and economic roots of prostitution, especially in respect to aboriginal communities, and instead plan to create new criminal categories that will add further to the need for additional prisons.

We do not need to look any farther than the United States to see the futility and stupidity of the government's approach on law and order. The United States has had a 40-year experiment in locking up large numbers of its citizens (one in four members of the Black male community has a criminal record); its prison population is now 2.2 million, the world's largest.

A recent report by the American National Academy of Science for the US Justice Department provides details on just how devastating this law-and-order policy has been. One commentator said that the United States "has gone past the point where the numbers of people in prison can be justified by social benefits" and that imprisonment now is itself "a source of injustice."

The *New York Times* in an editorial bluntly stated on May 25 "the American experiment in mass incarceration has been a moral, legal, social and economic disaster. It cannot end soon enough."

In another decision (Canada v. Harkat) on May 14, the Supreme Court sided with the government on the validity of the Security Certificate issued against Mohamed Harkat, a foreign national living in Canada. In an earlier decision in 2007, Charkaoui v. Canada, the Supreme Court ruled that the Certificate scheme "deprived named persons of their life, liberty, and security of the person in a manner not in accordance with principles of fundamental justice, contrary to s. 7 of the [Canadian Charter of Rights and Freedoms]."

As part of that earlier ruling the Court wrote that the scheme "violated the principle that a person must have the ability to know and meet the case against him, because there was not full disclosure of the government's case to the named person or any substantial substitute for full disclosure."

The Supreme Court even went so far as to suggest that the Special Advocates program adopted in the United Kingdom would meet its Charter concerns. Not surprisingly, the government did exactly that and in 2008 amended the Immigration and Refugee Protection Act so that Canadian Special Advocates could be appointed "who would protect the interests of the named person in closed hearings after having received disclosure of the entire record."

In its Harkat decision of 2014, the Supreme Court passed judgment on the very programme it recommended to the government in its 2007 Charkaoui decision. A slam dunk for the government.

What is missing from this debate and decision-making by the Court is the fact that any substantial recognition of a Security Certificate issued today means that the named individual will be locked up indefinitely or will be subject to strict release conditions. This is preventative detention.

There have been five major cases and all have been largely based on so-called evidence provided by foreign governments. These governments have not permitted their evidence to be tested in open court, and the Canadian courts have been left to evaluate in camera the validity of the evidence – and whether or not it is tainted by the use of torture. It is not unreasonable to assume that, in the five cases, torture was used, as the countries of citizenship of the five were Egypt, Algeria, Syria and Morocco.

It is also not an idiosyncratic jump to suggest that the use of Security Certificate today is akin to the use of internment by governments during the First and Second World Wars. During the first war, Ukrainians were forced to register and about 8,600 men, women and children were interned under harsh and abusive conditions.

During the Second World War, thousands of Japanese and Italians, many born in Canada, were declared to be enemy aliens and interned in camps across the country. In many of the camps the conditions were such that to be interned was to be given a death sentence.

The legal environment for the Security Certificate cases today has improved in comparison to that of those interned during the wars, but the cases today are surrounded by hysteria and hypocrisy similar to that prevailing decades ago. The detention of almost 500 individuals during the October Crisis of 1970 offers graphic evidence that governments are not to be trusted when faced with security issues they do not understand.

In reading the decision of the Chief Justice in the Harkat case, I have a strong suspicion that she was not completely convinced of the case she was making for the validity of the Security Certificate against Mr Harkat. Several times she referred to the fact that the IRPA program for Security Advocates "does not provide a perfect process," obviously a reference to the Court's 2007 decision in Charkaoui when it stated Security Certificates did not meet the principles of "fundamental justice."

However, in its 2014 Harkat decision, there is some sleight-of-hand wordsmithing at work since the creation of the Special Advocates represents the need for "procedural fairness." How the lack of principles of fundamental justice can be overcome by procedural justice is not explained by the Chief Justice.

At a minimum, this glides over a basic tenet of our rule-of-law system, that an individual has a fundamental right to know the details of the accusations, from where they originate, and to cross examine in open court the officials proffering the evidence. This does not happen, and will not happen, now that the Supreme Court has again legitimized Security Certificates.

Central to the Certificate scheme are the Special Advocates selected by the government to act as intermediaries on behalf of the accused individuals. Surprisingly, the government has been able to find these advocates from among legal professionals and have them act as the legitimizing force for the scheme.

In an analogous position, the American Medical Association has strictly prohibited physicians from participating in legally ordered executions. This policy is widely supported by members of the American medical profession.

Perhaps lawyers in Canada might wish to examine the role they are now playing in the Canadian preventative-detention scheme called Security Certificates. It is hoped that they would find their role contrary to their professional and ethical obligations. At this time, that is the only way this dastardly scheme will disappear from our legal regime.

Embassy

Alfred Dreyfus and Omar Khadr, bookends of injustice
March 4, 2015

OMAR KHADR. ALFRED DREYFUS.

One imprisoned today in a federal prison at the end of a corrupt legal process and miscarriage of justice; the other convicted and sentenced to lifelong penal servitude for espionage in 1894.

There is much to connect the two. Both are out of the great founding religions of the Middle East: one a Muslim, the other a Jew. Khadr, as a child, brought to war by a family dedicated to helping Afghans fight invading Western forces. The other was a successful officer in the French military from an affluent family in Alsace, then a German province. He was scapegoated by the rampant anti-Semitism in French society. Khadr was imprisoned by a vengeful American society and prolonged by his own spiteful government.

Dreyfus spent five years in a prison on Devil's Island not far from the Caribbean before he was pardoned and returned to military service, all within seven years. Ironically, Khadr spent 10 years in a prison at Guantanamo in the Caribbean in conditions even worse than those on Devil's Island. He is still in prison in Canada almost 13 years after his capture on the battlefields of Afghanistan.

He remains in prison scapegoated by a Canadian government's rabid anti-Muslim zealotry disguised as protecting Canadians. Dreyfus was able to recover his health after his imprisonment; Khadr lost sight in one eye and is slowly losing sight in the other, the result of a lack of and bungled medical treatment by his captors.

Dreyfus's nightmare ended through the dedicated work of a small group of supporters, especially his brother, who early on recognized and fought the attempt by the French military and anti-Semites in government to offload responsibility for the espionage to a Jew rather than to a known Catholic officer. Many knew it was an odious conspiracy. In the end the conspiracy was so ham-fisted that reading of the matter today leads to the conclusion that the willingness to see a Jew blamed reflected deep and abiding anti-Semitism throughout French society.

In large measure it took the work of the distinguished writer Émile Zola to pen an open letter to the French President in 1898 to overcome the conspiracy. Even then, Dreyfus was convicted at a second military trial when the court decided he was "already judged" and there was no need for a new verdict. It was only when the French President issued a pardon ignoring the decision of the military courts was Dreyfus released and his army rank restored. But the injustice lives on. In 1985 a statute of Dreyfus commissioned by President Francois Mitterrand was refused permission by the minister of defence to be installed at the École Militaire.

Khadr's prosecution and persecution goes on today with nearly half of his short life lived in prisons. His persecution started with his capture by American forces in August 2002. He was taken following a firefight between American soldiers and a Taliban unit. An American soldier, a medic, died following the encounter and Khadr, who was not the only survivor, was captured and transported to the notorious Bagram prison north of Kabul. It was a place of torture and Khadr was denied necessary medical treatment for his wounds.

The Canadian government learned of his capture, and fearful of his being transferred to the newly-opened prison at Guantanamo, in a diplomatic note, citing his age, asked the Americans not to send Khadr to the already infamous prison in Cuba. It was then and, remains today, a place beyond any norms of civilized behavior. The Americans rejected the Canadian request and Khadr was to spend the next 10 years of his life in the Caribbean prison, locked away from the sight of the tropical sun.

From the very beginning Khadr had dedicated supporters in Canada and even within the American military justice system. But they were unable to overcome the lunacy of the Guantanamo perversion of justice and the government of Canada was of little assistance. This, unlike other governments such as the United Kingdom and Australia, which succeeded in having their citizens (and in the case of the United Kingdom, residents) released from Guantanamo and returned home.

In the meantime the federal courts of the United States caught up with the perversions of the "military justice" system installed at Guantanamo by the Bush Administration and forced small changes which, unfortunately, did not significantly alter its denial of fundamental justice. Even after 2008 with a new president in the White House, dedicated to the elimination of Guantanamo, there was little success. The only success was the release of the many "shepherds" who ended up at Guantanamo.

Khadr's lawyers in Canada were equally active in promoting through the courts and there were four "wins" at the Federal Court. Sadly, those decisions were of little value when the Supreme Court, early in 2010, decided that while Khadr's "Charter rights were violated" by federal officials it went on to state that "it would not be appropriate for the court to give direction as to the diplomatic steps necessary to address the breaches of Mr. Khadr's Charter rights."

Unfortunately, the chief justice did not recall her comments to an Ottawa audience a few months earlier. Then she said: "The fear and anger that terrorism produces may cause leaders to make war on targets that may or may not be connected with the terrorist incident." In words that should be engraved on the walls of the Court itself or perhaps on a planned misplaced monument outside to the victims of communism, the chief justice went on to say, "or perhaps it may lead governments to curtail civil liberties and seek recourse in tactics that might otherwise deplore...that may not, in the clearer light of retrospect, be necessary or defensible."

Khadr has not yet encountered the "clearer light of retrospect" and remains locked in a federal prison. Even the Federal Court recently decided that the prison director was right when he ruled it was not possible to find appropriate space in the prison for Khadr to be interviewed by journalists.

The federal government, imitating the court martial decisions encountered by Dreyfus, continues to maintain that Khadr has already been judged and there is no need for a serious investigation of his conviction and sentence. Since Khadr returned to Canada in 2012 various Canadian public safety ministers, with all of the intelligence of those making robocalls, have parroted the view he was convicted of "heinous crimes" and the government has "vigorously defended against any attempt to lessen his punishment for these crimes." It is time perhaps for the current minister, Stephen Blaney, to change his name to Blarney.

Ironically, today it is possible Khadr may still find redress in the American judicial system. His American lawyers have launched an appeal of his conviction directly challenging the legality of the murder charge. Alfred Dreyfus would approve.

To complete the irony of these sad cases, history has recorded that the "inventor of Zionism" Theodor Herzl was strongly influenced in his promotion of a Jewish state by the anti-Semitism demonstrated in France by the Dreyfus convictions. The First Zionist Congress was organized by Herzl in August 1897. Fifty years later in late November 1947, the United Nations voted the partition of Palestine to include a Jewish state.

Embassy

Not all those who wander are lost.

—Bilbo Baggins

3. Canadian Abroad

IN THE LAST THIRTEEN YEARS OF WORK IN THE FOREIGN SERVICE I was first Director and then Director General for consular services for Canadians in difficulty beyond the borders of Canada. I arrived for this work in the fall of 1992 following three years of intense, successful diplomacy as ambassador to the countries of Central America – Honduras, Nicaragua, Panama and Costa Rica and for part of the time, El Salvador. That work saw the end of the civil and not so civil wars in Nicaragua and El Salvador. By the summer of 1992 the Americans ended support for the nefarious Contras waging war out of Honduras into Nicaragua, a peace agreement between the FMLN and the government in El Salvador was negotiated and the beginnings of a reduction of the violence in Guatemala was underway.

A UN peacekeeping force largely directed by Canadian military personnel was in place and it was one of the most successful such mission in the history of the UN organization. As well there was an international agreement to provide increased development assistance for the region. Earlier, over Christmas 1989 an American invasion put an end to the rule of Manual Noriega in Panama and in subsequent months oversaw the restoration of civil and political stability. Ten years later at the end of the century it saw the return of the Panama Canal to Panamanian sovereignty in line with the requirements of the treaty negotiated by Jimmy Carter in 1979.

The return to Ottawa was preceded by a month long stay in a Costa Rican hospital where parts of the anatomy were removed so the ending of the assignment was anticipated with the hope that a quiet new assignment would be part of the recovery. Personnel or in its modern nomenclature, Human Resources, thought that an assignment to Consular Affairs would be ideal. Little did they know as from the very first days of the new assignment the work was as intense as dodging bullets in El Salvador or flying in clapped out Russian helicopters in Nicaragua. Flying with Canadian military pilots was equally hair-raising especially on one occasion when one decided that we should inspect the insides of a caldaria north of Managua.

In those days of early September 1992 Consular Affairs did not exist as an operational unit of the Department. In the previous years it became part of the Immigration group or again using the nomenclature of the time, Social Affairs, which was merged with Foreign Affairs in the mid-1980s as part of the integration of disparate foreign operations into one department. In the summer of 1992 the immigration component of Foreign Affairs was returned to its domestic home, Immigration Canada. This was a result of an internal investigation of what was known as the al Mashid affair. Mr al Mashid was an Iraqi diplomat who it was alleged was given preferential treatment by the Canadian embassy in Austria and issued a visa for entry into Canada. Supposedly, Mr al Mashid had information on Saddam Hussein's military and political plans following his invasion of Kuwait in August 1990. Several persons in Foreign Affairs believed such information would be valuable to the Coalition planning to oust Hussein from Kuwait. Canada was part of the Coalition. The investigation of the issuance of the Canadian visa to Mr al Mashid suggested this was done in error and as a consequence the government of the day decided the Immigration component of Foreign Affairs should be reshuffled back to its domestic home.

At the time those making the decision on the reshuffle did not realize the consular function had been integrated into the Immigration group. As a result during the summer of 1992 there was some mild consternation as to what should be done for the consular function or in the vernacular – services to Canadians in difficulty overseas. The consternation was mild as services to Canadians had never been very high on the list of priorities for the Department of Foreign Affairs. John Hilliker in his book on the department *The Early Years, 1909-1946,* reflected on the efforts of early Canadian governments to avoid financial or direct responsibility for Canadians in foreign lands.

Even in the post-war period when Foreign Affairs was entering its "golden age" very little thought was given to the need for a professional cadre of people knowledgeable and experience in the needs of Canadians overseas. Rather the function became a backwater of departmental operations and those involved were not part of the best and brightest. Many of these factors are highlighted in the first article in this Section, titled "Canadians Abroad." The quality of consular services during this period was largely the result of the experienced and committed "locally engaged staff" at Canadian offices abroad. They remain central to the quality of these services today.

One of the results of the bureaucratic changes in the summer of 1992 was to place the consular function within the departmental legal affairs bureau. Serendipity is rare in the corridors of any bureaucracy but it was alive and well in the Pearson Building when I reported for work in the office of Barry Mawhinney, the departmental legal adviser, as the leaves were changing in the Gatineau. I had spoken to Barry before I left Costa Rica a few weeks earlier but had no earlier nor subsequent contact with him. It was instant rapport and we worked closely for the next few years or until another bureaucratic upheaval saw consular as part of a GOB (group of bureaux) that included financial services, protocol, physical property, information management and technology, inspection services and passports. A "common thread" was hard to find.

At the time of my arrival Mr Mawhinney was preoccupied with the Lamont and Spencer affair. Christine Lamont and David Spencer, two young Canadians had decided to provide help in the struggle to overthrow military regimes and support democratization efforts in South and Central America. In late 1989 they were arrested by the Brazilian authorities following the kidnapping of a prominent businessman in Sao Paulo. Before long there was a public and governmental campaign initiated by their families to have them released from prison and returned to Canada. It was alleged that they were wrongfully accused and there was no possibility that they would receive any measure of justice through the Brazilian courts. It was an intense campaign and Mr Mawhinney was relieved to see me in his office and the opportunity to transfer responsibility for Ms Lamont and Mr Spencer.

Up until that time I had never had responsibility for consular matters other than casual involvement in a variety of matters that affected Canadians in difficulty abroad. The Lamont and Spencer situation was a baptism of fire. Nevertheless, the threads of managing crisis were well honed from the years in Central America. Before long there were long conversations with family members and others involved (including a public relations specialist hired by the family to ensure the matter remained at the top of political and public agendas in Canada) in promoting the need for Ms Lamont and Mr Spencer to be released from their Brazilian prison and returned home.

By this time the Brazilian authorities believed they were unfairly characterized by Canada and were adamant the two Canadians were receiving appropriate attention within their judicial system; their care in prison was better than for other prisoners. As I would come to learn over the next decade it is the unexpected that will unravel difficult consular situations and create the opportunity for solutions. And the unexpected for the Lamont and Spencer matter was as unusual as could be expected.

An explosion at a service station in Managua, Nicaragua in 1994 uncovered a hidden cache of documents left behind by individuals who were preparing for revolutionary work elsewhere in Latin America. Among the documents were post-dated letters written by Ms Lamont to her family disguising her future activities. These letters became public and in the process destroyed political and public support for their cause.

In the aftermath, the Brazilian government now proven correct in its treatment of Ms Lamont and Mr Spencer signed a prisoner transfer treaty that had been on the desk of the President for several years. Within a few months Ms Lamont and Mr Spencer returned to Canada and within a few weeks were paroled and able to resume their Canadian lives. It was one of the more enjoyable telephone calls I was to make in the years following when I spoke to the family and assured them that the flight was now 18,000 feet and climbing after it had departed Sao Paulo.

I have detailed this matter as it provides an illustration of one of our current preoccupations. Ms Lamont and Mr Spencer were among thousands of Canadians who, since the American Civil War, have gone abroad to support the causes of others in foreign countries. The Spanish Civil War of the late 30s is the best known but thousands of others have done so in the wars associated with Israel, and its Arab neighbours, Vietnam, the Balkans and today the Ukraine and Syria and Iraq. Canadians have been largely tolerant of this wisely concluding that today's terrorist is tomorrow's freedom fighter. Today that tolerance is less in evidence and such travel is being exploited politically based on the bloody excesses of the wars in Iraq and Syria if not for electoral advantage in Canada.

The articles in this Section reflect the many consular matters in which I was involved before I retired and, in many cases, since I retired. There are several articles dealing with the standards and legal environment surrounding consular matters including the first two which detail the many changes that were undertaken after my arrival in late 1992. Of particular note is the second one, "The Modernization of Consular Services", detailing the development of a modern communications and computer system that is today the backbone of effective, timely and comprehensive service to Canadians in foreign places. I was a proponent of such systems for several years prior and was part of a small group that saw the early introduction of computer-based communications and data storage systems. This occurred when I was involved in both the United States and Asia Pacific South Bordeaux and the embassy in San Jose.

These were still early days in the "graphical user interface" revolution for applications but in less than six months after arrival in the Consular Bureau a contract was signed with an Ottawa based company, Amita Software (now WorldReach Software), to develop a comprehensive package of tools that would support consular work both in Ottawa and at the over two hundred service delivery locations throughout the world. This was COSMOS and it remains in full service to this day and still supported by WorldReach. This is a record in such matters where contracts with developers more often end up in the courts than a more than two decades-long collaboration. Equally more than seven countries have purchased COSMOS and use it to deliver consular services to their citizens throughout the world. WorldReach is today the leader in such service based software. COSMOS was awarded the Gold Medal of Distinction for such applications in 2000.

Of course such tools are only tools and it is their exploitation that provides benefits to Canadians. Based on the inherent data storage and communications capabilities of COSMOS fundamental changes were initiated in the mid-1990s in the delivery of consular services. The first which has had far reaching consequences was the development of a Consular Operations Centre in Foreign Affairs which is today the centre through which the Department manages its work 24-hours a day, seven days a week. Central to that work are services to Canadians throughout the world and to their families in Canada.

Associated with the Centre and based on new communications technologies was the development of the capabilities for the communication's systems at all offices abroad to be transferred to Ottawa during non-business hours or when there is a major political crisis or natural disaster requiring support for the embassy or high commission or consulate. As a result a person seeking assistance and calling the office will be helped by officials in Ottawa. Since the installation of this capability millions of dollars have been saved and services improved in the process.

Over the years there have been numerous situations in which large numbers of Canadians have had to be evacuated from dangerous situations. These have included wars and revolutions, natural disasters, accidents and epidemics. In many instances these evacuations included Canadians with a second citizenship and this was particularly evident in the 2006 forced departures from Lebanon.

Canadians were surprised to learn that upwards of 40,000 of their compatriots were living there and were in need of assistance. The government mounted a large scale marine evacuation to Cyprus and Turkey and in the end assumed the costs of close to $100 million.

In the aftermath of the evacuation there was considerable public comment on "passport Canadians" who were misusing their relationship with Canada and it would be appropriate to make changes in our laws to prevent such actions. Apart from the idea of creating two classes of citizenship, an inequitable and unworkable idea, the commentators did not realize that the Canadians assisted were fully paying for the help that is provided by the government when they are in difficulty overseas. In 1996 the government of the day as part of its budget process initiated a Consular Service Fee that is paid whenever a passport is issued. The fee has been in effect ever since and has collected well over a billion dollars for the government, far in excess of monies expended for consular services. There is strong evidence to support the contention that the government makes money in the provision of consular services. This is discussed in one of the articles in this section – "Are We Paying More For Consular Services Than Necessary" April 9, 2013.

Canadians Abroad
February 9, 2004

THE CALL CAME INTO THE OPERATIONS CENTRE AT FOREIGN AFFAIRS late in the evening. The voice was hesitant and faint. It was a young Canadian, touring South America by motorbike, saying that he was lying in a ditch along an isolated road in northern Bolivia following a close encounter with a truck. It was raining and he was injured. Within minutes the Operations Officer was in touch with the consul at the Canadian embassy in La Paz, provided the available information and instructed that assistance be sought from the Bolivian authorities. The caller was assured that help was on the way and before long he was receiving medical attention.

The call was one of thousands that come into Foreign Affairs' 24-hour Operations Centre each week from the four corners of the world. The system, based on the world's best communications and computer equipment and software, is the envy of most foreign ministries. The software backing the system, called *COSMOS*, was developed in Canada for Canadians. The British and Dutch governments recently purchased it for their own consular services. A first for Canadian-government-developed software.

It was not always this way. Consular service had been the handmaiden of the Department of Foreign Affairs' work since its inception. A lack of personnel, money and training gave constant reminders to the problems for those who visited the prisons and accidents, found missing children or negotiated the release of kidnapped Canadians. John Hilliker, in his book on the department, *The Early Years, 1909-1946*, reflects on the efforts of early Canadian governments to avoid financial or direct responsibility for Canadians in foreign lands. Regrettably, that policy continued for more years than was understandable.

Also, consular work never played an important role or place in the culture of departmental life either in Ottawa or abroad. Similar attitudes can be found in the foreign ministries of other countries. For most, life in the Foreign Service was not intended as one providing services to Canadians who were affected and afflicted by acts of others, god, or their own egos. Rather, for most, Foreign Service was for the 'loftier' pursuit of peace and commerce.

* * *

Nowhere is this better illustrated than the chequered history of the bureaucratic location and the identification of officers for consular services. Since the mid-1980s, the management of consular services has floated – independent of outside influence from a standalone bureau, to integration with immigration and passport, to inclusion in legal and environmental matters, and then on to trade and communications. Today, consular is part of a GOB (group of bureaux) that includes financial services, protocol, physical property, information management and technology, inspection services and passports. A common thread is hard to find.

These bureaucratic peregrinations were also accompanied by changes in the departmental officers designated for consular work. Historically, consular work was the responsibility of political officers; that changed in 1988 when immigration officers were assigned the responsibility. That changed again in 1992 when immigration officers were de-integrated (in the aftermath of the al-Mashad affair) from the department. At the time, little thought was given the fact that the removal of immigration officers from the department also meant serious disruption of consular services for Canadians.

This lack of thought was evidenced by confusion as to the future home of the consular function among departmental employees. It was these departmental employees, in the management group, who recognized the problem and made a proposal to have the consular function become part of their responsibilities. It was not a perfect solution, given their already overloaded responsibilities, but in the absence of other options it was accepted.

This change, in 1992, provided the stability on which wide-ranging and far-reaching changes could be made to the delivery of consular services. Nevertheless, there are suggestions today that these arrangements are no longer acceptable. As happens far too often in the department, personal and bureaucratic interests could once again take precedence over the interests of Canadians in difficulty overseas.

* * *

Canadians have been well served by the 1992 arrangements. But, as recent events have demonstrated, assistance to Canadians in difficulty overseas is no static matter – or one that can await bureaucratic perfection. The advent of the jet engine and chickens in the pots of many has made foreign travel as common as a trip downtown. Younger and older Canadians are travelling; they are travelling to more distant places; and adventure tourism brings its own special dangers. Wars, civil and not so-civil, terrorism, crime, earthquakes, volcanoes and storms have added immeasurably to the traveller's traditional problems of upset stomachs and sand fleas. In the Caribbean basin, sun, sea, sex and Seagram's are part of the background litany of afflicted Canadians.

Not so many years ago, governments and the travel industry worked to replace the archaic patchwork of rules and procedures that continued to dog the international traveller. In 1963, the Vienna Convention on Consular Relations was negotiated and represented a codification of historical international practise on the treatment of foreigners by nation states. It remains as the world's pre-eminent and, to a large extent, only international agreement that provides the basis for assistance to citizens in other countries.

Further to the Vienna Convention were efforts, largely through ICAO and IATA, for facilitation initiatives to ease the movement of the international traveller and to remove the barriers –many the legacy of the pre-aircraft era – that continued to make international travel an obstacle course. These efforts mirrored, in part, the efforts to facilitate the movement of goods and services which continues to make progress, even in a troubled world. Unfortunately, the efforts to facilitate and support the international movement of people have largely disappeared and, in the absence of world comity, the future of such efforts looks bleak.

In the early part of the 1990s, once the bureaucratic decisions were made, serious attention was given to improving consular services for Canadians. At the same time it was recognized that the future of consular services was dependent on creating a recognized and respectable place for the service in the daily life of Foreign Affairs.

* * *

A daunting task. The bureaucratic changes had decimated the trained group of Canadian consular officials, and it was largely due to the professionalism and dedication of locally engaged consular officers around the world that Canadians abroad continued to be assisted. Program reviews and other government-wide, expenditure-reduction exercises added to the bleak landscape. Resources for consular services, just as for other essential programs, were going south, and there were no expectations that this would change in the coming years.

In all of this, the objective was to maintain existing service levels and, as well, to improve and add to them. In this we were rebuilding the boat yet at the same time sailing it to the far corners of the world. During this period the demand for consular services was constantly outstripping the ability of the system to meet it. More Canadians than ever were travelling; dual-nationality problems were emerging as a serious impediment to providing assistance; parental child abductions were increasing, and there was a dramatic increase in the arrest of Canadians in other countries. In 1993, a preliminary inventory of Canadians in foreign prisons listed less than seven hundred. Today, there are times when the number exceeds three thousand.

Typical of the period were the calls to parents on Mondays to inform them that their teenage daughter had been arrested the night before in Jamaica – only to be told that was impossible. She was staying with friends down the road!

In bringing change to consular services it was assumed from the beginning that change would have to come from inside. There were no expectations that others would be willing or able to help. At the same time, it was assumed that there was a need to break with the hoary, historical traditions that so long encased and circumscribed consular services.

* * *

An early initiative was to broaden the travel information program. A limited version had been in place for a number of years and was largely centred on the publication *Bon Voyage, but* . . . . Country travel reports were created and, despite misgivings from lawyers on liability, these have blossomed into a central feature, informing Canadians of the problems that will be encountered and what can be done to avoid them. Today there are country travel reports for over 225 destinations. At the same time, country and subject publications were created and today there is a rich mixture, covering topics ranging from dual nationality to working overseas to retirement abroad, and to the woman traveller.

Early activities also included initiatives to improve the legal environment in which consular services are conducted. A League of Nations treaty which obligated Canada not to provide assistance to Canadians when they were in the country of a second citizenship was denounced, a first for Canada. Negotiations were begun for bilateral treaties with Egypt and Lebanon to assist in resolving parental child abductions. Treaty arrangements for prisoner transfers were concluded with a number of countries. In the United States, where there had been a treaty arrangement with Washington since the late 1970s, efforts were concentrated to improve its effectiveness and to increase the number of states active in the treaty. Today there is only one state - Rhode Island - that is not active in these treaty arrangements.

Throughout the period an overriding issue was to provide assured resources for consular services. The aim was to remove the large element of uncertainty associated with the 'lottery-based' allocation system that was and remains characteristic of the governmental process. This was achieved in 1996 when, as part of the budget for that year, a consular-service fee of $25.00 was approved. The fee is collected at the time a Canadian applies for a passport and today it, along with other fees, provides in excess of $50 million [today over $100] in revenue that is dedicated to consular activities.

The assured funding direct from Canadians and tied to the demand for passport services provided the foundation for the expansion in the recruitment of new people and expansion of services including new offices overseas. Resources for consular work has always been a small part of the department's budget, averaging in the single numbers, and the number of people directly involved worldwide less than three hundred. These cost recovery initiatives provided for significant increase in the personnel resources overseas and in the directing group in Ottawa. One example of this was the growth in honorary consuls who numbered in the low forties in 1993 to over one hundred today. These offices in places such a Puerto Vararta, Launda and Chang Mai are a low cost and effective way to provide consular help to travelling Canadians.

* * *

The assured funding also permitted the development and deployment of the *COSMOS* software. *COSMOS* is tied to the department's own computer and communications system, and provides Canada with the world's only dedicated consular software. It was developed in cooperation with *WorldReach Software*, an Ottawa-based development firm. Since its first deployment in 1993, it has provided consular officials overseas and in Ottawa with a thoroughly modern tool to support their work. In addition to improved case management, *COSMOS* provided the foundation on which the Consular Operations Centre was expanded so that services could be provided 24-hours a day in all corners of the world. Also there are software modules for the delivery of passport services overseas, registration of Canadians living abroad and contingency planning.

Today the tragic problems of Ms. Kazemi, Mr. Sampson and Mr. Arar demonstrate that consular assistance for Canadians in difficulty overseas will continue to occupy a significant place in public debate. Earlier the debate concerned assistance for Canadians, such as Raoul Leger, Stanley Faulder, Sean Kelly, Christine Lamont, David Spencer, Nguyen Thi Hiep and countless others.

Unfortunately for some, there was no satisfactory conclusion to the earlier debates and, as the new cases demonstrate, the current debate is as much characterized by wishful and confused thinking as it is by an understanding of what Canadians can expect when they venture beyond the borders of Canada. "Respect' for the Canadian passport or the 'rights' of Canadians overseas have become the demands of many and 'soft diplomacy' has become an all-encompassing accusation against the government.

Canadians overseas, just as it is for foreigners in Canada, do not have any special rights, nor can they expect to obtain preferential treatment from foreign governments. The best they can expect is that they are treated no worse than the citizens of the country concerned – and in many cases that is cold comfort. Canadian laws and rights end at the Canadian border and the laws and rights of another country begin when a Canadians crosses its frontier. For the vast majority of Canadian travellers this is not a problem. But for the few who encounter difficulty this basic rule is lumpy gruel.

Contrary to popular belief, there are few international rules, and certainly no effective "laws," that control the actions of states in their treatment of foreigners within its boundaries. The Vienna Convention of Consular Relations has more to do with the conduct of consular relations between governments than it has to do with the establishment of standards of conduct in the treatment of foreigners. In the Convention's fifty-seven articles only two establish standards of conduct. These provide limited requirements for notification in the event of the arrest and/or death of a foreign national. The Convention provides no support for the popular view that the Canadian government can "legally" demand standards of conduct on the part of other governments in their treatment of arrested or detained Canadians. The Convention provides no right of private communications with arrested persons, unlimited access, guarantees of medical or other services, or even a safe environment.

Equally troubling is that other international conventions on such matters as torture, the rights of the child, equality or human rights offer little direct benefit to Canadians arrested in foreign countries. There is a wide gap between the largely hortative objectives of such conventions and the need to assist individuals in trouble in foreign countries. In most instances there are no specific mechanisms through which breeches can be determined and remedies enforced. When feet are being beaten and fingernails shortened, threats of disruptions to the bilateral relationship or public embarrassment do nothing to improve the lot of victims. There is more than a risk that their lot would be made worse by such entreaties. When torture, coercion or mistreatment is used in connection with national security or large national interests, as was the case in some of the recent incidents involving Canadians, then there is little scope for redress based on national laws, international instruments or the quality of bilateral relations.

Persons and organizations perpetuating the myth that there is redress through such mechanisms do an enormous disservice. The disservice becomes more disturbing when the resulting public clamour results in foreign governments refusing to cooperate and puts on hold any expectation of positive action. Christine Lamont and David Spencer probably spent several years more in a Brazilian prison than was necessary as a result of the efforts of their supporters to portray them as victims, or demonstrate the unjustness of the Brazilian justice system. Foreign governments rarely read The *Globe and Mail* or listen to the CBC and, if they do, rarely heed their advice.

Canadians in difficulty in foreign lands do have a right to the full support and assistance of their own government. In times of trouble – deaths, accidents, kidnapping, illness and missing persons – most foreign governments are also ready to assist. However, it is common in such matters that the expectations of victims, friends and family are not always met. Persons naturally have high expectations and react badly when they perceive inattention or dismissal of concerns. In foreign lands such expectations are affected by language, practise and culture. Unfortunately, wrongful convictions, poor medical treatment, unfound missing persons and parental abductions are as much a part of the Canadian scene as they are of foreign countries and, despite the best will in the world, there will always be disappointments.

In the area of detentions and arrests the problems are more acute and the demand for action by those jailed or by family and friends in Canada more intense. The unfortunate reality is that some Canadians in foreign countries do pretty much what they do in Canada – they murder, assault, traffic in drugs, organize and carry out large-scale frauds and rob. In some instances Canadian law enforcement officials provide information to foreign governments that could result in the arrest of Canadians overseas. Also, Canada is one of the few countries that will extradite its citizens to foreign countries to face charges. Generally, Canadian law enforcement or justice officials admit to no obligation to assist in the defence of such persons, although there have been instances when they have cooperated with Foreign Affairs in doing so. For the most part, Canadians in such predicaments abroad are treated much the same as the citizens of the country in question. However, unfamiliar legal processes, lack of bail, barriers of language and custom, prison conditions and lack of direct support from family and friends all contribute to make the life of Canadians imprisoned abroad one of high anxiety, danger and illness. Many of the same conditions apply in Canada as well, but this does not lessen the obligation for action by Canadians officials.

In this fevered ferment it would be wrong to assume that Canadians have suddenly become the favoured victims of unsavoury regimes or friendly governments that have placed national security ahead of respect for human rights. The citizens of other countries encounter similar problems – some even in Canada. In this new world, the vast majority of travellers will continue to move and, while the movement is slower than we would want, only a very few fall victims to the misplaced or idiosyncratic vigilance of governments.

bout de papier, Vol. 20, No.3.

The Modernization of Consular Services: The Importance of Technology
March 17, 2004

GOVERNMENTS ARE UNDER INCREASING PRESSURE TO PROVIDE improved and increased consular services. Growing foreign travel and residency, increasing danger in many parts of the world, the expectation of citizens and the speed by which information now transcends time and space have come together to create urgency for governments to act.

Cost Concerns. This urgency comes at a time when the cost of providing services in foreign countries is increasing, and when fiscal caution and reductions at home are standard policies for most governments. As such, there is a requirement for careful consideration of the means and mechanisms that are used to improve and increase services. Improved services at a time of fiscal restraint are not incompatible – as the Canadian experience over the past ten years has demonstrated.

Canadian Experience. In the early 1990s Canada faced many of these same issues. More Canadians were travelling and their ages were lowering at one end while increasing at the other. They were going to more esoteric places with fewer local services, and in many places they were facing new dangers. In Canada, the media were suffused with stories based on the assertion that the government was not providing the level of service to its citizens that this changing environment required.

Improved Services. The governmental response was based on two factors. First, the demand for improved and increased consular services had to be met using roughly the same level of resources, and any new resources had to be funded by the clients. The second factor was the assertion that the achievement of improved services could only be made on the basis of increased productivity. At the time, it was concluded that increased productivity could be achieved by improved communications and the development of specialized computer work programs that would maximize the efficiency of the existing work force.

Consular Work Model. The work model at the time was one where most consular services were provided through Canadian missions overseas. As such, services were provided in the most expensive environment within the model. Very few services were provided through headquarter staff – the least expensive part of the system. It was concluded that the repatriation of services to headquarters to the maximum extent possible would permit the reorientation of overseas staff to those tasks that could only be performed in that environment.

Interacting Elements. At the same time an analysis of consular work was performed. Based on this analysis it was determined that there were three significant interacting elements which constituted governmental responsibility to its citizens overseas and the expectation of its citizens:

> providing authoritative, accurate and current information on conditions in foreign countries and advice as to what steps citizens could take to safeguard themselves before leaving home and. when overseas, as providing those services that could only be done by government at all possible locations where citizens encountered difficulty, and

> leaving to the private sector those services that did not require government intervention, especially when they entailed no danger to the well-being of the citizen.

Division of Labour. It was concluded that the first element – the provision of timely information and advice – could be carried out almost exclusively by staff at headquarters. With the second element – direct services to the citizen overseas – it was determined that many of these requirements could be performed by staff at headquarters, and where necessary missions could also be supported by timely intervention by headquarters. Regarding the third element – the shedding of some existing services – it was concluded that this had to be carefully presented to the travelling public, so as to avoid the impression that this would result in a significant and substantial reduction in services.

Relationships. The examination also concluded that consular services were an important element in the international-travel industry. As such, it would be mutually beneficial to cooperate closely with various elements of that industry. This was considered important in areas such as:

> travel medicine, medical insurance and travel insurance
>
> the distribution of security and safety information; and
>
> the development of new vacation destinations.

Information Management Technology. Central to the modernization of consular services was the development, implementation and deployment of dedicated information- management technologies. More than any other aspect of the strategy, it was with improved information management that productivity was increased significantly and the barriers of time and space overcome. Equally important, information-management systems provided the detailed data on which management-resource decisions were made on a more accurate and realistic basis.

Increased Productivity. In late 1992 Canada decided to implement an aggressive strategy to develop information-management tools to increase productivity that, in turn, supported improved and increased consular services over the past decade. This strategy, developed in close cooperation with the *AMITA Corporation* (now *WorldReach Software*), and continues to be the foundation on which Canadian consular services are provided.

Work Philosophy. Before there were any discussions with information- management specialists, consular professionals thoroughly analysed all aspects of consular work and determinations were made on how best to improve and increase service delivery through technology. This was not a "business case" but rather the detailed itemization of the philosophy that would surround the move to technology. The philosophy included the following key objectives:

Information. The core of consular work is the exchange of information between clients and officials. The move to technology had to store, transmit and protect this information, so that it was available in real-time to all officials who provided consular services. The system would retain all information online with expansion in storage capacity as and when necessary. All information would be backed up to disc at appropriate times in order to meet mandated archival standards.

Users. Access to the system would be centrally controlled. All consular employees – centrally or locally hired – irrespective of location would have access to the system. The system would be fundamentally intuitive, to maximize acceptability without dictation and to minimize training. Employees would be allowed to "come-to-the-system" at their own speed and comfort level.

Security. Risk management was the key. The nature of the work and those involved dictated that a balance had to be struck on security concerns and the achievement of an acceptable level of performance. The assertion was made that it was not necessary to include sensitive information within the system in order for services to be provided. In the rare instances when there was a need to transmit and store sensitive information, this could best be done outside the system, rather than hobble it with "worse-case" considerations.

Paper. There were no assumptions made with respect to whether or not the system would reduce paper use. It was left to the users to determine what level of paper retention was necessary for their own comfort level. It was assumed that over time, as confidence in the reliability of the system increased, users would reduce the need for paper – and this has happened.

Technical Specifications. These work-performance requirements established various technical specifications for the technological system that would be developed. They continue to surround the use and evolution of information-management technologies:

Reliability. The system must be available 100 per cent of the time;

Accessibility. The system must be available to all employees, both overseas and at headquarters. It should permit access for employees external to the normal place of work, using available communications systems;

Communications. The system would initially use proprietorial, departmental communications facilities, but, as the technology and security features improved, be fully capable of exploiting the ubiquitous Internet;

Expansion. The technology should permit the expansion of the system to new users and new points of service without the need for basic change to that system;

Upgrading. Development and operational tools and systems should be assessed as to their expected commercial endurance and only those with high commercial, survivable expectations used;

Inclusiveness. The technology should be capable of supporting the full range of consular functions, ranging from case management to the provision of travel advice to the registration of citizens;

Centralized Data. All data would be stored centrally and would be available to users in real time and online. (There were suggestions for data replications at overseas locations, but this was rejected on the basis of unnecessary complication without any resulting benefit);

Performance. The system response time was to be less than five seconds. This was considered one of the most important requirements as it, more than any other, provided user confidence. (This was not achieved initially due to bandwidth limitations at some locations overseas. However, it has remained a system requirement and today has been fully met.);

Data Convertibility. The system had to be capable of converting and storing information received in other formats (imagery, facsimile, scanning) and making it available system-wide

Data Conversion. Initially it was believed that data already available in an electronic format could be converted into the new system. However, the cost of doing so and the unreliability of the resulting product led to the decision not to pursue this objective. Rather old electronic data (mainly registration records) were left outside the new system and were only included as and when there was an operational requirement to do so. It was found that within a short period of time the old data were overlaid with current data in the new format;

Data Entry. Detailed rules were established in order to standardize data entry and where appropriate detailed "picklists" were included. These picklists became an essential element to ensure data comparability and analysis across time and place;

Report Generation. A key objective of the system was to provide users and program managers at the mission and headquarter levels with extensive reports detailing all aspects of work. These reports, identified as "operational" (Who were the Canadians arrested in the United States and Where were they?) and "managerial" (How many prisoner cases were there worldwide and in what countries?) quickly became a valuable and essential feature of the new system in order to analyze workloads and resource requirements;

Conclusions. The resulting systems (COSMOS and iCOSMOS [the Internet version]) have now been in use for over ten years. The total cost during that period for all aspects of development, operations and hardware was less than $15-million Canadian. The ongoing costs remain modest when compared to other systems and the derived benefits. The success of the system based on performance has been outstanding. Central to this achievement has been the willingness, over time, of employee utilization and support. The systems are now fully accepted as part of the Canadian consular-management culture. The current challenge is to ensure that the system does not degrade through inattention and remains current with new technological advances.

Improvements. Looking back over the past ten years it is difficult to envisage how Canada would have coped with its consular responsibilities without the support provided by technology. The improvements have been significant. These are:

Standards of Service. These have improved both quantitatively and qualitatively. More Canadians now receive consular services, and surveys demonstrate that there is a high level of satisfaction;

Work Satisfaction. A by-product of the use of technology has been a significant improvement in employee morale and job satisfaction.

Management Control. The use of technology for operational work provides managers with enormous amounts of data that are used to understand work patterns, work levels and resource requirements. In today's world these are essential requirements for consular managers to maintain support for their activities

WorldReach Software, Ottawa

Review

January 2006

Confessions of an Innocent Man: Torture and Survival in a Saudi Prison, by William Sampson. McClelland & Stewart Ltd, 2005

THIS IS A STORY OF TORTURE. AND IT IS NOT TORTURE 'LITE' – AS ONE of the contemporary faddish terms would have it in attempting to provide moral and political justification for such acts. It is not a book for the squeamish or for those who like their torture in the detached language of the reports of human-rights organizations.

The publication of the book rounds out a year in which Canadians have been inundated with first- and second-hand accounts of torture in the prisons of Syria and Iran. The accounts concerning Maher Arar, Ahmad Abou-El Maati, Abdullah Almalki and Zahra Kazami preoccupied and troubled Canadians and their government, raising large issues regarding the relationship of the state to its citizens and the state's protective responsibilities beyond its borders. Never before have Canadians seen, in such abundance, the ugly details that hide behind the word torture and its close companions abuse and intimidation. Heretofore, torture was something that happened to others – Canadians were somehow exempt from such inhuman behaviour.

Mr Sampson's well-written work provides an almost day-by-day account of the 965 days (the book reports 963 days) between December 17, 2000 to August 8, 2003 he spent in a Saudi prison. The book is remarkable in its recall of the detail associated with each blow – and there were many – the techniques of torture and other numerous degrading (rape) acts. Mr Sampson displays clinical detachment as he recreates the effect of the brutality on him and the emergence of his unique means of coping with his torturers and his expectation eventually he would be executed.

Mr Sampson was like many of the millions who flock to Saudi Arabia for the "easy" money. He had been "unemployed after a failed business venture" and the work in Saudi Arabia "sounded interesting . . . was reasonable well paid, with accommodation, car, holiday allowances, and comprehensive medical coverage." Shortly after arriving he was "eating pizza and drinking home-brewed beer" – and learning that there was a "ban on alcohol" which he was "breaking as this information was imparted" to him.

He reports that the Saudi authorities "had been turning a blind eye to a lot of the activities of the western expatriate community" and an "active social scene had developed." Mr Sampson was "amused" to encounter "more alcoholics in Saudi Arabia, among both the local population and the expatriates, than anywhere else" he had lived. It was a "fact of life" and, on more than one occasion, he found himself "in an elevator surrounded by a miasma of alcohol." He notes that he became a "regular" at the Coffee Pot bar and was "invited" to the other bars on the circuit.

* * *

Expatriates are a unique lot, and nowhere more so than those in Saudi Arabia. According to the Saudi government (2004) there were 8.8 million foreign workers in Saudi Arabia, about a third of the population and probably making up more than a half of the workforce. Most are from south and Southeast Asia (approximately 3 million are from Bangladesh, India, Pakistan, Indonesia and Sri Lanka) but there are significant numbers from the United States and the United Kingdom. It is estimated there are six- or seven-thousand Canadians, many working in the health services sector.

Saudi Arabia, as the Millennium approached, was a troubled place. And, while expatriates continued to enjoy the good life, as Mr

Sampson notes, there were troubling signs that while the presence of expatriates was tolerated "(at least on the surface) by the educated and affluent of Saudi society, it was actively resented in other quarters." The tightly controlled local media said little about the increasing numbers of Saudis who were dissatisfied with their lot – and were looking for answers even beyond their own radical school of Islam. Whabbism in its austerity describes both the religion and the land.

By the time Mr Sampson arrived in Riyadh in mid-1998, Osama bin Laden had been forced out of his refuge in the Sudan and was making common cause with the Taliban in Afghanistan. There is some information that Mr bin Laden sought to return to Saudi Arabia during this period, even though he had been stripped of his Saudi citizenship in 1994. The Saudi leadership, especially those at the very top, realized that his distance from Mecca was their best defence against his influence on many of their subjects. Bin Laden's involvement in the bombings of the American embassies in Dar-es-Salaam and Nairobi, along with other nefarious deeds, brought home to the leadership that their heads could be the first to burn should they play with Osama bin Laden's fire.

Up to this point there had been only a few violent manifestations of anti-American or anti-Western feelings in Saudi Arabia. In 1995 (November 13, car bombing) and 1996 (June 25), two American military installations were bombed killing 24 Americans. In the 1996 truck bombing of the Khobar Towers, 19 Americans military personnel were killed and hundreds were wounded. At the time, the American State Department attributed the bombings to the Saudi wing of Hezbollah, an Iranian-Syrian-supported group in southern Lebanon.

The November 17 and 22, 2000 bombings of vehicles carrying British expatriates were small- scale and amateurish in comparison to the earlier bombings like those in 2003 and 2004. The first bomb killed Christopher Rodway and seriously wounded his wife Jean. The second injured four Britons – all friends of Mr Sampson. There is no confirmed information on the type of bombs (Saudi CSI standards have not reached even those used on television), but it would appear they were either timed or remotely-controlled devices.

* * *

By this time, Mr Sampson had come to the attention of the Saudi authorities. The first instance was with police raids in April on two bars run by another expatriate, Gary O'Nions. Mr O'Nions and several others were detained. Sandy Mitchell, a close friend of Mr Sampson, informed him of the detentions. Mr Mitchell "had long acted as an unofficial prison visitor helping expats who fell afoul of the law" and on a number of occasions he "had managed to affect [sic] the release of those arrested." Mr Sampson notes that Mr Mitchell had called him because he had "recently begun to help him in these matters."

Probably this would have been of little consequence – except that later Mr Sampson in cooperation with Sandy Mitchell and others smuggled Mr O'Nions to Dammam in the Eastern Province of Saudi Arabia, from where he was smuggled across the border to Dubai. Mr O'Nions was arrested before he was able to leave Dubai and subsequently returned to Saudi Arabia, where no doubt his method of leaving Saudi Arabia was soon known to the authorities In the meantime in early October 2000, Mr Sampson and several friends were arrested by the Saudi authorities on liquor-related charges. After three days, Mr Sampson was released, following intervention by the Canadian embassy and others.

The November explosions first lead to the detention, on December 10, of Raf Schyvens, a Belgian national and close friend of Mr Sampson and Sandy Mitchell. Mr Schyvens was in a following vehicle at the time of the November 22 bombing and provided medical attention to the wounded. He was questioned by the Saudi authorities on two occasions prior to his arrest on December 10 – at which time he disappeared from view. A week later, on December

17, 2000, Mr Sampson and Mr Mitchell were detained and began their 965-days experience of the "theory and practice of hell." Oddly, Mr Schyvens, following his release on August 7, 2003 and return to Belgium stated that he had not been tortured by the Saudi authorities.

Mr Sampson has no doubts as to who was responsible for the explosions. Throughout his account he offers rebuttal information to disprove the Saudi accusations against him and Mr Mitchell. It is his view that the Saudi authorities themselves planned and carried out the November bombings. This view is augmented by what Mr Sampson regards as occasional unusual comments and actions by his Saudi tormentors.

Others are not so sure. There have been suggestions that these explosions were the work of Saudi extremists intent on making life miserable and uncertain for the expatriate community; others have suggested dissidents from the Eastern Province supported by Iran were responsible – hoping to create problems for the Saudi authorities. Still others have suggested that the bombings were carried out by dissident members of Saudi police or security organizations, or that the bombings were the work of the British security organization MI6 in collaboration with the Israeli security organization MOSSAD. (See http://cryptome.org/mi6-bombings.htm). [Interestingly, Mr Sampson writes that the Saudis during his torture and interrogation had him confess to being a British agent in Saudi Arabia].

* * *

There were bombings similar to those of November after the detention of Mr Sampson and his friends, and in these instances the Saudi authorities also tried to place the blame on expatriates. In the March 2001 bombing [again either a timed or remote-controlled device] near a downtown bookstore, another Canadian was detained along with a Briton and an American. They were in the neighbourhood at the time of the explosion. In these cases, relentless pressure by the Canadian and British governments, which did not differ markedly from the pressure in support of Mr Sampson and others, saw the men released without being charged after some 60 or so days. These men had been tortured in much the same manner as Mr Sampson. It was through the cooperation of one of them that a detailed account of the torture was assembled and presented to the Saudi Crown Prince in early September 2001 by a special envoy of the Canadian Prime Minister in the hope that it would be of help to Mr Sampson.

Mr Sampson is highly critical of the government of Canada and its officials. He was so during his detention – and his criticisms have continued since his release. It is understandable that 965 days in intolerable conditions would lead to questions of the government's commitment and the quality of its assistance. However, at the same time, there seems to be a deeper resentment to Mr Sampson's antipathy toward the Canadian government and its officials. Prior to his work in Saudi Arabia, he spent most of the previous twenty years in the United Kingdom, where he also has citizenship as a result of his father's birth there. In prison he tried to renounce his Canadian citizenship, but was thwarted by the Saudis who insisted that since he arrived in their country using a Canadian passport he could only leave using one. He maintains that Canadian officials "told me to my face on more than one occasion that I was guilty."

Indicative of Mr Sampson's state of mind toward Canada are his actions on the day he was to be released. Sandy Mitchell met with Mr Sampson and told him:

> *"The Embassy says you are to have a shower and get dressed".*
>
> *"Which embassy?" I asked.*
>
> *The British Embassy was his reply.*
>
> *"That is an order I can accept".*

Nelson would be proud.

Earlier in the book Mr Sampson relates his efforts to convey private thoughts to his father using references to P. G. Wodehouse, James Joyce and Rudyard Kipling's poem "If". Mr Sampson goes on to report that officials in Ottawa had to ask his father for the "import" of Kipling's poem. He writes his father cast "aspersions on their education" and providing "a none too brief sarcastic and pointed synopsis of the works of Rudyard Kipling." Like so much in Mr Sampson's incomplete understanding of the actions of Canadian officials on his behalf, he got this episode wrong – as he did on several other matters.

Mr Sampson goes on to write

At that time, I would accept such a request [to leave the prison] from British officials, but not from the Canadians, given their behaviour and crass stupidity. If I knew then what I know now of the British government's actions in our case, I would not have acceded to their request either.

* * *

After Mr Sampson's release, a detailed account of the actions of Canadian officials was prepared and made public. Jeffrey Simpson writing in The *Globe and Mail* on December 2, 2003 reported that Mr Sampson alleged that the Canadian government did not work hard enough for his release, accepted his guilt, and was leery of not impairing Canada's relationship with Saudi Arabia. Mr Simpson goes on to say that these allegations were accepted at face value by the Canadian media. However, in Mr Simpson's view, there is another side to the story. He wrote:

A letter drafted in Foreign Affairs and leaked to the Globe and Mail, but intended for Mr Sampson, outlined an impressive series of attempts by the government to help Mr Sampson. He refused many of the attempts for reasons he knows best, the most plausible being that he had convinced himself that the Canadian government was working against his release...

The record collected by Foreign Affairs shows that Prime Minister Jean Chrétien sent two special envoys to Saudi Arabia to press the Sampson case. In addition, four other senior government officials raised the Sampson cause with the Saudis. The Canadian ambassador in Riyadh repeatedly intervened on the file. Canadian officials met Mr Sampson 25 times in prison; he refused to see them on 24 other occasions. A Canadian-appointed doctor examined Mr Sampson once; he refused to see Canadian-appointed doctors on two other occasions. Three times, the government paid for a Canadian psychiatrist to visit Mr Sampson. The government offered to find him a Saudi lawyer. Mr Sampson alleges government officials accepted his guilt. They deny it.

The record compiled by Foreign Affairs undoubtedly puts the government in the best possible light. But even a sceptic must concede that the record amounts to a defensible, bordering on conclusive, case that the Canadian government did a lot to assist Mr Sampson. He doesn't think the government did enough, and obviously became so convinced while in prison.

Mr Simpson goes on to write that even Mr Sampson's assertion that the British were more aggressive in defending the interests of their incarcerated nationals "rings hollow." In his view the record demonstrates that "even if the British were more aggressive, a matter of judgment, they were not more successful in securing the earlier release of their nationals. He concludes that Mr Sampson had a "horrifying experience," but it is not clear from his allegations or from the government's "detailed defence" what "else could reasonably have been done to secure an earlier pardon."

Mr Sampson, hopefully, will continue to learn and arrive at a more complete understanding of the work done for his release. He may also come to understand that not all of the work that was done by his more-ardent supporters aided in that effort.

* * *

Mr Sampson throughout his account is critical of various governments (Canadian, British, Belgium and the United States) in their relations with the government of Saudi Arabia. "It would appear that appeasement of the Al Sauds is one of the highest political priorities in Canada, as well as in Britain and Belgium" and "[T]here was no government any more supportive of the Al Saud regime than the British government" and "[N]o longer would it be just my word against that of the lying bastards of the Saudi Arabian government and their counterparts in the governments of Britain, Canada, and Belgium."

All governments make Faustian compromises as they deal with the complex international environment. These compromises are apparent in balancing the supply-demand equation for petroleum. Saudi Arabia has been one of those compromises for several decades, but Mr Sampson is wrong to suggest that it is absolute or permanent. A new, unopened Saudi embassy building in Ottawa stands in stark testimony to the impact Mr Sampson's situation had on Canada's relations with Saudi Arabia.

Nor should it be said that such Faustian compromises are solely the sphere of governments. Mr Sampson and millions like him who go to Saudi Arabia and sell their expert services are the foot soldiers – ensuring the survival of the Saudi regime. Canadians, as much as any, are quite supportive of such compromises. The support of many Canadians for the relationship with the regime of President Fidel Castro based on a starry-eyed understanding of his social welfare policies (perhaps his Medicare system works better than ours) and his tweaking of the Americans' noses would make Faust blush.

Throughout his narrative, Mr Sampson details his large and small rebellions against his torturers and these give the book its great and lasting value. It is a tale of endurance, survival and personal heroism. His verbal and physical attacks on his captors, his "dirt" and hunger strikes, his lashing out against those who sought to help, and his no concessions to the very end (he refused to be moved into the company of other prisoners) places his book well above what is normally associated with the 'Black Hole of Calcutta' genre.

In some ways *Confessions of an Innocent Man* is reminiscent of the experiences of Commander James Stockdale who spent some 2714 days as a prisoner at the Hanoi Hilton during the Vietnam War. Jonathan Mahler writing in the *New York Times Magazine* on January 1, 2006 (to commemorate Cmdr. Stockdale's passing in 2005) had the following to say:

> **Stockdale gradually came to see heroism not as a matter of consistent good judgment but as a single act, or series of acts, performed in a particular context. And he came to see heroes not as people who had carried out their duty with distinction but as individuals who had, like himself, done something no reasonable person would ever have felt justified asking them to do.**

Stockdale called his actions "the rising of the few" and, ironically, his treatment at the hands of the American political system [he was Ross Perot's running mate in the 1992 presidential election] was more devastating than his seven-and-a-half years in a Vietnamese prison. For those amongst us who believe the money is easy in places like Saudi Arabia, they should read Mr Sampson's accounting.

Bout de papier, Vol. 22. No. 1.

They Do More Harm than Good
March 25, 2006

GOOD INTENTIONS, AS THE ADAGE GOES, PAVE THE ROAD TO BAD DEStinations. In today`s world, all too frequently good intentions are accepted – without regard for ultimate destinations and their costs.

Unfortunately, for Christian Peacemakers Teams, while the intentions of their work are laudable, the costs, as recent events in Iraq demonstrate, can be high. Their actions must be judged by Canadians on the basis of the dangers they bring to others when they get into difficulty.

Equally, the leadership of the CPT organization needs to use a larger calculus when making decisions about the placement of its teams. They must accept the limitation that their model of peacemaking does not fit all situations at all times.

We all joined the rejoicing that attended the rescue of three (James Loney, Harmeet Sooden, and Norman Kember) of the original four kidnapped team members in Iraq – although many details of what was involved are unavailable. Equally, we join them in the sadness that remains over the brutal killing of the fourth member, American Tom Fox, a short time ago.

Christian Peacemaker Teams have been active for less than 20 years. They developed out of a "consciousness" by Mennonites, Mormons and other religious groups that "by using the creative energy of non-violence together with organized groups, ordinary people could stand in front of guns and encourage less violent ways for change to happen. People were learning that courageous faith could overcome cynicism," according to the group`s website. www.cpt.org.

There have been Peacemaker Teams in Gaza, Haiti, Bosnia, Chechnya and Mexico. However, most of their operations, according to the CPT website, have been in the more familiar atmospheres of the District of Colombia, Virginia, South Dakota, New Brunswick, Puerto Rico, Nova Scotia, New York and Ontario.

The members of such teams, as interviews with their families and friends over the past few months have shown, are honourable, idealistic and dedicated. They see their work as supporting local efforts for non-violent peacemaking, getting in the way of injustice by being public witnesses to human-rights violations and being advocates for Canadian policy. These are all important roles in nasty and dangerous parts of the world.

It is one thing for people to volunteer their time and money to support such laudable efforts. It is something quite different for leaders of the organization to deliberately and continuously put them in harm's way in places like Iraq.

Since early 2004, more than 240 foreign civilians have been kidnapped and more than 40 killed – some with their heads rolling as the cameras rolled. On the order of more than two to one, most have been from non-coalition countries.

The kidnapping in October 2004 and subsequent killing of Margaret Hassan, the director of CARE International, demonstrated to most that even those with the best will in the world were as much targets as those with guns.

Why, in the face of such evidence, CPT leaders continued to put their volunteers in harm's way is something they need to explain. Daniel and his short time with lions is not a sufficient explanation. The killing of Ms Hassan and the bombing of the UN compound should have been sufficient warning to CPT leaders that they were dealing with something other than Daniel's experience when they placed volunteers in the Iraqi den.

Perhaps they were hoping American and coalition forces would provide their volunteers with protection, even though the presence of such forces was at the heart of the CPT rationale for being in Iraq.

The actions of the leaders since the kidnapping – organizing occasional candlelight ceremonies, public statements, along with presentations on their good intentions by others – demonstrate either the limits of their understanding of Iraq past and present or their overweening confidence in their own wisdom.

Early statements have provided scant details about the rescue of the two Canadians and one Briton. However, it is clear that it was a substantial military operation, spearheaded by the British SAS and involving civilians and military personnel from a number of countries – including Canada. An American statement indicated that someone they had detained on March 23 provided information about the location of the hostages.

A question that members of the CPT leadership may wish to ask themselves is the manner in which such information was extracted so quickly. One assumes the detainees were not read their rights.

The CPT has been quick to condemn the treatment of detainees in Iraq and elsewhere. By putting their own people in harm's way, the CPT leaders created conditions in which the injustices they are contesting are most likely to be perpetuated on their behalf. And it should be assumed that Iraqis will be part of the "collateral damage" successful operations entail.

Some Canadians may remember the Canadian miner who traded places with his kidnapped employee in Colombia in late 1998. The miner was hailed as a hero on his return to Canada and there was little attempt to detail the cost of his actions to others, especially the Colombians who arranged his release. Three Canadian reporters subsequently interviewed those involved. The story they reported in the *National Post* in February 1999 suggested that "good intentions" – if that was the motivation for the miner's actions – did incur serious costs.

At the request of the government of Canada, several Colombians, including members of the clergy, were involved in the delicate negotiations that led to the release of the kidnapped employee, as well as the miner. In doing so they put their own lives in serious jeopardy of being kidnapped or even worse.

The priest who was involved is quoted in the *National Post* article as saying: "From you, as Canadians, I ask the favour that Norbert Reinhart never come here again."

As with the CPT in Iraq, good intentions can lead to hell.

The Citizen

Canadians in Foreign Places
April 1, 2006

IT MUST BE SPRING. AND, AS LINDA DIEBEL IN HER MARCH 11 DIATRIBE (*Toronto Star*) would have it, Canadians are in deep trouble – if they get into difficulties abroad. Such articles are part of the rites of Canadian spring. They are about as accurate and explanatory as the weather forecasts associated with somnambulant rodents in early February.

Ms Diebel would have us believe that services provided by the government of Canada to its citizens abroad are inferior to those offered by the government of the United States. Her lack of knowledge is most apparent when she breathlessly reveals the United States has a special "Washington-based agency" within the State Department, named the Office of American Citizen Services and Crisis Management, and by implication suggests that Ottawa would do well to do the same.

Canadians should have expected something better from a reporter for the *Toronto Star*. It was almost four years to the day that the equivalent Canadian office, the Bureau of Consular Affairs in the Department of Foreign Affairs, reached into the wilds of Afghanistan and rescued a *Toronto Star* reporter who had been critically wounded in a grenade attack as she was driving south of Kabul.

Kathleen Kenna, her husband Hadi Dadshian and photographer Bernard Weil, all working for the *Star*, and their Afghan driver were travelling on the main road to Gardez when two attackers threw a grenade into the car – wounding her severely. Within hours an unconscious Ms Kenna, accompanied by her husband, was in a military hospital in Landsthul, Germany, from where ten days later she was medically evacuated to Vancouver for further treatment.

Ms Diebel's lack of knowledge is further demonstrated by her reporting of the "strict diplomatic protocol" the Americans use in such matters and, again by implication, suggests Ottawa is deficient in this area. She might wish to visit the Consular Affairs website where similar standards are displayed for the public and, hopefully, journalists to read. [See http://www.voyage.gc.ca/main/about/service_standards-en.asp].

There is also considerable confidence expressed by Ms Diebel in having national police forces involved in the delivery of such services to citizens abroad. There is reference to the murders of Nancy and Domenic Ianiero in Playa del Carmen earlier this year, the brutal slaying of Rebecca Middleton in Bermuda in 1996 and the involvement of the FBI in the investigation of the disappearance – and most likely murder – of American citizen Natalee Holloway in Aruba at the end of May last year.

* * *

There is, again by implication, the suggestion that involvement by national police forces would mean better investigations or speedier conclusions. However, in passing, Ms Diebel notes Ms Holloway is still missing, even though "the FBI took a lead in the investigation." A more accurate comment concerning who is in charge in such situations was the story in *USA Today* on March 29, 2006 which began: "*Netherlands police and Aruban authorities* scoured sand dunes and a beach in the search for missing Alabama teenager Natalee Holloway in this Dutch Caribbean island, an official said."

The hard reality is that local authorities, whether they be Mexican, Aruban or Bermudan, are in charge of and responsible for such investigations. Foreign experts and especially foreign police officers have no authority or right under international law to involve themselves in such matters – other than at the invitation of those local officials. Bilateral agreements between national police forces do not change that reality.

For the most part local officials are open to and accepting of outside assistance, but it is only on their terms. To suggest otherwise, as Ms Diebel does, is to mislead your readers and give Canadians false hope regarding how the world works in this area. Canadians in a foreign country can only expect the quality of care and the likelihood of success that are characteristic of such local authorities. That is not changed by the presence of foreign police officers.

An inept police force or an inefficient judicial system is not going to be improved by the arrival of foreign forensic experts or police officials. In judging such matters, Canadians would do well to remember that the files of the Association in Defence of the Wrongly Convicted (AIDWC) in Toronto are full of cases characterized by inept investigations by Canadian police, woefully inadequate prosecutions and attorneys who are asleep in defending their clients.

Canada's Consular Affairs office has sent Canadian forensic and police officials abroad to assist in investigations of crimes involving Canadians. Of particular note was the work of Dr James Young, the former chief coroner for Ontario, who travelled to the United States, Indonesia, Thailand, China, and Taiwan to assist Canadians in difficulty. He also reviewed several other cases in which Canadians were victims.

As well, the Consular Affairs office has sent RCMP and other Canadian police officers to places such as Belize, Trinidad, Vietnam, Equator, Gabon, Mexico, and the United States in support of efforts to assist Canadians. In all situations, the work of the Canadian police was in cooperation with local officials with whom conclusions were shared. However, their involvement did not materially affect the work of local officials or the outcome of the cases. In some cases their involvement did provide comfort to family and friends in Canada, but in others their work was equally criticized.

Ms Diebel refers to several cases in her story – all with the intent of demonstrating that Canadian officials were negligent or less than assiduous in pursuing the interests of Canadians in difficulty overseas. In doing so she accepts the judgement of family members as being the final authority on such matters without any suggestion that such judgements should be tempered with an understanding of the frustration and bafflement relatives undergo when dealing with traumatic and tragic events.

Her arguments are not enhanced by the self-serving comments of the former parliamentary secretary for Canadians abroad, Dan McTeague. Family and friends have established web sites where up-to-date information can be obtained – and readers are encouraged to do so rather than depending solely on what Ms Diebel has to say.

Frustration and bafflement are often characteristic of situations where the tragedy is within Canada. They are accentuated and deepened when the tragedy occurs in foreign countries with the attendant political, cultural, linguistic and criminal-justice-system differences. It is fair for the victims and their families to question the work of Canadian and foreign officials in such situations. However, it is also fair for Canadians to expect from journalists some measure of balance when they report on such matters.

Canadians will recall a few years ago when an American teenager was convicted in Singapore of public mischief. He, along with some friends, had scraped several cars with a metal object. As part of the sentence, the teenager was subjected to several lashes – which are permitted under Singaporean law. Americans along with others were justifiably outraged and pressure was applied to have the Singaporeans back down. The American President intervened with the Prime Minister of Singapore and the Singaporeans, in awe of this "powerful weapon not available to Canadians" as Ms Diebel wrote, reduced the sentence by *one lash*. As we have come to realize, "awe" even when it is accompanied with "shock" can be a limp weapon.

Not published by the Toronto Star

Border Follies
April 14, 2006

THERE WAS A TIME WHEN THE QUAINT IDEA OF "FACILITATION" WAS part of international travel. Nineteenth-century rules were to be eliminated and travel for Paul and Debbie would be seamless as they wandered the world. Even the International Civil Aviation Organization (ICAO), the godfather of international air travel, had a "Facilitation Committee." In those post-war days, there was heady talk of the disappearance of visas, and the real dreamers thought of universal citizenship for travellers.

How times have changed. Hijackings, shoe bombs, airplanes as weapon of mass destruction, suitcase bombs and box cutters have changed forever the wonderful world of travel. Today, a visit to your psychiatrist before embarking on an international trip is advisable. Even though airports and airplanes are better and more efficient, ubiquitous steely-eyed and tight-assed security officers turn the dream of travel into a series of hurdles that would give Perdita Felicien difficulty.

Not so long ago, Canadian Tire credit cards were enough to get you across the Peace Bridge. Today there is talk of digitized passports, smart cards, eyeball scans and Orwellian suggestions of a chip behind your left ear as preconditions for entry into the United States. And may the good Lord help you if you are a Canadian born in Syria or Iraq or some other country where Islam sways. Make sure you know the direction of east before you leave home.

Despite this damage to the dreams of travel, the security barriers that separate you and your luggage from an aircraft have been effective. Today air travel is the safest it has been since the heady days of the late '60s and '70s when to board an aircraft provided an opportunity to see Algiers or Havana. Equally, the likelihood of a bomb going off in the cargo hold is lower than at any time since Air India tragically disappeared from the radar scopes over the North Atlantic in June 1985. Global security measures have succeeded magnificently and, despite the aberration of 9/11, air travel today is less dangerous than driving The Queensway in Ottawa.

This is hard to understand when we are assaulted daily with news of mass bombings and killings in all corners of the world. It is not readily clear except to the discerning that these attacks and deaths have little to do with international travel. London, Madrid, Bali, Jakarta, Beslam, Manila, Moscow, Amsterdam, Casablanca, and Istanbul were not products of lax airport, airline or border security.

Rather these were "local" events carried out by citizens or residents of the affected country; a few days ago the British confirmed that last year's London bombings had nothing to do with al Qaeda. If this is the new paradigm for terror, it has little to do with the dramatic terrorism events of the previous forty years. Then, the aircraft was the target of opportunity for megalomaniacs and martyrs with small and large axes to grind. While some of these recent acts may be the product of a common, religion-based ideology promoted by Osama bin Laden – and the jury is still out on that – ideologies do not travel by aircraft, boat or train.

It is, therefore, extremely difficult to understand the decision of the United States to make enormous changes in the travel documentation required for intra-North-American travel. Such travel has nothing to do with North-American terrorism. All 19 hijackers on September 11 legitimately entered the United States several months earlier from overseas points. There was no apparent problem with their travel documents – but there were large problems in the ability of American officials to put together disparate pieces of available information that might have prevented the tragedy. In only one instance were they able to do so. Subsequent reviews have all concluded they should have done better.

It is normal for governments to lock doors after large events. Not surprisingly, wrong doors get locked and, more often than not, the addition of a second or third lock adds to the illusion that real action is being taken. Terrorists and their ideological directors do repeat themselves, but it is equally possible we will expend energy and resources on old doors and locks – while there is something new coming at us down the road.

The United States Western Hemisphere Travel Initiative (WHTI), its official name, has little to do with initiating travel. And it has very little to do with the prevention of terrorism. It does have much to do with changing decades-old, North-American-travel patterns. In so doing, the Initiative reflects the rigidities and emptiness of the American political system and its inability to rationally deal with immigration and terrorism issues. In that, Canadian performance is equally poor; one recent suggestion receiving serious attention would require immigrants to offer an oath to Canadian "values."

In the United States, the immigration issue has nothing to do with immigration from Chad or Iran or Vietnam or Poland. It is all about immigration or more accurately migration from Mexico. Less than two-hundred years ago, most of Texas, California and the flat pieces in between were part of Mexico. The wars of 1835-36 (remember the Alamo) and 1846-48 changed all that.

It is the view of one commentator that these areas remain "borderlands" and in American policy terms are similar to Alsace/Lorraine and Sudetenland which loomed so tragically in the European and world wars of the last century. In this view, contiguity between people and their previous country establishes a different dynamic for policy makers than for immigrants from Southeast Asia. And the large numbers make it different than immigrants arriving from Canada.

There is nothing as strong as an illusory answer to an illusory problem. Changing the travel documents for Canadians, Mexicans and Americans as they travel between the three countries of North America will not control migration from Mexico into the United

States. Like the drug trade, demand is a stronger force than interdiction. And, to repeat, it will do absolutely nothing to improve security against the scourges of international terrorism – no matter how it evolves.

The saddest part of this current episode in Canadian-American relations is that Prime Minister Harper got it right when he said, after his recent meeting with President Bush, "Washington won't budge on the border" and "I'm not sure Canadians are fully aware these requirements are coming." Canadians will adapt, and the run on the Canadian passport office will be enormous. However, for Americans, many of those planned and unplanned trips to Canada will become folklore. And it is so unnecessary.

Royal Prerogative and Consular Services
May 1, 2006

IN REVIEWING DOCUMENTS RELATING TO THE SEVERAL STATEMENTS of claim filed against the Department of Foreign Affairs, the issue of the status of consular services under Canadian law has been noted. The Manual of Consular Instructions states the following:

> *Extent of Protection.* ***Most consular services are provided as a matter of discretion by virtue of the royal prerogative; except as provided by statute; no one is entitled to claim such services as a matter of legal right.*** *Strictly speaking, protection and assistance can therefore be withheld by the Secretary of State for External Affairs at his or her discretion (although this in fact is rarely done). The nature and extent of protection and assistance is governed by these instructions and by the judgment of consular officers exercised in the particular circumstances of each case.*[1]

2. The reference to the "Secretary of State for External Affairs" suggests this section of the Manual is an old one, as the name was changed possibly in 1982 to Minister of Foreign Affairs, at the time the Trade Commissioners Service and the Immigration Foreign Branch were integrated into External Affairs and the name changed to Foreign Affairs. The official change may have occurred

---

1 **Manual of Consular Instructions, Volume 1**, 1993 Edition. EAIT 11(1). "Chapter 2, *Protection and Assistance*, Section 2.0 Introduction" page 2-1.

in 1985when the Department of Foreign Affairs and International Trade Act (DFAITA)became law.[2]

3. Uncertainty with respect to the position detailed in the Manual was created as a result of the recent decision of the Federal Court of Canada. In a decision released on August 18, 2004 in the case of Omar Ahmed Khadr versus the Minister of Foreign Affairs, Justice K. von Finckenstein said the following [the decision is quoted extensively since it touched on a number of germane issues] in response to a motion by the government of Canada to strike Mr Khadr's application for failure to disclose a cause of action:

> [22] Based upon the foregoing, there is a persuasive case that both the DFAITA [Department of Foreign Affairs and International Trade Act] and the Guide [A Guide for Canadians Imprisoned Abroad] create a legitimate and reasonable expectation that a Canadian citizen detained abroad will receive many of the services which Omar Khadr has requested. Indeed, Canadians abroad would be surprised, if not shocked, to learn that the provision of consular services in an individual case is left to the complete and unreviewable discretion of the Minister.
>
> [23] With regards to the foregoing, I note that the expectation in this case is arguably composed of both procedural and substantive elements. This type of expectation has been subject to significant judicial commentary in recent years. The Respondent submitted that prior jurisprudence has held that the doctrine of legitimate expectation can only compel procedural rather than substantive outcomes. However, it is notable that the majority of the Supreme Court was silent on whether there may be an expectation to certain substantive outcomes in Mount Sinai Hospital Center v. Quebec (Minister of Health and Social Services), [2001] 2 S.C.R. 281. Further, Binnie J. writing

---

[2] Department of Foreign Affairs and International Trade Act. R.S.C. 1985. c. E22. DFAITA.

in dissent in the Mount Sinai case noted that the procedural/ substantive distinction had been removed in England, Australia and other jurisdictions. At para. 35 he concluded:

In affirming that the doctrine of legitimate expectations is limited to procedural relief, it must be acknowledged that in some cases it is difficult to distinguish the procedural from the substantive. In Bendahmane v. Canada, supra, for example, a majority of the Federal Court of Appeal considered the applicant's claim to the benefit of a refugee backlog reduction program to be procedural (p.33) whereas the dissenting judge considered the claimed relief to be substantive (p.25). A similarly close call was made in Canada (Attorney General) v. Canada (Commission f the Inquiry on the Blood System), [1996] 3 F.C. 259 (T.D.). An undue focus on formal classification and categorization of powers at the expense of broad principles flexibly applied may do a disservice here. (Underlining added)

[24] The situation in this case is not unlike the UK case of Abbasi v. Secretary of State for Foreign and Commonwealth Affairs, [2002]_E.W.J. No. 4947 (C.A.), in which the Court of Appeal for England and Wales found that a legitimate expectation to some form of consular service had been created as a result of previous actions and statements by the British government. The logic of that case would appear to equally apply to the situation at hand.

[25] Accordingly, I am of the view that a persuasive case can be made that a legitimate expectation to consular services has been created through the DFAITA, the Guide and on the basis of the jurisprudence cited.

International Law

[26] Having found that a persuasive case for a legitimate expectation can be built on the basis of the Guide, I do not need to pursue the Applicants' other arguments related to section 10 of the DFAITA. Nonetheless, I note that the Applicants have made out an arguable case that section 10 should be interpreted with regard to the Vienna Convention on Consular Relations, U.N.T.S. Nos. 8638-8640, vol. 596, pp. 262-512 (VCCR), to which Canada is a signatory. As recently found by McLaughlin C.J. in in Canadian Foundation for Children, Youth and the Law v. Canada (Attorney General), [2004] 1 S.C.R. 76 at para. 31:

Within this limited area of application, further precision on what is reasonable under the circumstances may be derived from international treaty obligations. Statutes should be construed to comply with Canada's international obligations: Ordon [page101] Estate v. Grail, 1. [1998] 3 S.C.R. 437, at para. 137¼. (Underlining added).

[27] Specifically, the International Court of Justice's decision in LaGrand (Germany v. United States of America), [2001]_ I.C.J. 3 (27 June 2001) states that the VCCR does create individual rights to the services requested by the Applicants in this case. The Applicants should also have the opportunity to present evidence that an international custom has also evolved with regards to the provision of certain consular services.

CONCLUSION

[29] Given my findings with regards to reasonable and legitimate expectations, I find that the application displays a possible cause of action that the decision of the Minister not to provide the appropriate services (required under the circumstances) set out in the Guide may constitute a breach of his duties under

section 10 of the DFAITA. I also find that the Minister's duties under section 10 should be interpreted with regard to the VCCR, international jurisprudence and custom. As a result, I am not prepared to strike this application for failure to disclose a cause of action.[3]

4. As this citation demonstrates there are unresolved issues of law in Canada with respect to the government's "obligation" to provide consular protection and services to its citizens. However, at the heart of the Finckenstein decision were his comments that

> Indeed, Canadians abroad would be surprised, if not shocked, to learn that the provision of consular services in an individual case is left to the complete and unreviewable discretion of the Minister.

5. Justice von Finckenstein comment reflects a general level of expectation by the public to consular services. Successive Canadian governments have established through statements, documents and actions that there is an obligation to provide consular protection and services and increasingly there is support for the idea that in doing so a "right" has been or is being established. The Canadian courts, as they did in England and Wales, appear to be prepared to accept this when governments seek to assert otherwise.

6. A second element in the Finckenstein decision that should be noted was his reference to the International Court of Justice decision in the Lagrand case. The ICJ

> stated that the VCCR does create individual rights to the services requested by the Applicants in this case. The Applicants should also have the opportunity to present evidence that an

---

3 Khadr v. Canada (Minister of Foreign Affairs), Federal Court of Canada, Docket T-686-04, Citation 2004 FC 1145; August 18, 2004. http://decisions.fct-cf.gc.ca/fct/2004/2004fc1145.shtml

international custom has also evolved with regards to the provision of certain consular services.[4]

The ICJ decision in the Lagrand case (along with a subsequent decision involving several citizens of Mexico on death row)[5] caused the United States to denounce its ratification of the Optional Protocol to the Vienna Convention on Consular Relations Concerning the Compulsory Settlement of Disputes. Canada is not a signatory to the Optional Protocol.

7. No appeal has been made to the decision of Judge Finckenstein's in the Khadr case. As such it would be appropriate to have instructions from the Crown on the following:

> 1. Is an appeal being contemplated to the Khadr decision or has the appeal period expired?

> 2. If no appeal is being contemplated what is the status of the conclusion reached by Judge Finckenstein with respect to the (a) the obligation of the government of Canada to provide consular services; (b) whether the government of Canada agrees that the "VCCR does create individual rights to the services requested;"

> 3. Whether Section 10 of the DFAITA establishes a requirement for consular services as stated by Judge Finckenstein in paragraph 29 and quoted above:

>> Given my findings with regards to reasonable and legitimate expectations, I find that the application displays a possible cause of action

---

4 See LaGrand (Germany v. United States of America), [2001]_ I.C.J. 3 (27 June 2001)

5 See Avena and other Mexican Nationals (Mexico v. United States of America), 2004), No 128. Both the Legand and the Avena decisions can be found at http://www.icj-cij.org/icjwww/idocket/imus/imusjudgment/imus_imusjudgment_200403

that the decision of the Minister not to provide the appropriate services (required under the circumstances) set out in the Guide may constitute a breach of his duties under section 10 of the DFAITA. I also find that the Minister's duties under section 10 should be interpreted with regard to the VCCR, international jurisprudence and custom.;

and

4. The status of the comments quoted in paragraph 1 from the Manual of Consular Instructions that "Most consular services are provided as a matter of discretion by virtue of the royal prerogative; except as provided by statute, no one is entitled to claim such services as a matter of legal right."

How to Save Ramin
May 06, 2006

THE DETENTION OF PROFESSOR RAMIN JAHANBEGLOO IN TEHRAN has an air of déjà vu. Three years ago and in similar circumstances, photojournalist Zahra Kazemi did not survive. Information since, including the shocking testimony of Dr. Shahram Azam, paints a distressing and horrible picture of police and security officials backed by senior governmental and religious leaders who will brook no questioning of their hard-fisted rule.

The current standoff between Iran and the international community on nuclear matters adds to the siege mentality in Tehran – and Mr. Jahanbegloo is but the latest victim. Mr. Jahanbegloo's website (www.iranproject.info) shows a man dedicated to bridging disparate cultures and religions through reason and rationality. Articles such as "Globalization and Dialogue of Cultures," "Towards a Philosophy of Tolerance," "Secular Universalism and Cultural Particularities," "Iranian intellectuals; from revolution to dissent," and "September 11 and Prospects for Democracy in Iran" demonstrate a scholar dedicated to lighting small candles in some of the world's darkest spots.

From the limited information available, Mr. Jahanbegloo appeared discontented with the downtown towers of academe in Toronto and several years ago returned with his family to his country of birth. Working through an independent organization, the Cultural Research Bureau, he was assisting a small centre where reason and understanding might prevail.

In an interview published last year, he saw himself as a "bridge between Iran and (western) universities." But, in the same article, it was reported that Mr. Jahanbegloo saw some "signs that (his) ideas are gaining a toehold in Tehran." No doubt that "toehold" may have lead to his current problems. Mr. Jahanbegloo joins a long line of fellow Iranian intellectuals, students and journalists who strive for tolerance and civility in their own society and the outside world.

One of his articles, "The Role of the Intellectual in the Middle East," puts the issue this way: "One of the biggest problems of the Middle Eastern societies lies in the inability of the intellectuals in this region of the world to make up their minds about who they are. Are they specialized experts and professionals ... or independent souls whose only commitment is to truth and who add their voices to the public debates in the Middle East?"

Clearly Mr. Jahanbegloo saw himself as an independent soul with a deep commitment to truth. In that, Mr. Jahanbegloo was kindred to Ms. Kazemi. She used her camera as a lens into a world that most of us did not see or understand. Mr. Jahanbegloo uses words and ideas to illustrate to audiences, irrespective of the divide, that truth is still the only objective – if understanding is to occur.

Unfortunately, understanding may not be the main characteristic of the growing clamour that will surround his detention. Outrage will be its main characteristic and, at one level, deservedly so. But, if the objective is to help Mr. Jahanbegloo out of his nasty predicament, then there is a need for restraint, temperateness and calculation. It is easy to rush to the barricades and rain down invective and scorn on a government that would lock up a national treasure.

It is considerably more difficult in Canada and most western societies to exercise restraint in the face of such provocation. There will be questions in the House, editorials, and marches with candles, all designed to demonstrate that we care deeply about such matters. More important and much more difficult is that we must demonstrate we care so deeply about Mr. Jahanbegloo that we are prepared to suspend expressions of outrage – in order not to add fuel to his pyre.

It is not farfetched to note that, with the Iranian authorities in their current phase of sticking a stick into as many eyes as possible, "mobilizing scorn" and casting invective will not engender kind thoughts or humane treatment for Mr. Jahanbegloo.

In the aftermath of Ms. Kazami's death, every tool in the armoury of public and private diplomacy was used, but her remains still rest in the soil of Iran and her murderers are free.

Mr. Jahanbegloo's family and friends have urged restraint on the part of western supporters and Foreign Affairs correctly agrees. Right now, we do not know Mr. Jahanbegloo's condition, although there are disturbing reports that he is in a hospital. There have been conversations between the Iranian government and officials of the Canadian embassy, but there does not appear to be any softening of the Iranian policy on dual nationals.

Mr. Jahanbegloo is a citizen of Iran and of Canada. Most likely, as with Ms. Kazemi, he used an Iranian passport to enter Iran and presented himself as a citizen in his dealings with the local authorities. The Iranian government in such circumstances and in thousands of instances refuses to give status or credence to the second nationality. However, it has been Canadian policy and practice for a number of years to provide assistance and support to Canadian citizens outside of Canada – no matter how many other nationalities they possess.

Unfortunately, international law and practice is closer to the Iranian position than to that of Canada. The Vienna Convention on Consular Relations is silent on such matters, and the only international treaty dealing with dual nationality goes back to 1930; it prohibits Canada from intervening in circumstances such as Mr. Jahanbegloo's.

Canada was a signatory to the 1930 treaty, but because of this prohibition denounced it in 1996. In recent years there have been discussions around the concept of "dominant nationality," but unfortunately the factors that would be used in determining dominance would support the Iranian view in this matter.

It is in these dangerous and contested waters that Canada and Canadians – both publicly and privately – must exercise the utmost restraint if we are to help Mr. Jahanbegloo and not add to his misery. To do so would be the sign of a mature society; and from his writings, it would be the advice Mr. Jahanbegloo would give if he were able to do so.

The Citizen

Freedom to Travel
June 21, 2006

THE DECISION BY JUDGE MICHAEL PHELAN OF THE FEDERAL COURT A week or so ago concerning the denial of a passport to Abdurahman Khadr by Passport Canada provides interesting insights into the murky and confused world of passport entitlement in the current "Age of Terror." Members of the Khadr family have been prominent in the Canadian consciousness for the past decade, and are frequently referred to as Canada's al Qaeda family.

In early 1996 the family's patriarch Ahmed Said Khadr was first seen in an Islamabad hospital denying claims by the Pakistani government that he was involved in the bombing of the local Egyptian embassy when 13 died. At the time, Mr Khadr was working for Human Concern International, an Ottawa-based charity partially funded by CIDA. In some of the photographs, Mr Khadr was surrounded by some of his six children who today continue to claim public attention in their own right.

Following representations from the Canadian Moslem community, then Prime Minister Chrétien spoke to then Pakistani Prime Minister Benazir Bhutto and Mr Khadr was released. The connection between these events is tenuous at best as it is unlikely the Pakistanis would have released Mr Khadr if there was serious evidence of his involvement in the Egyptian-embassy bombing. If there had been, Mr Khadr would not have been resting in a local hospital, but instead, given the close relationship between Cairo and Islamabad, would have been in an Egyptian prison – the country of his second nationality.

Omar Khadr, the second youngest of the six children, has spent the last four years in American custody – first in Afghanistan and since 2003 at Guantanamo Bay. He has been charged with the death of an American soldier and is one of ten prisoners "indicted" under the highly controversial Military Commission system of justice. The Military Commission process is under review by the American Supreme Court whose ruling is expected in the next week or so.

Abdurahman Khadr describes himself as the "black sheep" of his family. He was detained by coalition forces in Afghanistan in November 2001 and, following his release from Guantanamo, according to his own testimony, worked for the CIA in Bosnia from where he returned to Canada in October 2003. Following his return he applied for a replacement Canadian passport and, when it was refused, launched his action in the Federal Court.

The June 8 ruling by Justice Phelan provides a window on the world of Canadian passport procedures and the rights of Canadians in this travel-conscious world. The clarity of the decision, its fidelity to the rule of law and the reasoning provide Canadians with greater certainty of their rights in this area than was heretofore evident.

Judge Phelan deals with Mobility Rights under Section 6 of the Canadian Charter of Rights and Freedom (which gives a citizen the right to "enter, remain and leave" Canada) by declaring that "the right to leave Canada is a hollow right if it cannot be exercised in a meaningful way due to the actions of the Canadian government directed against an individual or group of individual citizens." He goes on to argue that "it is no answer to say that it is not the Canadian government which prevents one from leaving Canada when a passport is denied, that the responsibility is solely that of the foreign country which requires it."

The Judge concludes that the "right to leave Canada is a sufficiently important aspect of an individual's freedom than any exercise of power which has an impact on that Charter value must be held to a high standard – of fairness – of review." He concludes that the importance of a passport means that the principle of fairness

– of which legitimate expectation is one – must be closely and rigorously adhered to."

Judge Phelan, without making any "findings" on whether Charter rights had been violated, did rule that the minister of foreign affairs (at the time Bill Graham) did not have the authority to deny Mr Khadr a Canadian passport. While the rules have been changed subsequently to include "national security" concerns as one of the conditions under which a passport can be refused, at the time Mr Khadr made his passport application he was entitled to receive one.

Judge Phelan's decision, however, did not leave the government bereft. He went on to write that "nothing in these Reasons should be held to conclude that the [Government] is prevented from immediately taking steps to revoke the passport on the grounds now enumerated in the amended Canadian Passport Order, if such grounds exist."

The ironic effect is that while Mr Khadr can receive a new passport today, the government can initiate action tomorrow to revoke its validity, if there are "grounds" for doing so. Originally, the decision to deny a passport to Mr Khadr was based on a report from CSIS expressing "national security concerns" – and these were central to the ministerial decision to deny the issuance of a replacement passport. Passport Canada had not taken any action to revoke his earlier passport, although it would appear the same reasons for denying a new passport would have been applicable. Should Passport Canada revoke a newly issued passport to Mr Khadr on national security grounds then it is more than likely that the case will be back before the courts once again.

It will be recalled that two years ago CSIS objected to the granting of a security clearance to Bhupinder Singh Liddar who had been named as Canada's Consul General in Chandigarh, India. He never went to Chandigarh (he now has a diplomatic appointment in Nairobi, Kenya), but Mr Liddar successfully appealed the CSIS conclusion to the Security Intelligence Review Committee (SIRC) which, after a ten-month investigation, recommended that Mr

Liddar be granted a top-secret security clearance. While the cases are different, Mr Liddar's situation illustrates the difficult task CSIS has in translating national-security concerns into language that withstands public scrutiny.

The Citizen

Evacuations and Departures
July 27, 2006

EDITORS AND TELEVISION PRODUCERS INCREASINGLY USE THE TERM "reality check" in the midst of reporting quickly moving and complex events. The idea suggests the ongoing reporting needs to be supplemented with a broader perspective of what is happening and to provide readers and viewers with an interpretation of fast moving events and where things are heading.

Three weeks into the Lebanese crisis there is a need for a reality check. The crisis carries with it broad issues of humanitarian, political, military and bilateral relationships each having their own complexities and uncertainties. As the efforts to suspend the fighting gather momentum, all of these factors will have considerable currency.

However, the objective for this set of negotiations will remain as it was for previous suspensions – to avoid the *status quo anti*. Many more on both sides will die if that objective is to be achieved. More likely death on the supper-time news will sap the will of all negotiators, including the Americans, and the dynamic that led to the current violence will be largely unaffected.

In the first days of this crisis the dominant issue for most Canadians is the well-being and safety of the thousands of Canadians who were in Lebanon at the time Hezbollah crossed into Israel and killed and kidnapped Israeli soldiers. Some have described the raid as the "tipping point" for what was already a fragile and deepening security situation.

Governments did not expect nor anticipate the raid and there is continuing speculation as to its timing and purpose. The spiralling downwards of security for all Lebanese and Israelis including the thousands of resident and visiting foreigners created an extraordinary dangerous environment for all. There can be every expectation things will get worse before there is any improvement. Hundreds have died civilians and soldiers alike; hundreds of thousands are on the move to safer places, both in Lebanon and Israel and beyond.

For Canadians there is an immediacy and direct connection to the crisis, again both in Lebanon and Israel. Tens of thousands of Canadians trace their origins to these countries and the connections, family, professional and religious, are current and deep. For millions of Canadians there is nothing unique in this.

Transfer the crisis to another country and the numbers would be similar. Greece, Italy, Hong Kong, Germany, the United Kingdom, Poland and the United States have large numbers of Canadians who live there on a permanent or semi permanent basis. Go to Mexico or any other sunny country during the months of the Canadian winter and there are tens of thousands of Canadians under the swaying palms. While Canadians love Canada many do not for all of the months of the year.

Canadian citizenship does not and should not carry restrictions on residency and the freedom to travel; at the same time there is no special protection for Canadians in other countries when things go bang in the night.

The July 12 Israeli raid into Lebanon created a complex set of actions within the government of Canada. The 24-hour Operations Centre for Foreign Affairs realized immediately the potential for a large scale humanitarian disaster and the concerns were immediately transmitted to all appropriate persons in the Department and the government. Our ambassadors in Beirut and Tel Aviv and elsewhere in the region were advised and within hours the outlines for an evacuation were in place, should matters spiral completely out of control.

The difficulties involved were understood right from the beginning. It was estimated that upwards of 50,000 Canadians were in Lebanon, only some 12,000 of whom had registered with the embassy and for whom there was detailed information on where they were and how they could be contacted. In the intervening days 25,000 thousand more registered and we now have a comprehensive picture of the Canadian community in Lebanon. While on a lesser scale, Canadians in Israel have also rushed to register their presence with the Canadian embassy in Tel Aviv.

The immediate concern was to find and deploy officials, both in Ottawa and in the region to deal with the crisis. For Foreign Affairs, the summer months is a time when thousands of persons are on the move, going elsewhere on transfer to embassies or back to Ottawa or are on vacation.

Most Canadian embassies, as they are for many countries, are relatively small and any crisis that is continuing and especially one involving the evacuation of thousands requires the influx of additional officials from all corners of the world. This was done; transfers were interrupted, vacations were cancelled and retirements foregone. The response was in the finest tradition of the Canadian Foreign Service. Other departments of the government, especially National Defence, quickly identified persons with special skills and these were quickly on their way to the region.

Evacuations are synonymous with transportation. The early bombing of the Beirut airport, key roads and bridges and the bombing of residential areas throughout the country destroyed the heart of the normal elements in any evacuation plan. Canadian military ships and planes were not available and, along with several other countries, Canada went into the spot leasing market for ships that could go to Lebanon and rescue the thousands of Canadians who indicated that they wanted to leave.

On the map, the distance between Lebanon and Cyprus and beyond to Turkey is not great. Ferries plied the route on a daily basis. The Israeli naval blockade of the Lebanese coast ended any normalcy in these waters. Ship owners and insurance brokers, while prepared to lease, wanted security guarantees from all of the contending parties and these were obtained, some with difficulty and most with narrowly defined windows. What could not be done was to calm the frequently stormy waters in the eastern Mediterranean and the nervousness of Israeli naval captains, following the earlier missile attack on one of their ships.

In the planning for the evacuation by sea, there was one guiding principle. In everything that was done including the timing of the first departures, adding to the dangers for evacuating Canadians was to be avoided. Discomfort was to be expected. It was also realized, based on the widespread experienced of many departmental officials in numerous other evacuations around the world, the first shipload of Canadians would be a time of testing for the various assumptions and plans that had been made.

Not surprisingly, some Canadians found the first voyage distressing and quickly voiced their discontent to the hovering media. But this is not a hundred yard dash; rather it is a marathon that can only be run over time and for Canada, the race is longer than it is for any other country given he numbers involved. However, even the best cannot calm the waters or reduce the nervousness of Israeli ship commanders.

Upwards of ten thousand Canadians have now been evacuated from war-torn Lebanon and it is expected more will want to leave, especially if the fighting intensifies. The Canadian government has stated that it is fully committed to removing every Canadian who wants to leave and extra officials will remain in the theatre until that is achieved.

Some have commented on the cost of this effort and the early commitment of the government not to charge those directly helped. There are long standing precedents for such decisions. For the many Canadians who are evacuated, the cost involved in re-establishing their lives in Canada will be significant and there is no need for the government to add to that burden.

It should also be noted that for the past decade the government has been collecting a Consular Service Fee from all Canadians who purchase a passport. This fee fully support the costs of maintaining and improving Canadian consular services throughout the world and is in part insurance for Canadians that assistance is available when they find themselves in harm's way far from home. Last year more than $70 million dollars was paid direct by Canadians for this purpose and over half a billion dollars collected over the past decade.

The fact that many of the Canadians in Lebanon also have Lebanese or other citizenships has led some Canadians to question the need for the government to provide assistance. This is an uncharacteristic narrow and perverse interpretation of citizenship and one that should find no support from Canadians.

Canada for many, many years promoted the freedom of all people to travel and to maintain ties to former countries of citizenship. Section 6 of the Charter of Rights provides for the right of every citizen of Canada "to enter, remain in and leave Canada." It should not be otherwise. Equally, the government should do what it can to assist all Canadians in doing so. The efforts of the countries of the European Union to provide for the mobility of its people involve principles that we could all emulate if we want to build a safer and more secure world.

The Rule of Law's Limits
December 10, 2007

AT 6 A.M. ON A RAINY APRIL 24, 2000, MS. NGUYEN THI HIEP WAS TAKEN from her cell in Trai Giam Prison in Hanoi, gagged and roughly bound to a post in the yard and executed by a firing squad. As she lay crumpled in the wet dirt another prison official provided a coup de grâce at the base of her skull.

Less than a year earlier, another Canadian, Stanley Faulder, was strapped to a gurney in Huntsville Prison, Texas, injected with various lethal chemicals and executed.

These two state-sponsored killings, more than any others, brought home to Canadians the barbarity of such executions. The distinction that one was done by a totalitarian state while the other by a functioning democracy where the rule of law is paramount was considered by most a quibble of no consequence.

The government of Canada protested the imposition of the death penalty at the highest levels in both governments. In the United States the protests included a filing with the Supreme Court and appeals to the then-Texas-governor, George W. Bush. In Hanoi the protests involved two visits by members of the Toronto police, who provided exculpatory evidence that resulted in written assurances from the Vietnamese government that Nguyen Thi Hiep would not be put to death. Fearful of the effect of such evidence, officials of the Hanoi government stealthily hurried the execution.

Most tragically, the protests did not succeed in these two cases. However, in several others, Canadian protests have been effective. In Singapore, the United Arab Emirates, Thailand and Washington State, the Canadian government has lobbied to ensure that

Canadians within range of the application of the death penalty were spared.

Canadian law during this period was extended to non-Canadians in Canada who were being extradited to countries where they could be executed. The decision of the Supreme Court in 2001 on Burns and Raffay effectively made Canada an abolitionist state (one of 133 in the world), for all Canadians and for foreigners within its jurisdiction.

Now the "new" government of Canada, in what can only be termed a fit of pique, has turned back the clock. It has done so in the most perverse and illogical manner. In less serious circumstances this would be risible.

Ron Smith was convicted of murder most foul and sentenced to death. For 25 years, his case has been wending its way through various stages of the American judicial system. In the meantime his accomplice has been transferred to Canada and released on parole. Throughout that period and more intensely since the early 1990s, the government of Canada made representations to various levels of the American government, and especially to state authorities in Montana, concerning the death penalty. These representations reflected the intent and spirit of the Charter of Rights and Freedoms.

A routine CanWest story detailing Canadian representations in support of Mr. Smith last October changed everything. A few hours after the story broke on Oct. 26, a spokesperson for Foreign Affairs confirmed that "it is the policy of the Canadian government to seek clemency ... for Canadians sentenced to death in foreign countries." However, on Oct. 31, there was a new policy. The minister of justice then stated that Canadians sentenced to death in other countries "can no longer count on the Canadian government to necessarily intervene where an individual has been tried in a democracy that adheres to the rule of law."

There is no evidence the new policy followed serious and prolonged discussion within the government. Rather it seems it was a case where ministers of the Crown with a responsibility to be fair and equitable to all Canadians decided that they did not like Mr. Smith and acted callously.

As one looks at the phantasmagorical world around us it is readily apparent that the new standard – democracy and adherence to the rule of law – for Canadian actions in such matters is not valid or workable. It is, however, a standard through which personal prejudice can be exercised.

It is all too apparent that democracy and the rule of law are not guarantees of fairness, accuracy or justice. A case close to home bears repeating. It took the Canadian criminal-justice system almost 50 years to provide some measure of justice to Steven Truscott who, at the age of 14, was sentenced to death by an Ontario court in 1959. In 2007 the Ontario Court of Appeal acquitted Mr Truscott, concluding, "based on evidence that qualifies as fresh evidence in these proceedings, we are satisfied that Mr. Truscott's conviction was a miscarriage of justice and must be quashed." Democracy and the rule of law took nearly half a century.

Mr. Truscott was and is not alone. There is an almost-daily litany of cases where Canadian courts, after years of fighting by lawyers from the Association in Defence of the Wrongfully Convicted and other counsels acting independently, have ruled there were serious miscarriages of justice. Guy Paul Morin, Donald Marshall and David Milgaard were the flag bearers for such cases. Democracy and the rule of law was not a standard of any validity.

If that is the situation in Canada, is it any wonder there should always be strong scepticism when Canadians are sentenced to death in foreign jurisdictions? Already, the Innocence Project in the United States has successfully obtained the release of more than 200 persons, using only DNA- based evidence. Thousands of others have been released based on the errors of judges, prosecutorial misconduct, defence incompetence and police and forensic mistakes. Thousands more of the wrongfully convicted still languish in prison, due to racism or mental incompetence factors or a lack of money to fight. In all of this it has been found that confessions are no guarantee of justice.

A few years ago the United States lost two cases before the International Court of Justice which indirectly involved the death penalty. The reaction of the United States was to withdraw from the treaty under which such cases were judged. Democracy and the rule of law guaranteed nothing.

Beyond North America, the situation is worse. There are 64 countries which retain the death penalty. Many are democratic and the rule of law abounds. However, as winter descends, Canadians who travel to Mexico may harbour some concerns, but they do not have to worry about the death penalty there. Mexico is an abolitionist state.

With Alex Neve *The Citizen*

Tears Are Enough
March 28, 2008

FOR BRYAN ADAMS, "TEARS WERE NOT ENOUGH" FOR THE TRAGEDY that was playing out more than two decades ago in Ethiopia. Today, for Brenda Martin, "tears are enough" to speed many Canadians into one of their periodic fits of hypocrisy and narrow moralization – when there is word that a Canadian has run into legal difficulties in a foreign country.

Ms Martin has been immensely successful, with the help of dedicated friends and supporters in Canada, to play the role of an innocent and badly-done-by victim of the machinations of an evil and corrupt judicial system in Mexico. And she may be right. At this point we do not know.

Before we accept the script written by others with a vested interest in ensuring that the play has a successful run, it might be wise to slow things down and consider what is going on.

There are precedents. Not too many years ago, two Canadians found themselves in serious trouble in Brazil. With a script that is being closely followed by the supporters of Ms Martin, Canadians, including the media, accepted the scenario as written – and for six years demonized the judicial system of Brazil and Brazilians. There were hysterical editorials and letters; the Commons justice committee met, and there were high-level exchanges between heads of government, as well as foreign and justice ministers.

Throughout those six years the Brazilians would have nothing of the Canadian breast-beating, believing that there was sufficient evidence for the conviction and that the Canadians had been treated fairly within their judicial system.

Then something happened. In Managua, Nicaragua, documentary evidence was found that proved conclusively that Brazil was right. Once the fuss subsided, the Brazilians agreed to transfer the two Canadians to a Canadian prison where, after a few weeks, they were released on parole. Most observers agree that Canada-Brazilian relations have never recovered.

Today the target country is Mexico. The superficial facts of the case are well known. Ms Martin was an employee of Alyn Waage, another Canadian, who used Mexico and Costa Rica as a base to run a worldwide "Ponzi" scheme. The scheme convinced 15,000 investors to commit some $60 million in the expectation that they would receive 120 per cent interest annually. Apart from the greed and gullibility of the investors, it was a machination that has had more imitators than there are rocks in Newfoundland.

Mr Waage and several others were extradited from Costa Rica to the United States where he, along with his son and others, pleaded guilty and were sentenced to numerous years in prison. Other trials are pending. All spent years in prison before trial. The investigation while directed by American authorities involved the police forces of Costa Rica, Canada, Mexico and Latvia. The role Ms Martin played, if any, in the investment fraud is at the centre of the charges in Mexico and it can be assumed that the police forces of other countries, including Canada, are involved.

The campaign of tears has increased in volume and speed in the last several weeks. Heads of government, foreign ministers and a special envoy are now involved and her cell at the Puente Grande Women's Prison in Guadalajara has become a place of pilgrimage for visiting Canadians. A former prime minister showed up and, as common as an undertaker at a funeral, the Liberal consular critic put in an appearance.

The media, which have been uncritical allies of Ms Martin, have fostered an atmosphere of fear and loathing. Canadians should boycott travel to Mexico (this one has not had much traction given the winter in central and eastern Canada); the Mexican judicial system is corrupt and malicious; Ms Martin is an innocent victim (even a letter from Mr Waage says so), and the Canadian government has to reach into Mexico and influence their judicial system.

No one would argue that Mexico has a fine judicial system. Equally, it is not the worst in the world by any means. And for Canadians to throw rocks south on such an issue, given the daily litany of wrongful convictions here, must be particularly troublesome to the Mexican authorities. The Mexican system of justice is different than what we have in Canada, following as it does the European continental or civil system.

There have been thousands of Canadians arrested in Mexico over the years and it would not be misleading to state that they have received judicial consideration as good as they would get in Canada. There is one large exception – bail is not generally available for a foreigner in a foreign country – just as it would not be in Canada or other countries in similar circumstances.

As with all such situations, especially in countries such as Mexico, the higher the political level of foreign interest and involvement, the less likelihood of success. Countries, including Canada, do not bear foreign criticism with any degree of equanimity. In this situation it may be time to call on the doctors who would prescribe an aspirin or two, rest, and quiet – if we really want to help Ms Martin.

The Citizen

The Consular Game
April 22, 2008

FOR THE PAST SEVERAL WEEKS, THE CANADIAN MEDIA HAVE PROvided a rich broth of the problems Canadians encounter in foreign countries. The number of such stories has caused many in the media to suggest there is an unusual catenation of events leading to the dire straits that many Canadian citizens have encountered.

Most of the events have involved the arrests of Canadians and their struggles with unknown or misunderstood judicial systems. The reaction of the media in most instances has been to accept that Canadians have been badly done by – and the problems can be attributed to malicious or mal-intended foreign governments.

However, for anyone familiar with the world of the consular, the recent stories have a déjà vu quality. These stories have happened before – and they will happen again. In between, the shortness of memory and the inability of the media to provide some measure of perspective cause reactions to be overdone and the remedies short-sighted.

The stories have run the gamut: two death-penalty cases, one in the United States, the other in Saudi Arabia; a middle-aged woman in a Mexican prison for over two years, awaiting the conclusion of her case; a woman sentenced for murder in Chang Mai, Thailand; a businessman jailed for ten months in northern India on visa problems, and numerous others in the far corners of the world.

A common thread in all of the stories is the quality of the help provided by the government of Canada and especially consular officers. An added factor has been whether the government itself is sufficiently committed or able to provide the assistance that Canadians and their families and friends demand in these circumstances.

Last fall, Hugh White, a Visiting Fellow at the Lowy Institute for International Policy in Sydney, detailed similar issues in Australia. Dr White's paper, written in the aftermath of the Israeli-Lebanese war and the evacuation of civilians on a massive scale, provided a variety of observations for reflection and consideration. His analysis of the source of the problems – more travellers to more destinations and increasing residence abroad – is reflected in Canadian numbers. These have been available to Canadian policymakers since the early days of the deployment of the COSMOS system and its associated mechanisms for measuring consular work in all of its manifestations. It was with the full understanding of those constantly increasing numbers that a number of steps were taken in Canada to avoid the problems that are now of concern in Australia.

Professor White's prescriptions for policy changes in Australia were all considered in Canada and were discarded as not being workable in the Canadian context. His concern that the resources needed for consular services should "not detract from the ability of Australia's foreign service to undertake critical diplomatic work" establishes a hierarchy of "services" that has little relevance in our democratic and demand-driven political systems.

Many have sympathy for foreign services that could be resourced to meet all needs; however, there is little expectation that this is a prescription governments are ready to meet over time or for all situations. Rather, crisis management has become the norm, and those of us who have lived and walked the talk believe there will be a magical point when the resources needed for all foreign-service tasks will ever be available. Rather, there will always be tensions within foreign services on the allocation of available resources and, in a world as troubled as today's, it is not surprising that consular services are obtaining an increasing share of the available resource pot.

Anyone with a longer-term perspective would understand that this rebalancing is more the result of past inequities when consular services were the poor cousins in all foreign services. Professor White is right when he states that there is a need for more resources for foreign services, but he is incorrect to suggest that this is a result of politicians pandering to the needs of their constituents when in trouble in foreign lands.

I would also take issue with Professor White's suggestion that the demand for consular services can be moderated by governments by informing their travelling citizens that "the safety of Australians abroad is the primary responsibility of the individuals concerned and of the governments of the countries they are visiting. Canberra should be forthright in making clear that there can be no automatic expectation that the Australian government will rescue citizens in trouble overseas."

This is a fine sentiment, but of no practical value. Governments who, in the abstract, make such declarations are the first to discard them when faced with the demands of injured or endangered citizens, irrespective of the circumstances. Many consular services a decade or two ago were premised on such declarations, and it was in reaction to the unacceptability of such that led governments to become more forthcoming and offer a wider range of services. To suggest otherwise would be similar to turning patients away from our hospitals because their lifestyles contributed to their medical problems.

There have been enormous changes in the world since the end of the Second World War. One of the most far-reaching has been the migration of people both on a temporary and longer-term basis. Unfortunately, while there has been considerable effort expended by governments to deal with the worlds of economic goods and services, little attention has been made to create an appropriate regulatory environment in which travellers are accorded appropriate attention.

Until that happens governments must and will ensure that the protection of citizens extends to the far reaches of this troubled planet.

Consularis

Another Sad Chapter
June 07, 2008

IT IS NOW ALMOST SIX YEARS SINCE THAT FATEFUL THURSDAY IN September 2002 when Maher Arar was detained by the American authorities and deported to Syria.

In Canada during those intervening years, there was unusual speed and interest in detailing the role of Canadian officials and their culpability. Compensation has been paid and Mr. Arar has emerged as an iconic representation of the evil a state can do when appropriate care is not taken by police and security officials in assessing and understanding information beyond their ken.

In this role Mr. Arar is a constant and stoical reminder of the harm done by government secrecy. Unfortunately, apart from compensation, other recommendations by Justice Dennis O'Connor have joined the numerous previous studies on the dusty shelves of government archives. Secrecy is more important for incompetence and ineptness to flourish than for the security of the state.

It was all the more surprising when, this week, one corner of the blanket covering the role of the American government in this tragedy was lifted. The Inspector General for the Department of Homeland Security (a sort of super auditor) appeared before a Congressional committee and provided some accounting.

After four years of investigating, the Office of the Inspector General (OIG) had little to say that was new and revealing. Yes, Mr. Arar was legally detained by American authorities and they followed all the rules in their book in arranging for his forced accommodation in Damascus. With unintended irony, the Inspector General in presenting his report to Congress revealed that American immigration officials "concurred" with his recommendations on the "understanding that the OIG concluded that INS (Immigration and Naturalization Service) did not violate any then-existing law, regulation, or policy with respect to the removal."

That is a bargain rarely available to most.

The furthest the Inspector General would go was to say that the assurances from Syria against torture were "ambiguous regarding the source of authority purporting to bind the Syrian government." On the issue of Syrian torture, the American government itself was the main author of reports that detailed such actions.

Ambiguity should have been the last consideration for those who made the decision to deport.

Beyond the Inspector General's central comments there are interesting tidbits in the report revealing the nasty machinations of senior American officials. Unfortunately, these machinations were mirrored in Canada during the summer of 2003 when efforts to have Mr. Arar released by Syria were interfered with by the RCMP and CSIS. Surprisingly, and for the first time, it was revealed this week that FBI officials by mid-afternoon on Sept. 26, 2002 – 65 minutes after Mr. Arar deplaned in Syria? – had concluded that he "was of no investigative interest."

For the next 10 days American immigration officials appeared to have acted on the conclusions of the FBI. Again for the first time, the Inspector General has now revealed that they were overruled by the acting attorney general (John Ashcroft was out of the country) who, on October 7, concluded that it would be "prejudicial to the interest of the United States" to accept Mr. Arar's request to be returned to Canada. Subsequent to that finding, the INS commissioner signed the memorandum authorizing Mr. Arar's removal to Syria.

It was apparent at the time that there was a very high level of interest in Mr. Arar within the American government. In part, an American official in conversation with Canadian consular officials indirectly suggested the decision to deport to Syria had been made at the highest levels of the American government. Equally, it was apparent from a conversation I had with Victor Cerda, the senior legal adviser to the commissioner for immigration, two days after the deportation that no information would be provided – not even confirming that Mr. Arar was then in Syria.

In some measure, Secretary of State Condoleezza Rice spoke of these problems when she was in Ottawa last October. At the time, she publicly stated that the Arar case was not "handled as it should have been" and "our communications with the Canadian government about this was by no means perfect. In fact, it was quite imperfect."

However, the words have had little effect in having Mr Arar removed from American no-fly lists.

It is unlikely there will be much more disclosure by the American government until such time as some of those involved retire after the November election – and memoir season is with us. Equally, the civil case filed by Mr. Arar in the U.S. is still under appeal. According to the Inspector General, that case – where individual officials have been sued in addition to the United States government itself – limited co-operation with his inquiries.

If there is any benefit to be taken from this sad case, it is that it will stand for some time as an example of the horrors that can be done by incompetent officials who believe they are acting in the best interest of their state. Unfortunately, good intentions when done in the name of national security only end in very dark, hot places.

I hope, however, the Arar Effect will have a long life.

The Citizen

The Real Reason to Bring Canadian Prisoners Home
September 3, 2008

IT IS EXTREMELY RARE FOR A FEDERAL COURT JUDGE TO BE HIGHLY critical of a ministerial decision. It is is normal for judges to give "significant deference" to such decisions. But in a decision (Getkate v. the Minister of Public Safety) released on August 25, Justice Michael Kelen pulled no punches and paid no "deference" to the minister.

The decision was rendered in response to a judicial-review request made by a Canadian imprisoned in the United States whose application for transfer to a Canadian prison had been rejected twice by Public Safety Minister Stockwell Day.

Justice Kelen, in his decision in favour of Arend Getkate, stated that the minister was "wholly unreasonable," that the "evidence points in a wholly opposite direction" to the decision and that the minister "unreasonably disregarded this evidence."

Over 30 years ago, Canadian officials were successful in promoting at INTERPOL and the International Law Commission a concept for a new international agreement. The concept was for bilateral and multilateral treaties that would permit convicted prisoners to transfer to their country of citizenship and serve out their sentences within a familiar environment close to family and friends.

The concept met an obvious need as, within a few years, there were numerous bilateral treaties and a multilateral one. The United States and Mexico were the first with a bilateral and Canada followed within a few months with its own treaty with the United States. The Council of Europe saw considerable merit in the concept and within a few years, in 1983, its member states agreed to a multilateral treaty in which all of its members could participate without needing to negotiate bilateral agreements.

The concept has stood the test of time and today there is an extensive network of such treaties and new bilaterals are signed every year. In the intervening years, in addition to the Council of Europe, both the Commonwealth and the Organization of American States have put in place their own treaties for the use of their members.

The concept and the treaties were not based on wide-eyed humanitarianism, although there is such an element in the results. Rather, they were based on the reality that Canadian citizens convicted in foreign countries had an absolute right to return to Canada following the completion of their sentences. More often than not, such persons would be deported directly to Canada. In those situations, once returned, there was no criminal record registered in Canada. Sometimes there was not even knowledge of the crimes committed, nor was there any ability by Canadian authorities to assess the individual's likelihood of re-offending or of being some measure of risk to Canadians.

The transfer treaties overcame these problems and, in the assessment of most countries, provided a valuable addition to international cooperation on criminal matters. Transferred prisoners were incarcerated upon return and, in doing so, there was an opportunity for correctional officials to assess the individual and come to firsthand conclusions on the individual and the danger he or she might pose once released.

In the intervening years, Canada negotiated treaty arrangements with countries in all parts of the world, with an emphasis on those where Canadians are frequently arrested and imprisoned. Today there are arrangements with 76 countries, ranging from Albania to Zimbabwe.

Between 1978, when Canada signed its first treaty with the United States, and 2005, more than 1,400 Canadians were transferred from foreign prisons to become inmates in Canada. The vast majority were from prisons in the United States, but there were significant numbers from Costa Rica, Mexico, Thailand, Trinidad and Tobago and the United Kingdom.

During those 27 years, only five were rejected for transfer by the then Canadian solicitors general/ministers of public safety – a rejection rate of less than one-half of one per cent. While precise information is not available, these rejections were based largely on an inability to prove Canadian citizenship by the applicant. All governments during that period, Liberal and Conservative, understood and accepted the value of such transfers for Canada and Canadians and made decisions accordingly.

It became apparent with the arrival of the Harper government that Mr Day had little understanding or sympathy for the well-tried concept of prisoner transfers. From January 2006 to January 2008, 117 Canadians were accepted for transfer by Mr. Day, but he rejected 61.

In the cases for which information is available, Mr. Day used various reasons, such as the return of the Canadian threatened the safety of Canadians and the security of Canada; there was no evidence that the individual could be rehabilitated, or that there was an "abandonment" of Canada by the applicant.

In the case of Mr. Getkate, who at the age of 12 in 1996 was taken to the United States by his mother and in 2002 was convicted of child molestation in Georgia, Justice Kelen summarily dismissed all three reasons for refusal, as given by the minister. The judge forcibly stated that the minister's decisions were inconsistent with the evidence presented to him by his officials, who on two occasions recommended that Mr. Getkate be transferred.

Justice Kelen's decision only has specific application to the case of Mr. Getkate, but there are many other Canadians who have been refused transfers by Mr. Day based on the same specious reasoning.

Some commentators have suggested that ideological reasons underpin Mr. Day's approach and form part of the "tough-on-crime" approach of the current government. It is equally apparent that the toughness of the approach is more illusory than real.

Certainly, in refusing to transfer Canadians from foreign prisons, the government is increasing the risk to Canadians when such persons return to Canada at the completion of their foreign sentences. We can hope that the clarity and reasonableness of Justice Kelen's decision will lead the government to change its approach. Unfortunately, the present fevered electoral atmosphere is not one where clarity and reasonableness prevail.

Embassy

At the Mercy of the Government
June 18, 2009

CANADA'S LEGAL SYSTEM IS SAID TO RESPECT PEACE, ORDER AND good government. Not always. Buried within the law books is an atavistic power unfamiliar to most Canadians, the Royal (or Crown) Prerogative – the residue of power untouched by Parliament. Most Canadian governments have used the prerogative sensitively, so that it attracted little attention. But since 2006, the government has been using it arbitrarily, even discriminatorily, to deny some Canadians the usual protections when travelling abroad.

The prerogative's dark side appeared most recently in the Abousfian Abdelrazik case. The government argued in the Federal Court of Canada that it could lawfully refuse Mr Abdelrazik, a Canadian who went to Sudan to visit his mother, a passport to return home to his children in Montreal.

Passports are a "matter of discretion falling within Crown prerogative," and the government argued that it has no "legal obligation in international law to even provide consular protection."

To translate: If you are in trouble overseas and go to a Canadian embassy, Canada's government believes that it has the option, but not the obligation, to help. If the government is fond of you, like Brenda Martin, it may help with papers or a private jet home, but if it scorns you, like Mr Abdelrazik, it may revoke your passport and exile you. The choice is the government's alone.

No laws govern this relationship, the government says. As then Mr Justice Konrad von Finckenstein of the Federal Court wrote in an earlier case: "Canadians abroad would be surprised, if not shocked, to learn that the provision of consular services in an individual case is left to the complete and unreviewable discretion of the minister." Except for the Charter of Rights and Freedoms, the minister's exercise of the prerogative is absolute.

What this means is that Canadian citizenship is less than it appears.

Other governments long ago passed laws that bind their discretionary hands and make it mandatory to help their citizens abroad. For example, the German Constitutional Court has written that the German state has "a constitutional duty to provide protection for German nationals and their interests in relation to foreign states." In the United States, a similar obligation is included in statutes requiring the government to provide consular services.

But in Canada, Parliament has never passed such a law, and consular officers have long been instructed that consular services are discretionary. That posed no problem when the prerogative was exercised sparingly, but today a litany of unresolved cases – not just that of Mr Abdelrazik, but of Omar Khadr, Amanda Lindhout, Beverly Giesbrecht, Ronald Smith and others – shows that the current government is taking arbitrary and capricious licence with the prerogative.

Currently, the only remedy these Canadians have is an expensive, slow appeal to the courts to assert their Charter rights. In Mr Khadr's case, Mr Justice James O'Reilly of the Federal Court ordered the Prime Minister to request Mr Khadr's return from Guantanamo Bay. In Mr Abdelrazik's case, Mr Justice Russel Zinn of the Federal Court ordered the government to issue an emergency passport and bring him home. The turn is revolutionary: Until a few weeks ago, Canadian courts had never overridden the Crown's Prerogative.

Rather than proceed with a haphazard judicial erosion of the prerogative, Parliament should pass a Protection of Canadians Act with rules to guarantee consular services for all citizens, irrespective of background or circumstance. The statute should require consular services to be non-discriminatory; should place a clear, positive duty on consular officers to assist Canadians in distress; should give

Canadians denied consular services access to a lawyer and a highly expedited appeal to court; and should permit them in a closed courtroom to see all personal information, including intelligence reports or diplomatic *démarches* that the government now hides as secret.

If a Protection of Canadians Act were already law, many of the most recent spectacles would have been avoided. The government could not hide behind secret evidence to justify its neglect of Mr Abdelrazik or Mr Khadr – evidence that, when finally revealed, demonstrated that the Canadian Security and Intelligence Service was knowingly complicit in their detention and torture.

The government also could not play favourites. When it negotiated with al-Qaeda to release elite Canadians, such as Robert Fowler and Louis Guay, it would also have to negotiate with other hostage-takers to release ordinary Canadians, such as Beverly Giesbrecht or Amanda Lindhout.

Perhaps it is not surprising for a government that attacks the Leader of the Opposition for having spent too much time outside Canada to be indifferent or hostile to the millions of Canadians who travel internationally for work or pleasure. But the freedom to travel is every Canadian's right, and when Canadians abroad land in trouble for whatever reason, they should not be subject to the whims of the government of the day.

For Parliament to extend statutory protection to the millions of Canadians who venture internationally would be a major milestone, and it would mean that Canadians are finally protected as Americans or Germans already are. To do otherwise leaves Canadians not only vulnerable to the vagaries of foreign governments, but to the sometimes-tyrannical vagaries of the Canadian government as well.

With Amir Attaran. The *Globe and Mail*

Some Will Be Helped, Others Not
August 15, 2009

FOR A YOUNG MAN (HE TURNS 23 IN SEPTEMBER), OMAR KHADR HAS had an exceptionally significant impact on Canadian politics – and equally upon our judicial system.

Friday, his impact was felt again. The Federal Court of Appeal, in a two-to-one decision, strongly affirmed an earlier Federal Court decision that Canadian officials, when they interviewed Khadr in the Guantanamo Bay prison, participated "in a process that was illegal under the laws of the United States and contrary to Canada's international human rights obligations."

The Court went on to say that the arguments of the Crown against responsibility for Khadr's mistreatment "were untenable" and wrote that the conduct of Canadian officials "amounted to knowing participation in Mr Khadr's mistreatment." In conclusion the Federal Court of Appeal agreed with the earlier Court decision that the remedy was for the government to seek Khadr's release from Guantanamo Bay and return to Canada. It wrote: "there is no legal or factual foundation upon which this Court can conclude that the decision not to request Mr. Khadr's repatriation is justified as a reasonable limit on his Charter rights."

This decision is consistent with several others made over the last few years. In nearly all cases, the Court has in forthright and unambiguous language criticized the government for its actions and set out in detail the redress that was appropriate. The most recent of these dealt with the Kafkaesque case, in the words of the court, of Abousfian Abdelrazik, who was imprisoned at the request of CSIS in Sudan – and then had to face the unswerving unwillingness of the government to assist in his return to Canada. The Federal Court was again highly critical of the government and, despite all of the reasons the government gave for not assisting Abdelrazik, under the direction of the Court he was quickly returned to Canada with little trouble.

One of the central arguments of the government in defending itself in these cases has been the use of "Crown prerogative" or in simple language the total discretion of the government to decide which Canadian citizens it will help and how, when they are in difficulty in foreign countries. The government argues that the Federal Court decisions in these cases are "an improper judicial intrusion into the Crown prerogative over foreign affairs."

Crown prerogative is an old doctrine of governments and was the basis on which Henry VIII arranged to have six wives. A lot has changed since the heady days of Henry. For a government with the standards and strictures of the Charter of Rights and Freedoms firmly in place to argue it has total discretion on these important matters, often involving life and death, suggests it is a government sadly and badly out of tune with the tenor of the country and the world.

It is not an exaggeration to state that when a government claims broad discretionary authority it is well down the road to discrimination. Some Canadians will be helped, others not. If the argument of the government is accepted, then the courts have no right to intervene on behalf of those who believe that there is discrimination.

This has been demonstrated in the policy of the government in seeking clemency for Canadians sentenced to death in foreign countries. The matter was the subject of another Federal Court case involving Ronald Smith, a Canadian on death row in Montana. The government decided to withdraw its support for clemency for reasons that the Court could not establish. Fortunately, the Federal Court did not agree and there is again support for clemency for Smith being addressed to American authorities.

Prime Minister Harper, in comments to the press, stated "one of the realities we have in this world with the increasing travel of people, increasing proliferation of threats ... this is a more and more difficult area. ... The government of Canada does not control affairs in other countries." Unfortunately these comments totally miss the mark.

Many of the problems that are frequently in the news or subject to Canadian judicial action do not involve the action of foreign governments. Rather it is the policy and action of the Canadian government that is disputed. It was not a foreign government that confiscated the passport of Suaad Hagi Mohamud in Kenya, nor was it the actions of the U.S. government that were adjudicated Friday by the Federal Court.

It is the policies and actions of the Canadian government and its officials that need to be corrected. Not to do so means that international travel for many Canadians will be even more a game of chance, with the government of Canada loading the dice.

Ottawa Citizen

All Aid Short of Help
August 17, 2009

THE HARPER GOVERNMENT HAS BEEN THE SUBJECT OF SEVERAL JUDIcial scoldings in the last three years. All have been at the hands of the Federal Court of Canada which took a dim view of governmental decisions involving Canadians in serious difficulty in foreign countries. Collectively the decisions represent the denial of the government's efforts to curtail assistance to such Canadians.

Omar Khadr had two favourable decisions from the Federal Court and even one from the Supreme Court that ultimately stated the government had to request his release from Guantanamo Bay prison; Abousfian Abdelrazik had his return to Canada ordered by the Court, despite the government's pleas that to do so was contrary to a resolution of the United Nations Security Council; convicted murderer Ron Smith was strongly supported by the Court in his request to have the government continue support for his plea for clemency; and in two other cases involving Canadians imprisoned in the United States, the Court ordered the government to reconsider their requests for transfers to Canadians prisons.

In all of these situations, and especially in its pleadings before the Court, the government sought to establish the principle that it had complete discretion in deciding which Canadians it would assist and those it would not. In the judicial decisions, the Courts did not deny the availability of discretion; rather, on a variety of grounds, they denied the basis on which discretion had been used in these specific situations. In the Abdelrazik matter, the Federal Court went so far as to state that his mobility rights under Section 6 of the Charter of Rights and Freedom had been denied. Thus, the Court has effectively gutted the belief of this government that it could determine who it would assist and who it would not.

The government has no one to blame but itself for this debacle. Its lumpy and idiosyncratic decision-making has created the perception if not the reality of playing favourites. The problem began when the then Minister of Public Safety, Stockwell Day, decided he would end the long- standing Canadian practise of transferring all Canadians in foreign prisons who requested a move to a prison in Canada. Mr Day, contrary to the recommendations of his officials, decided some Canadians would be transferred and others would not. In doing so he stated that those denied transfer would represent a threat to the safety of Canadians or possibly to our national security.

The Minister ignored the well-founded and internationally accepted rationale for such transfers. It was established so that Canadians who had been convicted in foreign countries could be assessed by Canadian officials before they were released. As matters now stand Canadians not transferred from a foreign prison will return to Canada at the end of their sentence – and be on Canadian streets without any assessment as to the danger they represent to Canadians.

The Court took a dim view of the Minister's reasoning. Justice Michael Kelen in his decision in one of the cases (Getkate) stated the Minister was "wholly unreasonable," that the "evidence points in a wholly opposite direction" to the decision and the Minister "unreasonably disregarded this evidence." Unfortunately, the Court decisions in these cases relate only to the individuals concerned, and the government continues to deny transfer to many Canadians incarcerated abroad.

The Court was equally critical of the government's reasoning in not seeking clemency for selected Canadians sentenced to death in foreign countries. In one case, the presiding judge stated that he could not find any basis in reality for why or how the new policy came into existence and that "it was made in breach of fairness, is unlawful and is set aside." Reading the Federal Court's decision it is apparent that members of the government did not like Mr Smith and acted callously. However, a judicial scolding for this government is not something that gets in the way of bad policy. Now the government has enshrined its discriminatory clemency policy in new clothing in the hope that this sleight of hand will deceive.

All of these court cases have surrounded the government's quite contrary approach to assistance for Brenda Martin. Then it was all hands on deck and for a while there was need for a traffic cop to direct Canadian ministerial visits to her prison in Mexico. There was absolutely nothing wrong with the effort the government expended (except perhaps for the chartered aircraft to return her to Canada) on behalf of Ms Martin. However, in a world where there is ample opportunity for comparisons, it is not surprising that some Canadians see discrimination and even some measure of racism when such assistance is not offered to an Abousfian Abdelrazik. There it took a court decision – one that the government fought tenaciously.

Today the case is that of Ms Suaad Hagi Mohamud. Here the insensitivity of the government in such matters has been unmercifully demonstrated. Overlooked in the reporting of the case is the fact that the government resisted DNA testing for Ms Mohamud for weeks. It was only when her lawyer filed a motion before the Federal Court that the government agreed to the testing on July 22 – two months after she had been detained in Kenya.

The Prime Minister a few days ago in commenting on Ms Mohamud observed the difficulty of dealing with such matters, especially when foreign governments may not be cooperative. He is right in making such an observation, as many cases depend on the cooperation of foreign governments. However, he misses the point completely when so many of the recent cases have nothing to do with the actions of foreign governments. Rather it is the action and policy of the Canadian government that has created the problems. Canadians should be rightly concerned with these developments. If not, the ghosts of Arar, El Maati, Almalki and Nureddin will haunt us for years to come.

The *Globe and Mail*

Dragging Through the Courts
August 25, 2009

THE MOVE BY THE FEDERAL GOVERNMENT TO SEEK PERMISSION TO appeal the recent decision of the Federal Court of Appeal concerning Omar Khadr to the Supreme Court again emphasizes the need for a better system to deal with such matters.

The Federal Court of Appeal in its August 14 ruling stated that the federal government had an obligation to seek the return of Khadr from the American prison at Guantanamo Bay. However, the increasing frequency of these issues and the lingering distress to those affected makes the courts a poor substitute for faster and more comprehensive action.

The Khadrs have been part of the Canadian political consciousness for well over a decade and the specific circumstance of Omar has been before the Canadian courts for the past three years. Above and beyond their issues is the question of the obligation of the government to assist Canadians when in difficulty in foreign countries. While many Canadians may be heartedly weary of the tribulations of the Khadr family, the central issue they represent should be of direct concern to all citizens.

Many will not see a direct connection between the Khadrs and Suaad Hagi Mohamud, Ronald Smith, Abdihakim Mohamed, Abousfian Abdelrazik or Brenda Martin. There is, nevertheless, a direct and important connection in that they represent graphically the range of reactions by the government in the assistance provided to Canadians in foreign countries.

The government has made abundantly clear in its arguments before the courts that it has and must continue to have the discretion to discriminate on the assistance it provides to Canadians abroad. This has been clothed in the doctrine of Crown or Royal prerogative, but essentially the argument assumes that these matters are aspects of Canada's foreign policy in which the government in its decision making is not subject to the intervention of the courts. The fact that the courts have become the last resort for such matters strongly suggests that a better system is required.

It is worth stating that assistance to Canadians in foreign countries, especially when it involves decisions made by the government of Canada, is not a matter of significant foreign policy. In international law, a distinction is made between foreign policy as represented by diplomatic or political relations and consular relations. There are even separate multilateral conventions for the two distinct areas.

Rather, the decisions made by the government of Canada in the recent cases that captured the interest of Canadians relate directly to the relationship of Canadians to their government and no other government. The concern expressed by many Canadians, including the media, strongly questions the willingness of the government to assist all Canadians with consistency, fairness and equity. Many Canadians do not see any of these characteristics in those recent decisions.

Relevant decisions of previous governments can be questioned as to their merits or effectiveness, but it can be stated with some certainty there was never an issue of fairness or equity or consistency – as there is today. Equally, a search of the records of Federal Courts previous to 2006 did not produce a decision in which the issues associated with the current cases were manifest.

The nature of Canadian society and the troubled surrounding world suggests the involvement of the courts is not a temporary aberration. Rather it is likely such cases will continue if the government continues to believe it has discretion in such matters and can be arbitrary and discriminatory toward Canadians. The concept behind Canadian citizenship does not establish categories of citizenship whether in Canada or outside, and for the government to act as if there were seriously undermines the citizenship of all Canadians.

Other countries are facing some of the same issues; and while Parliament is still away for the summer, the Foreign Affairs Committee is sufficiently concerned to meet on August 26 to discuss the treatment of Suaad Hagi Mohamud. As such, there is an opportunity for the committee to start consideration of an alternative mechanism to the courts to resolve these matters, bearing in mind that parliamentary committees are not a proper forum either.

Already there are suggestions that there is a need for legislation, as is the case in a small number of other countries, which would remove or limit governmental discretion. At the same time such legislation could establish in law (there is nothing at this time) the responsibilities of the government to provide assistance to all Canadians in difficulty in foreign countries. The legislation could also establish in law the rights of Canadians to obtain such assistance.

There can be every expectation, even with obligations and responsibilities established in law, that there will continue to be disputes and differences in what is done by the government and what is expected by a Canadian.

As we have seen, the courts are cumbersome and expensive in resolving such disputes, especially in a timely manner. In other areas where there are disputes between the government and the citizen, special offices have been established, often called ombudsman, to investigate and obtain solutions and redress. An ombudsman for consular disputes would provide a forum for resolving such matters.

In all of this, Canadians can hope the government will recognize there is a serious issue of public policy in the current situation. Surely the government, given the string of judicial defeats in the past few years, would agree that a better approach is needed.

The Citizen

When Tragedy Strikes in Paradise
November 23, 2010

POOR MEXICO. "SO FAR FROM GOD AND SO CLOSE TO THE UNITED States," as one of its former leaders aptly described a constant in his country's history. Today, with the predations of narco traffickers, that closeness is eroding the significant progress the country has made over the last fifty years. In that progress, tourism has been at the centre of growth in all parts of the country, and nowhere is that more important than on the Yucatan peninsula with its world-class Mayan Riviera.

Over the past thirty years the Riviera has grown from a backwater, known only to a few intrepid travellers to a hundred kilometers of five-star hotels, restaurants, white sand and weather that Canadians see only in their wildest dreams. Hundreds of thousands of Canadians walk the beaches with a confidence that is rarely available at distant, large-scale tourist resorts. There have been a few tragic incidents, but when placed within the context of the numbers involved, the Mayan Riviera provides the dreams that so many of us seek when our own sun drifts to the south.

The blast last Sunday at the Grand Riviera Princess Hotel in Playa del Carmen that killed five Canadians along with two Mexicans tragically illustrates the occasional dangers associated with tourism on this scale. The cause of the blast has yet to be determined with any degree of certainty, and it may be there will be no certainty in the end. However, even if it is determined that the blast was the result of poor planning or errors on the part of the resort's management, there is no reason to jump to large conclusions about the ability of Mexico to welcome Canadians – and provide for their safety and security. Events of this nature in Mexico are no different than an event, a few years back, in north Toronto where a gas facility was allowed to be located in a residential area with disastrous consequences.

However, where there is a need for examination and review is the ability of the government of Canada to provide support and assistance to Canadians who are affected by such events. Already there are comments in the press by the relatives of two of the victims, a father and his young son, that the services available to the mother in the aftermath of the explosion were inadequate. "We were all very frustrated by the lack of communication and the slowness in . . . finding out where they had been taken and the lack of support for her" a relative in Canada was quoted as saying.

Comments like these are common in the aftermath of such events and they are words that should be taken seriously by those responsible for providing support and assistance to Canadians in these tragic circumstances. At the same time there is a need to measure the comments against what is possible when things go bang and Canadians are killed or injured.

The explosion at the Princess Hotel occurred early Sunday morning and the information available suggests that the local authorities were prompt in their response and provided more than adequate support to survivors. However, in the middle of such events there is always a large element of confusion and lack of information available to those who have an urgent need for details about loved ones in the shortest possible time possible.

Canada has a consulate located at Cancun, less than an hour's drive north of Playa del Carmen, but it is not clear how soon officials from that office were on the scene of the blast. Most likely it was several hours before detailed information was available, but in this age of instant communication the media and relatives in Canada of those at the hotel and in the region were aware of the explosion and were seeking information from Foreign Affairs in Ottawa.

Again, from the limited information available, it appears the Mexican authorities were prompt in identifying those who had died and by Tuesday, less than three days after the explosion, arrangements were being made for the release of the remains and their transportation to Canada. In such situations, for that to happen in a relatively short time frame suggests considerable work was being done by Canadian officials. While relatives and friends would hope for even faster action, that is almost impossible.

Where Canadian officials increasingly fail in such situations is their unwillingness to communicate in real time with the public about their actions. It is this more than anything else that results in criticism and unnecessary uncertainty for those with relatives who may be involved.

For a number of years, it has been apparent that less and less information is released, with officials hiding behind the provisions of the Privacy Act. The Privacy Act was never designed for this purpose and there is an urgent need for those involved to speak to the public about their actions. Not to do so adds to the natural anxiety that attends disasters, such as the one in Playa del Carmen.

The Citizen

Canadians Abroad Deserve Our Help
March 3, 2011

DUNKIRK IT ISN'T.

Even before the last Canadian leaves Libya, the anti-immigration nativists are trotting out their threadbare arguments concerning the gullibility of the Canadian government and most Canadians – because we want to help our fellow citizens in difficulty in foreign countries. David Harris is no stranger to these arguments, and in the March 1 *Citizen* decided that the opportunity to do so again could not be missed.

Mr Harris, who does not deign to call these people citizens, prefers instead the label "passport-holders" in the hope that he can disguise who they are. They *are* citizens and, from the reporting, it is clear there are very few whose ancestors came from the northern edges of the Sahara – which is the assumption behind most of Mr Harris' argument. Instead they are the workers for and owners of small technical and oil and gas service companies and construction workers. As with thousands of others they have accepted that the world does not begin and end at the borders of Canada and have looked abroad for work, rather than look for handouts from their fellow citizens.

Canadians travel more than most. They do so for the full range of reasons – February, work, inquisitiveness, study and to see family and friends. Thirty years ago we saw fit to include international travel as one of the principles in our Charter of Rights and Freedoms. There was nothing startling in doing so; rather it reflected the very core of Canadian society. We were and are here as immigrants and fortunately, except for a few who hark back to some non-existent previous state of nature, Canadians and their governments take pride in what has been achieved. Those who measure the "costs" have Uriah souls, knowing nothing of the "values."

Canadians abroad are not any less "Canadian" for being so. To suggest they are pariahs harks back to a concept of Canada that has very little to do with the world as it is in the first years of the twenty-first millennium, or our collective image of ourselves. Are those of us who huddle along the American border more Canadian for doing so? Not in the least. The Canadians who venture forth – some back to the lands of their ancestors, others more broadly into a world that earlier Canadians fought to create – are to be encouraged and valued. The young Canadian Red Cross worker on the Tunisian border with Libya is representative of our collective futures.

Mr Harris sees great dangers for Canada in today's measured immigration. He erroneously cites "half a million in a single year," goes on to label this as of "unconscionable great social, economic and security cost," expresses the core of his argument as a warning that "passport-holders' connections with crisis-ridden countries" will expose Canada to "far-flung expatriates demanding Ottawa's assistance."

These fevered thoughts bear little relationship to reality. The arguments are akin to a business that does its books using only the costs of its activities and not including the income. It bears repeating that Canada without migration would be soulless and not the vibrant, dynamic and multifaceted land it is, where fellow humans from "crisis-ridden countries" come for relief and respite. Some return to their places of birth for many reasons, often no more complicated than to care for family members who have stayed behind, or for reasons of business. To label such persons as lacking "loyalty and commitment" to Canada assumes an idea that is without foundation.

Mr Harris gives some attention to the direct cost to the Canadian purse in providing assistance to Canadians needing evacuation from places such as Libya. Again his comments are inaccurate. There are no direct costs to the Canadian treasury. In 1996 the government of the day introduced a Consular Service Fee of $25.00. This is paid each and every time a Canadian applies for a passport. It generates millions of dollars annually. In 2010, some five-million passports were purchased by Canadians, generating revenue of approximately 125-million dollars which went to the Consolidated Revenue Fund. Since its inception in 1996, the Consular Service Fee has generated excess revenue over and beyond the costs of consular services, even when large evacuations, such as that from Lebanon in 2006, are included.

As well, a number of other consular services require the payment of fees and these generate several million dollars each year. As such, to suggest that Canadians in general are paying for evacuations or other services abroad is also without foundation.

There are problems in providing assistance to Canadians when they are in difficulty in foreign lands. Expectations are always higher than circumstances permit. That some of these Canadians needing assistance are former or concurrently citizens of a particular country or are there for narrow financial reasons is not sufficient reason to slash and burn the very policy that gives lifeblood to this country. It suggests a warped understanding of who we are and what we are about. Rather, we should take some pride in the fact that Canadians go out into the world and, we hope, contribute to the better world we all want.

The Citizen

Are We Paying More for Consular Services than Necessary?
April 9, 2013

IT IS WITH SOME RELUCTANCE THAT THIS ATTEMPT IS BEING MADE TO turn back the covers on a small aspect of the government's budgetary process. The Perils of Kevin (Page that is) come readily to mind when anyone tries to interpret financial data in ways that differ from the orthodoxy of government financial managers.

While the aspect in question is small, when set against the vast array of numbers thrown at Canadians throughout the budgetary process, the principle involved was sufficient to attract the attention of the Auditor General in 2008.

The issue concerns the fees Canadians pay for consular services and how those fees are administered by the government. Consular are those services provided by government to Canadians when they run into trouble outside of Canada.

The consular-service fee was instituted during the budgetary process of 1995-96 when it was one of the government's revenue proposals as part of a program review. It was a modest proposal: Canadian adults applying for a passport would be required to pay $25 in addition to the cost of the passport. The fee would be used exclusively to maintain and enhance the level of consular services. It was as much an insurance premium as a fee.

The implementation at the time was without serious opposition or comment, as most Canadians agreed with the principle that those who required exceptional services from their government should be expected to pay for those services.

The volume of passports sold (1.4 million in 1997) was expected to raise $35 million in revenue, the approximate cost of delivering consular services as measured by the rough tools of program costing at the time.

Under the enabling legislation and regulations, there was a requirement that such fees be used exclusively to finance the services to Canadians on which they were based. In March 2004, the government of the day enacted the User Fees Act aimed at "strengthening the elements of accountability, oversight, and transparency in the management of user fee activities." That requirement has been maintained with today's Travel.gc.ca website, stating clearly:"All the fees collected are used to maintain and improve Canadian consular services around the world." Unfortunately, there has been no reliable annual test of this assertion.

Problems from the outset
Right from the outset there were problems with how the fees were used. The money collected went to the Consolidated Revenue Fund of the government.

However, budgeting for consular services remained within the context of Foreign Affairs, and there was no willingness on the part of financial managers to bring the revenue produced by the consular fees and consular expenditures within shaking hands of each other. Rather, budgeting for consular services remained subject to the vicissitudes (or in the view of many, the lottery) of the allocation process.

Over the years the number of passports sold has quadrupled. In 1997, 1.4 million were sold, while in 2011 it was more than 4.8 million. That figure has been fairly constant for the past five years, reflecting the changed American entry requirement for Canadians. With very few exceptions, a passport is now required. Today more than 60 per cent of Canadians have a valid passport.

Consequently consular-service fee revenue has risen accordingly. Now it is close to a hundred-million dollars a year. Over the period since 1996, when the fee was implemented, almost a billion dollars in revenue has been collected. In the last four years alone more than $360 million was collected.

Over that same period the cost of consular services has risen as well and in 2012-13 is estimated at $65.7 million. For the next two years the Estimates show a reduction in the cost of the services, down to $62.9 million as part of the government's deficit-reduction process.

The Auditor General in a March 2008 report noted that in 2006-07 the government collected about $1.9 billion in service fees. In the section devoted to the consular-service fee, the Auditor General wrote that the department collected more "in consular fees than the cost of providing the related services."

The report went on to note that Foreign Affairs agreed that its "costing methodology for the consular services fee needs to be reviewed."

The department also stated that "over the past five years, including the costs of the Lebanon evacuation in 2006-07, there is a modest deficit from the consular services fee." It did not define "modest" and there is every reason to question the assertion.

Since then there has been little apparent effort by Foreign Affairs to bring the fees collected into some degree of balance with the cost of delivering consular services.

In the current fiscal year, it is expected that about $95 million will be collected in fees while the spending forecast is only $65.7 million. In its forecast of expenditures for the next two years the costs of consular services will be reduced by almost $3 million per year to $62.9 million.

There is no suggestion that revenues through the consular-service fee will be reduced as a result of fewer Canadians buying passports.

The audited figures from the Passport Office, which collects the consular-service fee on behalf of Foreign Affairs, are puzzling by themselves. Over the four-year period from 2009 to 2012 the collected fees sequentially are $86.6 million, $95 million, $86 million, and $94.5 million. However, the sale of passports through that period remained fairly constant. No reasoning is given for these variances, but they suggest there is need for an explanation before anyone accepts the government's assertion that there is a deficit in the consular-fee account.

An equally troubling aspect of the delivery of consular services is the government's steadfast assertion that such services are discretionary, forming part of the Crown Prerogative. Most recently the government successfully maintained this assertion before the Supreme Court in 2010. As is apparent from recent history there is very little difference between "discretionary" and "discriminatory" in the government's lexicon. It is equally ironic for the government to collect fees for a service that it maintains it has *no legal duty to provide.*

Embassy

Modernising the World of Consular Affairs
May 9, 2013

THE LOWY INSTITUTE'S ALEX OLIVER IS ONE OF ONLY TWO OR THREE researchers and commentators in the world of foreign policy who broadens foreign-policy matters to include consular issues.

For the most part, consular affairs is the ugly duckling of foreign-policy matters and rarely receives the intellectual attention it deserves – except when citizens are in difficulty in a foreign country and there is a national clamour for governments to mount up and ride to the rescue. The understanding of what is to be done or can be done is as scarce as water in the Sahara. And there are few signs that that understanding is becoming deeper or that there is even an urge for greater depth.

Ms Oliver has followed the consular-policy scene in Australia for some years and has done comparative research in other countries in the hope that there are examples, programs and policies that might be of value to those who make the decisions in Canberra.

For eleven years I was head of consular services for the Canadian government and, since retirement, I have continued to follow the matter in considerable detail. The problems highlighted by Ms Oliver in her latest paper, *Consular Conundrum*, are similar in Ottawa: more citizens traveling at both ends of the age spectrum; a government reluctant to provide additional resources and a blind adherence to the idea that more can be done with less; citizens and politicians who believe that mere waving of the national wand will produce miracles in a foreign land.

As part of the solution to these challenges, Ms Oliver recommends large, widespread publicity efforts to condition travellers to prepare for the problems they may encounter in foreign countries. I have serious reservations on the value of such efforts, as they are rarely successful, extremely expensive, and seldom sustained to the point that they influence behaviour. Canadian consular history is littered with a variety of such efforts and it is not unfair to say that they have bordered on the useless, except that they give ministers the illusion that they are doing something. One exception is the very targeted campaigns aimed at a select audience in a narrow time frame.

Another of Ms Oliver's recommendations is a consular fee or levy.

In 1996 Canada instituted the $25 Consular Service Fee that is collected at the time a passport is sold. Over the intervening years this has generated more thanC$1 billion in revenue and, in recent years with close to five-million passports being sold annually, annual revenue of almost C$125 million. The Consular Service Fee is paid by those likely to need consular services and is cast at a level sufficient to meet the costs. Interestingly, there was very little adverse public comment when the fee was implemented, and even today it is non-controversial.

Ms Oliver mentions technological innovation in her paper, but there is a much bigger story here. Australia probably trails most countries in its efforts to use technology to lessen the costs and burdens of providing consular services. Canada was the first to deploy the Consular Services Case Management System(COSMOS) to manage consular services, a system I designed and implemented. It has allowed a range of services to be more effectively delivered and managed and, at the same time, provided management with information on which services could be improved and costed.

Early on, I thought other countries could benefit from such software, and it has since been purchased by New Zealand, Spain, Ireland, Denmark, the Netherlands and the UK, with several other countries poised to purchase. Australia, since the late 1990s, has looked at COSMOS but has preferred to try and develop its own system, with little success. In the process it has spent many millions and today it is about to try again. It is a common failure in the IT world for those in the backroom to believe they can do better, even when 'off-the-shelf' technology is available. They rarely do.

Finally, the international consular policy environment is sadly deficient and has not had coherent attention since the signing of the Vienna Convention on Consular Relations in 1963. It is fifty years old this year and, even at the time of negotiation, it was such a compromised document that it offered little (except Article 36) by way of governmental commitments to assist those in consular difficulty. It was the sad result of lowest-common-denominator treaty-making, based largely on the historical norms that a diplomat at the Congress of Vienna would recognise.

I have suggested for a number of years that it is time for the UN to establish a review conference for the Convention to see if additional supporting mechanisms and principles can be included. The argument against doing so is the danger that we could lose what little protection there is in the existing document; I would argue thatlittle would be lost in trying to do better.

Great attention is given today to the globalisation of most areas of human activity. Last year one billion global citizens travelled to a foreign country. There is hope that the movement of people to the far corners of the world for education, tourism, business and family connections will bring about a long-lasting desire for peace, tranquility, fraternity and economic progress.

The signs are there, but happenstance is a poor guarantee that the casualties along the way will be not only minimised but helped. Of course, national governments retain responsibility for this, but there must be an acknowledgment that all governments need to work together. As we wander into the heart of the 21st century, no better monument can be created than a concerted effort by all governments to take the 1963 treaty and give it the norms that are necessary in today's world.

Lowy Institute

Diplomacy is always the final answer.

—Attributed to Gar Pardy

4. A Miscellany of Afterwords

IN 1975, LIFE IN OTTAWA AFTER THREE YEARS IN INDIA WAS BOLDLY interrupted with the suggestion that a posting to Beirut, Lebanon was in order to cement the ongoing efforts to become bilingual. The language lessons had continued throughout those years and there was receptivity to the idea that a few years in Beirut would complete the process and lend some fluidity to what was still a skill without mastery. But it was not to be. The simmering Lebanese civil war suddenly became hot and Beirut was at its epicenter. In a matter of days Beirut was of and instead our luggage was on its way to the Canadian High Commission in Nairobi, Kenya. Ever helpful Personnel suggested that the *Alliance François* in Nairobi might offer a suitable alternative for ongoing language studies.

Kenya in 1975 was dominated by the majestic President Mzee Jomo Kenyatta, one of the prime movers in the world-wide movement for African independence. He was an old man and a favourite diplomatic parlour game was to try and scratch the future as to developments following his death. He had led Kenya from its independence in 1963 first as Prime Minister then as President and Kenya in 1975 was a stable and increasingly prosperous country. The settler economy was largely dismantled and sharp edges from the fight for independence – the Mau Mau period – were disappearing with land redistribution favouring the major tribal group, the Kikuyu. Many of the settlers who had departed for Rhodesia during the early days of independence were returning and the wonders of Kenya's natural resources – wildlife and Indian Ocean beaches- were attracting thousands.

It was not long after arriving in June that the name Leakey and the importance of Kenya and East Africa to the world of paleontology leaped to the forefront. Richard Leakey was head of the Nairobi National Museum while his mother Mary was busy digging in nearby Tanzania's Olduvai Gorge where the footprints of one of our hot-footed ancestors gave dramatic and personal identification to a time when volcanos gave daily evidence of smoky violence. Louis Leakey, the idiosyncratic leader of the family died three years earlier but his influence on things paleontology in East Africa was still very much in evidence. Louis also played an enormous role in promoting research of primates within their natural habitats. Jane Goodall, Dian Fossey and Birute Galdikas were early recruits for this work and nearly fifty years later their impact on our understanding of our nearest cousins is still current.

For newcomers to Nairobi the influence of the Leakeys was enormous and provided the opportunity for firsthand experience and knowledge on these two fundamental fields of human enquiry. Richard a few years earlier doing field research on the eastern shore of Lake Turkana on the border with Ethiopia has unearthed fossils pushing back understanding of our human existence to millions of years. A copy of one skull (ER 1470 *Homo rudolfensis*) still sets among our treasures from East Africa. During this period the wonderment of human migration became an area of interest and in this section there are several articles on how a few hundred people some 60,000 or so years ago left Africa and populated the world.

But it was not all wonderment of the natural sciences. The High Commission was also responsible for the relationship with Uganda, then under the iron fisted and deadly rule of Ida Amin. I was the point person for Uganda and there was hardly a day when Ida Amin did not roil the international system with the nasty deeds of his government. Frequent trips were necessary, all by road requiring some 24-hours of driving and hours negotiating with border officials who were not inclined to be cooperative. Kampala and Uganda were gems of the tropics but five years of Amin misrule had destroyed all; agriculture was disappearing and it was a national holiday when the local brewery was able to bottle "fresh" beer. Bodies were a common sight and one of the world's most beautiful sites – where the Nile left Lake Victoria – had the most contented crocodiles in the world; they could hardly stir themselves at the sight of another body for the eating.

In late June 1976 Ida Amin and Uganda dramatically burst into the world's consciousness when the Popular Front for the Liberation of Palestine – External Command (PFLP-GC) successfully hijacked an Air France Airbus 300 to Entebbe with 248 passengers. A few days of negotiations resulted in the release of most of the non-Israeli passengers but over a hundred included the Air France crew remained. They were threatened with death and the Israeli government running out of options mounted one of the most successful hostage rescue operations outside of the Second World War. Sunday morning, July 4 was as usual a soft quiet day in Nairobi when reports of Israeli aircraft landing at the airport and before long the rescue operation dominated the news. The Kenyan government had cooperating closely with the Israelis and before long the planes were refueled and on their way back to Israel with the rescued hostages. One hostage was missing. Dora Bloch an Israeli-British dual citizen had the misfortune to be in hospital at the time of the rescue and in the aftermath of the rescue she was dragged from her bed and killed by Ugandan security officials. Her remains were only found in 1979 following the removal of Amin by the Tanzanian army.

Most western embassies had departed Kampala by the time of the hijacking but I continued making regular visits in order to wind up a variety of development assistance projects (mainly with the now moribund East African Community) and to bring comfort to the hundred or so Canadians still resident in country. These were mainly White Sisters and White Brothers, long time missionaries from Quebec who maintained schools and clinics for their Ugandan congregants. It was not long after the hijacking that I was on the road to Kampala with a load of Canadian whiskey and ginger ale the preferred drink of the White Sisters, and a request to see if any information was available as to what had happened to Dora Bloch. The White Sisters were their welcoming selves and it was an eerie feeling to relax in their inner rooms sipping rye and ginger in the candlelight while the distant sounds of gunfire could be heard.

Another stop on these periodic trips was with Dr Suzanne Corti and her husband Dr Piero Corti who ran a large regional medical centre – St Mary's Hospital near the northern city of Gulu. There the two doctors trained medical personnel and dispensed treatment to all who showed up in their clinic often during the political violence that raged in the region. My occasional visits included various supplies that could be collected in Kenya and smuggled through the border as diplomatic shipments. The Cortis along with Ugandan doctors were the first to identify AIDS in its early African manifestations and both died living among their patients a few years ago. Their daughter continues to work in support of the medical centre.

One of the more unusual matters during the East African years was a visit by Gerald Utting a journalist with the Toronto Telegram. Gerald was one of the Telegram's foreign correspondents and a few years earlier had been detained by the Palestinians in southern Lebanon. He was only held for a few weeks and after his release wrote of his experience with some acclaim. In late 1976 he decided that a period in Idi Amin's Uganda would make a good story and one morning he was in my office discussing his intentions. Caution was not Gerald's watchword and before long we had arranged for signals should he run into trouble. Of course he did and before long I was on my way to Kampala once again to see if he could be pried out of the clutches of the Amin regime.

Fortunately, earlier I had established contact with Bob Astles, one of the British hangers-on who served Milton Obote following independence. He was detained by Amin but was rehabilitated and became an informal functionary able to achieve things that the Foreign Ministry would not touch. Bob was helpful and before long Gerald was on his way to London on one of Amin's resupply of things British. Gerald once again wrote of his experience in a Ugandan jail again with widespread interest. I just developed a bad pain in the back from walking the Uganda walk where your head was closer to the ground than your ass. Astles received considerable notoriety when he was the model for Dr Nicholas Garrigan in Gilles Forden's novel *The Last King of Scotland.*

While in Kamala during these visits I often met with the French Ambassador, Pierre Renaud, who continued to maintain a western presence during the last violent years of the Amin regime. Renaud's residence was next to one of Amin's more notorious prisons and the noise was such that Mme Renaud returned to Paris. Often in the soft Kampala evenings Ambassador Renaud (he helped my French more than the Alliance in Nairobi) and I sat outside and discussed whatever was available for news in Uganda while nibbling cheese and sipping fine cognac. Our discussions were often interrupted by the sounds of animals in the nearby trees and the animals at work in the nearby prison.

The Amin regime limped along until 1979, a year after I had left for Washington. Then the neighbouring Tanzanian army marched in and in a matter of days overthrew the regime. Amin eventually was given "religious" protection by Saudi Arabia. A previous president, Milton Obote was restored to power but it was to be a short interregnum, as in 1985 there was a military coup and he was again driven from the country. Shortly thereafter the coup leaders were replaced by Yoweri Museveni, a rebel leader, who thirty years later still rules with a hard hand. In the intervening years the civil wars in Uganda, Rwanda and Congo have merged into a nasty regional war that continues to roil all. Fortunately outside powers for the most part have stayed aloof from these nasty wars and time as with most conflicts in Africa will be allowed to dampen these post-colonial tribal conflicts.

I left Kenya before the death of President Kenyatta. He died in August 1978 at a time I was adjusting to life in Washington during the sad last years of Jimmy Carter's Presidency. The end of Kenyatta presidency was peaceful but before long the forces of corruption, tribalism, regional differences soon came to dominate the country and almost inevitable lead to the horrendous tribal conflicts of the late years of the first decade of this century. Kenyatta's son Uhuru played a part and it was his political ally, Mwai Kibaki, who won the December 2007 presidential elections which lead to further tribal violence. Uhuru's actions were sufficiently causal that the World Criminal Court in The Hague indicted him on charges of crimes against humanity. The Court was caught in a wide scale push back by African leaders and the indictment was withdrawn. Uhuru is President today and ironically Kenya is now part of the tribal and religious conflicts from neighbouring Somalia. It remains a tough neighbourhood. (April 2015)

Book Reviews
September 26, 2006

The Saddest Country: On Assignment in Colombia, by Nicholas Coghlan. McGill-Queen's University Press, Montreal, 2004.

Far in the Waste Sudan: On Assignment in Africa, by Nicholas Coghlan. McGill-Queen's University Press, Montreal, 2005.

HOW NICHOLAS COGHLAN BECAME A MEMBER OF CANADA'S FOREIGN Service should be closely investigated. The selection process, the questions asked and those asking the questions should be identified, so that the information can be used to ensure persons of similar striking qualities are recognized and welcomed. Mr Coghlan's two books under review provide ample evidence that he is the sort of representative Canada needs, as it struggles to re-establish its place in the world and deal with the asymmetrical problems of a unbalanced international system.

Anyone in the space of a few years who can write comprehensive, understanding and perceptive books about two of the world's most difficult countries obviously has the talent to be on the front lines of our foreign service. Not only are the books well-written but Mr Coghlan has an eye for telling details which, while overwhelming at times, when synthesized provide the reader with a sense of place – and an understanding of why Colombia and the Sudan are the way that they are.

Of Colombia he writes that a massacre is "defined as the killing of four or more persons at one time and in one place" or, in the Sudan: "More court cases involved litigation over cattle and marriage dowries gone wrong with the horn size and skin colour of bulls providing much grist for learned legal debate." In both countries, it is amply clear that outsiders have not had or will ever have sufficient import to materially alter the inevitable direction of their national roads to ruin.

In many ways the books document his (and those of his ever-present Jenny) extensive travels in both countries. (Some of his trips must have caused sphincters to tighten on Sussex Drive in Ottawa). And it is not aimless travel. It is in the great tradition of the 19th century when the traveller frequently brought understanding and a nimble mind that provided the basis for discovery and insight.

In Colombia there was hardly a river (and there are many) that Mr Coghlan did not navigate and, in doing so, saw the country for what it is – an Eden where too many apples have been eaten. In the Sudan, the clash of some of the world's great civilizations and religions, African, Arab and others continues to dominate. And these are places where inept, to be kind, or more accurately, exploitative leaders and outsiders ensure that even time, the greatest of all solutions, will not bring redress or resolution.

Colombia is the more familiar of the two for Canadians. However, the Sudan with its latest festering boil, Darfur, is closing the gap and is becoming one of those international flashes that Canadians adopt – and then turn away from with easy aplomb.

Colombia is where insurgency is a business. It overlaps with the drug barons and the oil companies. Whatever the original reasons for the creation of the ideological insurgent groups of FARC, the ELN or the EPL some fifty years ago, or even longer, if one accepts "root" causes as a justification for such violence, these have long faded – and today the FARC and EPN dominate territory, exercise many of the attributes of government and ensure that for the long-suffering Colombians, long-suffering will remain.

The emergence of the paramilitaries, or the paras, as a not-so-secret weapon for the Colombian military, government and large economic interests, added another volatile chemical element in an already explosive mixture. Along with the government and the drug barons, the paras are, as Mr Coghlan writes, according to the Colombians themselves, the "actors" in their dance macabre. And ironically, as actors their "roles" cannot be assumed in advance of specific events.

Mr Coghlan describes the interplay between these elements in one small battle:

> *It looked as though what had happened was that the guerrillas had attacked, but the paras had then encouraged the population to leave and in turn then pressure the military to reinforce the garrison at Jurado – thus providing a shield for a renewed para presence.*

He goes on:

> *The remains of the police station were an awesome sight. For one hundred metres all around, the dirt was pitted by ten-foot craters left by the launching of the FARC's now trademark propane canister mortars. . . .*

> *At the Marine base, the scene was even grimmer. . . . You could work out which were the last holdouts by piles of used rocket-propelled grenade cartridges.*

As he left this scene, Mr Coghlan writes:

> *All this, of course, in that South Seas location. We boarded the Belalcazar at midnight for a ride back to Bahia Solano; the stars were so bright you could read by them, and the dolphins left phosphorescent trails as they dived under and around our bows. Another day in paradise.*

Mr Coghlan's book is replete with such scenes and their cumulative effect is one of Dante-esque despair, and no doubt the reason for the title of his book, *The Saddest Country*.

There is hardly a section of the country, that Mr Coghlan's cool but sympathetic eye does not take in. From the Darien Gap on the border with Panama in the north (". . . Cacarica Watershed. Cacarica, translated literally, mean 'Rich Shit.' ") to Puerto Asis, Putumayo, in the south where "80 percent of the department's economically active population, i.e., 97 percent of the rural population, is directly engaged in one phase or another of the cocaine business." And, despite focussed attempts to limit the trade, "forty tons of finest Putumayo cocaine still reached North America and Europe every year. A fitting epitaph to the decades' long 'war on drugs.' "

Colombia, in addition to its well-known reputation for cocaine (and increasingly for poppy by-products, as Mr Coghlan wearily notes), is also known as the kidnapping capital of the world. Kidnapping, drugs and an extensive protection racket provide all of the main actors – the insurgent groups, the paras, the drug barons and the government – with the grease that keeps the present sad system humming. It is a successful "failed" state.

It is, however, kidnapping – both for its lucrativeness and its widespread intimidation value – that continues to dominate Colombian life. As Mr Coghlan notes, middle-class Colombians form the "vast majority" of those taken and, as "an increasing number of couples make living will pacts that stipulate that if one is kidnapped, the other will not pay – kidnappers are turning more and more to children."

Mr Coghlan discusses two such cases, involving Canadians, in which he too was involved and, while he does not say so directly, it is clear that, as we have known for years, everyone pays. Purist far from the scene of such events decry these payment, but anyone who has been on the front lines knows that the higher moral duty is to ensure the release of these unfortunate victims. Coghlan gives true and well-deserved credit to his locally engaged consular officer, Ida, "our long serving and highly reliable," official. In these days of doubt about the Foreign Service Ida Isaak and Mr Coghlan are valuable examples of the quality of persons we need to see more often.

Weaker persons might have reconsidered their decision for a career in the Foreign Service upon learning that, after three years in Colombia, you were assigned in 2000 to open an "office" of the Canadian embassy in Khartoum. However, Mr Coghlan did not miss a step; in his words "you cry when you learn you have been posted to Sudan, but you cry harder when the time comes to leave."

The book from this assignment, published in 2005, and titled *Far in the Waste Sudan*, provides another example of Mr Coghlan seeing a country from the ground up and the people down. His travels were as extensive as in Colombia and, if that is possible, more dangerous. While *The Saddest Country* is almost exclusively about Colombia, *Far in the Waste Sudan* provides a compelling account of such associated issues as the politics and effectiveness of humanitarian and development assistance in such situations, the effect and politics of the discovery of oil, the machinations of leaders whose first interest after decades of war was more personal than enlightened, and Canadian commercial interests in the Sudan.

Mr Coghlan left the Sudan just as Darfur ("Home of the Fur People" which gives a sense of the climate just a few miles north of the Equator) was becoming critical – but just as another peace agreement bought a welcomed respite to the war in the south. Except for two short aid-related trips to Dafur and several days hiking throughout the area centered on the fabled mountains of Jebel Marra ("a lake rich in myths and legends, whose depths were reputed to be the home of evil itself."), there was little going on in the Sudan at that time to indicate the birth of another insurgency – nor the ferocity and obtuseness of the reaction by the government in Khartoum.

However, there is much in the book about the war in the south. Mr Coghlan's descriptions of the pig-headedness of the government in Khartoum, the rebels with political headquarters in Nairobi, and their respective international supporters clearly demonstrates that any eventual permanent solution in Darfur will be long in coming and involve untold suffering.

The discovery of large quantities of oil in south-central Sudan in the late '70s and early '80s, much of it in the contested areas, introduced a new dynamic into the decades-old civil war. As Mr Coghlan notes, oil was the reason Canada opened a diplomatic office in Khartoum in 2000 – not because it needed the oil but because a heavy hitter from Calgary, Talisman Energy (formerly BP Canada), bought out the interest of Arakis, another Canadian firm, in 1998. Talisman brought new capital (25 per cent interest in the project) but also modern oil technology and, within a few years, hundreds of million in revenue for Khartoum – which by 2001 amounted to "40 percent of the Sudanese government's budget."

As Mr Coghlan wryly notes, "Talisman had done its geological and financial homework, but it had no idea of the political and public relations quagmire into which it was wading by acquiring Arakis and pursuing the Sudan project." It was not long before it did, as Talisman became a sitting duck for Canadian and international humanitarian organizations (with Canadian government hand-wringing on the side), and by 2003 it threw in the towel and sold its share to the Oil and Natural Gas Corporation (ONGC) of India (a clone of the early days of Petro Canada) for $1.1 billion.

A footnote to the Talisman story occurred in September 2006 when an American judge denied a claim by the Presbyterian Church of Sudan. The claim, filed in 2001, alleged that Talisman aided and abetted the Sudanese government in a brutal campaign of ethnic cleansing and rights abuses in south Sudan. The company is reported to have been "pleased" with the ruling.

This chapter should be required reading for any Canadian resource company (or others, since the field for humanitarian concerns are broadening as we read) interested in investing in a country with a record such as that of the Sudan. However, there are ups and downs to such investments and Mr Coghlan ably highlights them. While he does not go so far, there are four conclusions that might be reached:

- While forced out by domestic and international pressure, Talisman's continued presence in the Sudan might have brought greater interest in and resources for community development and emergency relief work than its successor, the ONGC. Certainly, by the time that it left, it was actively involved in humanitarian work in its areas of activity.

- Secondly, the new capital invested by Talisman meant that the oil pipeline to Port Sudan, the expansion of the oil fields, along with the increase in oil prices after 2001 provided the Sudanese government with resources allowing it to become more robust and bloody in its fight with the southern rebels.

- By the same token, the rebel commanders in the south, seeing the ever-increasing revenue accruing to Khartoum probably made the calculation that the only way they were going to get their hands on any of it was though a peace agreement. Accordingly, in 2002 peace agreements were signed – one dealing with the Juba Mountains region and the other, the Machakos Protocol, covering self-determination for the south and the separation of state and religion. These agreements appear to be holding and southern leaders are now part of the gravy train in Khartoum. (John Garang, the leader of the Sudan Peoples Liberation Army for many years, became Vice President of the Sudan following the peace agreements. He died in a helicopter crash on July 30, 2005 in southern Sudan. There are questions still as to the cause of the crash.)

- Fourth, it might be extrapolated that the hard-nosed reaction of Khartoum to the emergence of the insurgency in Darfur in 2003/04 was supported by the ever-increasing oil revenues. Having forced the south to accept an agreement, after fifty or so years of conflict, it is likely that Khartoum believes Darfur is an easier problem. And certainly, no one will suggest that Sudanese oil be internationally sanctioned.

Mr Coghlan's frequent observations on humanitarian and development assistance in war torn Sudan should be required reading for those who make large decisions concerning these issues. There is no doubt that delivering assistance into Sudan in the midst of a civil war was a daunting task. That people did succeed, as Mr Coghlan notes, was a tribute to the hundreds of organizations, governmental, non-governmental and international that were involved. However, there was a "niggling doubt":

> *What would happen when back in London, Washington, and Ottawa people started to lose interest and there was nothing left for the planes to carry? The SPLM/A had been in control of a very large portion of territory for nearly twenty years now – wasn't it about time they started to feed their own people? And what kind of self-sufficiency and resilience were we encouraging by dropping hundreds of thousands of tons of grain out of the back of planes, however accurately, month after month, year after year?"*

In some ways the most discouraging chapter in the book is the fifth which records Mr Coghlan's conversations with the political "elite" of Khartoum. These are all honourable, (not a too- formal word to use), educated, experienced men (there are no women, of course) and democratic politicians. There is little sense that they preside over one of the world's more reviled political systems. One is almost left with the impression that, if only General Omar Bashir were to leave the scene, they would see that a new Sudan appeared. However, in one conversation with a former President, Mr Coghlan records what may well be the epitaph for the Sudan: "There are many Dafurs in Sudan."

These are rare books about two of the world's most troubling countries and, being written by a person who walked the ground and talked with those involved, are all the more enlightening. Not many, if any, members of Canada's Foreign Service have produced books of this quality and importance. Perhaps Mr Coghlan's example will lead more to do so, as Canadians and the world need all the help they can get on the issues that both books so ably portray. I have already suggested to the personnel department of Foreign Affairs that Mr Coghlan's next assignments should be to Papua New Guinea and Albania.

bout de paper, Vol. 22. No. 3.

The Definition of a Nation
October 11, 2006

LOOKING FOR IDEAS IN THE CONTEXT OF A POLITICAL-PARTY LEADership race is akin to looking for elephants in spruce trees. Experience shows that neither is likely to be found.

It was thus a surprise when Michael Ignatieff a month ago declared that the "future of Canada includes the recognition of Quebec and aboriginals as nations in our Constitution." Apart from in Quebec, the reaction among the country's pondering pundits was as if Mr. Ignatieff had broken wind at the Governor General's. The "n" words were again out and about in the land.

A few years ago, following the Charlottetown and Meech Lake imbroglios and the near-death referendum experience in 1995, the country – again except for Quebec – gave a collective shudder, and there was a silent consensus that "not in our lifetimes" would we open Pandora's constitutional box again.

What has been surprising, and it has again surfaced in the reaction to Mr. Ignatieff comments, has been the division over the current status of national unity. One editorial in a national paper stated without equivocation that "the current approach to national unity is working" and "national unity is not threatened."

Commentators from Quebec do not share that breezy view from Toronto. There, the reality is closer to home – and the view is common that the next national-unity crisis is no further away than the next provincial election. Independence has not gone away and remains a favourable option for more than 40 per cent of the Quebec population.

A victory for Andre Boisclair and the Parti Quebecois and we are all on the referendum road again. Most agree that Premier Jean Charest and his Liberals are a very thin defensive red line – and the political confusion in Ottawa does not offer a soupcon of comfort either.

The Clarity Act offers as much protection as a fig leaf in downtown Baghdad. The Supreme Court has already ruled that a clear majority in a Quebec referendum for separation requires the federal government to begin negotiations for the break-up of the country.

And does all of this hinge on a six-letter word that spells the same in English as it does in French? "Nation" and its associated culprits "nationality" and "national" approach nails-on-blackboard intensity for many English Canadians, while, in Quebec "nation" may be simply another way of saying "distinct society" – and perhaps "We love you."

In the minds of many English-speaking Canadians, "nation" is equivalent to "state" or "country" or, in another political sense, "kingdom. It is none of these in any legal sense, as is readily evident from history, particularly European history, from which we all sip on such matters.

Confusion is intensified when nation is combined with state to give us, in English, the Nation State. In its idealization, the nation state combines both a geopolitical and an ethnic/cultural/religious/linguistic unity. As is readily apparent, even with a modest understanding of this phantasmagorical world, there are few true nation states – and migration and immigration ensure that there will soon be even fewer.

Iceland is often cited as the only modern nation state. Whether more existed historically is hotly disputed by sociologists and political scientists and, as usual with such matters, they also dispute which came first, the nation or the state.

A word analysis of the works of Shakespeare illustrates how recent the word "nation" is in English. Writing in the late-16th and early-17th centuries, Shakespeare only used the word "nation" 27 times in his works – which more often than not involved issues of governance. On the other hand, he used "state" 237 times, "country" 144 times and "kingdom" 102 times. This in a land that today acknowledges at least four nations (without getting around to Yorkshire, the Isle of Man or the Channel Islands) within its bosom.

There would appear to be little reason for the rest of us to get upset about such a matter. All modern states are an amalgam of peoples with widely varying cultural, religious and linguistic backgrounds. Most are becoming more so.

The modern era of the state that is largely European originates out of the Peace of Westphalia, which in 1648 brought a negotiated end to the Hundred Years War. (There may be some lessons from that era for a Middle-East peace now that we are beyond six decades of war in that troubled region).

The 1648 peace treaty by no means gave Europeans peace for very long, but it did give them the outlines of an international system that provided recognition for each country's sovereignty and territory. It also allowed for the emergence of "national" independence movements and the creation of states, such as Italy and Germany.

Once the philosophers and propagandists had a go, it was not long before the mythical and destructive concept of the nation state emerged. It did so more on the basis of the need for rulers to deliver large messages – or as an attempt to create national unity. In all of this, racism was never far from the centre.

Europe, which has suffered the most from the extreme application of nationalism and the concept of the nation, is today on its way to becoming the world's first supra state. In the European Union the concept of nation is beating a retreat in the face of liberal labour mobility laws, as was epitomized recently by the "Polish plumber in Paris" drama. A shared flag, a national anthem, open borders and a common currency and passport illustrate what reasonable leaders can achieve.

Compared to many countries, Canada has less diversity than most. Here, however, the fog of political debate allows obscurantism and bigotry to get in the way of reasonable compromises and political bargains. We should know better than to expect that, by ignoring and avoiding the problems and the issues surrounding national unity, there will be anything more than short-term and false comfort.

The ugly old bear of national unity when out of sight does not become less fierce. Rather, time and the increasing success of the Quebec nation are simply adding to the magnitude of the problem and could easily lead to the need for a passport to travel from Ontario to New Brunswick.

It is hoped that these are the considerations that led Mr. Ignatieff to stick his finger into our eye a few weeks ago. It is uncharacteristically bold for a leadership candidate to do so. Perhaps 30-odd years of travelling other roads and seeing Canada from a distance provided for some measure of vision and perspective – and the courage (some would say foolhardiness) to act.

Those who stayed at home have no particular claim to wisdom or understanding on this issue and so far, collectively, they have adopted the sunny view from Toronto.

Ottawa Citizen

Nuclear North Korea: The Road from Chalk River
October 18, 2006

IT WAS A VERY DIFFERENT WORLD ON DEC. 8, 1953, WHEN THE recently elected U.S. President, Dwight D. Eisenhower, spoke to the General Assembly of the United Nations. In a speech that many today would fondly label as a "What if ...?" model, the President spoke of a different future than what had already come to pass. Eisenhower, the former Supreme Commander of the Allied forces in Europe, laid out for his global audience a vision of a new world in which the atom bomb, then only eight years old, would be put into the service of world peace and human progress.

The 1953 speech, called "Atoms for Peace," opened with the observation that, "Never before in history has so much hope for so many people been gathered together in a single organization." With a modesty and balance rarely seen today on such occasions, the President went on to detail an agenda where the United States, in co-operation with the other nuclear and near-nuclear powers, would take nuclear weapons "out of the hands of the soldiers" and put them "into the hands of those who will know how to strip its military casing and adapt it to the arts of peace."

Canada and the United Kingdom were acknowledged by the President as possessors of the "dread" atomic secrets and as countries "whose scientific genius made a tremendous contribution to our original discoveries, and the designs of atomic bombs."

A lot of water, both heavy and otherwise, has passed under the spans that bridge the period from 1953 to recent events in North Korea. But there are real connections because Canada – sometimes with honour and other times crassly commercialistic and naïve

– has been one of the main players in the spread of nuclear technology around the world.

Much nuclear technology, in the language of disarmament, is "dual use" and runs along a continuum from peaceful application to weapons development. However, there is a large area of overlap that has been a conundrum for the believers in peaceful use and non-proliferation experts. In the early days after Eisenhower's 1953 speech, there was a taking up of the ideas and an enthusiasm for the spread of nuclear technology, that in today's light seems breathtakingly naive. Nuclear reactors in everyone's backyard were seen as the road to a future in which peace and prosperity would reign.

Canada was ahead of most countries in promoting the value of nuclear technology in the service of humanity. Despite (or, some would say, because of) its significant involvement in the development of the first nuclear weapons, Canada in the mid-1950s was promoting its unique natural uranium/heavy water technology as the best – and there were eager customers.

An agreement with India in April, 1956, led to the delivery of an updated version of the Canadian NRX (National Research Experimental) reactor at Chalk River, called CIRUS. It was in operation by 1960 at the Bhabha Atomic Research Centre near Bombay. It was supported by an extensive exchange of scientists and the training of hundreds of Indian nuclear scientists, engineers and technicians in Canada. In nuclear technology terms, there is nothing with a greater "dual use" than knowledgeable, experienced people. India was in the nuclear age and on its way to having nuclear weapons.

This was followed in 1963 by an agreement to build a nuclear-power plant in the Indian state of Rajasthan, modelled on the CANDU reactor that was under construction at Douglas Point, Ontario. It was financed by Export Development Corporation funds on World Bank terms. Three years later, another agreement covered the building of a second reactor in Rajasthan on similar financial terms. There were safeguard agreements for both reactors (but not the NRX reactor near Bombay) that reflected the non-proliferation standards of the time.

In geopolitical terms, these were not auspicious times to be taking chances on nuclear technology in an unstable region. In 1962, India lost a disastrous war with China and only sued for peace when it was clear that the Chinese army was on its way to Calcutta. Shortly thereafter, China became a nuclear-weapons state with its first atmospheric test in 1964. The then Soviet Union provided considerable assistance, but that ended soon after with the Sino-Soviet split – and the Chinese nuclear program was indigenized.

In these circumstances, no Indian leaders – no matter how Gandhian they were inclined to be and, for the most part, they were not so inclined – could ignore the nuclear threat now represented by China. It was in the midst of the implementation of the Canadian agreements that the Indian decision to go "nuclear" was taken. A few years later, in 1974, the Indians held their first underground nuclear test, Operation Smiling Buddha. Not surprisingly, India used plutonium from the Canadian NRX reactor and another experimental reactor for the explosion.

As anyone familiar with the affairs of the Indian sub-continent will attest, there was a time when countries sought to be even-handed in dealing with India and Pakistan. So the Canadian government, reflecting the good work done with India on nuclear technology, agreed to provide Pakistan with a power reactor similar to those being built in Rajasthan.

Canadian General Electric, with the permission of the government of Canada, signed a turnkey contract in 1965 – and full power was achieved by October, 1972. Again, hundreds of Pakistani scientists, engineers and technicians were educated and trained on the nuclear technologies involved. And no one suggested that the Pakistani generals and civilian politicians did not accurately read what was going on in India.

By this time, the Eisenhower ideal of "Atoms for Peace" was in tatters, shredded by the harsh international environment in which nuclear powers used atmospheric tests to demonstrate their prowess – atomizing all peace efforts. For many, there was a realization that nuclear proliferation was on the march. In 1998, India again tested nuclear weapons, and Pakistan did so for the first time a few days later.

Canada sought to improve the safeguards it had with both India and Pakistan, but that horse was well and truly out of the stable. So, when both India and Pakistan refused to sign the Nuclear Non-Proliferation Treaty, which entered into force on March 5, 1970, Canada terminated all nuclear co-operations with them, except for safety-related material and assistance.

The connections between Pakistan and North Korea on nuclear matters remain murky, but enough is known to suggest that it has been a substantial two-way collaboration (nuclear technology for missile technology), lending considerable credibility to the recent claims by North Korea of having exploded a nuclear device. The Canadian assistance to and collaboration with Pakistani nuclear scientists and engineers, going back to the 1960s, has been transferred to North Korea, and is an integral part of the North-Korean nuclear-weapons program – no matter how limited or tentative it may prove to be.

It would be easy to be cynical about these developments or to second-guess the motivations of those who made the decisions 50 years ago that have led to the proliferation of the nuclear weapons we see today. However, what is significant is that the proliferation is as limited as it is.

There are now five nuclear-weapons states (the United States, the United Kingdom, Russia, France and China), as defined by the Non-Proliferation Treaty; there is one nuclear-weapons state (India) that has been given semi-official status by the United States; two declared weapons states (Pakistan and North Korea); and one widely perceived weapons state (Israel). There are also suspicions that Iran and Saudi Arabia have clandestine nuclear programs. One ray of hope is South Africa; it had nuclear weapons, but renounced them and signed the Non-Proliferation Treaty in 1991.

On the other side of the equation are the 188 states that are party to the Non-Proliferation Treaty, and, for the most part, provide no indication that they want to see their nuclear status change.

In many ways, the Non-Proliferation Treaty has been one of the most successful disarmament efforts ever, and the attention given to Iran and North Korea – while hesitant and reluctant on the part of some – augurs well for continuing effective control of this dangerous technology. Recalling the words of Eisenhower, it would be better if all of this culminated in "Atoms for Peace," but that ideal was for a less-cynical and less-complex world. Today, it is important that bombast and threats are met with balance and common sense.

Kingston Whig Standard

A Species on the Move
January 08, 2007

THE MODERN DIVINERS, SCIENTISTS WHO DECODE THE SHREDS OF DNA from the far corners of the world, have concluded that all Homo sapiens descended from a small group – possibly as few as 150 people – of migrants who left east Africa via the southern end of the Red Sea some 50,000 years ago.

The descendants of this group, within 5,000 years of leaving Africa, spread throughout Europe and Asia and reached Australia. Between 15,000 and 25,000 years ago, their descendants reached the Americas, but it was only about a thousand years ago that New Zealand was peopled. Predecessors in Europe and Asia, Homo erectus, while overlapping with Homo sapiens, disappeared in the process – an evolutionary dead end.

Ever since the departure of Homo sapiens from Africa, migration has been a constant element in human development. The urge or the need to move is as human as language. The diviners have also concluded with some confidence that there are more genetic differences within large groups than there are between them. Thus Canadians will have greater genetic diversity among themselves than they will have with Mongolians.

The migrations of the last two millennia established today's world. The Visigoths and Ostrogoths sacked Rome, leading to the arrival of the Angles, the Saxons and the Jutes in Britain, following the collapse of the Roman colony there; Slavic and Turkic peoples moved into and around Eastern Europe; Genghis Khan spread war and genes from China to Iran and Russia, and Europeans, in the second millennium, started a secondary migration to Australia, New Zealand, the Americas and various bits in between.

These migrations continue. Today, in just one small European country of about 16 million, there are large numbers of Berbers from the Rif Mountains of Morocco, Moluccans from Indonesia and more than 200,000 Surinamese from the shores of the Caribbean. That country is the Netherlands. The Hispanicization of the United States and the human kaleidoscope that is Canada demonstrate that the migratory urge remains one of this world's most characteristic features.

The amazing genetic commonality has done little to mitigate the phantasmagorical baggage of mind and soul we have inculcated since climbing down from the acacias. Language, music, religion, ethics, culture, and ethnicity emerged and, when influenced by climate and geography, have given us the diversity that leads to the best of times and often the worst of times.

The Age of Reason or the Enlightenment of the 17th and 18th centuries stands as a very large rock around which much of the baggage of the mind and soul began its evolutionary erosion. The importance attached to individuality and reason fundamentally altered our emotional and intellectual concepts. Most importantly, it led to standards requiring changes in our views of our fellow humans – and the relationship of the ruled to those ruling. While purveyors of cultural and intellectual relativity attempt to limit the effect of this 18th-century tsunami, it is still the tidal wave on which our intellectual and social evolutions are carried.

The migratory instinct today has been hugely influenced by the mainstays of the modern world – worldwide communications and transportation systems. Historically, migration was mainly a one-way affair with often-total severance of contact with home countries and families. Today, airlines have a special category of passage for migrants – VFFs (visiting family and friends), and communications companies strive to make international calling as inexpensive as that within a city.

Increasingly, this is causing the concepts of citizenship and its cohort nationality to lose their historical exclusivity and dominance. Instead, the human spirit and the actions of many demonstrate that our genetic commonality, our true humanity, strives to place reason and individuality at the forefront of human progress.

Europe, the birthplace of modern rationality, is leading the way on this enlightened path. Today there are hundreds of nationalities within 27 states and more to follow – striving and succeeding in lessening the bonds of tradition and ignorance to be European. Not many of our recent ancestors would be so foolish as to suggest that the "cockpit" of all modern wars would become the cauldron out of which the structure of a truly modern and peaceful world can be witnessed/observed.

In Canada there are those who would turn back the clock on the one truly great and unique Canadian value – our open door to the peoples of the world. The 1914 Komagata Maru incident, when Sikhs were not allowed to disembark in Vancouver, the internment of Ukrainians and Japanese Canadians, the Chinese head tax, and the words of one senior federal official in 1938 that none were "too many" in denying entry to Jewish refugees from Europe demonstrate just how far we have come.

Today the barriers against migrants are more subtle. Efforts to curtail dual citizenship, lengthening the citizenship-application process, taxation measures for Canadians living outside of Canada and, silliest of all, concerns that a facial veil will rock our domestic tranquility are current examples. These ideas and their underlying concerns demonstrate the willingness of some to narrow and limit the unique Canadian open door – and need to be resisted.

Those promoting such measures and concern do so in the name of promoting national security, obtaining a few more tax dollars, protecting our medical-care system from fecund aliens, limiting access to our educational system or, most insidiously, the maintenance of an "us and them" mentality, despite our genetic commonality.

While many of these underlying prejudices have long been with us and will not end soon, it is nevertheless troublesome when the federal government casually mentions that all of these matters may be subject to correction.

It is even more troublesome when many of these issues have long been with us and were not considered important when they involved tens of thousands of Italian, British, or German Canadians, or when a million or more Canadians live in the United States. The realization that several thousand Lebanese Canadians had returned to Lebanon or that many thousand more Canadians live in Hong Kong or India does not provide either the need or the rationale for corrective action.

Election talk abounds. Immigrants, being such a significant part of our body politic, will, as in the past, steady the nerves of those politicians who believe that accentuating differences and discord or establishing different classes of citizenship should be part of the Canadian value system.

The Citizen

Book Review

January 21, 2007

Nixon in China: The Week That Changed the World, by Margaret MacMillan. Viking Canada Penguin Group, Toronto, 2006, 395 pp., $45.00

SOME FIFTEEN YEARS AGO HISTORIAN FRANCIS FUKUYAMA PUBlished *The End of History and the Last Man*. His book, an expansion of a 1989 article, argued that the end of the Cold War and the break-up of the Soviet empire represented the end of the ideological struggle between principles of liberal western enlightenment and those of totalitarianism, as represented by the Soviet system. It was his view that the future would see democratic forms of government dominating the world's political systems. Unfortunately, his provocative and misunderstood title, especially the "end of history" part, lead to popular debunking of his analysis. (The Last Man element in the title is a concept of Nietzsche). Samuel Huntington's *Clash of Civilizations* is but the latest critical effort, but his suggestion that ideological conflicts are being replaced by "civilization"-based conflicts offers less intellectual rigour than that associated with Professor Fukuyama's thesis

As with many novel intellectual theses, that of Professor Fukuyama was adopted and adapted by others; many neo-conservatives both in the United States and elsewhere did so in support of their own action-agenda for the world. Assuming that Professor Fukuyama's interpretation of the future was reasonable, many neo-conservatives went one step further and argued that hastening the end of many of the remaining illiberal and nasty regimes was a laudable objective for American foreign policy. Never was the distance between thought and successful action greater – and today neo-conservatives are in ragged and disappearing retreat. Unfortunately, the thesis of Professor Fukuyama, which in intellectual terms should have provided some measure of unity between left and right, will suffer historical ignominy based on the actions of others.

The "end of history" metaphor now has a life of its own, and the "beginning and end of history" is a useful starting point when interpreting books dealing with recent events. It raises the question, looking backwards, when does history begin? Is it a few moments ago? A few months? Or a few or many years ago? History today, current history, modern history and recent history have all been used to describe books that promise to provide perspective on recent events, even though the perspective may be short-sighted or astigmatic.

Chou En-lai when asked for his views on the importance of the French Revolution replied that it was too early to come to any conclusions. A history professor many years ago put the time factor right when he offered the view that "history is argument without end." Along the same lines are the aphorisms of many reporters that today's news story is the "first version of history" or history is written by the victors.

These musings are more than applicable to Margaret MacMillan's latest book, *Nixon in China: The Week that Changed the World*. The book provides a detailed accounting of President Nixon's 1972 visit and, while it attempts to recount the Chinese, Russian and other roles, thoughts and actions associated with the event, it is very much the American version that Professor MacMillan provides. The vast majority of the references and the associated bibliography are overwhelmingly American-centric. As such, it will not be the final word on the visit, as important as the work may be, but rather the starting point for others who may be able to reflect access to a greater range of relevant material or a longer time span.

The sub-title of the book, *The Week that Changed the World*, is reflective of the sub-title of the professor's earlier book, *Paris 1919: Six Months that Changed the World*. Even in that case the title was a bit over-the-top – the jury is still out on some of the issues discussed and decided in Paris. As Richard Holbrooke wrote in the Foreword to *Paris 1919:*

> *Some of the most intractable problems of the modern world have roots in decisions made right after the end of the Great War. Among them one could list the four Balkan wars between 1991 and 1999; the crisis over Iraq (whose present borders resulted from Franco-British rivalries and casual mapmaking); the continuing quest of the Kurds for self-determination; disputes between Greece and Turkey; and the endless struggle between Arabs and Jews over land that each thought had been promised them.*

If the word "change" is used in its ordinary sense, then there is no doubt that events such as Nixon's visit to China, as with the Paris Peace Conference, did change the world. However, if "change" is used in a larger historical sense, then there is a need to adopt the Chou En-lai caution when ascribing historical importance to what are in essence recent events. There is perhaps enough perspective to agree that the events in Paris in 1919 did change the world in an historical sense, but I am more sceptical as to that claim for Nixon's visit to China which was less than forty years ago. There is even more scepticism when it is acknowledged that the phrase is one that President Nixon used to describe his visit. Professor MacMillan reports [page 307] the following:

> *. . . Under the influence of the maotai, or so Kissinger suspected, Nixon got carried away and suggested that the United States stood ready to defend China if any foreign power tried to attack it. Their joint communiqué, he said proudly, would*

make international headlines the next morning. After all, 'This was the week that changed the world'.

The central strength of Professor MacMillan's book is her vivid and, at times, psychologically deep portrait of one of the most complex men in American history, Richard Nixon. This is equally the strength of *Paris 1919*; her deft portrayals of Georges Clemenceau, David Lloyd George and Woodrow Wilson – and a supporting cast of hundreds of others – gave that book its lasting character. Richard Nixon is more than a match for any of that trio, having travelled the American road of Red-baiter, a shrewd reader of international omens and a manipulative and disgraced domestic politician. Professor MacMillan writes:

> **Even historians who disapprove of psycho-history find themselves tempted irresistibly when it comes to Richard Nixon. It is partly that he inspired such strong feelings. It is partly the contradictions. The statesman of distinction who, as his tapes revealed, could talk with insight and understanding about the role of the United States in the world and then flail the next moment at his enemies, real or imagined, in crude, racist and scatological terms. . . . The man who wanted to be great, who told himself at the start of 1970, 'Be worthy of 1st man in nation and in world', yet who was capable of such petty meanness and did so much to damage American public life. He was vicious and relentless in attacking others;**

The other protagonists in the book are less completely sketched than Nixon. Henry Kissinger, who was initially sceptical of the trip to China, is there in broad terms only and the overall impression is not reflective of the major impact he had on world affairs for almost a decade. His paranoia regarding secrecy and demand for control while in the White House make Prime Minister Harper's PMO appear as a flowery wind-blown open field. Clearly several books have yet to emerge from the Kissingerian mine to supplement his own abundant hagiographies. William Rogers, the Secretary of State at the time of the China visit and an honourable man, attracts some attention, but overall the impression is one of a lone dik-dik encircled by lions.

The Chinese crew is not well or uniquely demarcated. The portraits of Mao Tse-tung and Chou En-lai, still very much at the centre of everything Chinese, who were in their last days (Mao died in 1976 and Chou a year earlier) rely on two main sources. The first and most significant is Jung Chang and Jon Halliday's monumental study, *Mao: the Unknown Story*; the second being Zhisu Li's autobiography, *The Private Life of Chairman Mao: the Memoirs of Mao's Personal Physician*. Both are unique books and probably the best sources available, but, in her use of this material, Professor MacMillan does not add much of unique value to our understanding of these men. Again it is going to be a matter for future historians with longer perspectives and possibly new material to complete the picture of what was probably the most unusual partnership in the 20th century.

The Sino-Soviet Union dimensions are surveyed at a high level, but again the lack of original material or use of available material limits the authenticity of the discussion and the conclusions. More than any other country, the Soviet Union had the most to lose by Nixon's efforts to create a tri-polar world. However, surprisingly, while there were threats and sinister noises from Moscow, the Soviets did very little to disrupt the looming Sino-American engagement. The sense of bewilderment in Moscow is perhaps reflected by the Soviets having Victor Louis (described by Professor MacMillan as "a Moscow-based journalist who acted as a conduit for Soviet views") publish an article in a London newspaper saying "how easy it would be for the Soviet Union to launch a surprise attack on China, perhaps against China's own nuclear facilities in Xinjiang province." Professor MacMillan's description of Louis is hardly complete. There is evidence that Victor Louis was the KGB agent, Vitaly Yevgenyevich Lui, who operated as an agent of influence in Europe and North America and whom some credit with leaking Nikita Khrushchev's memoirs.

A harbinger of the Sino-American rapprochement was Canada's own successful negotiations with China to establish diplomatic relations. Professor MacMillan devotes several paragraphs to this early phase in China's reopening to western countries. She states that "Most significant of all, it [China] opened talks with the United States' neighbour, Canada." This discussion opens with a bit of a clanger in suggesting that "Canada still looked to Britain for leadership" and goes on to over-simplify the various issues in play for Canada, both domestic and foreign, that led to the decision by newly minted Prime Minister Trudeau in January 1969 to seek negotiations with China through Canada's ambassador in Stockholm. After less than two years, agreement was reached in October, 1970, and a month later the first Canadian diplomats arrived in Beijing.

Unfortunately, Professor MacMillan fails to name the various Canadians who were engaged in this effort, unlike her detailed information on the Americans. For the record, Arthur Andrew was the Ambassador in Stockholm who began the negotiations and he was succeeded by Margaret Meagher. Bob Edmonds was at the Stockholm embassy and was very much involved in the process. Back in Ottawa Ralph Collins was the responsible Assistant Under-Secretary; Blair Seaborn was head of what was then the "Far Eastern Division," and John Fraser was the China desk officer. John travelled to Stockholm for most of the substantive meetings. Ralph Collins, who had been born in China of missionary parents, was Canada's first ambassador. For persons interested in the dynamic of why Canada did not maintain relations with China after the revolution in 1949, Chester Ronning's *A Memoir of China in Revolution* is an excellent source. Unfortunately it is out of print, but there are copies in used book stores around Ottawa.

Professor MacMillan mentions the role Dr. Norman Bethune indirectly played in the Stockholm negotiations; a new Canadian film occasioned a dinner invitation to a Chinese official who was known to the Canadian third secretary at the embassy in Beijing. Dr. Bethune is an iconic, if not a cult figure in Sino-Canadian relations – and the degree to which this is a conscious creation of the Chinese authorities based on limited reality has not been appropriately addressed. Teasingly, Chinese-born, British author Jung Chang does not mention or make any reference to Dr Bethune in her exhaustingly detailed account of the long march and the thousands, including doctors and stretcher bearers, who were directly involved.

Leaving aside my earlier quibbles about "early" history books, works such as this one have an enormous value in demonstrating that leaders can and do change the course of events and create their own destiny. The role Taiwan played in American politics and foreign relations from 1949 on and the American pathological antipathy towards Communist China are difficult to recapture today. "Who lost China" was a rallying cry – one that Richard Nixon was not averse to using. But twenty years later he foresaw the importance of China in world and American politics, and acted accordingly. There are lessons in this for all leaders, but most importantly, for Americans. The cost of enmity and unconditional support for one's purported friends needs to be carefully calculated and open to recalibration. Nowhere is this recalibration needed more than with the countries of the Middle East, including Israel.

bout de papier, Vol. 23, No. 1.

A Little Tibetan Political Theatre Playing Out
August 15, 2007

IT WAS A FINE PIECE OF POLITICAL THEATRE.

Six members of the Students for a Free Tibet and the group's executive director, three of whom were Canadians, boldly intruded on Chinese countdown celebrations for the 2008 Olympics. They successfully draped a large banner on the most iconic of all Chinese symbols, the Great Wall, calling for a Free Tibet in 2008. Pictures were instantly flashed around the world.

The Great Wall caper was preceded by an earlier protest in Tibet where five activists protested China's plans for the Olympic torch journey to include Mount Everest.

In both cases, Chinese authorities detained the activists for a day or so, made rude and threatening noises, and promptly deported the lot.

The Chinese are no slouches at political theatre and fully realized that such theatrics are only made worse by their prolongation. The speedy removal of the actors from their stage and their quick release from a Chinese jail, which was an intended part of the stage, minimized the effect of the protest.

Tibet has been an episodic and almost ephemeral issue in the lexicon of current international problems. The rich history of the region and the machinations through treaties devised by the British approximately a hundred years ago created a confusing and conflicting record against which the legal status of Tibet must be judged.

Chinese authorities established Tibet's current status when, in 1950, the People's Liberation Army marched in and put paid to the suggestion that Tibet had any status other then as part of the

People's Republic of China. Even the government of Taiwan agrees – one of the few issues on which there is unanimity between Taipei and Beijing. No country recognizes Tibet as anything other than a part of China.

A few years later, Tibetans living in the Kham and Amdo regions (which are separate from today's Tibet Autonomous Region of the PRC) revolted and, with clandestine support from the Americans, the unrest spread to Lhasa. The revolt was brutally suppressed; American support evaporated, and the Dalai Lama, along with many members of his government, went into exile in India in 1959.

Thousands died and over the years tens of thousands more have gone into exile in India, with many resettling in other countries. Canada began its modest resettlement program in 1971 with several hundred Tibetans settling in Ontario and elsewhere. Today there are some 4,000 Tibetans in Canada, mainly in Ontario. Here their descendants have kept the fire of a free Tibet burning and are significant contributors to the New York-based Students for a Free Tibet.

In Canada, previous governments have feted the Dalai Lama as a spiritual leader and last year Parliament voted unanimously to grant him honorary citizenship. Canada's "new" government has made references to the issue, and one junior minister, with his own bit of political theatre, prominently displayed a portrait of the Dalai Lama during a courtesy call by the Chinese ambassador.

Nevertheless, Tibet remains in the twilight of international issues. To the extent that governments and international organizations take note, it is in terms of human rights and genocide – and not with respect to its international legal status. Tibet is accepted as an integral part of China and no government has energetically or consistently questioned that fact.

The Dalai Lama and the Tibetan government-in-exile have tacitly accepted that reality. Increasingly, the demands have moved from independence to guarantees of greater autonomy within the Chinese system. Earlier this year, the Dalai Lama was quoted as saying that what he wants "from the Chinese authority is more autonomy for

Tibetans to protect their culture." He went on to say that Tibetans should accept that Tibet is part of China.

The actions at the Great Wall and in Tibet by the Students for a Free Tibet demonstrate that there is a body of Tibetans who do not accept that the cause of a free and independent Tibet is lost. They are a new generation and, using the Internet and other modern technologies, they are determined to keep the issue alive.

When the International Olympics Committee voted to have China host the 2008 games, there were significant mixed and conflicting motives on both sides. In agreeing to have the Games held in a thoroughly undemocratic country for the first time since the 1980 Moscow Games, many countries were hopeful that the Olympic spotlight would create conditions for an easing of China's harsh political system. Not so many years ago, the Chinese used ping pong to begin the end of their international isolation. Now, however, the Games are seen as an opportunity to validate their current political system and successful economy.

The playing out of this dichotomy is now underway. The Tibetan demonstration is among other wide-ranging protests in which China is the centre of attention, including human organ harvesting, the environment, the death penalty and tainted food and other exports. Already there are calls for countries to boycott the Games, and these calls will become shriller and more insistent and persistent in the next twelve months. There are opportunities and dangers in these conditions – and countries will need to act carefully so that only the opportunities are exploited.

Embassy

Book Review

October 21, 2007

Borderless Deceit, by Adrian de Hoog. Breakwater Books Ltd, St John's, NL, 2007

I BEGIN READING A BOOK WITH A SENSE OF WONDER. WONDER ABOUT what is to be expected. For many authors, experience has shown what lies ahead. Wayne Johnson's books will always have a combination of geography, climate and character as their central features; Ian Rankin can be expected to deliver a whodunit where the detective deduces largely from the inside of a decent whisky bottle, and Robertson Davies can be trusted to detail the human condition in any of many frailties and, one hopes, an occasional success.

A new novelist, as is Mr de Hoog, has a more limited track record on which to judge what to expect. His first novel, *Berlin Assignment,* published last year, capped a thirty-year career in Canada's Foreign Service and, following the advice of all handbooks to write about what you know, Mr de Hoog's first effort detailed aspects of Canada's Foreign Service against a background of the destruction of the Berlin wall and the reunification of Germany. If that was all it offered, it would still be a most readable and insightful book.

It was much more; it was fine satire in the great traditions of that style. His new book, *Borderless Deceit,* is very much of the same style.

There are not many novels extant that deal with the Foreign Services of the countries of the world. What there is largely deal with secret missions, carried out by people with cloaks and daggers in total disregard for the structures and protocols that give some measure of order to today's often-chaotic world. The only exceptions of any note are the four delightful books of Lawrence Durrell (Esprit de Corps, Stiff Upper Lip, Sauve Que Peut and Antrobus Complete), detailing his experiences in a British embassy in central Europe after the Second World War. His was satire of a rare high order.

This lacuna is surprising since a constant theme of today's world is the need for vision and action to create societies where the worth of the individual far exceeds, hopefully, the needs of the nation state. After all, the UN Charter begins, "We the peoples of the United Nations. . . ." No one, despite the heaving and sighing of many (for example the fascination of a former prime minister for The *New York Times*), has been able to create a world where national and international diplomats do not have a central and unique role. The increasing flabbiness of the military muscle of the United States in the face of unique opposition merely demonstrates the point even more strongly. Even North Korea and Libya succumbed to the blandishments of diplomats.

All the more reason to welcome de Hoog's literary light into the recesses of Canadian diplomacy. *Borderless Deceit* is the story of four diplomats, three of whom haunt the halls of the "Service" in Ottawa. The fourth, Rachael, a "high flyer" in the language of the "Service," moves from the mission in Vienna to Geneva and is finally appointed as the Ambassador to Romania – the youngest in the history of the "Service." Two of the three in Ottawa are timeworn caricatures of any diplomatic service, and all the more accurate for that. One is a "Czar" of various foreign "Operations" while the other is a brilliant analyst of arcane intelligence, working closely with the Americans.

The third one in Ottawa is a computer geek who is brought in to save the Service when a foreign-sourced virus (a refused immigration applicant) invades and wipes out in seconds the departmental records and its ability to communicate with its far-flung foreign empire. She is *sui generis* and her generational uniqueness provides freshness and flip that adds new features to the characters of her two

Ottawa colleagues. The book plays with the interactions of these four with humour, depth and sensitivity – and in that alone is of considerable value.

However, while the characters are significant, the satire that permeates Mr de Hoog's writing is what gives the book lasting and unique value. The Canadian Foreign Service is not known for its openness or frankness in dealing with the public and for many there is an ancient religiosity about its work and processes. Mr de Hoog picked up on this aspect in his first book, and now in his second, he again provides his own titles for the various offices of the Foreign Service in Ottawa. For the most part these are taken from the world of the church, convent and monastery. The author's deputy minister, Étienne des Étoiles, and head of the "High Council" is characteristic of the many around Ottawa who know less and less about more and more – and have a shelf life of less than a piece of pop music.

The collapse of the communications network brings its own religiosity and Mr de Hoog shows unusual command of its arcane nature.

> *The bug arrived in stealth, without warning. And it was virulent, so bad that some – the closet mystics amongst us – supposed it sprung from the occult. A visitation? . . .*
>
> *Cyberspace velocity and a voracious appetite for ruination – these were the overt symptoms. But the bug also possessed an inner wizardry, because it was precisely targeted, like a smart bomb.*
>
> *Vital spirits gushed from the Service as water through a burst dam. Ten thousand linked computers scattered over all the diplomatic outposts were sabotaged with one stroke. . . . Our shocked techies stood by, helpless and slack-jawed. Outside in the rest of the world all the other networks went about their business in robust good health. Why us? Why no one else?*

Of course the diplomat outside of Ottawa, Rachael, continues her work and search for personal salvation, seemingly indifferent to the cataclysmic events in the capital. For those in Ottawa, the world stopped for a few weeks, and it was only with the restoration of the network through the display of technical artistry – exclusively available in a good novel – that life returns to normal. However, for the four characters, it is a new life and the ending provides the surprise that can be expected only from a good novelist.

bout de paper, Vol. ?.

Change Isn't Always Good
January 23, 2008

THE POLITICAL PACE IN THE UNITED STATES IS QUICKENING. IN WHAT has probably been the longest episode of political foreplay in the history of the country, the results from Iowa and New Hampshire foreshadow surprises yet to come. The November 4 elections are still ten months away and it is not hyperbolical to suggest that these elections, more than any other recent ones, are not only for the United States but for the world.

Hope, vision, change and new departures have emerged as the focus for the Democrats and for some Republicans. This should not be surprising since the last sixteen years have been calamitous ones for the Republic, moving from issues of farcical loose zippers to a deadly attack on the United States to the start of wars in places that are not amenable to superpower military might. We have seen some of this before and, while *déjà vu* is not something politicians running on promises of super-Herculean performance are attuned to, for the rest of us it should serve as a caution on the difference between rhetoric and reality.

The 1976 and 1980 elections, which saw the election and defeat of Jimmy Carter, had many of the same features as today's United States. Living in Washington during this period and observing at first hand the disintegration of the Carter presidency and the ascendancy of Reagan created still-evident twinges in my neck from that American *volte-face.*

Jimmy Carter inherited an America not unlike today's. The failed Vietnam War was still a raw and exposed nerve, and the meltdown of the Nixon administration shook the very foundations of the nation. The economy was in what was colourfully called "stagflation;" budgetary deficits were inexorably climbing; the dollar was adrift, and OPEC was flexing its energy muscles by reducing oil production. The brief interregnum of Gerald Ford with his early pardon of President Nixon did nothing to bring the nation together – and the 1976 election was seen as an opportunity to restore some lustre to the "City upon a Hill."

No one could have been more unusual than Carter as a candidate for President. A one-term governor of Georgia, peanut farmer and graduate of the Naval Academy, he rode onto the American political scene as the ultimate outsider and the harbinger of change. His mother, when told that he was running for President, caustically opined "President of what?"

With initial name recognition of only two per cent, Carter forged a national campaign that saw his election on November 2 by the narrowest of popular-vote margins – 50.1 per cent over Gerald Ford. He did slightly better with Electoral College votes, obtaining 55 per cent. He was the first President elected from the Deep South since Zachary Taylor in 1848. Carter was a professed "born-again Christian" – and no one before or after was so badly treated by God or by the gods. His Presidency was a litany of disaster after disaster, and any hope of change and restoration of confidence in the American dream became hostage to a daily quest for survival.

The first year of Carter's administration gave early evidence of his promise. Large activities abounded to deal with the energy crisis; the start of a Middle-East peace process centered on Egypt, and the signing of the Panama Canal Treaty. But the economy with ever-increasing unemployment and inflation, along with the erosion of the value of the American dollar, was a large background noise that was not amenable to foreign policy successes or rhetoric about change.

In 1979, the wheels on the Presidency were wobbling before January was done; the Shah of Iran was out and Khomeini was in. And the rest of the year provided an agenda of *annus horribilis* for leaders ever after. The Three Mile Island nuclear accident cut short one of his proposals for the energy crisis; the identification of a Soviet brigade in Cuba undercut his arms limitation talks with the Soviets, and the decision to admit the Shah to the United States for medical treatment in late October led directly, three weeks later, to the capture of the American embassy in Tehran – and the imprisonment of fifty-two American officials. Seven weeks later, the Soviets marched into Afghanistan. Midway through 1979, President Carter made the fatal error of attributing his problems of leadership to the American people. In a nation-wide speech in mid-July, now referred to by historians as his "malaise" speech, the President opened by saying that he wanted "to talk to you right now about a fundamental threat to American democracy. . . " This was not a traditional threat but an "invisible" one; one that "strikes at the very heart and soul and sprit our national will."

By this time no one was listening and in the coming months the Administration survived on the basis of its constitutional right to a four-year term. The *coup de grâce* was delivered on April 24, 1980 when the airborne mission to rescue the American hostages in Tehran crashed ignominiously in the southern desert of Iran. By this time the gods were sneering, and less than a month later Mount St. Helens erupted.

President Carter soldiered on and eventually was re-nominated by his party – overcoming an attempt by Senator Edward Kennedy to win the nomination. At the time, his national support was 21 per cent – less than that of President Bush today. In the election he faced Ronald Reagan and John Anderson, an independent candidate. Carter received 41 per cent of the popular vote but, due to the vagaries of the Electoral College, Reagan won by a landslide of 91 per cent.

As the failed Carter presidency demonstrates, change is an inchoate policy and a cheap novelty for potential leaders. Even an electorate's desire for change – or perhaps it is more a need for inspirational leadership – is not without its limitations, as the dropping by the wayside of some fringe candidates has demonstrated.

Change in American terms, as in any mature democracy, means keeping what you have and, ideally, providing some measure of leadership against a fickle and fitful world. Hopefully the electorate will understand the difference and elect a President with whom we can all live comfortably. At least one historical change is already underway: there will be either the first woman or the first Black candidate representing one of two major parties for the Presidency.

The Citizen

The Mobility of Labour
February 29, 2008

LAST SEPTEMBER, THE PREMIER OF QUEBEC ANNOUNCED THAT HE was optimistic about signing a labour-mobility agreement with France within a year. The announcement received scant attention, suggesting that it was the kind of announcement most Quebec governments hang on the line from time to time. For Quebecois, agreements with France have some of the same buzz as the fascination of other Canadians for British pageantry and royal peccadilloes.

There is every reason to think otherwise. Governments are awakening to the spectre of declining or stagnant population growth, greying and longer-lived populations, and narrowing labour resources. The boomers are increasingly of the age when "Depends" are more important than the workplace. This at a time when the sustainability of economic growth requires greater certainty of assured labour.

Aldous Huxley's prescient "Malthusian belt" no longer contains simply chemical contraceptives. The Pill was a great emancipator, but there are now other factors of equal importance. The increasing and almost equality of genders in the remunerative workforce for social, political, and economic reasons, postponement of marriage, delay in having children, high divorce rate, and the demands of aging parents are all negative factors affecting the future availability of indigenous labour. Neither Malthus nor Huxley foresaw these events.

The United Nations in a report last year detailed the aging of the world's population. The report suggested that global aging is "a process without parallel in the history of humanity." It went on to predict that humans over 60 would outnumber those less than 15 in forty years.

Canada, along with most industrial countries, is not immune to these forces. The outward migration from the Atlantic provinces into western and central Canada – more recently accentuated by the economic boom in Alberta and the death of the traditional fishery – the unique, seasonal farm-workers program out of the Caribbean and Mexico, the influx of foreign temporary workers, and the high levels of immigration have all successfully provided the Canadian economy with needed labour and, equally, labour mobility. However, with un?employment now hovering at historic highs, there are reasons to question whether our past performance is a harbinger of the future.

Most European countries are facing similar questions. The historic low-fertility rates for many European countries (almost as low as 1.0 in some countries, with 2.1 considered to be the replacement rate) are slowly edging upwards – the case in Canada – as is the age of the women having children. In Germany, however, there is little change; one expert has stated there is "exponential negative growth" for the population with deaths outnumbering live births since 1972. Canada, even with a fertility rate of 1.54 (the highest since 1998), remains considerably lower than most western European countries and other industrialized nations. Rewards for birth have been one ironic answer.

The European Union and its member countries have raised the issue to the top of their agenda, based on the belief that migratory flows have a significant contribution to make to future economic growth. Last September a High Level Conference was held in Lisbon in which member countries agreed to develop common policies and practices on legal migration. The Conference documents acknowledge that this should be done in cooperation with source countries, as it is acknowledged that one serious side effect is "brain drain" from many third- world countries.

Legislation is now under discussion in the European Parliament for a "Blue Card" modelled on the American Green Card (although the European Plan is much more restrictive) in order to meet the need for 20-million skilled workers over the next twenty years. The EU Justice Minister noted that only 5 per cent of the persons who migrate to member countries were skilled workers – as compared to 55 per cent of those arriving in the United States. The Blue Card will fast-track skilled, third-country nationals, which could lead to EU citizenship after five years.

The United States' recent bruising and unsuccessful efforts to reform immigration law illustrates some of the difficulties involved. Essentially, the reforms failed over how to amnesty the twelve-million illegal workers in the United States – and not call it an amnesty. There is little dispute of the need for such workers, and reform will be high on the to-do list of the new Administration.

Other than on the amnesty/illegal-workers issue, the United States does well in attracting highly skilled employees from the rest of the world. It is estimated that there are eight to twelve million valid Green-Card holders (legal immigrants) in the United States – and that number keeps increasing. One side effect is reflected in a recent United States Census Bureau report which stated that one in five people over the age of five spoke a language other than English at home last year. In California 43 per cent of residents spoke a language other than English at home and in Los Angeles the number was 53 per cent. Spanish was the most common.

This is the global environment with which Canada must contend, if it expects to maintain an edge in obtaining the skilled workers the country needs in the coming decades. The existing Canadian system, which has not had a major overhaul since the late seventies, needs attention. First and foremost it must overcome its bias towards family-class migrants, establishing it as a humanitarian program – not an economic one. Instead the system must give much greater emphasis to economic, independent migrants based on broad criteria that are expected to be factors in Canada's economic future.

Equally important, the reforms should overcome the long, painful process through which refugee determination is made. In its present form it is fruit for a Dickensian epic which brings neither honour to Canada nor an easy new start to troubled persons who have already made a decision to be Canadian. One simple reform might be to offer many of those seeking refugee status an opportunity to enter the economic-migrant process, which many are. And above all, let's drop the nonsense that dual citizenship is a problem; rather it should be seen as a benefit in the increasingly competitive world of global labour.

Embassy

Toward Self-Determination
November 16, 2008

LIVING AT THE EDGE OF EMPIRES IS NOT KNOWN FOR ITS PEACE OF mind or even peace of country. Georgia is but the latest example of what the Romans learned when they took on the Caledonians.

While the geographical entities we call states adapt and adjust to the forces of ethnicity, religion and language, Georgia and Kosovo provide fodder for reflection as we grope our way into the future. These states may well be harbingers of things to come; importantly, however, they are modern examples of the complexities surrounding the unity of states – in comparison to the unity of peoples and their freedom to choose.

In historical terms it does not matter whether the President of Georgia, Mikheil Saakashvili, acted recklessly when he shelled the South Ossetian capital of Tskhinvali last August in his attempt to put an end to insurgencies in South Ossetia and Abkhazia. As we know, small events, such as the assassination of an archduke, can trigger large consequences.

Equally, it does not matter whether the Russian military response served narrow Russian interests or was a humanitarian intervention. It is also worth emphasizing that the first Georgian president after the break-up of the Soviet empire sowed the seeds of secession with his harsh treatment of the Ossetians and Abkhazians.

Rather, the larger issue is whether the conflicting principles of territorial integrity and self-determination can be balanced in a way that will, over time, satisfy the Ossetians, the Abkhazians and the Georgians. At the same time the grey shadow of what the Russians call a "zone of privileged influence" hangs over the region and has to be accorded due diffidence.

And while this is not Hungary circa 1956, Western statements about the situation, initially at least, demonstrated a robustness that clearly exceeded the West's ability, if not its willingness, to intervene. Not surprisingly, the chickens associated with the creation of Kosovo as an independent country are now roosting as Ossetia and Abkhazia.

Territorial integrity is the large rock around which the modern world is organized, stabilized and managed. Formerly it came to the modern world through the treaties of Westphalia in the 17th century and, during the intervening years, royal births and marriages, wars and insurrections. It has largely shaped the countries of Europe and their destinies. Since the Second World War in Europe it has been a writ of the most holy. Today it is a worldwide phenomenon, imbued in law and treaty – and to suggest that it may need to be tempered is akin to shouting fire in the proverbial theatre.

While good fences may make for good neighbours, it is the principle of territorial integrity, in one guise or another, that has been the rallying cry when forces of disruption – either foreign or domestic – try to rip the fabric of a country's territorial coherence. Georgia is but the latest in a long history. Today there are many more Georgias where territorial integrity will be tested, including places like the Ukraine which, more so than Georgia, is part of the zone of Russian privilege.

Self-determination is today's countervailing force. It has many historical antecedents, such as the American and Irish wars of independence, but in terms of global impact it is a product of the 20th century. While not a declared part of the President Woodrow Wilson's Fourteen Points issued in early 1918, it was an important element in many of the specific discussions during the Paris Conference that under-pinned the break-up of the Austro-Hungarian and Ottoman (Turkish) empires.

However, in the aftermath of the Second World War and the documentation associated with the formation of the United Nations, self-determination of people was given legitimacy and vibrancy, and formed the philosophical basis on which the dismantling of European empires in Asia, the Middle East, Africa and the Caribbean took place.

For the most part, decolonisation maintained a significant continuity with territorial integrity and paid little attention to minorities who over time were adversely affected. The wars or insurgencies in Cyprus, Palestine, Kashmir, Sri Lanka, Burma and the Philippines are daily reminders that self-determination for a majority more often than not meant domination for minorities.

Adding to this already volatile, confrontational environment was the effort, largely propelled by Canada, to give form and substance to humanitarian foreign interventions. Dressed in fairly thin legal, but thick moral, clothes, the concept of Responsibility to Protect (R2P) seeks to hold governments to a high standard of conduct in their treatment of their own peoples – specifically from genocide, war crimes, ethnic cleansing and crimes against humanity. So far supporters of the concept have sought to see its use in such disparate situations as Burma and Darfur with little to show. Somalia is a dark hole which few want to approach.

In these complexities Canada has been both an enthusiastic and a hesitant participant. While it pushed the R2P concept to recognition in a Security-Council resolution in 2006, it waited a month before giving reluctant recognition to an independent Kosovo. And its statements on Georgia give new meaning to abstraction: "Canada is gravely concerned..."

Quebec, of course, represents the fox in the Canadian chicken coop. Here territorial integrity and self-determination have been successfully balanced by successive Canadian governments to the point where autonomy rather than secession has been increasingly institutionalized within the Canadian and Quebec polities. While Quebec secession still finds resonance among some Quebecers, it is increasingly a romantic view of what was, rather than what is or could be.

The Citizen

The Border
December 1, 2008

ONE OF THE SPECTACLES ASSOCIATED WITH THE ELECTION OF A President in the United States is the emergence of soothsayers, prognosticators, and policy wonks who, as with the diviners of old, seek to foresee the future and offer advice on how to get there. A subset of these in Canada stand on The Border and issue forth learned analyses and pie-in-the-sky hopes for Canada's relations with the new President.

2008 is no different. The election of Barack Obama, carrying with it the mantra of "change" and a limited spoken record – that in some instances is at variance with Canadian interests – has occasioned a heady mixture of fear and hope north of the 49th. The combination has already resulted in several research pieces and articles, seeking to give a framework for the future of the Canada-United States agenda.

Numerous historians have observed that a key to the relationship is the chemistry that exists between a President and a Prime Minister. This was most evident when two pseudo Irishmen were able to create the political environment first for a bilateral and then for a three-state trade agreement. These deals were cemented when the unlikely chemistry of a former governor of Arkansas and 'le petit gar de Shawinigan' were able to make common cause. There was nothing magic in these deals based as they were on converging national interests as much as they were on personal chemistry.

We should not forget the other side of the coin. In the early 1960s there was a dance macabre between John Diefenbaker and John F.

Kennedy, then Lester Pearson, around the issue of American nuclear weapons on Canadian soil.

Unfortunately, there is little evidence that the existing Prime Minister has either the interest or the skill to develop the personal chemistry that would help make Canadian interests a part of the new President's agenda. If it does, it will be due more to alchemy than chemistry.

A second element in achieving Canadian objectives in Washington is that there is a need for some clarity in Canada as to what the agenda should be. One minority government followed by an even shakier one does not inspire much confidence that there will be a lot of coherence in Ottawa that would obtain a favourable response in Washington.

To the extent that Canadian issues will be on Obama's White House agenda, it will be wonderment as to what is going on at the confluence of the Rideau and the Ottawa Rivers. Certainly, the developments over the past few days will not create any interest in putting Canada at the top of the new administration's list of urgent things to do.

In some measure there is little ambiguity as to the big bilateral matters – economics and finance, trade, energy, the Arctic, environment and security (including the "thickness" of the border) will be on most lists. However, the problems these issues present in Washington will seem very different from those they present in Ottawa.

Adding to the challenge of getting attention in Washington is the tendency of Canadians who should know better to characterize Canadian interests as also being in the best interests of the United States. A few days ago a former ambassador in Washington was reported to have advised that when we go to Washington we have to go with a list that says, "this is as much in your interest as ours." This presumption that we can or even should try to work both sides of the table in any negotiations with the Americans bespeaks an immodesty bordering on the delusional.

The same tendency is revealed with keeping the Mexicans in the tent. There are many involved with Canada-United States negotiations that see the Mexican factor as a large and unwelcome hindrance rather than as a valued ally. The Mexicans are well aware of this and despite the polite smiles they accept that the spirit of the "Three Amigos" is somewhere behind "Remember the Alamo" in the public memory.

Shortly after the elections on November 4, senior Canadian ministers were quick to make public comments about negotiating with the new administration. The Finance Minister, Jim Flaherty, was reported to have said that Canada is prepared to use its "emerging energy superpower" status in order to prevent the Americans from seeking changes to NAFTA. Others have suggested that this "superpower" is an important club to wield in ensuring less trouble along the border or, in the current jargon, a thinner border.

Coming from Ontario, Mr Flaherty might be forgiven for not remembering the National Energy Program of 1980 or the fact that energy policy is very much the sovereign prerogative of the provinces. There are few signs that the premiers of Alberta, Saskatchewan, British Colombia and Newfoundland are any more ready to salute Ottawa today on a new national energy policy than Alberta was almost three decades ago. Blowing wind might seem good politics in Canada, but it is recognized for what it is in the United States.

In all of this it is safe to say that Canadians can relax over the issue of large or even any significant or wide-ranging negotiations with the new administration in the coming months. Rather it will be business as usual, dealing with irritants large and small in the bilateral relationship. At the same time there will be an urgent need to understand what part we will play in the larger global gestalt that will be an important characteristic of the new administration in Washington. In that, Afghanistan will again loom very large.

Cadillos and Balconies
July 9, 2009

HONDURAS IS NOT A PLACE THAT OCCASIONS POSITIVE IMAGES AND good thoughts. Historically oligarchic, unduly open to foreign influence, largely from Washington, and prone to natural disasters, especially hurricanes, it has had little success in moving its people to an acceptable level of economic and social progress. It remains in the second hundred of countries on the United Nations human development index and is probably close to the bottom among Latin American countries.

But for the last thirty years it has been reasonably democratic in its public life, shaking off to some extent its designation as the original "banana republic." This has been a significant achievement, especially because it occurred as Honduras became the American "aircraft carrier" in assisting the Salvadoran government in its civil war and the contras in their war against the Sandinista government in Nicaragua. These wars were negotiated to a more or less peaceful conclusion in the early 1990s and, apart from Guatemala, the level of violence dropped significantly – so much so that the region largely disappeared from our consciousness.

That all changed on June 28 when suddenly the world awoke to find that the Honduran President, Manuel Zelaya, had been forcibly exiled to Costa Rica. The rhetoric and the drama surrounding this act by the Honduran judiciary, congress and military continue. The ex-President has appeared before the UN General Assembly in New York where he obtained a resolution by acclamation that member governments should not recognize the new government in Honduras. In Washington the OAS gave a three-day deadline for the restoration of Zelaya as President or face suspension from the organization.

For extra drama, the ex-President, accompanied by several other senior Latin American politicians, overflew the airport at Tegucigalpa attempting to land. He did not succeed and his air farce of bravado flew off to neighbouring Nicaragua. We can all heave a sigh of relief; as someone who has landed many times at the Tegucigalpa Airport, I know that even on good days with all of the gods in your corner, it is a white-knuckle adventure.

Now there is a period of second thought about what has occurred in Honduras in the past ten days and perhaps out of this reflection an appropriate response will be crafted. The quick rush to label the events of June 28 as a *coup d'état* is undergoing scrutiny. It was certainly not a *coup* in the Latin American tradition. That tradition usually involved the military taking action against a civilian administration, followed by the emergence of a military strong man who quickly did away with the trappings of civilian dominance – and looked for a balcony from which to declaim.

In Honduras on June 28, from the available information, it was an earlier decision by the Supreme Court that led to the crisis. The Court declared as illegal an attempt by the President to create conditions in which he could run for a second term, contrary to the constitution. The President sought to circumvent the decision and, in doing so, the Congress, supporting the Supreme Court, declared the President was acting illegally and had to go. It then elected its own leader, Roberto Micheletti, as President. The exact role of the military still lacks precision, but it can be said with some certainty that it was close to all of the decisions that were made.

So far as can be determined in this highly charged situation what the Supreme Court and Congress did was in accordance with the Honduran constitution. Perhaps the detention of President Zelaya and his exile to Costa Rica was over the top. In earlier times most likely he would have been shot. Progress, if it can be called that.

Nevertheless, outsiders were quick to side with President Zelaya and his reinstatement was the single demand of the international community. Hugo Chavez, the President of Venezuela, charged that the United States was responsible for the removal of Zelaya. In part this resulted in American policy staying with the international rush to judgement; Canada remained with the pack as well. A Venezuelan opposition party probably got the dynamic right when it stated that "Hugo Chavez has become the George Bush of Latin America."

The important element in this crisis is the means by which countries like Honduras deal with their internal problems, at the same time keeping onside with an international community that is quick to condemn but short on helping. All countries skirt with the rules of democracy and do so without attracting the opprobrium that Honduras has encountered.

The American Supreme Court decision in 2001 declaring George W. Bush elected President is clearly regarded by many as a partisan political decision unworthy of that great court. Similarly, Stephen Harper's decision to seek prorogation of the Canadian Parliament last fall rather than face possible defeat falls in the same category. These decisions were certainly contrary to the spirit if not the content of democratic rule, but in our countries these were judged to be part of the warp and woof of partisan politics.

Perhaps in the coming days, and there are already signs of this, a compromise will be reached on the Honduran crisis. The idea of an outside mediator is now in play. Oscar Arias, the President of Costa Rica, is one possible candidate, as is the President of Brazil, Luiz Lula da Silva. Peter Kent, Canada's minister of state for Latin America, who earlier described the events as a coup d'état, on July 4 was more restrained. He told the OAS that suspending Honduras would not be enough to restore democratic order. Rather the OAS had to "maintain diplomatic initiatives" and engage the new government in Tegucigalpa in order to end the crisis. We can expect others will come to the same conclusions.

Canada's 2012 Bid for the Security Council
September 29, 2010

WHY, AFTER NEVER BEFORE LOSING, DID CANADA GO DOWN TO defeat in its bid to join the United Nations Security Council? It is easy to blame "the system" or to accuse outsiders, and that seems to be what many sore losers are doing. But that sort of petulant, even childish response is exactly the wrong one if Canada is to understand the reasons for its failure, and do better at the next election in 2012.

As defeats go, Canada's was terribly humiliating. In the first round of voting, this country came in last place in a field of three candidates. In the second round, Canada placed last again – but only after losing more votes. Foreign Affairs Minister Lawrence Cannon then conceded defeat, preferring that to a third, certainly unsuccessful vote.

We think that the loss is traceable to a sea-change in Canadian foreign policy. In the past, Canada was a shoo-in for the Security Council because it was a middle power that, although not always popular, nevertheless strove to achieve friendly relations with all. But, under the misdirection of Prime Minister Stephen Harper, Canada has shed both the eager internationalism of Lester Pearson, and the compassionate conservatism of Brian Mulroney. The result is that Canada today thumbs its nose at international law and exhibits a selfish, beggar-thy-neighbour attitude on major issues that matter to the UN.

Consider peacekeeping: It used to be that Canada was a generous contributor of police and soldiers – the "blue berets" – to UN operations worldwide. When Canada last sat on the Security Council in

1998, thousands of its peacekeepers had done service in the Rwanda and Yugoslavia genocides. But today, Canada provides many fewer peacekeepers to the UN than even the poorest third world countries – including Rwanda. There are so few Canadian peacekeepers worldwide today (just 221) that they could fit onboard a single airplane. By shunning peacekeeping in favour of a shooting war in Afghanistan – a war that most countries outside the West view as unjustified – and electing a Prime Minister who wanted to go to war in Iraq too, nothing cost Canada more votes in the race for the Security Council.

On climate change, Canada signed a UN treaty (the Kyoto Protocol), which no Canadian government, Conservative or Liberal, ever tried to honour. The treaty is international law, and requires Canada to reduce its greenhouse gas emissions six per cent by 2012. What sharper rejection of international law than the Harper government's decision to release an official plan increasing emissions 25 per cent by 2012. That gesture put Canada in the bizarre, contradictory, and hopeless position of declaring its intent to break international law, while vying to be elected to the Security Council.

Canada also failed the test of the Security Council's most crucial area, which is peace. Since age 15, Omar Khadr, a Canadian child soldier who was brainwashed by his father into al Qaeda at age 9, has been held prisoner in Guantanamo Bay; today he is the last Westerner there. But, rather than reintegrate Khadr as international law requires for child soldiers, Mr Harper says he should be tried for war crimes. Canada rebuffed the UN's requests to seek Khadr's release, and ignored American requests to take detainees like Khadr back. All this plays havoc with numerous UN treaties and Security Council resolutions on child soldiers – now that Canada is the first (and only) country in the UN's history to endorse prosecuting its children for war crimes.

The Harper government's usual defence to these failings is to argue that Canada weathered the global recession with the strongest, fastest-growing economy of any G8 country. This is true, but as a pitch for Security Council membership, it backfires. Canada needed the votes of dozens of poor countries to win the election, yet the Harper government's 2010 budget froze foreign-aid spending for the coming five years. The budget freeze means that, as Canada's economy grows, development aid as a proportion of our wealth will shrink about 15 per cent by 2015 – which, unhappily, is the UN's deadline to achieve the Millennium Development Goals (MDGs). As strategies to win an election, squeezing the world's poorest and the MDGs while bragging about Canada's wealth was never likely to succeed.

These examples give truth to Mr. Harper's canard that Canada is "a consistently reliable and responsible participant in UN initiatives." If Security Council membership is earned by hard work, the countries that won deserved to beat Canada. Germany reduced its greenhouse gases ahead of deadline, and Portugal took in prisoners from Guantanamo Bay who were not even Portuguese.

None of this is to say Canada should never be elected to the Security Council, for it has been an asset to that institution before. Winning the election in 2012 will be even harder, now that Canada's unbroken string of victories is destroyed. The fact that Canada is led by a Conservative minority that prefers clinging to power alone and by its fingernails, rather than lead by a stable coalition also gives other countries little reason to cut deals with us for that future vote.

Therefore, merit will matter in the 2012 vote. For Canada to avoid another embarrassment, this country has to repair the awesome damage that the Harper government has done to Canada's international reputation. There is no free lunch.

With Amir Attaran

More Huffing and Puffing about Immigration
November 30, 2010

THE CREATION OF A NEW PUBLIC-POLICY CENTRE, ONE DEDICATED to the study of immigration issues, should be an occasion for quiet congratulations. The past months, following the arrival of a few hundred Tamils from Southeast Asia onto the shores of British Colombia, have occasioned more breast-beating and gnashing of teeth than long guns. At the same time other immigration issues, especially refugee determination, multiculturalism and dual citizenship, are never far from the surface of public comment and political manoeuvring.

As such, the need for coherence and independent thought on immigration matters has long been evident. The possibility of a centre on such matters that might bring unbiased research free of cant would be of great value to the public debate. Unfortunately, the Centre for Immigration Policy Reform, which has been in the news recently, along with the appointments to its advisory board, offers few prospects of adding greater understanding to the public discourse.

The website for the Centre certainly provides little hope for that greater understanding. In its opening statement the Centre's participants set out its ideology. The opening comment that "immigration is having a major impact on the life of Canadians" borders on the trite, but then it gets downright nasty. "High immigration intake discourages Canadians from acquiring the skills necessary to fill shortages in the workforce." It goes on to blame immigration levels for the difficulty in achieving "Canada's environmental objectives and inhibit[s] efforts to reduce the extraordinary size of our ecological footprint; . . . and creates pressure on health care and education facilities as well as increases in congestion and pollution." Further, immigration causes a lack of "social cohesion" as a result of the concentration of "immigrants of similar backgrounds" in our larger cities.

The Centre labels as "myths" the idea that immigration provides "a practical means of providing . . . enough workers to pay the taxes needed to support our aging population." And, with the certainty of attendees at parties where tea is the main drink, it asserts that Canada does not "require a constantly growing workforce and population to achieve greater prosperity." As a sign of the times, the organizers of the Centre baldly state that "Canada's national security needs are being compromised by inadequate immigration and refugee screening while the immigration platforms of political parties, too frequently based on myths and out-of-date orthodoxies, seek short-term political gain rather than what is best for the country." Stirring language, but containing its own myths and orthodoxies. The only problem not attributed to the ills of immigration is probably dandruff.

This descent into *ad hominem* arguments reflects the all-too-common nativist approach that dominates discussions about immigration. In a country where we are all immigrants and the only distinction is that some are more recent than others, it passes all understanding when a group of researchers seeks to create public debate on the basis of half-truths and tendentious assumptions which create more heat than light.

A number of individuals associated with the Centre have long been active in stressing the evils of immigration, its first cousin multiculturalism, and the dangers they represent for Canadians. Not surprisingly their huffing and puffing have had little effect on Canadians and the body politic. Apart from aboriginals, there is today a large and growing body of citizens who see immigration as the essential life force of this country. Even some of those critical of the system that has bought millions to our shores and irrevocably changed this land admit grudgingly that, "Immigration has played a major role in Canada's development." The Centre suggests that there was some other force that created today's Canada; aboriginal Canadians were migrants and, fortunately for them, there were no naysayers around to cast judgement on the value of their arrival.

A former academic associated with the new Centre is one of the more extreme in denouncing the value of immigration and multiculturalism. For him, there is a need for a "moral contract" with immigrants that would clarify the responsibilities of citizenship. Even more troublesome, he would propose a system of "graduated citizenship" that would reflect different degrees of commitment to the country. (See *Ottawa Citizen*, June 7, 2008). The academic goes on to suggest that we should have different colours of passports to reflect these levels of commitments. Not so long ago, tens of thousands of Canadians died on the fields of Europe fighting such errant nonsense.

The Centre website scribes do not suggest that some immigrants be returned to their country of birth; however, they clearly do not want to see immigrants entering this country in the numbers of the past. Equally, they are of the view that many of the problems that form the base of public discussion today can be attributed to immigration. Sadly, the Centre could have provided a lot more than its Sarkozy-lite approach to immigration matters. There is a need for such public debate, but we can only hope that those who participate in it can look beyond counting their toes – and regard with greater perspective and understanding what made this country what it is.

The Citizen

The New Nuclear World
February 25, 2011

IT HAS BEEN MORE THAN SIXTY-FIVE YEARS SINCE THE BOMBS OF August 1945 abruptly ended the Asia Pacific War. Since those fateful August days, the world has fretfully lived with the threat of nuclear weapons. Over the intervening years a variety of international mechanisms and arrangements have come into being that provide some measure of comfort as we live in the shadow of "the destroyer of worlds." To many it is amazing that the August 6th and 9th explosions over Hiroshima and Nagasaki have been the only examples of the military use of nuclear weapons. And, down to today, the decision by Harry Truman to deploy these weapons has been subjected to ongoing analysis, criticism and applause.

Out of this continuing discussion has come a rare world-wide commitment, ragged at times, to prevent the development and use of such weapons. The numerous treaties, agreements and statements that have become part of that commitment have proved effective in limiting their use. But, as numerous media reports have documented, the international commitment has been less effective in preventing their development.

Last May the quintuple Review Conference for the Nuclear Non-Proliferation Treaty (NPT) of 1970 – the centre-piece treaty on the subject - took place in New York. Unlike its predecessor in 2005, there was some measure of success in that there was a consensus "Final Document." The intervening five years reflected the sea change in Washington, where today there is a strong commitment by the Obama administration for a nuclear-weapons-free world. It also reflected another fundamental change from the Bush administration. Then, the policy was to carry hammers and look for nails; today, American policy reflects a more sophisticated approach and a commitment to diplomacy, non-military action and economic pressure.

The NPT with close to 190 members represented an act of faith when it was negotiated in 1970 and today is the most widely supported arms-control treaty in history. The treaty legitimized the nuclear-weapon programs of the United States, the Soviet Union, China, the United Kingdom and France. In exchange there were commitments for the transfer of peaceful-use nuclear technology and the reduction of nuclear weapons in the inventories of nuclear-weapon states.

This treaty reflected a *realpolitik* approach to international treaty making and, despite a number of serious national aberrations, remains the flagship for the eventual elimination of nuclear weapons. Supporting the treaty is the work of the International Atomic Energy Agency (IAEA) which has been tough, consistent and persistent in policing the hidden roads of nuclear proliferation.

One proliferation scenario is the over-heated speculation involving terrorist organizations gaining access to and using nuclear weapons of varying lethality. Accentuated by the media and often supported by "leaks" from national-security organizations, this scenario has become a minor industry – directed at making our nightmares more scary than necessary. While dreams of nuclear weapons may infuse the fevered minds of terrorists and suicide bombers, the weapons of choice continues to be IEDs and the AK47. These represent a clearer and present danger to many around the world.

As with so many of our modern-day security problems, nuclear proliferation is at the crux of increasing national ambitions, and the belief that such weapons provide an added level of protection and national throw weight in an increasingly non-polar world. These national aberrations are serious and could become more so. Unfortunately, these aberrations infect others with the nuclear-weapon-proliferation virus and while dominos are an exact and overused metaphor, it has some value in this element of international gamesmanship.

Before the ink was dry on the 1970 NPT its basic compact was violated. Israel's policy of "don't ask don't tell" created ambiguity concerning its nuclear-weapon program, but there are few if any who do not believe it has nuclear weapons, some dating back to the late 1960s. Israel's nuclear-weapon program was aided and supported by both France and the United Kingdom and was unique in that there has not been a verified test of its weapons. It is possible that the September 1979 nuclear explosion in the distant reaches of the Indian Ocean was an Israeli nuclear test. While Israeli ambiguity softens criticism in the West, it does little to calm the nuclear ambitions of many of its neighbours.

In the intervening years Israel has also used its superiority in intelligence and military might to ensure that nuclear programs of neighbouring states do not advance much beyond the tyro stage. In 1981 Israeli warplanes destroyed the Iraqi nuclear reactor south of Bagdad and it repeated the same feat by destroying a nuclear facility in Syria in September 2007. More recently there is evidence that Israel was behind the assassination of Iranian nuclear scientists and the wounding of another in 2010. More recently still Israel, with American assistance, was responsible for the introduction of the Stuxnet worm into computers controlling Iranian uranium-enriching centrifuges.

India was more open with its nuclear-weapon ambitions, exploding its first device in 1974 using Canadian nuclear technology and nuclear material from a Canadian research reactor. While Indian security needs had more to do with a nuclear-armed China, it was not surprising that Pakistan's reaction to the 1974 explosion was to intensify its own nuclear program and by the late 1980s it had its own nuclear weapons – an acknowledged underground test was carried out in 1998. As with India, Canada was instrumental in assisting Pakistan with its nuclear ambitions going back to the mid-1950s.

Israel, India and Pakistan did not sign the 1970 NPT, but their actions fuelled dissatisfaction with its basic compact. Pakistan, in particular, through the activities of its senior nuclear scientist, A Q Khan, provided assistance to North Korea, Libya and Iran in their clandestine nuclear-weapon programs. North Korea, which has withdrawn from the NPT, carried out its first nuclear explosion in 2006 and there are confusing assessments as to the status of the Iranian program. However, no one disagrees that there is an Iranian nuclear-weapon program and, importantly, a missile-delivery system. So far, Iran remains a member of the NPT.

On the other side of the ledger throughout the past forty years, two countries, South Africa and Libya, have ended their nuclear-weapon programs.

The world has adjusted to the nuclear weapons of Israel, India and Pakistan (except for the security of its weapons). In the case of India, an agreement with the United States in 2007 legitimized its nuclear-weapon program through segregation from its nuclear-power program. As a result most countries, including Canada, have resumed nuclear cooperation.

The North Korean and Iran nuclear-weapon programs continue to attract sustained countering action through sanctions and enticements and, as mentioned, sabotage. So far these efforts have had little effect on North Korea and its nuclear weapons have added considerable uncertainty to the north Pacific security equation. Equally, there has not been much success in deterring Iran from its nuclear-weapon ambitions. Sabotage may have slowed their efforts, but there are few signs that Iranian nuclear aspirations are either short-lived or controllable.

North Korea and Iran represent the most serious attack on the hopes for a nuclear-weapon-free world. Already there are signs that their nervous neighbours are looking for their own countering weapons. While the American nuclear umbrella is of some value to South Korea and Japan, both of these countries have the capabilities to produce their own weapons.

In the Middle East a more complex equation is playing out and the nuclear horsemen are in full gallop. Iran, assuming that the forces of liberation and democracy will have little effect on the "direct-from-god" sanction for its nuclear program and its willingness to intervene politically into the affairs of other countries in the Middle East, will remain a large causal factor in the nuclear policies of other countries. Saudi Arabia's nuclear intentions have always been circumspect, but the weakening of American support for authoritarian regimes will lessen the existing circumspection – and in the coming months there will be expressions of Saudi needs for nuclear technology in order to prepare for the day when its oil and gas runs out! In the past there have been reports that Saudi Arabia helped finance the Iraqi nuclear program and its ties with Pakistan provide considerable uncertainty as to what role nuclear issues play in that relationship.

In the past Egypt has been a firm advocate of a nuclear-free zone in the Middle East, but various parties have suggested that it should pursue a more active nuclear-weapon program. It already has two nuclear-research reactors, favourite instruments for proliferating countries, and in an unsettled political environment there can be every expectation the nuclear issue will receive more attention. It is a member of the NPT and any suggestion that it might try and slide away from those obligations could be costly, especially if international financial sanctions were to be considered.

The Israeli bombing of a nuclear installation in Syria three years ago suggests that there are those in that country who continue to see nuclear weapons as a necessary element in Syrian security in the years ahead. Its close ties with Iran and Pakistan could provide some shortcuts, and there is no shortage of scientists and technicians in the region who could be used. Iraqi history demonstrates that it has the capability to exploit nuclear technology and to believe that that history will remain dormant is simply whistling past a graveyard.

The possession of nuclear weapons by Israel, coupled with its inability or unwillingness to come to terms with the Palestinian issue, will continue to provide fertile ground for those in the Arab world who insist that countervailing nuclear weapons are urgently needed. The 32 years of strategic peace that Israel's peace agreements with Egypt and Jordan provided are now part of the region's history, challenged recently by the brave and uncertain new world of Middle Eastern politics. The flames ignited by the police abuse of a fruit seller in southern Tunisia suggests we may have already been closer to stability, let alone peace, than the region will see for some time.

Prism

Canada Will Pay a Steep Price in Border Talks
September 12, 2011

LAST FEBRUARY PRIME MINISTER HARPER AND PRESIDENT OBAMA signed a joint declaration *Beyond the Border: A Shared Vision for Perimeter Security and Economic Competitiveness*. The declaration stated that both countries intended to "pursue a perimeter approach to security" in order to "accelerate the legitimate flow of people, goods and services" and to do so in ways that would "support economic competitiveness, job creation, and prosperity."

There was little public discussion of the ideas in the declaration at the time, but in recent weeks there have been several pieces – "the first, potentially major, bilateral initiative in more than two decades" writes a former Canadian ambassador to the United States. For the most part these articles concentrate on border issues which "frustrate rather than facilitate trade." Largely missing from the public discussion is any understanding of the price that would be paid by Canadians in order to open wider border doors for Canadian trucks and Canadian services.

The declaration comes after ten years of failed initiatives to remove a variety of border restraints and constraints imposed by the Americans in the aftermath of 9/11. First there was the bilateral Shared Border Accords and then, with the inclusion of Mexico, the Security and Prosperity Partnership (SPP). In the midst of these partnership-based efforts, the United States unilaterally announced in 2005 the Western Hemisphere Travel Initiative (WHTI) – which had the direct result of curtailing travel between the United States and the countries of the Western Hemisphere. The WHTI required all travellers, including Americans, to carry passports or other government-issued identification when entering the United States.

Initiatives to improve access to the United States by Canadians, their goods and their services foundered on continuing American security concerns. While Canadians and Mexicans argued that prosperity was dependent on freeing the border, American responses were always coloured by and filtered through the prism of national security.

Throughout the decade hardly a year passed without some senior official reminding Americans of the threat Canada presented to the United States. Recently, Janet Napolitano, the American Homeland Secretary, spoke of the need to treat the Canadian border much the same as that with Mexico. She wanted "a real border" in the north. Since she is from Arizona, no doubt "real" in her mind includes a lot more guns, walls and continuing self-delusions.

Subsequently, the American Government Accountability Office (GAO) also weighed in and complained that the threats on the Canadian border were much higher than those on the Mexican. The American Commissioner for Customs and Border Protection, earlier this year, went even farther when he testified before Congress, claiming there are more cases "where people who are suspected of alliances with terrorist organizations, or have had a terrorist suspicion in their background – we see more people crossing over from Canada than we have from Mexico."

The Shared Vision declaration represents a dramatic and desperate change in strategy on the part of the government of Canada in seeking changes to the border. In the earlier post-9/11 initiatives, security was part of the package but was presented as a needed element for both governments. Increased security cooperation and integration were justified on their own merits. Shared Vision, on the other hand, includes security measures as a trade-off by Canada in order to buy American cooperation on border issues.

The essence of the security measures in the Shared Vision declaration requires the transfer of information to the United States on, potentially, millions of persons, most of whom would be Canadian citizens. Officials with the Canadian Shared Vision working group negotiating with the Americans, briefing interested Canadians this summer, were frank in declaring that increased Canadian cooperation on security was the price to be paid for the removal of border restraints and constraints. They were equally frank in stating that the privacy rights of Canadians could be affected in paying that price.

While these officials noted that the Canadian government had established "red lines" on privacy matters over which it would not cross, there was no confirmation that existing Canadian laws on privacy would not be changed. Following an August 15 meeting in Winnipeg with Janet Napolitano, Public Safety Minister Vic Toews mused to the press, "How do we share information in an appropriate fashion in order to ensure that security interests are met and yet that it doesn't thicken the border?" While the roles of privacy commissioners in both countries were discussed, Ms Napolitano laconically commented that "privacy issues between the United States and Canada are not nearly as great as is suggested."

The negotiations have now reached the point where it was leaked on the past weekend that an agreement had been reached on an implementation action plan for almost forty initiatives. There is no confirmation of this, as earlier Mr Toews revealed that Prime Minister Harper and President Obama will meet early this fall on the Shared Vision discussions. Mr Toews indicated that the negotiators needed "further directions" on the action plan. The leak may be nothing more than a crass attempt by the government to surround the Shared Vision initiative with the memories of 9/11.

President Obama is already in re-election mode and it is a certainty he will concede nothing to Canada on the border without large and dangerous concessions from Canada on security. Even a partially assembled presidential bus in Canada has become part of the rubbish on the presidential-election trail.

The protection of privacy is the subtly acknowledged elephant in the room in these discussions. In the last few years there have been two commissions of inquiry, which revealed that the privacy rights of Canadians were violated by the sharing of information with the United States. The men affected became guests of nasty regimes with life-changing consequences.

Both the Auditor General and the Privacy Commissioner have added their voices on the need for greater privacy protections. This and previous governments have ignored recommendations for changes and have been reluctant to improve existing protections by updating the out-of-date Privacy Act of 1983. If Canadians are not vigilant they may soon discover that the Americans have more control over their privacy rights than we do at home.

The Citizen

How the U.S. Blackmailed Canada
December 8, 2011

FINALLY, THE STARS ALIGNED AND AFTER A 10-YEAR EFFORT THERE IS consensus with the Americans on what might be done to ease border restrictions. Prime Minister Stephen Harper and President Barack Obama announced Wednesday a plan establishing an agenda for improvements to cross-border goods and services traffic. In exchange, Canada will provide the United States with personal information on millions of Canadians and become part of a North American security zone.

Fundamentally, the consensus signals Canada signing on to the American-centric view of the world on security matters. In the process, Canadian security institutions will be more closely integrated with those of the United States.

The February 4, 2011 meeting between Harper and Obama produced a "Declaration," an intent document on "a shared vision for perimeter security and economic competitiveness." This week's meeting produced an "Announcement" on the same subject. It should be emphasized that these are not formal treaties or even formal agreements, although there could be greater formality in the future. They are expressions of hope.

The documentation resulting from the two meetings do not provide suggestions that the people of Canada can use to make judgments based on the wisdom of this agreement, negotiated in the backrooms of both capitals.

Instead, Canadians are given a large dose of bromide with the statement that both countries will work "together in co-operation and partnership"; suggesting, at least for the government of Canada, that the troublesome details implicit in the agreement will be hidden behind the wall of national security. Equally, as a sign for our future, the consensus will not include issues, such as "buy American" laws or the building of pipelines, or the willingness of the United States to act unilaterally when its interests are under stress.

The need for such an agreement grew out of the policy mistakes of the United States in the aftermath of 9/11 when the border was closed for several days, and the implementation of border-security measures which, at their heart, suggested Canada was the source of danger to the United States.

The 1988 and 1992 free trade agreements which, in the words of the American negotiator at the time, would "open the doors between Canada and the United States" with "awesome" economic benefits as we move into the next century, were less than prophetic.

Throughout the 10 years since 9/11 there has been a drum roll of comments by American leaders that Canada represents an existential threat — a threat that needed to be countered by tough American measures, including the arming and hardening of the border. Only last May, in congressional testimony, the American Commissioner for Customs and Border Protection stated that there were more persons "suspected of alliances with terrorist organizations, or have had a terrorist suspicion in their background … crossing over from Canada than we have from Mexico."

The earlier bilateral Smart Border Accord, its associated Action Plan and the trilateral Security and Prosperity Partnership for North America in 2005 were all touted as mechanisms to improve border security, while at the same time freeing the forces of economic competitiveness. They all failed miserably and the failure was again reflected by unilateral American action to limit and control cross-border travel through the Western Hemisphere Travel Initiative. Again, these unilateral American restrictions on travel will not be altered by the Beyond the Border consensus.

These long-running train wrecks had little effect on the United States. Instead, the American-centric trade community in Canada accepted the drum beat out of Washington that "security trumps trade." It was that acceptance by the government of Canada that led to the Beyond the Border approach in the hope that it would neutralize American concerns on security. In the announcement Wednesday, Canada sold its national-security independence in exchange for hoped-for minor changes to American border restrictions.

It is not an overstatement to suggest that the United States blackmailed the government of Canada into making this deal. It was the American way or no way. Reducing restrictions for Canadian exports to the United States hold little political value for the Obama administration in the fervour of an election year, nor can there be much hope that the environment will be much better after November 2012.

The lesson for Canada is that it should not be lured into negotiations of large comprehensive agreements which include unrelated matters. History has demonstrated that Canada is more successful in negotiations with the United States when disagreements are narrowed and offsets in unrelated areas avoided. The Beyond the Border initiative is so large and so nebulous that neither the security of Canada nor its access to American markets will be helped. Like the Maginot Line of old it provides a temporal sense of success. It offers nothing for a rapidly changing future.

The Citizen

Harper Takes a Page from Assad Playbook
January 18, 2012

PRIME MINISTER STEPHEN HARPER AND PRESIDENT BASHAR AL-ASSAD of Syria have little in common.

Mr Assad, fighting for his political survival and that of his minority Alawite dynasty established by his father more than 40 years ago, has created a regime as repressive as any in the world.

Mr Harper is fighting ruthlessly and tenaciously to stamp his brand of conservatism upon the land. The bloodless passion he brings to the effort is reminiscent of cyborgs in recent science fiction whose refrain is "resistance is futile."

Mr Assad, from the early days of the Syrian revolution in February of last year, has laboured loud and hard to blame his troubles on foreign hands. In doing so, he is relying on a time-trusted trope that desperate despots throughout history have used.

Now Mr Harper and his Energy Minister have taken a page out of the Assad playbook. They, too, see the hands and money of foreigners at work in the opposition to the Enbridge Northern Gateway Project.

The Prime Minister was bruised by the success of the American environmental movement and the people of Nebraska in delaying permits for the Keystone XL pipeline. This was in spite of the enormous amount of Canadian money and Canadian-government support that went into the effort to obtain American approval for the project.

In the aftermath, Mr Harper and others in his government publicly stated, in a theme common to such disputes, that they knew what was best for the United States, and surely the wisdom of pipe-lining Canadian bitumen to refiners in Texas was a "no-brainer."

In his more-hurt-than-sorry rhetoric at the time, the Prime Minister went on to muse that Canadian energy products had other suitors and, with all of the subtlety of the meeting of the iceberg and the Titanic, suggested China would be a more welcoming place for Canadian energy.

To make sure that his message was understood south of the border, in recent days the Prime Minister and his Energy Minister have claimed that the foreign hand is American, carries American money and provides support determined to thwart his policy of moving Canadian energy offshore through the Northern Gateway pipeline.

The sad and immoral part of this strategy by the Prime Minister is its devaluation and dismissal of the opposition to the project by the aboriginal peoples who live on the land most directly affected by pipeline. There are very few large consensuses in this country, but one of the most fundamental is the belief that the indigenous peoples have not fared well in the more than five- hundred years since the arrival of the Europeans.

It is only now, through the use of the courts, the regulatory system, and the support of large numbers of non-aboriginal Canadians, that there is some hope the future could be better than the past. Land, of course, is the foundation on which that hope is based, and for the Prime Minister to imply that aboriginal opposition to the Gateway project is a product of American money and influence creates a new low in the management of this country's affairs.

A China agenda

An earlier proposal to build a pipeline in the Mackenzie River Valley to carry gas from Alaska to the continental United States was studied for more than three years by Commissioner Thomas R. Berger. Mr Berger left a large and unique legacy of understanding the importance of aboriginal land. He concluded that the pipeline should not be built because of its impact on the lives and well-being of the resident aboriginal peoples.

At the time, the proponents of the pipeline promoted the idea that the very future of Canada was tied up with having the pipeline built. Surprisingly, Canada and Western Canada have done quite well without it.

Almost four decades later, the same claims are being made for the Gateway project. Even the name promotes its inherent value. Proponents have released figures on its economic benefits that make the European debt problem seem manageable.

Ironically, the main beneficiary of the Gateway project, if built, will be China. Not so long ago the Prime Minister spoke with great scorn of the Chinese government and stated that it was not one with which Canada should do business. At times he seemed to have been suggesting, in the words of Ronald Reagan in another context, that China was an evil empire.

Times have changed, and in a few weeks the Prime Minister will be making his second visit to the Middle Kingdom. There can be every expectation Canadian energy will be at the top of the agenda. At the bottom, if at all, human rights will hardly get a mention.

All of this is coming at a time when the government is promoting northern Alberta energy products as being "ethical oil." A non-government organization has been created with that name by both members of the government and the energy sector.

Obviously, those involved in the promotion of the ethical oil message come from the marketing departments of universities, and not philosophy. As with President al-Assad, when oil or your very survival is at stake, ethics have very little to do with your arguments.

Embassy

Chain Reactions
February 24, 2012

THE VOLATILE MIXTURE OF IRAN, OIL, NUCLEAR PROLIFERATION, economic and political sanctions, assassinations and computer viruses, Israel, and Presidential elections in the United States forebodes a dangerous agenda for the rest of the year. Central to this complex agenda is the Iranian nuclear program and whether or not its associated nuclear-weapon activities have already crossed the Rubicon – and are about to provide the Iranian state with usable nuclear weapons

This issue has been part of the international agenda since Russia's decision to assist Iran in finishing a nuclear-power reactor in 1996, a project that began with German assistance when the Shah was still in charge.

There is an iron rule of nuclear-weapon proliferation. If a country has nuclear weapons or is determined to build them, then an adversarial country will do the same. India followed this rule with determination once China obtained nuclear weapons in the mid-1960s; and, once India did so in the mid-1970s, Pakistan was not far behind in developing its own nuclear arsenal.

Both India and Pakistan had prepared for the development of nuclear weapons through the assistance provided by Canada for a nuclear-power program. The associated transfer of technology and the training of hundreds of scientists and technicians by Canada provided the rich intellectual capital for the development of nuclear weapons by both countries. In the case of India, fissile material from a Canadian experimental reactor at Trombay, near Mumbai, was used for its first underground-test nuclear explosion in 1974.

This approach, nuclear-power reactors as a precursor to the development of nuclear weapons, is in contrast to that followed by the five nuclear-weapon states. The United States, the (then) Soviet Union, the United Kingdom, France and China all developed nuclear weapons prior to the development of nuclear-power reactors. Israel did the same, and was the first to introduce nuclear weapons into the Middle East in the mid-60s. It never did develop a nuclear-power program.

The incomplete Iranian nuclear-power plant at Bushehr on the north-eastern shore of the Persian Gulf was bombed by Iraq during the First Persian Gulf War (1980 to 88). With Russian assistance in 1996, one power reactor was rehabilitated and came on line in 2010. As part of the deal the Iranians agreed that the spent fuel would be returned to Russia.

Today the Iranian nuclear program is a complex one, including uranium enrichment and spent- fuel reprocessing, both capable of providing fissile material for nuclear weapons. These and other associated facilities are located at some fifty different locations across Iran, many deep underground or at hardened sites. Associated with the weapons program is the development of missile-delivery systems capable of reaching Israel and most of the Middle East east of Suez, from deep within Iran.

Both Israel and the United States (and probably most countries) have concluded that Iran is within months of having nuclear weapons or the capability to produce them. Israel believes this will happen within the next nine months while the United States suggests a slightly longer time frame. Only the United States, Western Europe and a few other allies guardedly believe economic and political sanctions will deter or slow Iranian determination to possess nuclear weapons. Israel, understandably, is much more pessimistic and has given every indication that it will not wait until there is confirmation of weapons before it moves from covert assassinations and bombing operations inside Iran to overt aerial attacks on key facilities of the Iranian nuclear-weapon program.

It is almost a certainty that Israel will attack Iranian facilities before November this year. A singular element in the Israeli decision to attack is to ensure the maintenance of American support and assistance. In the fervid atmosphere of American election politics the Republicans have already delivered promises of unquestioning support. It can be assumed that Obama and the Democrats will be no less supportive if they are put to the test in an election year. Ironically, with one or two exceptions, Israeli military action will find firm support from most of the countries of the Middle East.

The more troublesome aspect of an Israel attack will be its ability to ensure serious disruption and setbacks to the Iranian program. The Israelis have a reputation for effective decisive action, based on its 1981 successful bombing of the French-supplied nuclear reactor at the Al Tuwaitha Nuclear Center near Baghdad and on its 2007 destruction of a North-Korean-assisted reactor in the Deir ez-Zor region of Syria.

An attack on Iran will have risks far in excess of those single-site bombings. It will require a much larger effort; it will be over a much longer distance; it will be against multiple dispersed and hardened targets; and there is certainty of retaliatory action by the Iranians and its Hezbollah allies against Israel. Shipping in the Persian Gulf will be affected. The Israeli attack will have some of the intensity of the shock and awe that came with the American invasion of Iraq in 2003, but it could be a "bridge too far" even for the Israelis.

Shakespeare got it right as usual with his "Cry 'Havoc!', and let slip the dogs of war". The Israeli attack on Iran presages a period of violence and uncontrolled events, even by Middle East standards. The use of nuclear weapons in such a conflict cannot be ruled out.

Mission-Sharing: Baird was Ambushed by Brits
September 26, 2012

IT HAS BEEN 16 YEARS SINCE A BRITISH FOREIGN SECRETARY HAS MADE an official visit to Ottawa. On his way to the annual meeting of the UN General Assembly, British Foreign Secretary William Hague thought that it was time to meet his "first cousins."

In the absence of any pressing bilateral matters, he and his Canadian counterpart, John Baird, thought it was time to recreate an earlier bond by announcing the sharing of diplomatic premises and consular services.

Both countries had gone their separate ways on such matters since the British Parliament passed the Statute of Westminster in 1931.

The Statute provided legislative equality between the Parliament of Canada and that of Westminster and was the constitutional basis on which Canada began its engagement with the world. In large part that engagement established an international Canadian personality with its own interpretation of worldly matters and its own range of policies and activities, reflecting the unique requirements of Canadians.

The international environment in which Canada came to play a unique role has undergone changes of great magnitude in the past 80 or so years, but one of the great rocks has been the need for each and every country to establish itself as a separate and independent actor.

The main instrument of doing so is the establishment of representative offices in other countries. All countries have created embassies, high commissions, consulates general, consulates, and offices of honorary consuls. They remain the post offices for all official bilateral communications, and the place where citizens can seek assistance when travelling abroad.

Equally, some countries have established arrangements to offset the costs of such offices by administrative arrangements with other countries to assume responsibility for specific diplomatic or consular functions on its behalf.

Such arrangements are frequent, and seldom is there a suggestion that something other than minor exceptions to a national presence is in play. These arrangements are not meant to alter the bedrock of modern international relations in that each country is totally and exclusively responsible for its relationship with another country.

Not surprisingly, that bedrock of modern international relations has become more solid as the world erratically strives towards representative and responsible governments for all, with full observance and support for the laws of human rights tortuously built into this phantasmagorical vision.

Both the banal and the evil have wrapped themselves in the principle of national sovereignty to avoid such change. "Responsibility to protect" and its military outrider "regime change" have emerged as collective responses.

It is in this larger context that the British and Canadian foreign ministers entered into a minor administrative arrangement for work and, dreamingly, cost reductions in the delivery of diplomatic and consular services in inconsequential locations around the world.

But for Mr Baird, who has brought vivre and energy to the Harper government's management of foreign policy, it appears he was the victim of a British ambush.

Mr Hague is part of a coalition government where the Kiplingesque nostalgia of many backbench Conservatives has to be reconciled with the worldly and especially pro-European views of its Liberal Democratic partners.

It is in this British frame of reference that the idea of initiatives having a Commonwealth or, in the view of some, a British Empire context must be judged. Clearly, someone in London with a small axe to grind decided to give Mr Hague's visit to Ottawa some British political flavour by leaking the agreement of joint embassies. It was not long before someone suggested Australia and New Zealand might be part of such arrangements.

In the absence of details, it was not surprising that the idea took on wings of fancy, if not fantasy. "Canada and Britain to join diplomatic forces," "Canada, Britain plan to open joint embassies," and "Canada, Britain eye joint embassies" ran the headlines. Questions and comment followed even before the foreign ministers had signed the initiating documents.

For a government that has made it part of its sacred duty to burnish the British connection, the idea had obvious appeal. Pictures of the Queen in all embassies and the adding of "Royal" to parts of the Canadian armed forces were already in play, and the idea of closer association with Britain internationally fitted this nostalgic worldview.

But before the ink was dry there was a realization that the agreement launched a rock and not a bird. Mr Baird quickly labelled the arrangements as being "small" and "administrative" while another minister suggested that we would be sharing "photocopiers" with the British, and not embassies.

Even before the launching of this agreement with the British, there were one or two minor co-operative arrangements in place. There have been other such arrangements with other countries and, undoubtedly, there will be more in the future.

Canadians have come to live with a complex constitutional arrangement with the Queen as head of state. However, the reaction of many Canadians to the idea that closer association with the British government internationally can be easily added through shared diplomatic premises will now, hopefully, be returned to the quiet back rooms of diplomacy where it belongs.

Foreign relations should not be confused with being first cousins.
Embassy

Canadian Cheerleaders on the Sidelines in Mid-East Diplomacy
November 21, 2012

WAR DOES NOT NEED CHEERLEADERS, ESPECIALLY WARS IN THE Middle East. Yet that has been the essence of Canadian policy in the region for the last six years. Conservative government statements since the recent surge in violence have emphasized only one principle — the right of Israel to defend itself.

This might be comforting for the government. But, if those who control Canadian policy were to move beyond the narrowness of writing election-time speaking points, it would be apparent that this one principle was and is of little value in today's Middle East. Rather, any realistic policy must acknowledge the historical injustices of the peoples of the region and seek to create a climate in which discussion and negotiation can take place.

The current policy on Middle Eastern issues reflects, more generally, the dismal state of today's Canadian foreign policy. More often than not when an issue arises, there is an immediate polarization of thought and the government seeks to attach itself to a piece of policy driftwood, irrespective of its value for long-term survival.

For hundreds of years, the Balkans epitomized the intractability of issues that combined religion, geography, language and history. Balkanization became a metaphor for fragmentation and division and a signal of insolubility. Yet in a concatenation of events, the world and its governments were able to come together and give effect to policies that are remaking the region, giving new hope that there are few problems beyond solution. There are still rough edges to the solutions in the Balkans, but increasingly the benefits of peace and the prospects of prosperity have overshadowed ethnic and religious strife.

The issues of the Middle East are no less complex than those that faced the world in the Balkans. As the events of the Arab Spring suggested, even the most obdurate of situations can be bested by the concerted efforts of the people of the region and long-term involvement by the international community.

Canada, unfortunately, maintains a "Johnny-one-note" approach to the region, summed up by Foreign Minister John Baird at a fundraising dinner in Ottawa Tuesday when he stated that Canada "stands by Israel's side." Our government has effectively removed itself from the playing field. Irrespective of passionately held views by some Canadians, most would argue that the creation of a state for the Palestinian people with full sovereignty is a necessary starting point to peace and prosperity in the region. Instead, it remains an area that vacuums effort and resources away from other matters needing attention from the international community.

In the dark shadows of the violence of recent days there was an opportunity for the international community, in full co-operation with the people of the Middle East, to once again return to the tables of diplomacy and negotiations. A re-elected and reinvigorated President in the United States, an increasingly high level of frustration on the part of many Israelis, and a growing realization by the peoples of the Middle East that they have been badly and cruelly served by their own leaders combine to offer a small modicum of hopefulness for the international community to once again attempt to cut through the obduracy of history and religion.

Outsiders have a variety of interests — political, economic, security — at play in the Middle East. But the ongoing stalemate centred on the lack of any progress on the emergence of Palestinians from Israeli colonialism colours all and defeats efforts in addressing other problems.

It is a truism that only the United States has the authority and the legitimacy to yet again begin a new Middle East process centred on the establishment of a sovereign state of Palestine. The January parliamentary elections in Israel provide an opportunity for Israelis to introduce some measure of balance to their national government in the knowledge that "Iron Domes" and invasions of Gaza do not a sustainable security policy make. Equally, there is an opportunity for President Barack Obama to demonstrate that Israeli involvement in American politics has reached unconscionable and unacceptable limits.

These are dark hours for both Palestinians and Israelis. The one bright spot has been the willingness of the President of Egypt, Mohammed Morsi, to emerge as a broker for peace, playing a key role in negotiating a ceasefire announced Wednesday with U.S. Secretary of State Hillary Clinton.

Egypt has been a guarantor of regional peace since its peace treaty with Israel several decades ago and Morsi's willingness to retain that role needs the support of all, including Ottawa. One can only hope that the Israeli leadership understands this and starts looking beyond the ends of its guns for security.

For Canada, we are the far outriders of any involvement in future developments in the Middle East. As we wander the planet looking for trading partners, it is time that attention is given to the world in which freer trading arrangements would flourish.

Ottawa Citizen

Book Review

Winter 2012

On China, by Henry Kissinger. Allen Lane Canada, The Penguin Group, Toronto, 2011, 586 pp., $38.00

HENRY KISSINGER NEEDS NO INTRODUCTION IN THIS MAGAZINE. FOR the past sixty years his has been the voice of foreign policy *par excellence*, at the perihelion of the numerous momentous events that shaped the second half of the 20th century. At 89 his views remain central to many of our major policy conundrums and it is rare that he is not consulted on large issues of public policy both American and beyond.

He has published some sixteen books on foreign policy, ranging from the 1957 *Nuclear Weapons and Foreign Policy* to three volumes of memoirs dealing with his years in the public service of the United States. His years (1968-1977) as National Security Adviser to President Nixon and Secretary of State to both Nixon and President Ford were ones during which the shape of today's world was initiated and constructed. It is on those achievements that his legacy is based.

Nowhere is his legacy more profound, more fundamental to today's world than his work on China. While he has discussed this work in earlier books, his latest *On China* provides a comprehensive understanding of what was wrought through the events of the subsequent forty years, since the late February 1972 surprising arrival of the typical American cold warrior in Beijing. The world has not been the same since and the full impact of that event remains at the centre of one of our world's most complex issues. The integration of

China into the modern world's international system and its debut as the second largest global economy, soon to be first, presents opportunities and dangers that will affect all for the rest of this century. Today the speed and scope of China's "re-emergence" means that we are only now in the early days of needed global and bilateral adjustments, if we are to avoid the deep and dangerous fissures that attended the end of the Second World War.

Kissinger makes clear that the "re-emergence" of China is the most accurate term that can be used in describing what has happened since the arrival of European colonial powers along the coasts of China in the 18th century and the subsequent collapse of its imperial system in 1912. The first three chapters provide a tightly written presentation of the major social, political, economic, philosophical and military elements of China before Mao started his destructive war on many of them. As Kissinger makes clear, *realpolitik* was not first a European technique but rather a central element in how the Middle Kingdom dealt with those on its borders wanting to cause harm. His descriptions of the Chinese approach to its relationships with those on its borders provides clarity on many aspects of Chinese foreign policy, which remain important today as we come to grips with this heaving behemoth.

The end of the Second World War and the associated close alliance between the United States and the Soviet Union gave rise to a debate in the United States as to how to deal with a Soviet Union that many in the West saw as intent on world revolution and domination. It is out of that debate that George F Kennan, a member of the American embassy in Moscow, wrote his "Long Telegram" providing the analysis for American policy. The Truman Doctrine, as the policy became known, proposed "containment" as the guiding principle of American policy towards the Soviet Union. For the next two decades containment remained at the centre of American foreign policy, and there were few initiatives suggesting alternative approaches.

Kissinger broke with the containment policy, promoting instead the idea of *détente* in order to reduce tensions between the two countries. At the time, late 1960s, China's relationship with the Soviet Union was undergoing considerable stress with thousands of Soviet troops along its borders and regular military clashes. The American policy of *détente* with the Soviet Union and the deteriorating relationship between the Soviet Union and China provided the environment for the reconciliation between the United States and China. At the time the United States was still embroiled in a bitter and unwinnable war in Vietnam, an ostensibly close ally of China. However, for China, bigger stakes were at play – and Vietnam was cast overboard in the larger game of triangular superpower relationships

The three-way relationship between the Soviet Union, China and the United States post-1972 provided the basis for the management of the international system down to the breakup of the Soviet Union in 1992. All three countries played predestined roles, allowing China to make the transition from the revolutionary policies of Mao and Zhou to the boardroom approaches of Deng, Jiang Zemin, Hu Jintao and soon, Xi Jinping. It is this predictability in Chinese leadership that has provided social stability and constancy of policy, leading to its extraordinary economic gains.

The most serious exception to the steady evolution of China during this period was the uprising at Tiananmen Square in May, 1989. Kissinger quotes the American academic Andrew J. Nathan, on the uniqueness of the situation in China, who believed that neither the students nor the regime wanted confrontation. However, "Through miscommunication and misjudgment, they pushed one another into positions in which options for compromise became less and less available."

Kissinger describes the international reaction as "stark" with China described as an "arbitrary authoritarian state" where "popular aspirations to human rights" were "crushed" and the American relationship "came under attack from across a wide political spectrum." One side argued for "confrontation" while another argued that progress on human rights could be better attained through a policy of "engagement." Since the 1972 visit of President Nixon, the American policy of engagement had withstood the philosophical differences and policy vicissitudes of varying American administrations. Through the almost two decades the bipartisan approach on the importance of China to the United States ensured stability in both philosophy and policy.

Kissinger, twenty years later, provides the essential arguments for the matter and his comments have currency far beyond the example of China. He writes:

> There are instances of violations of human rights so egregious that it is impossible to conceive of benefit in a continuing relationship; for example the Khmer Rouge in Cambodia, and the genocide in Rwanda. Since public pressure shades either into regime change or a kind of abdication, it is difficult to apply to countries with which a continuous relationship is important for American security.

He answers his own question by writing that "China would be a major factor in world politics, whatever the immediate outcome of the Tiananmen crisis. . . . Isolating China would usher in a prolonged period of confrontation . . . [and] there were objective limits to American influence on China's domestic institutions, whether confrontation or engagement was pursued."

The Harper government in 2006, coming late to the issue, decided it did not like the government of China and engaged in a policy of low-level confrontation. However, three years later, experience demonstrated that there were no benefits to confrontation and in the last three years unreserved engagement has come to the fore. Kissinger's concluding comments on the matter, which remains relevant to countries far beyond China, bear emphasis:

> The basic direction of a society is shaped by its values, which define its ultimate goals. At the same time, accepting the limits

of one's capacities is one of the tests of statesmanship; it implies a judgment of the possible. Philosophers are responsible to their intuition. Statesmen are judged by their ability to sustain their concepts over time.

In his final chapter "Does History Repeat Itself?" Kissinger attempts to provide perspective on the evolution of China from 1949 with its ever-increasing political, military and economic might. He makes a comparison to the evolution of North Atlantic states where there are "divergent assessments of international issues and the means of dealing with them; even at their most bitter, they retain the character of an interfamily dispute. Soft power and multilateral diplomacy are the dominant tools of foreign policy, and for some Western European states, military action is all but excluded as a legitimate instrument of state policy."

Kissinger draws a sharp contrast with the situation prevailing in Asia. He writes:

> In Asia, by contrast, the states consider themselves in potential confrontation with their neighbors. It is not that they necessarily plan on war; they simply do not exclude it. If they are too weak for self-defence, they seek to make themselves part of an alliance system that provides additional protection.... Sovereignty, in many cases regained relatively recently after periods of foreign colonization, has an absolute character. The principles of the Westphalian system prevail, more so than on their own continent of origin.

China has land borders with fourteen countries, three of which (India, Vietnam and the then USSR) it has engaged militarily since 1962. Close at hand there are other countries (South Korea, Japan, the Philippines, Cambodia, Thailand, Burma, and Indonesia), with which it has had unresolved disputes, either strategic or marine boundaries. There is as well the issue of Tibet which, despite more than fifty years of effort, Beijing has not been able to obtain legitimacy in the eyes of most Tibetans or the world. It is not necessarily an area of instability but it is one where miscalculation, misunderstanding, misjudgement or exploitation can quickly deepen into issues that affect interests far beyond the region.

Kissinger draws parallels with pre-World War I Europe with its Anglo-German rivalry as "an augury of what may await the United States and China in the twenty-first century." As an example of the future, Kissinger writes that "China would try to push American power as far away from its borders as it could, circumscribe the scope of American naval power, and reduce American's weight in international diplomacy. The United States would try to organize China's many neighbors into a counterweight to Chinese dominance."

There is some measure of pessimism in Kissinger's writings at this stage because of the inability of most countries to deal with large-scale political events. So far he does not see in Asia a sense of an emerging discussion that might start a process for a regional consensus. Kissinger's policy prescription is for the development of a "Pacific Community" similar to that which has emerged in the North Atlantic, even though it was an initiative aimed at containing the Soviet Union. Kissinger sees such a Community as inclusive of China and not one by which China is "contained". All of the countries of the region, inclusive of India and Australia, would be part of such a community. More than anything else, Kissinger is hopeful that future policies and actions by the United States and its regional allies do not result in a standalone China, confrontational to the rest of the region.

There are few signs that such efforts are underway and the recent decision (post publication of this book) to create an "Asian pivot" to existing American foreign policy with the opening of a military base in Australia, and the possible reopening of bases in the Philippines, does not provide encouraging auguries for the future. These initiatives are seen by most as being directed at Beijing. Kissinger has little to say on the extraordinary growth of the Chinese economy, suggesting that convergence of economic interests remain significant.

For the most part, he sees this development as almost a return to the days before the Taiping civil war when China's economy was larger than that of most of the other countries of the world.

He closes his book with an observation on a meeting with Premier Zhou Enlai. He quotes Zhou as saying "This {Nixon's visit] will shake the world." Kissinger goes on to say "What a culmination if, forty years later, the United States and China could merge their efforts not to shake the world, but to build it." As with events in the Middle East, "Inshallah."

bout de papier, Vol. 27, No. 1.

The Iran Caper: The Washington Scene - Getting the Americans Interested in the Six
January 15, 2013

JIMMY CARTER WAS NOT HAVING A SUCCESSFUL PRESIDENCY. ELECTED by the slimmest of margins – 50.1 per cent of the popular vote - in November 1976, two years into his mandate, he still remained an outsider to many Americans. More troublesome, he was taking on the air of an ineffective leader at that.

The promise of a sharp break between the sordidness of Watergate and the future gave Mr Carter his slight edge with the American people. In some ways he represented something more than a change of administrations, rather he personified regime change at a time when the term had little currency.

I arrived in Washington in the summer of 1978 on a cross-posting from East Africa, after three years of coping with salubrious Kenya and murder-ridden Uganda under Idi Amin. It was a welcome change and the new job was an interesting one – intelligence liaison with the CIA and the Department of State. It was the start of a four-year university-level course on the world.

There was a miasma about the city suggesting the promise of the Carter presidency was in trouble. Not unlike today, the economy was unresponsive to the normal nostrums; reliance on foreign oil seemed impossible to counter; and, less than a year after arriving in the capital, President Carter, in a nation-wide speech, unconvincingly sought to offload his responsibility for these problems to the American people.

There were successes, but these were largely in foreign affairs. A historic treaty with Panama was negotiated and ratified by Congress to return the canal to Panamanian sovereignty at the end of the century; the Camp David Accords started a process in the Middle East for reconciliation between the Israelis and the Palestinians, underwritten politically by Egypt and Jordan; a second round of strategic-arms-limitation talks led to an unratified agreement with the Soviet Union; and, most significantly, President Carter gave voice to the view that the morality of human rights had a role to play in American foreign policy and the management of the international community.

Events in Iran, however, created a worrisome backdrop. Carter visited the country early in his presidency and, contrary to his views on morality in foreign affairs, lavishly praised the Shah, seeing him as a force for stability in the region. It was not a view shared by most Iranians who harked back to the illegitimacy of the dictator's coming to power by British and American machinations in 1953.

1978 was a year of regime-shaking civil conflict that the Shah and his main instrument of control – SAVAK – brutally tried to counter, but with little success. In the process the Shah lost his limited legitimacy and, before January, 1979 was out, so was the Shah. HIs nemesis, Ayatollah Ruhollah Khomeini, in exile in Iraq and France for the previous fourteen years, triumphantly returned to Tehran on February 1, 1979. He was a man with a plan and within a year he was not only the supreme religious leader of the country and Shia everywhere, he was also Iran's supreme political leader.

In Washington these events were carefully followed, but there was little understanding or appreciations of how fundamental were the changes in Iran. The initial issue was how to deal with the Shah in exile in Egypt. Rifts in the administration were clearly evident. Cyrus Vance, the Secretary of State, wanted to cut all ties with the Shah and did not want to see him in the United States, even for critical medical treatment. Vance and his colleagues at State emphasized that the United States needed to recast its relationship with Iran in the aftermath of the Shah's downfall, and diplomacy had to dominate confrontation. Vance was not without influence. In the early days of the administration he was highly successful in the handling of the negotiations with Panama on the canal and with the Middle East discussions leading to the Camp David Accords.

Over at the White House, Zbigniew Brzezinski, National Security Adviser to the President, had a decidedly different approach to the world. Born in Poland between the wars, Brzezinski had built a reputation as a realistic interpreter of the Eastern Bloc, especially the dominated countries of Eastern Europe. In the process, he became known as the Democrats' "Kissinger," favoring peaceful engagement with the region over détente. In Carter's government he was seen as a wily opponent of Vance, who still saw détente as a guiding principle in the management of East-West relations. Their strongly held views became polar points in the administration and often led to ambiguous policies – which played out in counterproductive responses during the hostage crisis.

The news on November 4, 1979 that Iranian students had taken control of the American embassy did not occasion serious concern in Washington. Prompted by the decision of the United States on October 22 to allow entry by the Shah for medical treatment, the takeover was considered similar to what had happened earlier in February, 1979 when students took control of the embassy, but left after a few days. This benign view was soon overtaken when, unlike in February, the Ayatollah backed the action of the students; it was only then that the policy community in Washington realized that it was in the midst of major crisis.

The CIA in those days was *hors de combat*. Stansfield Turner was appointed by Carter as his Director of Central Intelligence in early 1977 and it was soon apparent that it was not one of his better decisions. The Agency was still coping with Seymour Hersh's 1974 allegations in the *New York Times* dealing with covert activities, including assassination efforts involving foreign political leaders and the undermining of foreign governments. These activities were collectively known as the Agency's "family jewels." As well, Hersh alleged that the Agency was collecting intelligence on the political activities of American citizens. Mainly based on Hersh's allegations, Congressional investigations (Church and Pike Committees) provided substantive confirmation of the Agency's illegal activities and recommended major changes in the management of American intelligence activities at home and abroad.

In the midst of these externally imposed and wrenching changes, Turner decided there was a need to reduce the size of the Agency, especially on the Operational side. Over eight-hundred officials were fired (known as the Halloween Massacre in Agency lore). It was years before the CIA returned to overconfidently believing it had a significant role to play in American foreign policy. As an intelligence liaison officer I was part of a small group (British, Australians, New Zealanders) which had official status with the Agency, as well as with the Intelligence Bureau of State. Our role was to provide the Americans with our own information of events in the world and our interpretations. Equally, from the Americans, we sought and were freely given access to their intelligence, analysis and conclusions.

It was clear from the very start that the United States did not have a coherent understanding or appreciation of what the overthrow of the Shah represented for American policy. The takeover of the American embassy complicated what was initially a foreign-policy matter and turned it into a major domestic issue. Iran under new and radical leadership was one thing; Iran capturing and torturing 52 American officials was a crisis of an entirely different order.

The overwhelming concentration in Washington was concern for the 52 hostages held by the Iranians. Vance and officials at the State Department sought action at the United Nations and the International Court of Justice, but even when successful there was no reaction from Tehran. At the While House Brzezinski was promoting direct military action to rescue the hostages, an idea he continued to promote and organize until it led to disaster in the southern desert of Iran on April 24, 1980 with nine dead rescuers and two crashed aircraft.

There was little action within the administration on the six Americans now safely sequestered at the home of John Sheardown and the official residence of Canadian Ambassador Ken Taylor. The prevailing assumption was that they were out of harm's way and would be accommodated within any larger effort concerning the 52. However, it was clear by early December 1979 that this assumption was not only erroneous but dangerous as well – not only for the Americans being sheltered by Canadians but for their Canadian rescuers.

The press by this time were counting bodies and it soon became evident both to Jean Pelletier, the Washington correspondent of *La Presse* in Montreal, and the *New York Times* that the numbers being used by the State Department in describing the hostages did not add up. Pelletier even sought confirmation from the Canadian embassy as to whether Canada was sheltering some of the hostages. Fortunately, both *La Presse* and the *New York Times* agreed that to publish the story at that time could well lead to increased dangers for the hostages and their Canadian friends.

In Ottawa these developments rang the alarm bells. In early December it was decided that the Americans had to be convinced that the six hostages with the Canadians in Tehran must be dealt with urgently – before they joined their colleagues as hostages in the American Embassy. Pat Black, the Under Secretary for Intelligence and Security at Foreign Affairs, called in early December and asked that I approach appropriate persons within the CIA and lay out for them the need for urgent action on getting the six Americans out of Tehran. He mentioned that Flora MacDonald would be meeting with Vance in a few days during a NATO meeting in Brussels and she intended to raise the matter as well.

Frank Carlucci was the Deputy Director of the CIA and was highly regarded as the person in the Agency who could get things done and done well. I met with Carlucci soon after the call from

Black and laid out the case on the need for urgent American action to exfiltrate the six from Tehran at the earliest possible moment. Carlucci appreciated the dangers the six, along with the Canadian staff, were in, realizing that it would only be a matter of time before the situation in Iran became public knowledge. Within a week or so of this meeting Tony Mendez was selected by the Agency to organize and carry out the exfiltration of the six from Tehran.

The exfiltration operation has now been celebrated in books, documentaries and a Hollywood movie. Each in their own way, some more accurately than others, captures the operation in all of its detail. The Hollywood movie, unfortunately, eliminated the role John and Zena Sheardown played in the drama and, as it becomes part of the American mythological historical record, it is appropriate that Canada and Canadians stand their ground on the roles that were played by so many. It was not only a hugely humanitarian and personally dangerous effort by Canadians in Tehran but also one of the finer efforts by Canada's Foreign Service in a long, long time.

In the immediate aftermath of the rescue operation on January 28, I accompanied Frank Carlucci to Ottawa where he expressed the appreciation of the United States government to Flora MacDonald. It was a cold, snowy day in early February when he met with Ms MacDonald just prior to the February 18 federal election. Kind words were offered and Ms MacDonald rushed off for last-minute electioneering. As we put on our winter clothes outside her office in the Pearson building, I helped Carlucci's security man with his large jacket. Unexpectedly, the coat was much heavier than anticipated and it fell to the floor was a muffled clunk. I picked it up and looked questioningly at the security official in the full knowledge that the matter of Americans carrying weapons in Canada was a perennial issue. The security man looked at me with a slight smile on his face and simply said "lifesavers."

As a postscript to these events, in late January this year a general in Iran's Revolutionary Guard criticized the 2011 storming of the British Embassy in Tehran, saying students and activists should "avoid actions driven by emotion." The general went on to say that Iranians must deal with their enemies "more intelligently" and "avoid shallow and emotional actions" that damage Iran's image abroad. Insha'Allah.

bout de papier, Vol. 27, No. 2.

The Confusing World of Economics
January 23, 2013

THE WORLD OF ECONOMICS AND THE ARCANE PRACTITIONERS OF the art dominate all aspects of our lives. It was probably always so, but today's intensity and scope is without precedent. Its large assumptions about our behavior and especially its willingness to make large and small prognostications suggest that casino owners in Las Vegas make more frequent deposits at their friendly banks. In a very large sense, there are good reasons not to pay much heed to these forecasts about our future conditions. They are largely without merit.

Several decades after the publication of Adam Smith's seminal book, *The Wealth of Nations*, another Scot, the poet Andrew Lang, put into words a pithy criticism of economists that still echoes down through the ages. Mr Lang wrote: "he uses statistics as a drunken man uses lamp-posts ... for support rather than illumination."

I am not an economist, but the specialty loomed large when a long time ago I was part of the Meteorological Service of Canada (now eponymously known as Environment Canada) and coped with another inexact science in places such as Gander, Goose and Frobisher bays (now Iqaluit). On badly forecasted days, we derived some satisfaction knowing that economists were pushing an even larger rock uphill – with little expectation of ever reaching the top.

Since then, weather forecasting has reflected the enormous changes in the worlds of mathematics and physics. The relationship expressed by the butterfly in Jakarta and snow in Regina metaphor has pushed meteorology into the realms of fractals, chaology and dynamic systems, developed largely by Benoit Mandelbrot.

Mandelbrot was probably the most important mathematician since Isaac Newton and, as a result, weather forecasting today is ever-increasingly edging towards a fuller understanding of nature.

Unfortunately, the same cannot be said about economics.

Since the days when *The Wealth of Nations* provided the world with a comprehensive and reasoned understanding of wealth, especially at the national and international levels, economics and economists have laboured in vineyards that have rarely produced wine worth drinking – or advice to governments and individuals that reached the status of vintages.

Rather, in the nearly 250 years since Mr Smith gave form and substance to the study of economics, the discipline has wandered from pillar to post in its effort to provide coherence and understanding of the world of labour, capital and resources.

It is not surprising that the field of economics was the last addition to the Nobel prizes, and then only in 1968. Reflecting the softness of the subject matter and criticism of the selection process, the prize, in 1994, was broadened to include persons in such fields as political science, psychology, and sociology – all equally bereft of coherence and sustainability.

Today broad economic policy is dominated by the writings of two economists who, characteristic of most economists, crossed pens and conflicting thought throughout the 1930s.

These two economists – or perhaps "political economists" as was a commonly used description of the times – John Maynard Keynes and Friedrich Hayek created the intellectual capital that continues to confuse many who plot public policy.

Equally, this historical intellectual capital has stalled the evolution of economics into a respectable discipline, based on intellectual rigour and professional honesty. For many, the practice of economics today is similar to having physicists contend with two concepts of gravity.

Keynes, who is the best known of the two, taught at Cambridge and, in his *Treatise on Money* in 1930, provided a bankrupt world with ideas on how governments could put an end to the ups and downs of business cycles. His ideas, when filtered, called for governments to stimulate economic demand and employment during recessions through large spending programs.

Classical economists at the London School of Economics were affronted by Keynes's proposals and reached out to the Austrian economist, Friedrich Hayek, to provide a counterpoint. While there are various interpretations today on Hayek's writings (he largely ignored economics in his later writings and teaching), essentially he argued that the answer to the peregrinations of the business cycle were to be found in the decisions of individuals relating to large wealth-generating projects.

This is reflected in modern economics by the use of Adam Smith's metaphor "the invisible hand of the market" and associated with the idea that unfettered capitalism provides the answers for guiding our economic lives.

Today the proposals of Keynes and Hayek, although amplified and brought up to date, dominate both economic and political discourse. As in the 1930s the departments of economics at some universities have become ideological bastions of either governmental stimulus or unfettered markets. The most prominent of these was the School of Economics at the University of Chicago, which has dominated American thought from the 1960s onwards. Not unfairly, it can be said that its ideas led to the economic collapse of 2008. A pale imitation at the University of Calgary had some currency a few years ago but, as with Chicago, has seen the cold water of reality dash its pretensions.

Throughout the world, as in Ottawa, governments continue to search for answers to the confusing world of economics. Not surprisingly, economists have little sound advice to offer that is not tainted by ideology.

In Canada the government has given Canadians both a dose of stimulus and significant reductions in government services, while throughout promoting the idea that the marketplace provides the road away from our economic troubles.

In doing so, there is more faith than understanding in its various proposals and, as history has shown, time more than intellectual understanding provides the path to a better future.

In the meantime governments and economists have taken a leaf from the pages of early meteorology: If you want to know which way the wind is blowing, wet your finger and stick it into the air.

Embassy

No Slam Dunks with Uncle Sam
February 20, 2013

THE SECOND RULE IN INTERNATIONAL NEGOTIATIONS WHEN THE first rule of matching concessions does not apply is to seek asymmetrical cessions. The Obama administration, through the American ambassador in recent days, has been trying exactly that in the Keystone XL muddle. The Ambassador has never been one to ruffle the smooth ebb and flow of Canadian-American relations, preferring instead the purring of a small feline in a Panglossian world.

The Ambassador, David Jacobson, expectedly coming to the end of his four years in Ottawa, was quick to pick up on one of the central themes in President Obama's State of the Union address on February 12. The President's speech, which caused ringing in the ears of most Republicans, re-established himself as a man deeply concerned with our collective future as a result of a lack of action on climate change.

"But for the sake of our children and our future, we must do more to combat climate change," he told his audience. And, in words that are almost heresy in Ottawa, went on to say that we must "choose to believe in the overwhelming judgment of science and act before it's too late."

The "slam dunk" characterization by the Prime Minister a few months ago on the Keystone XL decision, just after the American election, is no longer in play. Even the new Secretary of State, John Kerry, who has never wavered in his promotion of policies to deal with climate change, is already officially burnishing his environmental credentials. In a speech on February 20 Kerry's rhetoric was unconstrained: "We as a nation must have the foresight and courage to make the investments necessary to safeguard the most sacred trust we keep for our children and grandchildren: an environment not ravaged by rising seas, deadly super-storms, devastating droughts, and the other hallmarks of a dramatically changing climate."

Any inclination on the part of some White House staffers to "take one for Canada" is more hope than reality at this stage. Planning for the mid-term congressional elections in 2014 is underway and the White House will need all of its allies, including environmentalists, to retain its current position in Congress – if not to improve it. As such a "No" decision on Keystone XL or a punt down the road is a safer bet than a "Yes."

It is in this context that Ambassador Jacobson's suggestion for a more forthcoming approach by Canada in its policies on climate change might be helpful in Washington. In an interview the Ambassador is quoted as saying "there are an awful lot of folks who are trying to make up their minds, and trying to draw the right balance between these two things, who I think will be moved by progress" [on climate change].

The Ambassador's suggestion, carefully staged from Washington, only has one purpose; that is to offload responsibility for a "No" decision onto the Canadian government. There are many in this country who are supportive of Canada doing more on climate change and angry at the Conservative government for its Neanderthal policies. Its recent efforts to throw numbers at the public in an attempt to demonstrate that it has created a "silk purse" will do nothing other than add confusion to Canadians' appreciation of what is happening to federal policies on climate-change.

Embassy

"Those Who Take Us Away" – and Those Who Look Away

February 22, 2013

IN 2010 THERE WAS COLLECTIVE SCOFFING AS PUBLIC SAFETY Minister Vic Toews and then Treasury Board President Stockwell Day cited an increase in "unreported crimes" as the basis for the government's "strong on crime" polices, along with claims of a "lack of confidence in the justice system" by Canadians.

This was one of very few instances when the Conservative government was prepared to use statistics (or more accurately survey data) collected by Statistics Canada in support of one of its most controversial policies. More typical was the government's decision to eliminate the long-form census, leading to the resignation of the country's Chief Statistician.

With this history, there might have been some expectation that the government's response to the February 13 report by Human Rights Watch, dealing with "unreported" crimes committed by members of the RCMP against indigenous women and girls in northern British Colombia, would be robust. As the HRW report details, there are enormous amounts of information available that demonstrate that life for many indigenous women and girls in northern British Colombia is poor, brutish and, too often, short. The HRW personalizes this information with interviews of fifty persons who report in detail their experiences with the RCMP in recent years.

Part of the backdrop for the report is the murders and disappearances along Highways 97 and 16 in northern BC. These roads have become "infamous" for the dozens of women and girls who have been reported missing or were found dead in the area over the past fifty years. There are hundreds of similar cases across Canada.

The response of the government has been pathetic. The Prime Minister said that the government has sent "appropriate information" to the useless Commission for Public Complaints Against the RCMP. He then went on to offload responsibility to HRW and the Liberal Party by stating that they provide their information to the "appropriate police." The "appropriate" police are, of course, the RCMP. Even the RCMP shamelessly asked aboriginal women and girls to come forward and provide their complaints to their officers. Sadly, both responses totally ignore the central fact that the allegations made by aboriginal women and girls involved officers of the RCMP!

The suggestion that a special Commons committee be struck to investigate the matter demonstrates how out of touch Members of Parliament are on this matter. Such committees, in the past, have demonstrated less of an interest in establishing an understanding of a particular matter than in partisan bickering and personal scoring.

One of the key points made in the Human Rights Watch report is the observation that "researchers were struck by the fear expressed by women they interviewed. The women's reactions were comparable to those Human Rights Watch has found in post-conflict or post-transition countries, where security forces have played an integral role in government abuses and enforcement of authoritarian policies."

It is no accident that the title of the HRW report is *"Those Who Take Us Away."* The RCMP has been the coercive arm of Canadian government policies towards aboriginals since its inception one hundred and forty years ago. It was the outside enforcement arm for residential schools and, when aboriginals were needed in the high Arctic to demonstrate Canadian sovereignty, it was the RCMP who ensured that people along the eastern shore of Hudson Bay were moved to places near Resolute Bay.

It is this history that sees aboriginal groups trying to appeal to the Crown and to the United Nations for redress for their grievances. Central to these grievances is the lack of any recognition by Canadians that it is the policy of colonialism that has guided the policies of Canadian governments towards the aboriginal people. The actions of the Idle No More movement, the hunger strikers and the Chiefs all have a common denominator – the absence of any coherence by governments today, and by Canadians generally, in seeking equitable and fair approaches to the problems of aboriginal peoples.

Governments come and go and so do our aboriginal policies. If Canadians paid attention to the health needs of the peoples along the Labrador and west Hudson Bay coasts, our church basements would be filled with outrage. Add in the other basic needs of water, housing and education and we would all have to move to our "iconic" hockey rinks to fit in the protestors.

Of course this is not going to happen, as it is far easier to have outside accountants examine books and confirm our prejudices that any problems are the fault of the aboriginals.

The Human Rights Report, however, creates a very large and tragic question mark that should remain in the minds of all Canadians. When those responsible for providing safety and security for the most vulnerable of aboriginals are identified as a major danger then it is more than time that we all took notice and demanded action. To suggest that the victims go to those who abuse them is beyond reason. It is time for independent examination and corrective action.

A few years ago, the American satirist Pat Paulsen had a few words to say about immigration policy. To adapt his words to north of the border (which I am sure he would not object to) Mr Paulsen said, "All the problems we face in Canada today can be traced to an unenlightened immigration policy on the part of the Canadian Indian."

iPolitics

Borders and Edges
April 22, 2013

NOT SO MANY YEARS AGO, A CANADIAN COULD ENTER THE UNITED States using a Canadian Tire credit card. It was then an age when international travel was an early harbinger of the globalization of humanity. Even the International Civil Aviation Organization had a "facilitation" committee aimed at making international travel as seamless as possible.

As with most dreams, the intervention of the nightmares of political, economic, religious and ethnic strife have harshly pushed national policies of control and entry in an entirely different direction. While international air travel today is at the billion-person level it is not an experience with much joy.

The only exceptions to this deeply disappointing trend are the countries of the European Union. Some of these bravely seek to maintain the dreams of the Rome and Maastricht treaties, and the Schengen Agreement for borderless conditions for travel and work. But it is doubtful those dreams can be maintained in the face of the economic crises at home, and the dark torments at the edges.

The scene at the Canada-United States border is even more depressing. There, the dreams inherent in the 1988 and 1994 free trade agreements have given way to the nightmares that crowd the minds of American officials. The benign view of Canada and Canadians and the "longest undefended border in the world" is now one of apprehension.

In the words of Janet Napolitano, the American Homeland Secretary, there is a need to "change the culture" surrounding the American treatment of the Canadian border and to make it clear to all that "this is a real border." More recently Ms Napolitano has been promoting the idea of a border-crossing tax for Canadians entering the United States by land. That will ensure that there are no misunderstandings about the Canada-United States border being "a real border."

These American fears have been manifest since 9/11, and one could almost feel the palpations in Ottawa that the recent Boston bombings and murders might have Canadian connections. The identification of an articulate aunt to the alleged perpetuators in Toronto will, in the minds of many American officials, confirm the view expressed by the Commissioner for Customs and Border Protection in 2011. Then the Commissioner testified before Congress that there are more "cases where people who are suspected of alliances with terrorist organizations, or have had a terrorist suspicion in their background – we see more people crossing over from Canada than we have from Mexico."

In the twelve years since 9/11 there has been an elimination of all efforts to facilitate travel between our two countries. The American requirement for passports for re-entry by its own citizens has decimated any inclination by Americans for tourist travel to Canada. Canadians, however, have nimbly adapted with over sixty per cent now holding passports. Cheap air travel from American airports and cross-border shopping continue to draw Canadians south of the border, draining the Canadian economy of some of its increasingly scarce lifeblood.

Surrounding these developments is the new lexicon we now use to describe the border. It is no longer "undefended", it is now a "thick" border with urgent prayers for a "thin" one. There are strong signs that, as with life, "thin" is more metaphorical than real. Instead there are drones that monitor the border nearly as much as they do over Afghanistan and Pakistan; Canadian border-security officers now carry weapons similar to their American counterparts; and there is now joint policing on shared waterways with continuing efforts to extend this to land areas as well. Do not be surprised that in the coming months the knock on your door could be an FBI officer.

The 2011 Shared Vision Declaration announced by Prime Minister Harper and President Barack Obama and its promise of advancing prosperity and defending our values and freedoms is a maple tree in December barren of its leaves, but with hope for syrup in the spring. The American ambassador bravely asserted a few months ago that we are safer and better off as a result of the Declaration. He pointed to wait times at airports as having improved and less missing baggage on connecting flights. He did not acknowledge the possibility that this may be due to Canadians making their initial flights from American airports.

On the other hand, one of the creators of the free trade regimes and another who has vainly supported the hope for benefits of the 2011 Declaration have come to different conclusions. A few months ago Derek Burney, writing in *Foreign Affairs,* described Canada-United States relations as "while civil have seldom been productive." John Manley, the President of the Canadian Council of Chief Executives, was even more despairing. "To be perfectly honest, it's more promising than actual results." Mr Manley should know, as he was the author of an earlier failed attempt to "lighten" the border through the Smart Border Plan.

In all of this the Shared Vision myopia lives on, more in hope than any real expectation that the border will ever be a thin one again. The Shared Vision boat may still be afloat, but the orchestra is playing Nearer My God to Thee.

Embassy

The Canadian Legacy of Margaret Thatcher
May 1, 2013

NONE OF THE EULOGISTS AT MARGARET THATCHER'S FUNERAL ROSE to the equivocation of Marc Antony in his testimony at the funeral of Julius Caesar. Marc Antony mastered Imperial Rome's divide by describing both Caesar and his assassin, Brutus, as honourable men.

The eulogists today took an easier route, deciding that they were there "to praise" Ms Thatcher. In doing so they ignored the duality of Ms Thatcher's legacy.

Her rock-in-the-handbag approach to Britain's economic, social, and loss-of-status issues in a changing world gladdened many. Yet, as evident since her passing, she deepened and sharpened the fissures of British society.

Funerals are not occasions when such fissures are bridged. This is especially so with a government that has adopted a Thatcherlite approach to some of the same problems that Thatcher acolytes claimed she eliminated during her 11 years as prime minister. A reasoned argument can be made that today's problems grew out of her policies.

As Marc Antony would claim, ceremonies sometimes are occasions to hide deep fissures. By placing Ms Thatcher within the pantheon of Nelson, Wellington, and Churchill, the British government of today is attempting to cover up her failures and place her within the reflected glory of these earlier leaders.

Fortunately, time and historians, not today's politicians, will be the arbiters of her legacy. And the healthy streak of revisionism among today's historians will ensure that it will be a spirited debate. It will be one Ms Thatcher would enjoy.

One of the unusual features of the encomiums offered following Ms Thatcher's death was the response from Canadian politicians, especially those who came of age during and after her time in office.

Prime Minister Stephen Harper led the parade, referring to her as "a giant among leaders" and saying Ms Thatcher "had the rarest of abilities to herself personify and define the age in which she served" and her economic policies "defined contemporary conservatism itself."

Foreign Minister John Baird – who throughout his political career has moments suggesting he is a character out of the Boy's Own Paper – has often given testimony to the importance of Ms Thatcher in his own political formation and life. He reportedly named his cat in her memory and, in an undergraduate paper at Queen's University, touted her economic philosophy.

In her passing Mr Baird saw the world as losing "a legend...an icon and a personal political idol."

Speaking from a region of the world, the Middle East, with more illogical convictions than most, Mr Baird described Ms Thatcher as a "conviction politician," adding that the world needed more "of those." He went on to offer her to the ages: "In many ways it will be less about what she accomplished in the United Kingdom than what she accomplished in the world by inspiration."

Other members of the government spoke firmly in support of these ukases. The President of the Treasury Board, Tony Clement, attempted to rewrite history when he declared that Canada was "still in the midst of Pierre Trudeau statism, and that was the consensus among the intellectual elites and political elites."

Pierre Poilievre, a parliamentary secretary, saw Canada implementing "Thatcherism gradually over the past quarter-century," using the free trade agreement with the United States as an example – ignoring Ms Thatcher's blind opposition to closer European economic and political co-operation.

Barbara McDougall, a member of Brian Mulroney's cabinet, was more objective in her comments. She and Ms Thatcher "bore not one whit of resemblance to each other," when Ms McDougall began to see herself as a serious politician. "It was the woman thing, and I finally pushed myself off the starter mark and won."

Brian Mulroney, whose time as prime minister largely overlapped with Ms Thatcher, was more balanced in his views. Mr Mulroney did not have to sit at anyone's knees to learn about politics, and, as such, Ms Thatcher was a colleague with whom he fought as much as they agreed.

Mr Mulroney had very little to say about her domestic policies, rather emphasizing her international role. While agreeing on such matters as the role of Gorbachev in the G7, free trade, and the expansion of NATO, he had "their most difficult conversations about apartheid for more than five years."

Reflecting his own experience, Mr Mulroney went on to write that "it is always tempting for one generation to regard the leaders of the generations that follow with some condescension." However, he was of the view that at a "crucial chapter" in the history of the United Kingdom, "without Margaret Thatcher's resolute leadership, the United Kingdom would have suffered far more deeply."

No other group of foreign politicians was as large or as laudatory in their praise of Ms Thatcher. This praise went far beyond the requirements for such occasions and says more about those offering it than her achievements.

It suggests that Ms Thatcher validated for many in the present government of Canada characteristics of bloody-mindedness, personal decisiveness and divisiveness and ideological purity. The long haul into government for many of these persons against long-established norms of Canadian politics also suggests there was a need for foreign validation of what they were about.

In this, the death of Ms Thatcher and the associated assaults by many in Britain strike at the very heart of both personal and party convictions in Canada. This comes at a time when, after six years as a government, the wens and the warts of that government are starting to show. Over-the-top laudations of Ms Thatcher will not change that.

Embassy

Qatar's Quiet Understanding of Canadian Politics
May 8, 2013

CANADIANS CAN BE FORGIVEN IF THEY HAVE TROUBLE RECOGNIZING Qatar or its significance to Canada. That has changed in the last few days. Qatar, with surprising adroitness, has offered to host the International Civil Aviation Organization and, in doing so, wrest it away from its 66-year home in Montreal.

That this is a serious matter is readily apparent from the government's shrill reaction. Immediately, a "Team Montreal" was formed, including a minister from the separatist government in Quebec City, a beleaguered, temporary mayor from Montreal and John Baird, the Canadian Foreign Minister, who a few weeks ago was boasting about his successful repairing of relations with several Gulf states, including Qatar. From the Prime Minister down all hands are now on deck to beat back this dastardly attack on an international institution that has helped make Montreal into a modern cosmopolitan city.

The government for its part readily understands what is at stake with the Qatari offer, even though it has refused to admit that it is connected to its policy of uncritical support for Israel. First, it is a direct attack on Canadian foreign policy, which in the last seven years has bled dry the support of many countries around the world. Despite Mr Baird's whirl-wind visits to nations around the world and his polite reception, countries in the Middle East, Africa, Asia and Latin America have been dismayed, if not alarmed, at the significant changes in Canadian foreign policy. A foreign policy that, since the days of the Second World War, has carefully and successfully sought to bridge some of the deep international divides and provides support for amelioration of the human condition.

One would not expect it from such a distant country but, second, the Qatari offer for ICAO represents a quiet understanding of Canadian politics. The Conservative government is in single-digit support mode in Quebec and, in some measure, this is a direct result of its foreign policy, which finds little support in that province. As the issue continues to develop over the next several months, there can be every expectation that members of the Quebec government and numerous others in the province will publicly conclude that Ottawa's foreign policy is the root cause of the problem. The mad rush by Mr Baird to puff up Canadian defenses against the Qatari offer says more about electoral support in Quebec than anything else.

It is still early days in the playing out of the Qatari offer, but it is not an issue that will disappear. The failure of Canada to find sufficient support for a seat on the Security Council against Portugal in 2010 should have been a large warning to the government. Instead it has made its international position even worse by its ever-deepening support of Israel, even to the extent of trying to generate allies against Palestine obtaining observer-state status in the UN General Assembly.

As with the Keystone XL pipeline issue in the United States, the Harper government refuses to understand the connectedness of policy. Its earlier rejection of the Kyoto Protocol to the UN Framework Convention on Climate Change and a variety of other decisions strongly support the view that it is a denier of climate change. This provided the solid backdrop for a wide variety of American and Canadian organizations to attack the building of the pipeline. In recent days the government has sought to portray its sow's ear environmental policy as a silk purse, but this is seen as a move of desperation and certainly not one involving "principle" – Mr Baird's favourite word.

So with the government's policy on Israel. The divide with the 22-members of the Arab League and even the 57-member Organization of the Islamic Conference is now beyond reconciliation. There are, of course, deep and profound differences between the countries making up these organizations, but the one issue around which they can usually coalesce is that of Israel and Palestine. These countries represent nearly half the votes needed by Qatar to support its offer for the move of ICAO from Montreal.

As well, the Qatari move fits into a broader effort for the diversification of who manages world affairs and from where it is done. The move from a G7 "directing" body to a G20 one has been painless and regarded by most as reality-based. At the same time, of the 17 specialized agencies of the United Nations, of which ICAO is one, none is headquartered south of 35 degrees north (approximately Washington, D.C.). London, Paris, Geneva, Vienna, Rome and Madrid are all headquarter cities, some with more than one specialized agency. But Beijing, Pretoria, Tokyo, Sao Paulo, Doha and New Delhi have been bereft of such international enhancement.

Perhaps in all of this Mr Baird's naïve and nativist approach to foreign policy will undergo some change. Already there is an indication of this. He is quoted as saying that "If we can make that deal [to retain ICAO] even better, we're prepared to do so. . . ." And in another interview Mr Baird said that Canada will not be "outbid". It is novel to see Mr Baird move away from foundational "principles" in the conduct of foreign policy and see the edges of old-fashioned money emerge. If the CEO of SNC-Lavalin were to say that, the RCMP would probably pay him another visit.

Embassy

Obama: Pivots and Divots
December 4, 2013

A YEAR AGO BARAK OBAMA HAD JUST BEEN RE-ELECTED PRESIDENT and today he continues his historic journey as the first black American elected to the office. While much of the early shine of his presidency has faded he continues to provide justifiable hope for a deeply troubled world, even while the American foreign-policy house is undergoing serious renovations. However, reflecting our topsy-turvy world, his approval ratings have soared and fizzled like July 1 fireworks on Parliament Hill.

Today the President's ratings are fizzling as he and his administration attempt to escape from the very-modern-day snaring of troublesome software, which is unable to take orders for health-care insurance. For many of us conditioned to the idea that such problems are with the user, it is an understandable situation. At the same time our personal experience tells us this is transitory.

Commentators have been quick to analyze each twitch of Obama's ratings, seeing in them large portents for the future. In doing so they ignore the basic principle that today such twitches have little value for longer-term understanding. They are like the six learned but blind men of Indostan who, upon examining an elephant, in the words of John Saxe "Thought each was partly in the right, /And all were in the wrong."

The CNNing of contemporary American political reporting causes difficulty in distinguishing between descriptions of elephants and gnats. In the continuous 24-hour news cycle to which we have become addicted there are few helpful clues in distinguishing the enduring from the transitory.

A few days ago one commentator wrote about the President: "Barely a year later, the aloof loner has become a lame duck in a second-term collapse of such historic proportions that it is prompting people to compare him to, of all people, George W Bush."

Another piece by two commentators, one of whom was a former Canadian ambassador in Washington, wrote that the present software situation "has the force and political fallout of the Hurricane Katrina debacle." They went on to write "Inevitably, a president weakened on the home front – as Obama is now with the problems engulfing Obamacare – is diminished globally as well."

Such large conclusions have more to do with sizzle than with any large understanding or appreciation of the American political process. Like the blind men of Indostan, such comments offer little understanding of the unusual animals that we meet on the road to the future.

Nowhere is this more apparent than in American foreign policy. President Obama has been an outlier on foreign policy from the earliest days of his Presidency. American troops are now completely out of Iraq and the signs are favourable that they will be largely out of Afghanistan by the end of next year. In each case the withdrawals have been helped by the turmoil created in both countries with the original invasions.

Unintended consequences can be as much positive as negative and the withdrawal of American troops and the lightening of American involvement will be the spark for longer-term political arrangements for both countries.

The freshly minted nuclear accord with Iran is contributing enormously to the Obama urge to eliminate the Middle East as the central pivot for all American foreign policy. The initial harmonic statements from Israel and Saudi Arabia ironically illustrate how fundamental is the accord for a variety of relationships in the Middle East cauldron.

The accord puts American foreign policy into an ascendency where the examiners of gnats are seldom found. Overlooked in this achievement has been the rare cooperation of the five permanent members of the Security Council, including Russia and China, in managing one of the world's most complex and sensitive foreign-policy issues. Single flowers do not a spring make, but they do give hope of more to come.

While there is a long way to go in building down the Iran nuclear-weapon threat, there is little reason for Canada to act like a skunk in a small elevator. Nowhere is Joe Clark's description of Conservative foreign policy of "lecture and leave" more apt than Mr Baird's performance on Iran. Mr Baird may insist that his is a "made-in-Canada foreign policy"; however, it would be more accurate to state that it is a foreign policy "announced in Canada."

Equally, in the midst of these initiatives, the Obama-directed "pivot" to things Asian should be seen as adding to the lightening of American involvement in the Middle East. While the contending forces in Asia are large, they are less neuralgic within the American political system than those associated with the Middle East. As such Asian issues might contribute to the return of a greater degree of bipartisanship in American foreign policy.

The ability of electronic news organizations and couplet-sized social networks to deaden our senses and faculties has become a sad aspect of our modern world. This impulse needs to be countered with the understanding that a leader who breaks with the past still has an enormous role to play.

Nowhere is that more urgently needed than in our understanding of American foreign policy. In recent years American leaders have emphasized that the physical border between Canada and the United States is a "real one." Canadians need to recognize that our government's aloofness to those who continue to ameliorate the world's sharp divides needs strong, consistent support. Not comments from a growling peanut gallery.

The Politics of Numbers
December 11, 2013

WE ARE A STRANGE PEOPLE. NO SOONER HAS AN INTERNATIONAL economic agency released a 65-country survey on the teaching of science, mathematics and reading for 15-year olds than, in the words of one business leader, there is a "national emergency." He went on with the clarion call of those who scale imaginary walls: "We need skills, we need knowledge-workers to really improve our prosperity and build our society."

It did not matter that a careful reading of the numbers for Canada's 21,000 mid-teens who took the test revealed they were good. Most commentators, misleadingly, started from the illusory conclusion that the rest of the world is standing still – while Canadians attempt to make our education system work in the full knowledge that national leadership on the matter is a long-forgotten hope.

But, as with all such matters involving national comparisons, the issue is less with the results than with the perennial Canadian self-serving assumption that we are among the very best in the world. Over past decades all Canadian governments have loudly re-echoed every positive international conclusion and clad themselves in the self-righteous garments of their own policies. The various Conservative government reports on its Economic Action Plan are replete with bragging that only North Korea surpasses.

But the reaction is different when the shoe goes to the other foot. When an international observer is sent to Canada to observe and report on deep-seated social and economic issues, Canadian government indignation is deep and wide. A few months ago a UN official saw fit to be critical of the state of our indigenous people. He was almost run out of town on a rail. The unsolved murders of some 600 Canadian aboriginal women are left to the vicissitudes of police forces that seem to have trouble finding Parliament Hill on July 1.

One commentator at a recent meeting of the Canadian Political Science Association, using the "bully" word now widely associated with some teenagers, accurately wrote: "It [Canada] has played nice when necessary, broken its promises when it could, and used military, police, political and bureaucratic power to dominate, marginalize, delegitimate and assimilate Aboriginal peoples . . . Like most bullies, Canada doesn't like critique. It diminishes those who offer it, preferring the mythologies with respect to its goodness in the world."

If there is a surprise in the recent OECD report it is that Canada continues to do so well compared with other countries. As most education commentators have stated, provincial educational policy in Canada has had all of the consistency associated with the weather in Newfoundland or the legitimacy of the prime-ministerial assertion that the North Pole belongs to Canada – based, apparently, on the snaps he took during his annual summer sojourns north of 60.

The sky is not falling and the Canadian education system, while not at the head of the international class, is doing well. The large problem it is facing is the perpetual calls from a variety of interested clients for changes based on narrow self-interest. Do we need more tool- and-die makers in a time of 3-D printers or MBAs with the ethics of warthogs or fewer students with a sense of history or critical faculties sufficient to understand a phantasmagoric world? All, from time to time, are thrown into the educational mixer and, unfortunately, there are political leaders who are either incapable or unwilling to look beyond their shoes or the next election.

Rather, the success of the Canadian education system has less to do with the environment in which it has to operate than with the quality of the students that do well in spite of those who see education in narrow selfish terms.

Economic prosperity based on the rising-tide model of lifting all yachts is one of the most pernicious myths that our political system currently peddles. Intellectual prosperity based on equity and equality (both sadly lacking in government educational programs for aboriginals) must be restored and maintained at the centre of any successful educational curriculum. If that were to happen, there would be a lot less need to pay attention to international scoring.

As to mathematics, it is doubtful that one in any 100,000 Canadians would recognize the name Robert Langlands. Yet he is one of the world's most renowned mathematicians. He was a graduate of the New Westminster and UBC educational systems (1940s and '50s) and then went on to teach at Princeton, Yale, and is today Professor Emeritus at the Institute for Advanced Study at Princeton where Albert Einstein spent his post-European years.

Dr Langlands is known for his Langlands Program, conceived in the 1960s, in Einstein's old office. The Langlands Program, in the words of a review in the *New York Review of Books*, "aims at being a grand unifying theory of mathematics." In recent years the Program has "expanded beyond pure mathematics to the frontiers of theoretical physics." One writer has stated that "it is the source code of all mathematics."

Reflecting my own mathematical weaknesses I will not try to explain Dr Langlands' work. Rather I leave it to readers to seek understanding elsewhere. However, his work in awards ceremonies has been described as . . . *extraordinary vision that has brought the theory of group representations into a revolutionary new relationship with the theory of automorphic forms and number theory.;* and . . . *path-blazing work and extraordinary insights in the fields of number theory, automorphic forms, and group representation.*

Not bad for the BC education system during the Second World War and shortly thereafter. The record is incomplete, however, on how well Dr Langlands scored on his math exams at the age of 15.

Embassy

Russian Roulette at the North Pole
December 16, 2013

CANADIAN DIPLOMACY DIED ON THE FLOOR OF THE HOUSE OF Commons on December 10. The occasion was Question Period when a question by the Liberal leader about the Senate scandal prompted the parliamentary secretary to the Prime Minister to loop off into the wonderland of the North Pole – and a Liberal denial that Santa was Canadian. Completely lost in this holiday nonsense was any sense that the ice, waters and undersea land around the North Pole remain one of the most critical issues facing today's world and the future of humanity.

The absurdity of the exchange in the House of Commons is commonplace and provides evidence that a Canadian Theatre of the Absurd is alive and well and has replaced seriousness as a national characteristic. The conflation of the Senate/PMO problems with a joke concerning the control of the North Pole illustrates a government with an empty tank, and no understanding that Canadian prosperity is firmly attached to efforts to promote a well-ordered world. It also supports the contention that the Prime Minister is playing Russian roulette with an unregistered gun.

The North Pole sovereignty issue has been a relative sleeper in the body politic for years, clouded by robust talk in support of an Arctic policy but little action. After decades-long study by experts, costing more than $200 million, the Prime Minister decided on a dramatic intervention. This intervention appears to have been based on the sudden awareness in the all-seeing PMO that the Canadian submission to the United Nations Commission on the Outer Limits of the Continental Shelf lacked any supporting evidence of Canadian claims in the High Arctic. The submission, in preparation since the early 1980s, provided evidence supporting claims for the extension of the Canadian continental shelf only in the Atlantic.

There are two reasonable conclusions. First, governmental experts, both scientific and legal, who prepared the UN submission found very little or no evidence that would support Canada's claims extending the outer limits of its continental shelf to the area around the North Pole. Second, the mandate given the experts was deficient in not stressing the need to do exhaustive research to support the extension of Canada's continental-shelf claim in the North Pole area.

Research on the matter was underway long before Canada became a party to the Law of the Sea Convention in 2003 and the completion of related negotiations in 1982. However, at the time of acceding to the Convention in 2003, Canada had 10 years to file a submission with the UN Commission on the Outer Limits of the Continental Shelf, providing evidence in support of its various offshore claims. In its recent partial submission, it was indicated that information on its claim in the Arctic would be forthcoming later. This is particularly surprising since Canada successfully negotiated the inclusion of Article 234 in the Law of the Sea Convention, which deals with the "delicate ecological balance" in ice-covered areas.

The current process and its attending publicity suggest there is only one option open to Canada with respect to the Arctic: to quickly do the needed research and try to counter the claims of Russia, Norway and Denmark, who have already provided the UN with submissions.

What is missing from this calculation is any sense of the time it will take for a firm conclusion to be derived from the Law of Sea process. Some commentators throw out a 20-year horizon but that has no basis in fact or reality. Given the issues involved in the North Pole waters and the range of interested parties, particularly the United States and China, it should be assumed that, as the Irish have long known, there is no gold to be found at the end of rainbows.

There is, however, an alternative for Canada and one that would likely obtain considerable support within the international community. The alternative is for Canada to strongly promote the idea that the waters and seabed around the North Pole be declared part of the "common heritage of humanity." It was the common-heritage concept first proposed by Ambassador Arvid Pardo of Malta at the United Nations in 1967 that prompted the negotiations for the Law of Sea Convention. Article 136 of the Convention states that "the seabed and ocean floor and subsoil thereof, beyond the limits of national jurisdiction" are part of the common heritage of humanity.

The common-heritage principle has had a long intellectual history and has found legal expression in several multilateral treaties dating from the middle of the last century. The 1954 Hague Convention for the Protection of Cultural Property in the Event of Armed Conflict, the 1967 Outer Space Treaty and the 1979 Moon Treaty included common-heritage references. While not expressly mentioned, the common-heritage principle was central in resolving the many conflicted and conflicting national claims to Antarctica and the 1959 treaty making that continent part of the common-heritage legacy. While the Antarctic Treaty largely deals with matters scientific, it does provide a conceptual basis for dealing with the conflicting claims in the Arctic.

Canada has been missing from those seeking international order on a grand scale. Since its successful efforts on the creation of the International Criminal Court and the Land Mines treaty, Canada has done little to resolve large international issues. The North Pole offers such an opportunity and, in taking it on, Canada might start a new golden age for its diplomacy.

The Citizen

High Stakes in the High Arctic
January 20, 2014

AN UNUSUAL EVENT OCCURRED ON JANUARY 15. PRIME MINISTER Harper sat down with a journalist and, one on one, answered detailed questions on the government's strategy and policies for the Arctic. It was an unprecedented and rare occasion, and one that could usefully be followed for other issues of concern to Canadians.

The interview came only a month after the Prime Minister decided that Canada's submission to the UN Commission on the Outer Limits of the Continental Shelf was deficient. In his comments at the time, Mr Harper was reported to have been dismayed that the submission to the UN Commission did not provide evidence supporting Canadian claims in the High Arctic, including the North Pole.

Unfortunately, his comments on January 15 added further confusion to what remains a major issue in Canadian foreign policy. Throughout the interview the Prime Minister confused existing Canadian sovereignty in the Arctic with efforts to provide legitimacy through the United Nations for Canada's claims to the waters around the North Pole and the associated seabed. It bears repeating there are no serious counterclaims to Canadian existing sovereignty over the islands of the Arctic or to the associated 200-nautical-mile exclusive economic zone.

There are three disputes in the Arctic two of which involved counterclaims by other countries. The first is by Denmark, acting on behalf of Greenland, over the 1.3-square-kilometer Hans Island located in the Nares Strait between Ellesmere Island and Greenland. Over the last two years bilateral negotiations between Canada and

Denmark/Greenland have largely resolved the issue with a possible agreement recognizing each country's sovereignty for half of the island or possibly a condominium arrangement whereby both countries jointly administer the small rock. The second dispute is with the United States and involves maritime delimitation in the Beaufort Sea. It is a traditional maritime dispute similar to several others that Canada and the United States have submitted to international arbitration with satisfactory results. It is a relatively easy dispute to settle, assuming that both countries are interested in seeing it resolved.

The third dispute involves the Northwest Passage that provides a commercial-shipping route from Baffin Bay in the east to the Bering Strait in the west. Canada claims sovereignty over this area, based on the fact that these are "internal waters." The Passage is surrounded almost entirely by Canadian sovereign territory or waters of the exclusive economic zone. Only the United States has taken consistent exception to this claim of Canadian sovereignty. The Americans see the Canadian claim as undermining the unfettered operation of its naval forces in the area.

Neither Canada nor the United States have sought to inflame matters and in 1988 signed an agreement on cooperation in the Arctic. A clause in the agreement states that the "Government of the United States pledges that all navigation by U. S. icebreakers within waters claimed by Canada to be internal will be undertaken with the consent of the Government of Canada."

Apart from these three issues there are no serious counterclaims to the exercise of full and exclusive Canadian sovereign rights over the land masses of the Arctic Archipelago and the associated territory on the mainland. It was noted in a recent Library of Parliament report that "Canadian sovereignty over the Arctic islands is legally uncontroversial, and any concerns that Canada is not sufficiently present and active to fulfill the principle of occupation are unlikely to weaken its claim."

In his interview on January 15 the Prime Minister stated that "Canadian governments have claimed the North Pole since I believe at least the 1930s." He went on to say "there is no compelling reason" to "surrender that claim." This is where the confusion occurs. It is the Canadian "claim" to sovereignty for the North Pole which is entirely different from the "exercise" of sovereignty in the Canadian Arctic.

Canada's claim to the polar waters was based on a 1907 proposal by Pascal Poirier in the Canadian Senate. Senator Poirier served in the Senate for 48 years and was the longest-serving member of the upper chamber. His proposal for claiming sovereignty over the polar waters was based on his Sector Principle which called for the projection of a country's longitudinal borders to the North Pole. In 1925 Canada verbally extended its arctic-water boundaries lying between 60° west and 141° west longitudes all the way to the North Pole. Since then Canadian leaders have been ambiguous if not muddled in the promotion of this claim.

In response, the Soviet Union, Norway and the United States advanced similar claims based on their Arctic territories based on the Sector Principle. While Denmark could make a similar claim it has not done so since the Sector Principle has faded from use and does not find support in the UN Convention on the Law of the Sea. UNCLOS provides its own formula for determining marine boundaries. Rather than using the Sector Principle for marine boundaries and their delimitation, UNCLOS uses the outer limits of continental shelves. Once these "outer limits" are determined then the external waters are considered the High Seas, subject to a different administrative regime run by the United Nations. Canada has accepted this approach in seeking extension to its marine boundaries in the Atlantic Ocean, largely involving the Grand Banks and Flemish Cap areas. This claim was submitted to the UN Commission on the Outer Limits of the Continental Shelf in December last year.

In these circumstances it is understandable that Canadian experts did not support the use of the Sector Principle in the demarcation of marine boundaries in the Arctic and probably left it out of the original Canadian submission to the United Nations. Now that the Prime Minister has intervened and wants waters to the North Pole included in the Canadian submission and, as such, a Canadian "claim," the experts will have to fall back on measurements for the continental shelf in the polar area. It is a difficult area to measure and, if it has not already been done in any complete and conclusive manner, then the second part of Canada's submission to the UN will be a long time coming.

Embassy

Gods, Caesars and Elections
January 29, 2014

PRIME MINISTERIAL FOREIGN VISITS ARE SUFFICIENTLY FREQUENT and follow such a common pattern that there is very little that is unique one from the other.

In diplomatic speak they are an effort to "broaden and deepen" a bilateral relationship and are often reduced to "B&D visits" in background shorthand.

In such visits there is a ceremonial greeting on the tarmac, a motorcade to downtown, a speech or two to a receptive audience, bilateral discussions with local leaders, meetings with local business leaders in order to emphasize that "Canada is open for more business," possibly a town-hall-type meeting or discussions with the "younger" generation, the signing or witnessing of a hortatory agreement or two and visits to places of local significance.

Each prime minister tailors foreign travels to his or her own idiosyncrasies and specific interests. A few years ago Pierre Trudeau visited India when Indira Gandhi was prime minister, a country Mr Trudeau had visited when he was a randy young man. In the preparations for the visit the requisite instructions came from Ottawa, including the requirement that the Prime Minister wanted to visit Khajuraho, known universally as the temples of love. There, there are hundreds of stone sculptures over a thousand years old, showing men and women doing what came naturally.

With tongue in cheek, the High Commission detailed the exact nature of Khajuraho and suggested that pictures of the Prime Minister gazing at these frozen-in-time sexually explicit poses would be fertile ground for images that many in Canada might find objectionable – or lower the tone of the visit meant mainly to support Ms Gandhi's policy of dismembering Pakistan.

Initially Ottawa resisted, but when Max Ferguson, known to CBC listeners for decades as Rawhide, got wind of what was being planned and did one of his hilarious verbal sketches suggesting the athletic Prime Minister could show the ancient lovers a pose or two, Khajuraho was quickly cancelled. If I recall, the Taj Mahal by moonlight was substituted.

Needless to say, Prime Minister Harper's foreign travels do not include such unusual idiosyncratic elements. Nevertheless, his recent visit to Israel, the West Bank and Jordan was sufficiently idiosyncratic or, in the view of many, strange as to ensure that it will live on as one of the more unusual visits in Canadian diplomatic history.

There is nothing unique in this government's support for the State of Israel and its willingness to come to its defence whenever dark forces gang up or when there is legitimate criticism of the policies of its government – that are widely recognized as being in contravention of international law. These have been a constant element in Prime Minister Harper's foreign policy.

This was dramatically affirmed, four years ago, in a declaration by the then Minister of State of Foreign Affairs, Peter Kent. Then, Mr Kent stated "an attack on Israel would be considered an attack on Canada." Mr Kent, now a backbencher, seeking a higher authority for his unprecedented statement, went on to say the "prime minister has made it quite clear for some time now and has regularly stated that an attack on Israel would be considered an attack on Canada."

The strangeness of the Prime Minister's visit to Israel is not even in the laudatory rhetoric that sought biblical support and justification for his policies. Father Raymond J. de Souza, a Roman Catholic priest and member of the Prime Minister's accompanying party, wrote that the use of the words "through fire and water" found expression in the Old Testament "when you walk through fire you shall not be burned, and the flame shall not consume you."

The uniqueness of this visit is rather to be found in the extraordinarily large official delegation and accompanying party. Some 237 persons were listed in a PMO release and, while the government left for a later announcement the specifics of who paid their own expenses, separate reporting suggests that a sizable number were paid for out of public funds.

Even stranger was the large number of divines and leaders from the Canadian Jewish and Evangelical communities. As far as can be ascertained, apart from Father de Souza there were no representatives from other Canadian religious communities.

It can be fairly stated that never in the history of Canadian diplomacy has such a delegation left our shores and been used in support of a contentious foreign-policy issue.

Canadians, apart from in Quebec, have never sought a sharp distinction between the activities of the state and those of its religious communities. Unlike in the United States and many other countries, the separation of church and state does not find expression in Canadian law and the Charter of Rights and Freedoms is silent on the matter. When separation comes into question, it has been largely on the matter of public funding for parochial schools, most recently in Ontario and a few years ago in Newfoundland and Labrador.

In Quebec the situation is different, as the present debate on the Charter of Values has demonstrated. In a sense, Quebec, since its own social revolution 50 years ago, now adheres to the tradition in France where, for more than 100 years, the policy of Laïcité is followed. Laïcité provides for a strict separation of church and state, particularly in public policy.

The debate over the Prime Minister's delegation will continue, but it is already being overtaken by events. Perhaps a more accurate interpretation of the visit was provided by one of its members, a Conservative MP from Ontario. In an effort to have his photograph taken with the Prime Minister at the Western Wall in Jerusalem, the MP was heard to exclaim: "It's the re-election! This is the million-dollar shot."

As of old, sometimes it is the remarks of children that tell us the emperor is not wearing clothes.

Embassy

The Break-Up of States and Lessons for Canada
May 3, 2014

TODAY IT IS UKRAINE.

In recent years, it was Sudan, Ethiopia, the former Yugoslavia, the former Czechoslovakia, and the granddaddy of all break-ups, the former Soviet Union.

Tomorrow it could be the United Kingdom, Belgium, Nigeria, Mali, Myanmar or even Canada.

Unsuccessful efforts include the Tamils of Sri Lanka, the Basques of Spain, the Moro in the Philippines and the Irish of Northern Ireland.

Historically, the creation of new countries out of the bodies of "united" states has been a regular aspect of wars, both civil and otherwise. Rarely is it a peaceful process. Language, religion, race, economics and even cultural differences have led people in all parts of the world to seek independence from dominating national governments – and create a new government reflecting their own national aspirations.

The lamentation and neuralgic reaction of the international community to such developments has been uniform: They have to be contained and fought against, even though there may be legitimate and practical reasons supporting separation. In part, this can be credited to the uneven and often tragic results that separation can produce, or to the fear that it can stoke similar passions at home.

Few would argue with the need for separate states in the Balkans or for a new state in southern Sudan, but some would point out that the results missed expectations by a wide margin. Unfortunately, more often than not, the fight for separation subsumes differences within the separating territory or creates inadequate arrangements for the post-separation government.

In South Sudan, the tragic civil war that is now underway reflects papered-over differences between the two dominant peoples, the Dinka and the Nuer. Unfortunately these differences were accentuated by the post-independence political leadership with tragic results.

Bosnia and Herzegovina emerged as an independent state from the chaos associated with the breakup of Yugoslavia in 1992. The subsequent war, including the siege of Sarajevo, ended with the Dayton Accords and it remains an independent state. Its continuing independence, despite its complex history and cultural and religious divides, is remarkable and gives testimony to political skill unmatched anywhere in the world.

A country of only four-million people, it is lumbered with a governmental system, according to a recent article in The *New York Times*, consisting of 142 municipalities, two highly autonomous entities, ten cantons, a special district, and a national government. This has resulted in 180 ministers, 600 legislators and a swarm of about 70,000 bureaucrats. Topping the whole system is an internationally appointed high representative with executive authority to overrule anything that happens below him.

In both cases, South Sudan and Bosnia and Herzegovina, independence brought nasty wars to an end and, despite the lacklustre results, they will over time remain independent if not prosperous.

Different issues

Today's Ukraine presents an entirely different set of issues than those of South Sudan and Bosnia and Herzegovina and the loose talk of separation for parts of the country should be taken seriously.

George F. Kennan, the world's most trenchant observer of things Russian, observed in 1944 to the then Polish prime minister, "the jealous and intolerant eye of the Kremlin can distinguish, in the end, only vassals and enemies, and the neighbours of Russia, if they do not wish to be one, must reconcile themselves to being the other."

The history of Russia since, and even before the 1917 revolution for that matter, has demonstrated the wisdom of Mr Kennan's observation. During the Soviet regime, Poland, East Germany, Hungary and Czechoslovakia were subject to the full range of Soviet interventions. Since the downfall of the Soviet Union, there is ample evidence that little has changed in Russian policy towards it neighbours.

The two wars in Chechnya and the security clamp on any separatist urging in neighbouring Dagestan give ample evidence of the ability of Moscow to pay any price for maintaining the unity of the existing Russian state.

Even more relevant to today's Ukraine was the Russian reaction to events in Georgia in 2008 just down the Black Sea coast from Crimea. Then, the Russian army and navy intervened to prevent Georgia from militarily attacking separatist groups in South Ossetia and Abkhazia. The Russian military intervention quickly overcame Georgian resistance and both South Ossetia and Abkhazia are today de facto parts of Russia.

Georgian leadership at the time was particularly inept and reckless in that there was some expectation of Western intervention. As with Hungary in 1956 and Czechoslovakia in 1968, the Kremlin adroitly read the West. There were hot words and empty threats only, and today the chastened Georgians accept that they are both vassals and enemies of Mr Putin.

The history of Ukrainian independence has been short, and so far its leaders have displayed an amazing inability to understand the world in which they must live. The barricades, the tragic deaths and the overthrow of a corrupt president (who was not unique in the Ukrainian system) are stirring events for all of us far removed from the action. The Ukrainian émigré community has been loud in demanding supporting action and the Canadian government has foolishly jumped into the fray without serious consideration, apart from domestic electoral ones, of the implications for Canada's own fragile national-unity debate.

Over the years Canadian foreign policy has maintained as fundamental articles not to create foreign enemies, or supporters for Quebec independence. Prime Minister Stephen Harper and some of his ministers have tossed this fundamental aspect of our foreign policy overboard and are often eager to engage in the fissiparous debates of other countries, especially if there is a domestic community that can be exploited for electoral gain.

As the Georgians discovered, and the Hungarians and Czechs before them, Western words do them no favours. In fact we do them a disservice to suggest that Canadian and Western statements and rushed trips by foreign ministers have any value either in Kiev or Moscow. Ukraine is part of Putin's sphere of influence and will remain so. For a leader who was prepared to spend over $50 billion not to win a hockey game, the cost of keeping Ukraine within his orbit will be small potatoes.

Embassy

The Malicious Concept of Mother Canada
April 9, 2014

THROUGHOUT THE TROUBLES IN UKRAINE AN OLD WORD AND AN old-world concept has been at the centre of Russian policy. This is Motherland. In the Russian context "Mother Russia" has been used for a thousand years by Czars, Soviet leaders and now post-Soviet leaders to create a deep mythical attachment of the Russian people to themselves and their land. In the Ukrainian context and elsewhere in the border regions, President Putin has used it to justify Russian claims of responsibility for Russians living in lands beyond the Russian Republic.

In his March 18 speech at the Kremlin, Putin appealed to all of the ethnic groups living in Crimea and went on to say "this is their common home, their motherland." He went on to stress that "In People's hearts and minds, Crimea has always been an inseparable part of Russia." In his own rise to power Putin used the ultra-right Motherhood (Rodina) Party and subsequently co-opted it into his own United Russia Party.

Many have dismissed Putin's words as lies, with one Western divine ironically stating that it reflected a "tendentious" sense of history. Such characterizations more often disguise the lack of principle in our own motivation.

Large concepts, such as Motherland, Fatherland, Homelands and Heartlands, have been used extensively in Europe and elsewhere by authoritarian leaders to provide legitimacy for their regimes and to create allegiance from their people. In most cases such concepts place the "state" at the centre of the political system with people relegated to supportive roles. Particularly, Motherland and Fatherland were used extensively by the governments of Germany and Russia/ the Soviet Union – with the disastrous results which still bedevil the international system.

More recently South Africa used the concept of Homelands (and their physical manifestation) as part of its apartheid regime. Even the United States has not been exempt from this malicious concept. In the aftermath of 9/11 it created public support for policies and programs that were the antitheses of those underpinning the foundation of the Republic by establishing a super-security organization. This was the Department of Homeland Security and a decade later it still demonstrates that it is more the concept of "Homeland" that drives its activities rather than the provision of greater security.

Even Peggy Noonan, a far-right-wing Republican ideologue, objected, saying that the name "grates on a lot of people" and "isn't really an American word." Unfortunately there was little comment from the American Black community on the use of a word employed by white South Africans to try and soften the effect of moving millions of Blacks into large geographic ghettos.

An ironic if not sad aspect of all of this was Prime Minister Harper's words during his recent travels in Europe. For the most part he contributed little to the construction of an effective policy. Rather his role, like the man who shouted "fire" as he left the theatre, consisted of rhetorical shouts for others to rise up against President Putin.

In doing so he gave support to Joe Clarke's recent accurate and caustic description of current Canadian foreign policy as "lecture and leave." The Prime Minister went so far as to pretend that he understood the Russian people better than President Putin. "I don't believe that's where the Russian people are, particularly the younger generations in Russia. I've been in Russia several times and I find the ordinary Russian people, especially the younger people, to be very Western in their outlook, their values and desires."

Without attributing ulterior motives to his comments, such as Canadian electioneering or the possible sale of Canadian energy to European countries deprived of Russian supplies or deflecting Canadian political woes, the Prime Minister takes on an enormous burden when he places his own understanding of another country ahead of those of its own indigenous leaders, no matter how offensive they may be.

Even more Machiavellian was the breaking of the story that the Harper government is giving financial and political support to the construction of a "massive monument" on the shores of Cape Breton Island at Green Cove. The frosty lips of Vladimir Putin must have smiled when it was revealed that this monstrosity is to be called, now wait for it, Mother Canada. The ten-story statue is the dark dream of a Toronto businessman and Parks Canada to build the "Never Forgotten National Memorial." Surrounding the statue will be the "We See Thee Rise Observation Deck", "The Commemorative Ring of True Patriot Love" and the "With Glowing Hearts National Sanctuary." Tacky will have to be re-defined.

One Cape Bretoner with an understanding of federal government largesse on their beautiful island is quoted as saying: "If they put it down at Green Cove, all you're going to see is her arse."

Embassy

Nigeria Beckons
May 21, 2014

THE GLOBAL ABHORRENCE TO THE KIDNAPPING OF NEARLY THREE-hundred schoolgirls in the northeastern Nigerian state of Borno by Boko Haram continues. Unfortunately, the global reaction will do little to assure their safety or rescue the young students or deal with the problems that groups such as Boko Haram feast upon. More likely it will make matters worse, giving the kidnappers global recognition that has largely been missing so far.

Boko Haram, in one guise or another, has been around for almost two decades. The political and religious divide it exploits goes back hundreds of years. That divide is between an Islamic world north of the Sahara and an African one to the south. As the struggles in Nigeria, Mali and the Central African Republic show, like the expanding desert, Islam is now a major and growing factor in the lives of millions of Africans south of the Sahara. In this historical migration of religion there can be little expectation that there is an easy or an early conclusion to the associated violence.

These post-colonial failed states are poorly equipped to deal with the fanatical tumult rendered by groups who claim a special relationship with a god. Mali needed outside assistance from France to contain an invasion from the north while the Central African Republic, even with African regional military support, has not been able to quell its horrific internecine violence. Nigeria has been quietly obtaining assistance from the United States and other Western states for several years, but, as the current violence shows, this has not been successful in quelling the aggression of Boko Haram in several of its northeastern states. Nor have leaders in the neighbouring states of Niger, Cameroon and the Central African Republic had success in dealing with Boko Haram. There can be every expectation that this bloodshed will continue.

There is a tendency to attribute the increasing violence to outside forces and influences. To some extent there is some legitimacy to this view. Egypt for years has exported extremist religious leaders and fighters. Many fought for change within Egypt and, following frustration and torture in its notorious prisons, left to fight in other places. Al Qaeda's present leader, Ayman al-Zawahiri, is an example of this process.

The turmoil in North Africa, especially Algeria and now Libya, has contributed leaders and weapons for the violence around the Sahara. The lack of any progress on political reform in those countries will ensure that many will see the vastness of the desert as a safer arena for their activities. Western leaders falsely celebrate the success of their departing military forces from Afghanistan, claiming al Qaeda has been quelled. In doing so they ignore evidence to the contrary and naively hope that this graveyard of failed hopes will be controlled by its newly (nearly) elected President. Al Qaeda is alive and well in such places as Pakistan, Yemen, Iraq, Syria and perhaps in the Sahara. Before long there will be overt signs of al Qaeda life after "death" in Afghanistan.

Unfortunately, while the gunslinger originators of the War on Terror are no longer in power in the United States, the War lives on in the Western responses to the violence in places such as Nigeria and other affected countries. The word terrorism has become the knee-jerk description by governments everywhere for all acts of rebellion no matter the cause or the effect. For the most part the violence is not understood and only prompts pious statements about the obvious. Like its failed precursor, the War on Drugs (which after several decades of failure may be debated at a 2016 UN Conference), the War on Terror remains as one of the world's largest global-policy failures. Since the failures of the Wars on Terror in Iraq and Afghanistan, the policy largely consists of drone strikes in

Yemen – where the largest blowback centres on whether or not the United States President has the authority to authorize the deaths of American citizens supporting the Shia-based insurgency there.

The response to the latest violence in Nigeria assumes that Boko Haram operates in a vacuum – an imposed force operating independently apart from the religious, ethnic and cultural complexities of Nigerian society. Nigeria retains the legacy of a British pastiche of regional kingdoms left to fend for itself – with the world offering pious complaints when the Igbos tried to leave the Federation shortly after independence to form Biafra or when the military, having larger pockets to fill, decided it could do better than corrupt elected governments. Nigeria, with a growing population that will soon exceed two-hundred million and an oil-based economy, will remain a fragile state – always waiting for the next disaster to strike.

The reaction of the government of Nigeria to the insurgencies in the north, and as well to smaller-scale ones in the south, has been violent and ineffective. Boko Haram continues to exist and operate unopposed over wide swaths of the north. The governmental responses have been indiscriminate, making little distinction between perpetrators and victims. The predominant consequence is more recruits for the insurgents.

Canada's response to the kidnappings has been especially egregious. Canadian politicians from all persuasions clamoured for the government to take an active role and seek the same from a beleaguered Nigerian government. After a few days it appears that several Canadians were sent to West Africa with vague suggestions that they would combine with American and British personnel "to work on the freedom of these young girls." It is not clear if these are "military boots on the ground," security personnel or some combination. One does not need to be especially skeptical to assume that the safety of the girls has not been enhanced by this ad hocery.

It is especially ironic that it is now only a few days since the RCMP told Canadians that the number of missing and murdered aboriginal women over the past three decades is now nearing 1200.

Some of these women are, of course, girls as well, if that distinction is necessary. Yet the response of Canadians to this horrific information is one of indifference, accepting the government prattle that it is taking action to deal with the matter. It was easier to send a few Canadians to Nigeria than to look seriously at our own problem at home.

Embassy

Canadian Foreign Policy – The World to Come
May 28, 2014

LOOKING DOWN THE ROAD OF CANADIAN FOREIGN POLICY IS A BIT of a mug's game best left for late evening discussions with old friends, including Laird Lagavulin. With that caveat there are two matters that will bedevil Canadian foreign-policy mavens in the years ahead, especially if the current unilateral counterproductive approach were to continue.

The first is the need to bring the waters around the North Pole under international governance. The second is for the world to develop standards for use when existing states succumb to fissiparous pressures. The nature of Canadian society makes this of relevance to millions of Canadians.

The inexorable changes to the world's climate envelope place international governance of our common atmosphere at the very top of our collective responsibilities. The increasing number of extreme weather events gives daily warning of the need for greater collective action; so far collective action has failed to overcome differences of geography, economics and disbelief of the science. The disappearing Arctic ice cover is but one of the many consequences of worse things to come. The interest of the world in shorter shipping routes and access to imagined resources under these seas and in the Arctic lands will not be lessened or prolonged by the lack of an internationally accepted management regime.

The eight countries of the Arctic Council (Canada, Denmark, Finland, Iceland, Norway, Russia, Sweden and the United States) have assumed responsibility for the world's Arctic. In the 1996 Ottawa declaration which brought the Council into existence, it is stated that it will provide a means for promoting cooperation, coordination and interaction among the Arctic states. The declaration goes on to include the involvement of the Arctic Indigenous communities and other Arctic inhabitants on issues, such as sustainable development and environment protection.

Eighteen years ago when the Council came into existence the disappearing ice cover, while feared by many, did not have the potency it has today. The future in 1996 is already here and there are few signs that the government of Canada is able or willing to provide the leadership that the matter requires. A few issues over the past few years give graphic illustration of the lack of understanding or vision on the issue.

- The annual summer visits by the Prime Minister surrounded by weapons of war from another era and different circumstances do not constitute policy leadership. All it has done is create the most promised military force in the world. President Putin could be forgiven if he were to quote a previous Russian leader about the armies of the Pope.

- Last year's submission to the UN Law of the Sea on the possible extension of Canada's exclusive economic zone in the High Arctic did not initially include reference to any claim by Canada. Then, to compound the problem, the Prime Minister referred to an unwritten historical Canadian claim based on principles long ignored by the rest of the world. To cover this serious omission, the government sought to joke about the matter by talking about Santa being Canadian.

- There are ongoing references to threats to Canadian sovereignty over the Northwest Passage as if these are real. They are only real in the sense that Canada has done little if anything to prepare the region for the shipping that other countries will direct through the Passage. The world will use the Passage and patrol vessels, surveys and navigational aids are needed now if disasters are to be averted, or to put an end to any questioning of the legitimacy of Canadian sovereignty.

- From time to time Canada grouses over the inclusion of non-Arctic observer states in the work of the Council. There are twelve such states now, ranging from China to India to Italy to Singapore, and there can be every expectation that this interest will grow as the ice-cover lessens. To believe that the Arctic is the exclusive preserve of Arctic states is akin to those denying the reality of the disappearing ice pack. What happens in the Arctic does not stay in the Arctic and there is a need to include a broader international community in ensuring that the looming climatic disaster is not accentuated.

This sad record does not constitute a Canadian policy. Instead it invites others to step into the vacuum and play the area for their own advantage.

The state of States
Ukraine for the past six months has illustrated the problems with the Nation-State concept that emerged in the 17th century with the Treaties of Westphalia. The concept was based on the false idea of the comprehensive internal unity of the State. Of course during a period when the divine right of leaders still had some credibility, this false idea found acceptance. Today as we look at a phantasmagoric world, the false idea has been exposed for what it is – a useful construct for a world that no longer exists. Perhaps only Iceland and maybe Japan still meet the 17th century ideal.

The emergence of the need for consent from those governed to those who govern is an absolute for our 21st-century world. This absolute is often ragged at its edges but there is no countervailing force that undermines its legitimacy even in China or Russia. Today the force that is with us is the reduction of the state to its constituent elements, requiring the protection of the majority from unaccountable leaders and the protection of minorities from majorities.

The countervailing forces of fusion and disintegration of States has been a constant in the post- War period and there are few signs that it will lessen anytime soon. There is no absolute legitimacy for the continued existence of a State any more than there was an absolute legitimacy for the divine right to rule by persons who manipulated the false concept that it was god given. The streets give us political theatre but do not give us government.

For the Scots to decide that they want a future separate from the English, based on little more than a feeling that there was a bad deal four-hundred years ago creates its own legitimacy. Although to spend an evening in a Glaswegian pub suggests there is a language divide as well. The role for the rest of the world is to ensure that there is a fair opportunity for the Scots to express their preference. There is no role for the English.

Closer to home the two referenda in Quebec on independence or, confusingly, sovereignty did not provide a fair opportunity or legitimacy for the process. Despite recent events and, perhaps because of them, the issue will return. If there is a successful fair opportunity for independence, then there should also be a fair opportunity for minorities in Quebec such as aboriginal peoples or the English, to express their own views on a separate existence or unity with a neighbouring State.

The world is bereft of any fundamental guiding principles to deal with these problems as the situation in the Ukraine demonstrates. Crimea has become part of Russia without a fair opportunity for the people to demonstrate their own preferences. The result is that a minority, the Tatars, who were as badly abused as any people by former Russian governments, did not have a fair opportunity to express their opinions.

For Canada with a significant population which does not accept its continuation in its existing form, this will be a forever problem. Shouting from the sidelines when other countries go through their own national traumas is neither appropriate nor wise. Neither is going to war in such places as Afghanistan, Iraq or Libya in the hope that it will heal large internal divisions. The reduction of these states to weak federations or the creation of new ones is their inevitable future.

Embassy

Satire and Irony: Bedfellows for Today's World
January 10, 2015

OUR UNDERSTANDING OF SATIRE AND ITS IMPACT ON OUR DAILY lives, especially in Europe, will dominate the short news cycle for another few days. The justifiable inclusion of all religions in the weekly fare of *Charlie Hebdo* is not only appropriate but requires the excesses which drew violent reactions. Hopefully *Charlie* will remain as a bright star illuminating the excesses of religions everywhere.

Historically and in today's world satire has been an essential tool of our collective enlightenment. But in our reaction to the attacks on *Charlie Hebdo* it is equally important we understand and appreciate that satire's close cousin, irony, must be valued and understood as we decide on our collective reactions.

Central to our collective actions is the ongoing belief that "we have to fight them over there, for our protection at home." It is a mindset that is a pernicious post-colonial hangover and as recent history demonstrates of little or no value. In fact it adds to our insecurity.

Most of the world's colonial powers, and these were mainly western, prior to postwar decolonization and self-determination were successful in keeping their foreign subjects under control with a few troops from the metropolitan country supported by local allies.

This worked as the colonial powers were not limited in their willingness to kill, bomb and contemplate the use of poisonous gas. But the colonial gerrymandering left behind by the breakup of empires after the First and Second World Wars created a hodgepodge of colonial centric countries with little historical or modern legitimacy.

In Africa the seeking of national coherence has dominated but surprisingly except in a few instances (Ethiopia, Somalia, Sudan, Mali, Libya and the Congo) the colonial legacy has held. Nigeria, the largest country in Africa, cursed with serious tribal and religious divides and a petro-fueled economy, remains without national legitimacy. Fortunately, former colonial powers have stayed out except for occasional and short-term peacemaking operations.

The same cannot be said for the arc of countries stretching westward from Pakistan to Egypt. The colonial legacy of created countries along with the United Nations mandated establishment of the State of Israel provides the bullets that lead to deaths in all parts of today's world.

Unfortunately, it is a region where western powers collectively have decided that present day national interest demands intervention. There have been many and the irony is that we are collectively surprised that successes have ranged from the limited to the nonexistent and to making matters worse.

Egypt, Lebanon, Jordan, Syria, Iraq, Iran, Saudi Arabia, the Gulf, Yemen, Pakistan, and Afghanistan have all seen western interventions, both military and political since the end of the Second World War. Without exception they have solved little except adding to the regional ferment. It is easy to see religion as a significant motivator given its excesses in the region. However, it should be noted that religion is more of a tool for those who are unwilling to accept the continuing colonial legacy, including the creation of the state of Israel.

When faced with the death of citizens at the hands of persons who use the religious tool, western leaders do two things. First, they reach for their speech writers so they can outdo each other in describing the violence. The French Prime Minister last week reflected this when he remarked "It is a war against terrorism, against jihadism, against radical Islam, against everything that is aimed at breaking fraternity, freedom, [and] solidarity."

Such instantaneous analysis and flowery concepts provide some measure of comfort but they do little to deal with the violence from diverse volunteers from around the world. Recent reporting include among them: A Nigerian banker's son; a British college student; two Central Asian immigrants to Massachusetts; three Frenchmen; and a variety of disaffected Canadians and Australians.

Second in their reaction to such violence at home many western leaders decide that violence and war in another country is part of the solution. The experiences in the first fifteen years of this century demonstrate its folly. Afghanistan, Iraq, Yemen, Libya and Syria give sad testimony to how bankrupt this policy has been.

No one has demonstrated this fallacy more than Prime Minister Harper. There has not been a war which he did not like. Even before he was Prime Minister he promoted the Canadian role in Afghanistan and a role for Canada in the 2003 invasion of Iraq. Since becoming Prime Minister he has ensured a role for Canada in Libya and today in Iraq. Even his statements on the Ukraine suggest that a larger western response, including the use of the military to events in the Ukraine would be appropriate.

The irony is that there is no evidence that such involvements have lessened political violence at home or in the invaded countries. Rather there is evidence that they have produced more violence at home and will continue to do so. In these circumstances it would be appropriate for the west to get over its colonial mindset and attempt to create policies at home and internationally that could see a reduction in such violence.

The Prime Minister's recently suggested that a change to Canadian laws governing preventative detention at home might be a starting point. Obviously his understanding of history is weak as that was the favourite tool of colonial powers everywhere.

Embassy

Speech: Writing and Writers
January 21, 2015

I AM NOT SURE IF THEY STILL BRING COAL TO NEWCASTLE OR EVEN IF Newcastle still uses coal. But in historical terms the old adage of "Bringing coal to Newcastle" amply describes the idea of talking to you today about writing. It strikes me that talking to professionals whose life was preoccupied with writing in all of its manifestation is akin to the idea about bringing coal to Newcastle.

But there are a few minutes to fill in order for your chicken to stop flapping and your beer and, courtesy of Mr Kohler, cheap wine or should I say cheaper wine, to settle and so I must say something hopefully intelligent to an audience that should be all experts on the art of writing.

I would point out that my last comment illustrates what writing is all about. I could have left it at "cheap wine" but in deference to Mr Kohler I said "cheaper wine" which has a wholly different context.

I confess that when I arrived on the banks of the Rideau almost fifty years ago writing still had its classical definition of putting pen to paper and making sense of things of which readers needed some measure of enlightenment. That was until I had the good fortune to work with a lady by the name of Mary Q. Dench. We later suggested that the Q stood for "Quarrels" and it is fair to say that "Quarrels was both her name and her philosophy."

When Ms Dench discovered I was from Newfoundland her first reaction was that English was my second language. Her task then became one of correcting the many years of bad teaching by persons who did not believe that the letter "H" had any relevance in the English language.

This she did with both alacrity and showed no mercy on an early occasion when what I thought was a fine piece of exposition about events on the Malay Peninsula came back from her office looking as if Colonel Sanders' chickens had revolted.

The historical context for this was that the Commonwealth Division was a geographic one and our job was to try and keep our irrepressible High Commissioner in Kuala Lumpur, John Hadwin, under some measure of control. Many of you will remember that this was no easy task for someone new to the ways of Foreign Affairs.

John was demanding Ottawa support the Malays as they sought to keep the Singaporeans within the federation. At the time the CAF were trying to sell outmoded CF-86 Sabres and John thought they would make a fine gift for the Malays. I must have had some measure of success as I seem to recall the F-86s ended up in Turkey.

In any event Mary was as close to a teacher of English I ever had. Her rules of structure started with the word and slowly moved up the mountain side to such things as phrases, sentences and paragraphs and, voila, a whole document.

Mary is no longer with us in body but as slovenly habits of age and authority intrude on my writing, I can easily recall Mary's cardinal rule that what we wrote was our own personal legacy. It was not whether we were able to stop the attacks on the royal family of Ruritania by the Swiss Conspiracy.

Since those heady days of the late 1960s and especially since retirement I have seen writing as the quintessential legacy of my professional live. One of the joys of retirement is you can immediately or attempt to, share your writing with the world where the critics are less merciful than Mary Dench ever was.

The offset, of course, is in doing so you carefully cultivate the moderate self- deception that your experiences, ideas and views may be of some relevance in our phantasmagorical world. But as most of you also know members of the Canadian Foreign Service have never been known for their modesty.

My experience is that I have developed a set of observations on post retirement writing that may be of some relevance to those of you still thinking about entering this world of moneyless work. I should emphasize that I am largely talking about non-fiction writing although some of you would suggest that much of what I write is fiction. I leave that discussion for an evening at the Fart and Groan on Clarence Street.

Let me leave you with my observations.

The foremost observation of course is that if you want to write, than write. There is nothing that will get you a rejection or even silence from editors and publishers than you offering ideas for articles or books that you intend to write. If the editors and publishers are kind, a rare event, they might go so far as to say "fine," let me have your piece once the words are on paper. Until that happens you are just part of the great unwashed or as we say in Newfoundland "you'se is from de bay boy"

The second observation is that the more authority you can bring to your writing then the greater the likelihood it will be considered. Being a former member of the Foreign Service might have had a measure of cachet a few years ago. Increasingly, however, as with the government itself, being a member of the foreign service does not bring loud hosannas and automatic approval from the reading public.

So if you can surround yourself with claims of association with law firms, ngos or universities there is immediate and greater credibility for your writing. Such honorifics as senior advisor to the Bluff and Poof Legal Chambers; or a member of a penurious NGO such as End Excrement Now; or involvement with a social policy organization that examines the space between a dog and a fire hydrant will open doors that you did not think even existed.

My third and last observation is that having written something and having it published then be prepared for the making of enemies that you did not think possible.

More often than not any comments on your writing have less to do with your actual writing then the fact that you have deeply offended someone or some group. These persons or groups immediately assume that you are part of a secret cabal of former diplomats who having lived of the fat of hard working Canadians for years are now trying to perpetuate your high life style.

Having views on the value of a few hundred Canadian troops trying to turn around several thousand years of Afghan cultural and political traditions and you are immediately fighting the battle of the Somme once again. Tell the world that there are occasions when the Rose Maries cannot tell one end of their horses from the other and the value of the Battle of Batoche to the history of Canada dominates your email. And of course the granddaddy of all subjects is to say something to the effect that the Palestinians have had a bit of a bad deal over the last seventy-five years and you might as well leave the country.

But in all of this there is great personal pleasure in seeing your ideas and words dropped into the Canadian market place and knowing they will find as much acceptance as they find opposition.

Even the medical profession has suggested that writing more than any other activity – perhaps there is one other I leave to your imagination - will protect your brain from the ravages of your earlier high living. There is a suggestion that you will even catch up to Ernst Cote who recently celebrated his 101st birthday by dealing with a nasty intruder.

So my advice to all is to write, write and keep writing. At least that may get you an email like a recent one I received. It suggested that as a recent immigrant to Canada I knew little of its great traditions and public life. It went on to say Mackenzie-King made a terrible mistake when he agreed to the inclusion of Newfoundland as the tenth province some sixty-five years ago.

My tempered response suggested the writer did not know his history very well. With tongue firmly in cheek I wrote it was not an accident that union happened at one minute before midnight on

March 31; this was done by Newfoundlanders so that mainlanders did not know it was an April fool joke. I have not yet had a reply. Thank you.

RHOMA Monthly Meeting

Baird's Version of Harper's Kool-Aid
February 4, 2015

IF TRAVEL MAKETH A FOREIGN MINISTER THAN JOHN BAIRD WAS A well-made foreign minister. A casual examination of his travel last year shows that he made fifty-three visits to other countries. Except for Africa no one was overlooked. Countries in Europe (even Liechtenstein), Asia (East Timor) and Latin America (Paraguay) were blessed. In all places his presence saw the "broadening and deepening" of bilateral relationships.

The keeper of oddity records, Guinness, has yet to pronounce but it is likely that former American Secretary of State Hilary Clinton has been displaced as the world's most travelled foreign minister.

Supplementing the travel has been a blizzard of press releases from the minister's office commenting on the ills of the world and often, the dastardly efforts by many to make things worse. The Ukraine and the Middle East showed up regularly but not forgotten were press releases dealing with the Windsor Hum and attempts by the distant Maldives to hold national elections.

Not to be out done the minister's efforts were ably supported by press releases by the Ambassador of Religious Affairs who made sure that we were reminded of the various religion-based attacks throughout the world. These bring to mind the dictum of John Foster Dulles to the effect that the Middle East would be a better place if they all acted as good Christians.

In today's world where religious-based strife is common it is not difficult to find but to have its own designated "ambassador" offers cynicism equal to that of Stalin who had questions about the armies of the Pope. Even more cynical is that the Ambassador for Religious

Affairs is the only non-elected person in Foreign Affairs allowed to issue press releases in his own name.

These press records carry their own standards. The minister "strongly condemns" the Assad regime for a variety of atrocities and used the same words to attack anti-homosexuality legislation in Gambia; he was "sickened" by another kidnapping of young women in Nigeria; and "deeply concerned" by a EU General Court decision concerning Hamas; and earlier, his concern was equally deep by the movement of Russian troops near the border with Ukraine. There was some bewilderment when he expressed his concern and trouble (in four separate press releases) to the Maldivians during their national election process. Like the Minister excess was the guideline not brevity.

Mr Baird was the fifth foreign minister during the Harper era. He was preceded by Peter MacKay, Maxine Bernier, David Emerson and Laurence Cannon none of whom stayed around long enough to establish a lasting memory. So when Mr Baird arrived after the 2011 elections, the novelty of his appointment, gave way to the idea that the least diplomatic person in the Harper government would bring new leadership and direction to the dispirited keepers of the Pearsonian legacy.

It was not to be. Mr Baird, as with his immediate predecessors, were all drinkers of Harper cool aid and, instead of being on a high road, were on the potholed road of "principled" positions in dealing with a phantasmagorical world. But surprisingly when these positions were given thought it was evident our principles were situational and influenced not by the complexities of the world but by the complexities of the Canadian electorate.

In the Middle East especially Canadian historical efforts to loosen the Gordian knot of impasse surrounding the creation of a Palestinian state, today's policy is largely a talking point for the Prime Minister of Israel. Equally, efforts by Egyptians to create diversity within their political system were largely ignored. But similar efforts in Ukraine were supported to the point that it was possible on some days to have a Canadian cabinet meeting in downtown Kiev.

Not a word is said about the fact that the only freely elected President in Egyptian history still languishes in prison and during a recent visit Mr Baird announced assistance and training for his jailers.

Mr Baird was particularly fond of visiting the Arabian Peninsula with the colonial era rulers that perpetuate a Gilbert and Sullivan scenario with real guns. Saudi Arabia needs military equipment made in Southwestern Ontario; done with financial support from the government of Canada. Or Saudi police need assistance from Canada; it is done with a short press release. And reports that the Saudi government has had a hand in financing al Qaeda there was absolute silence.

To ensure there was no dissention within the bureaucracy, the keepers of the tattered tradition of "principle" in our foreign assistance budget were all bundled off and hiddened within the bowels of the Foreign Affairs never to be heard from again.

The encomiums surrounding Mr Baird's resignation as Foreign Minister have been many but they have more to do with his personality than with his actions and policies over the past four years. He was certainly a person one could spend a comfortable evening with at the corner pub but there is very little to suggest that he added anything to our collective ability to manage the complexities of the 21st Century.

Perhaps he summed it up best in his end of last year press release when he added Canadian "interests" to his guiding principles. There is little to argue with if that was so but to try and disguise it with the use of "principle" cheapens both the idea and the man.

Mr Baird is now with his predecessors – MacKay, Bernier, Emerson, Cannon – names that appear on the list of Canadian Foreign Minister but easily forgotten. He was a quirky placeholder. He did little for the troubled world and sadly even less for the possibility that Canadians could help.

Embassy

Book Review
February 2015

DON'T TELL THE NEWFOUNDLANDERS: THE TRUE STORY OF NEWFOUNDLAND'S CONFEDERATION WITH CANADA by Greg Malone, 2012, Viking Canada Edition [2014], Toronto, 314 pp., $22.00.

SIXTY-FIVE YEARS AGO THIS SPRING NEWFOUNDLANDERS ENDED their nearly half- millennium of convoluted and unique constitutional history by voting narrowly to become the tenth province of Canada. In many ways this constitutional history did not differ materially from other parts of the British Empire except in its final denouement.

There is a weak historical consensus that the Island was "discovered" in June 1497 by an itinerant Genoese sailor in the employ of Henry VII. John Cabot or Giovanni Caboto, claimed this "new founde land" for England, Less than a century later a foppish and frequently penurious nobleman, Sir Humfrey Gilbert, accompanied by minstrels, Morris dancers and a Hungarian poet sailed into St John's harbour in August 1583 and re-iterated English ownership. Gilbert's ship along with all hands sank before it made it back to England. Nevertheless, through the magic of faux historians, we have Gilbert's last words before he sank beneath the North Atlantic. Echoing the sentiments of thousands of Newfoundlanders ever since, Gilbert is "recorded" as shouting "Courage, my lads! We are as near to Heaven by sea as by land." The accompanying Hungarian poet, Stephanus Parmenius, drowned earlier during the voyage but not before he left us with the unofficial motto of the Island *Piscium inexhausta copia* or in the vernacular, Fish Without End.

As with most of the bits and bobs of empire managed from London, Newfoundland experienced the full range of British colonial administrative mechanisms. First were the "Fishing Admirals" – government by the first-arrived ship captain in a port each spring; next came several Proprietary Governors who had visions of cotton and other crops emerging from the rocks; and then British naval officers with an excess of rum, lash and buggery were put in charge.

It was 1832 before the Island had its first elected assembly along with an executive council run by a governor out of London which as a group simply added to the abundance of fog. In 1855 there was "responsible" government, seven years after it occurred in Canada (then roughly Ontario and Quebec) and Nova Scotia. In 1907, Newfoundland along with New Zealand was granted Dominion status by London. Party politics emerged largely reflecting the religious differences between southern Ireland Catholics and west England Protestants. Fish dominated and its world price determined standards of living. It was a harsh mercantile system were money stayed with the merchants on land and the dangerous work done by fishermen on the stormy waters of the North Atlantic.

The cost of an oversized contribution, both in men and money, from the Island to the First World War coupled with the earlier disastrous decision to build a railway (from fish stage to fish stage) lumbered the Island with an oversized debt. The 1929 global economic crash was fatal creating near fiscal bankruptcy conditions. The British were not doing much better and any help from the Mother Country was conditional on the surrender of responsible government and direct control of finances by London. The elected Newfoundland Assembly agreed and from 1933 onwards there was government by a secretive commission consisting of four British, two Newfoundlanders and one Canadian all appointed by London.

This 1933 decision by the Newfoundland legislature to temporarily yield its status as an independent country was a unique one in the history of the world. It is the major theme in Greg Malone's book, *Don't Tell The Newfoundlanders*. Malone is a well-known

Newfoundland actor having help develop the television series CODCO and appearing in the *Republic of Doyle*. He has been an occasional politician having lost as the NDP candidate in a 2000 Newfoundland Assembly by-election. More recently he has been associated with Elizabeth May and the Green Party

The Joey Smallwood version of Confederation has dominated post-1949 history. While there have been occasional weak assaults on its basic tenet that the process was a democratic one, the overall success of the venture has dampened interest in any background story. One such assault was the 1992 movie *The Secret Nation* starring Mary Walsh, Cathy Jones and Rick Mercer. Ms Walsh, a graduate student in history at McGill, returns home looking for information on the referendum conspiracy that led to the 1949 union. Needless to say, while a good movie, it was seen by fewer people than live on Funk Island.

Mr Malone's book is the first serious attempt to put a measure of investigative scholarship into the issue. His interest in the matter was triggered by St John's lawyer James Halley who from his student days at Dalhousie Law School in 1949 harboured doubts on the Smallwood version of events and over the years assembled "a large collection of research materials relating to Newfoundland's federation with Canada." Malone also pays tribute to the work of Paul Bridle who between 1974 and 1984 produced three volumes of *Documents on Relations Between Canada and Newfoundland*. In over 3500 pages Bridle details Canadian activities between 1935 and 1949 that led to Newfoundland becoming the tenth province. His interest and involvement in the matter goes back to 1944 when he was assigned to the Canadian High Commission in St John's which had been opened the year before. Needless to say the sheer scope of Bridle's work ensures it is even less read than those who saw *The Secret Nation*.

Malone's central thesis is that the British controlled and dominated unelected Commission of Government in St John's manipulated the 1948 referendums to create the majority decision to become the tenth province of Canada. Malone states this was contrary to the 1933 understanding that post-Commission decisions on the future of Newfoundland were to be made by an <u>elected</u> Newfoundland government. "The constitutional arrangements whereby confederation between Canada and Newfoundland was effected were extraordinary, dubious and as controversial in London and Ottawa as they were in St John's." Neither Canada nor Britain wanted to use the British North American Act which had provisions for additional provinces, instead "Canada preferred to negotiate with Britain while Newfoundland was temporarily under British control."

The British sidestepped its decision to have an elected Newfoundland assembly make final decisions on the constitutional future of the Island. The British Newfoundland Act of 1933 promised that "as soon as the Island's difficulties are overcome and the country is again self-supporting, responsible government, on request from the people of Newfoundland, would be restored."

Instead the British decided there would be an elected National Convention in Newfoundland that would "consider and discuss" the future constitutional status. As Malone makes clear this was a dramatic change from the original proposal that would allow the National Convention to "discuss and determine" the future for the Island. In making the change the British retained the right to override any and all recommendations made by the National Convention. This it did when the Convention at the end of its work in January 1948 voted for two options to be decided in a referendum – retain Commission of Government or return to Responsible Government as it existed prior to 1933.

Smallwood and his allies in the Convention had pushed to include Confederation with Canada as a referendum option but were defeated 29 to 16. After the vote and dissolution of the Convention Smallwood mounted a vigorous campaign directed at London to have Confederation included as an option in the June1948 referendum. The British first consulted with Canada and in March 1948 ordered that confederation with Canada be included as a third option in the planned referendum. A fourth option – economic union with the United States – was promoted by a group of St John's merchants but never had much traction and was not included in the referendum.

Once Atlee replaced Churchill as Prime Minister in 1945, the British secretly created conditions that would not see a return to Responsible Government even though the main condition in the 1933 Newfoundland Act for its return was met – "financial difficulties overcome," probably in the fear that American interests would come to dominate on the Island. A National Convention delegation to London in 1947 had trouble even finding a hotel and led the *London Daily Express* to comment "How cold, graceless, ungenerous and chuckleheaded is the attitude of the Government towards Newfoundlanders. . . ." Once the British decided that it wanted confederation then there was little room to maneuver for those who promoted a return to Responsible Government. Lord Beaverbrook, formerly one of Churchill's most able ministers in charge of aircraft production during the early days of the war and now out of government, charged that "our rulers spoke for Britain with the voice of a shark lawyer."

The role Canada played in the years leading up to the 1948 referendum was one of caution so as not to be seen as fueling the possibility of another Newfoundland rejection of confederation. Norman Robertson even went so far as to caution the Canadian High Commissioner in St. John's, Scott Macdonald, that "All correspondence on our Newfoundland policy should be marked 'Confidential' since . . . it may be difficult to prevent correspondence, which might conceivable be embarrassing, from becoming public unless it is given a security marking."

The British visited Ottawa in September 1945 and, as described by Prime Minister Mackenzie King, for the purpose of "very confidential and informal discussions on matters relating to Newfoundland." Mackenzie King went on to say in a message to Scott Macdonald in St John's "Ostensibly [the] mission would be for other purposes, and therefore this information is for you alone." Peter Clutterbuck from the Colonial Office headed the British delegation and in a separate note prior to the visit noted that "You should know that we have been careful not to give Newfoundland Government any inkling of [his] impending visit or its object."

Reporting on his discussions in Ottawa Clutterbuck noted that earlier "the Canadians had themselves been giving a good deal of thought to the Newfoundland problem and had certain ideas which they were anxious to discuss with us before conclusions as to future policy were reached." To his surprise, Clutterbuck wrote that "the initial reaction of the Canadian officials to this approach was almost entirely negative." Clutterbuck with the presentation of this Canadian view simply stated that "who would be surprised if Newfoundlanders began to think seriously of turning to the United States?" This "entirely negative" view was typical of Mackenzie King's approach on all large issues but with C. D. Howe pushing hard for the inclusion of Newfoundland the hard Canadian interest was never far from the centre of the discussions.

Clutterbuck when on to note the mention of American interest quickly turned the discussions around. "At this stage the Canadian officials became more helpful . . ." In his report Clutterbuck then wrote the Canadians asked what the British government's reaction would be if "the Canadian Government were to indicate to us that they would welcome a recommendation by the proposed National Convention in favour of Newfoundland joining up with Canada." With his reply Clutterbuck set the stage for eventual confederation: "I said that any such invitation would be warmly received by my Government; it had always been felt . . . that union with Canada was the Island's natural destiny."

Malone goes on to write "Newfoundland's fate was sealed. Canada had the dollars – it was the buyer and would set the terms. Britain was the vendor and would deliver the goods – Newfoundland." Three months after these discussions Clutterbuck was knighted and appointed British High Commissioner in Ottawa to "preside over the final transfer of power."

Nevertheless the June and July, 1948 votes were near run things. The results of the June 3 vote as reported from St John's by Paul Bridle were:

> Commission of Government for a period of five years 21,944
>
> Confederation with Canada 63,110
>
> Responsible Government as it existed in 1933 69,230

The results did not provide a majority for any of the three options so the British scheduled a second vote for July 22, 1948 to decide on the two leading ones – confederation and/or responsible government. Bridle in his reporting noted that the appeal of the "proposal [for] responsible government should endeavour to negotiate economic union with the United States." He went on to comment that Chesley Crosbie's "sincerity appears to be so taken for granted" and that a "substantial body of people" were willing to accept his views and "give him a chance." Mr Crosbie was the leader of the economic union with the United States political grouping and, of course, the father of John Crosbie who has enriched Canadian politics with the same level of sincerity.

The second vote on July 22, 1948 was decisive but not overwhelmingly so. Confederation received almost seventy eight thousand votes while responsible government received just over seventy-one thousand. Confederation won with 52% of the vote cast; 150,000 Newfoundlanders voted out of a possible electorate of 176,000. The total was about 5,000 less than those who voted on June 3.

In ending his documented account of how Canada and Britain conspired to ensure confederation was the final outcome of the postwar constitutional process in Newfoundland, Malone deals with the largely underground belief of many that the British rigged the results of the second referendum. (This was the main theme of the

1992 movie *The Secret Nation*). This has been an ongoing controversy since the referendum and Malone presents the largely circumstantial evidence – the tallying of the votes in the governor's office, the destruction of most of the ballots shortly after the once and only counting, no poll-by-poll compilation, no recount despite the narrowness of the results, elliptical statements by those involved – with some completeness. He concludes "From London to St. John's there were many who cried foul about Newfoundland's entry into Confederation, but none of them could hold raw power to account. However the very "very nasty taste," as one British MP put it, has never gone away."

The double dealing of the British and the Canadians and their common perfidy is well summed up by Malone title *"Don't Tell the Newfoundlanders."* The history of Newfoundland's rejection of Confederation on three earlier occasions was known and as the results from the 1948 votes demonstrated remained a strong force in the land. The British wanted out and were prepared to manipulate arrangements to achieve that end. Ottawa, despite the suggested reluctance of Mackenzie King reflecting his personal operating characteristic, wanted Newfoundland for a variety of geopolitical and economic reasons but realized that overt action on its part would make this even more difficult to achieve. Smallwood served Canadian and British interests but it was his own personal commitment to union with Canada that as much as outside manipulation that led to Confederation in 1949.

Greg Malone tells the story of confederation with the accuracy of the historian with an exhaustive documentary record. It is a compelling account. No one argued that the British were more than normally perfidious in the postwar period and that Canada was prepared to play the game as the prize in Canadian terms was an immense one. But what is missing from the account are details of the larger game Britain was playing.

Central to the Newfoundland issue was the condition of Britain in the immediate postwar period. It had just emerged from a war that was a close run thing; millions died and its infrastructure was in ruins, its economy was non-existent and central banks everywhere were not generous in offering financial assistance. Equally the Empire was not only fading it was disappearing. In 1947 the Subcontinent was partitioned; India and Pakistan along with Burma and Ceylon emerged as independent countries and in less than a decade the forces for decolonization of the Empire in Africa and elsewhere was well underway.

In all of this Britain played a short game of divesture of places and matters of marginal value. The 300,000 Newfoundlanders in this game were very small potatoes and appeal to their contribution to the wars of Empire found little resonance in London. The detailing of British perfidy as Mr Malone has done provides a valuable account of the death of what for many of us was a "home, in the place where the Irish mystics dreamed of going." That home lives on for many even though many Newfoundlanders live in it as a poetic abstraction. Camelots still have a role to play.

Bout d'paper. Spring 2015

Cuba: An island looking for more sun
March 18, 2015

FOR MORE THAN 50 YEARS CUBA HAS PLAYED REGULARLY ON THE international stage transcending others by constancy and uniqueness. Its proximity to the United States and the influence of its migrants on the American political system guarantees there is not much on the island that does not play large in Washington and, as a consequence, on the rest of us.

Its late independence from Spain and the subsequent gratuitous military involvement by the United States created a semi-colonial environment with American political and economic domination. Corruption was endemic starting at the very top. The successful 1959 revolution by Fidel Castro and his younger brother Raúl spun heads in Washington to the point that one of the world's most inept military operations was attempted two years later at the Bay of Pigs or more poetically, *Invasión de Playa Girón*. It set a pattern for American policy until recent days.

Castro's economic decisions, particularly the nationalization of American-owned industry and land and close relations with the Soviet Union, guaranteed retaliation by the United States. Before long Cuban sugar, its only significant export, was prohibited from entry.

Some eighteen months after the Bay of Pigs invasion Castro persuaded the Soviet Union to install nuclear weapons on the island. For the Soviet Union it was a counter to the installation of American medium-range nuclear missiles in Turkey and Italy capable of reaching Moscow. Once the Soviet intentions became evident a 13-day naval standoff took place to the northeast of Cuba.

It was a near-death nuclear standoff, but in the end the Soviets agreed to remove their missiles from Cuba in return for an American promise not to invade Cuba. Not made public at the time, the Americans agreed also to remove their nuclear missiles from Turkey and Italy.

Castro learned playing on the world's strategic stage had consequences and ever since those fateful days of October 1962 he played a more limited international game. He sought to export his revolution to other countries and gave military help to several countries in Africa. He also occasionally provided support for insurgencies in Latin America with little success.

Castro's domestic reforms were more successful especially on education, medicine and social services. Today these survive and will be the lasting legacy of his regime.

But it is a regime that has run its course. Fidel is sidelined with medical issues and his aging successor, brother Raúl, has announced that he will not run again as president after 2018. But as they saw with their acolyte Hugo Chávez of Venezuela, such plans can be easily abruptly shortened.

President Raúl Castro has already begun to remove some of the sharper edges of his brother's economic policies. As one commentator put it, he has "corrected some of the mistakes" of the past. Economic differentiation was introduced allowing for the buying and selling of property, small retail businesses are permitted and, perhaps most important, foreign travel is allowed for all Cubans. Also restrictions on electronic communications, both domestic and foreign, are being eased.

US-Cuba détente
United States President Barack Obama's decision to open discussions with Cuba, a détente Canada helped broker, with a view to the normalization of relations has completely changed the dynamic on the island. American economic sanctions and embargoes have kept Cuba a relatively poor island while most of its Latin American neighbours have joined the global economy. Any easing of these

sanctions will have an immediate and positive effect. Americans negotiators were back in Havana this week and there was little to suggest President Obama will want to see this initiative stay at the discussion stage much longer.

Raúl's international intentions are also forward-looking. He has resumed discussions with the Paris Club, which co-ordinates solutions for countries with debt payment problems. President François Hollande of France is expected to visit in May and a possible agreement on debt might be in place before then. Equally, there is widespread support in Latin America to see Cuba resume its membership in the Organization of American States and this could occur at its April meeting in Panama.

Nearly two million Cubans have migrated to the United States with more than a million in Florida. It is a potent political bloc but one that is by no means monolithic. Both Republicans and Democrats see opportunities arising from the normalization of relations and this more than anything provides President Obama with more than reasonable chance of erasing one of the more egregious foreign policy failures of the past half century.

Cuba is not the dark place that many try to present. There is little or no chance of a Cuban Spring. Raúl Castro's economic reforms and the expectation of better relations with the United States provide strong incentive to stay with the regime. But that only goes so far.

The two old men will not be around for much longer. As with all such regimes, there is little succession planning and the transition to new leadership could be fragile if not dangerous. There are no apparent heirs to the Castros except for a couple of cronies who are almost as old. The next generation of leaders is not readily apparent. If Raúl has plans in this area, nothing has been said and there is little likelihood anyone will step forward until both of the Castros are interred.

I witnessed a sense of the times when I walked on a large pedestrian walkway in downtown Havana last week. An American journalist was doing interviews with passing Cubans seeking views on the future. The subject was incoming American investment with the journalist suggesting it would be valuable to fix many of the rundown and dilapidated buildings surrounding the walkway. The Cuban disagreed, replying it "all looked better than Gaza" to him. Let's hope it stays that way.

Endnote

THESE ARTICLES WERE WRITTEN BETWEEN 2004 AND THE SPRING OF 2015. Most were published in daily and weekly newspapers and in other publications. I am grateful to these publications for accepting my writing and giving them prominence to a wide audience. These publications include:

bout de papier: Canada's Magazine of Diplomacy and Foreign Service

Embassy: Canada's Foreign Policy Newspaper

Diplomat and International Trade

Globe and Mail

iPolitics (Online)

Kingston Whig Standard

Ottawa Citizen

Prism Magazine (Online)

Printed in Canada